THE CULTURAL POLITICS OF U.S. IMMIGRATION

NATION OF NATIONS:
IMMIGRANT HISTORY AS AMERICAN HISTORY

General Editors: Rachel Buff, Matthew Jacobson, and Werner Sollors

The Cultural Politics of U.S. Immigration

Gender, Race, and Media

Leah Perry

NEW YORK UNIVERSITY PRESS
New York

NEW YORK UNIVERSITY PRESS
New York
www.nyupress.org

References to Internet websites (URLs) were accurate at the time of writing. Neither the author nor New York University Press is responsible for URLs that may have expired or changed since the manuscript was prepared.

Library of Congress Cataloging-in-Publication Data
Names: Perry, Leah, author.
Title: The cultural politics of U.S. immigration : gender, race, and media / Leah Perry.
Description: New York : New York University Press, [2016] | Includes bibliographical references and index.
Identifiers: LCCN 2016014067| ISBN 978-1-4798-2877-7 (cl : alk. paper) | ISBN 978-1-4798-2386-4 (pb : alk. paper)
Subjects: LCSH: United States—Emigration and immigration—Social aspects. | United States—Emigration and immigration—Government policy. | Immigrants in mass media. | Mass media and race relations—United States
Classification: LCC JV6475 .P47 2016 | DDC 325.73—dc23
LC record available at https://lccn.loc.gov/2016014067

New York University Press books are printed on acid-free paper, and their binding materials are chosen for strength and durability. We strive to use environmentally responsible suppliers and materials to the greatest extent possible in publishing our books.

Manufactured in the United States of America
10 9 8 7 6 5 4 3 2 1

Also available as an ebook

To my parents.

CONTENTS

ACKNOWLEDGMENTS

This book was written with the help of many people, and its strengths are due to their interventions, suggestions, and support; any flaws or unintended harms are entirely my own. First and foremost I thank *Nation of Nations* series editors, Matthew Frye Jacobson and Rachel Ida Buff. This project would not have been possible without their suggestions, expertise, encouragement, patience, and overall generosity. Matt has been a co-traveler on this project from the very beginning. I am overwhelmed with gratitude for his invaluable mentorship; my words are entirely inadequate. I am also indebted to both Matt's and Rachel's path-breaking American Studies scholarship, which has been crucial to my intellectual development as a scholar. Both model the kind of ethical, rigorous, generous scholar and teacher I strive to be.

I am very grateful to Eric Zinner and Alicia Nadkarni at New York University Press for their support of this work. The rigorous and thoughtful comments of my three anonymous reviewers made this book much stronger, allowing me to expand it in ways unimaginable without their careful feedback. Many thanks to production editor Alexia Traganas for making my words clearer.

I want to give special thanks to Karen Adams for her thorough early edits of this manuscript, which helped me to clarify and develop my arguments. An early version of some of this research appeared in a special issue of *Cultural Studies* titled *Cultural Studies and/of the Law* and in a book edition of the special issue, *Cultural Studies and the "Juridical Turn": Culture, Law, and Legitimacy in the Era of Neoliberal Capitalism*. I thank issue and book collection editors Sean Andrews and Jaafar Aksikas for their very helpful critiques. A version of another portion of this work is included in the anthology *American Shame: Stigmata and the Body Politic*. Editor Myra Mendible and the anonymous reviewers provided insightful comments, which helped me to clarify my thinking, and improve my work.

At SUNY Empire State College (ESC), I received a generous faculty research grant, which was crucial to the completion of this project. I thank Dean Michael Spitzer for his substantial support, as well as senior faculty member Ian Reifowitz. He kindly mentored me through the publication process, helped me adjust to ESC's nontraditional system, and has had confidence in me when my own faltered. My colleague and punk rock sister, Donna Gaines, makes every day more fun and interesting. Both Ian and Donna set the bar high with their scholarship, and I greatly appreciate their intellectual companionship and friendship.

I could not have written this book without the mentorship of the scholars who trained me. I am a more analytical and competent scholar thanks to the efforts of Paul Smith, Alison Landsberg, Scott Trafton, and Roger Lancaster. Special thanks to Larry Levine, who continues to be a role model in terms of scholarly rigor, transformative teaching, and activism; I am so grateful for the time that I had to work with him before his passing. I am indebted to Carl Grindley, my first academic mentor. Many thanks to Suzanne Scott: under her tutelage in a supportive feminist community, I learned how to teach Women's, Gender, and Sexuality Studies, and do all that I can to empower and nurture my students.

My students enliven my work and life. Brian Picone especially was my colleague, friend, and teacher more than my student. I miss his sharp intellect, unwavering commitment to social justice, bravery, and knack for dancing in heels; the world is far better for having only briefly had him in it.

My gratitude to my intellectual community in graduate school and after: Jessi Lang, Rebecca Forrest, Lia Uy-Tioco, Fan Yang, Sean Andrews, Jaafar Aksikas, Allison Lakomski, and Rob Gehl, my fellow Cultural Studies warriors. Katy Razzano and Pia Moller helped me to ask difficult questions and have been important sources for research materials, discussions, and camaraderie. I have been challenged and inspired by our subsequent collaborations, and my work has been enhanced by their meticulous feedback. Rachel Martin, a uniquely insightful feminist teacher and scholar and beloved friend, continues to be "my person."

Upon my move (back) to New York City following graduate school, Dharma Punx gave me a soft place to land (or perhaps helped me to sit with not-so-soft places). My *mittas*, Kathy Cherry, Mirza Molberg, Rachel Durga Page, and Carla Snow remind me of the vital importance of breathing, laughing, savoring a cookie, and beach days. Many thanks also to Adam Groff for his friendship, care, and technical assistance *dana*.

Finally, I thank my parents, Camille and Al Perry, for their unwavering support and patience, particularly through my teenage years and lengthy graduate studies. They did indeed work assiduously to provide me with a better life, as did my grandparents on both the Guarnierri and Perry (formerly "Perrera") sides before them. My curiosity about our family's immigrant stories provided the impetus for this project, and my parents' love and encouragement were vital to its fruition.

Introduction

Media, Gender, and Immigration

Migration throws objects, identities and ideas into flux.
—Kobena Mercer, *Exiles, Diasporas and Strangers*

In February 1984, Madonna released the single "Borderline" from her first, eponymously titled album, and by June, it became her first top-ten hit on the Billboard Hot 100.[1] Soon in heavy rotation on MTV, the two-sequence video depicted Madonna struggling to choose between two men and two worlds. Her desire for her Latino lover and his multicultural working-class world conflicted with her desire for celebrity, which was offered by another suitor, a white male photographer. Filmed in an urban Latina/o neighborhood, or barrio, in Los Angeles, and directed by Mary Lambert, the video juxtaposed the colorful world of the Latino boyfriend and his multiethnic break-dancing entourage, who hung out on rooftops and in bodegas and pool halls, with the drab, sanitized, colorless world of the photographer, with his luxury sports car and private studio space—its classical statues standing in for Euro-American high culture—and his offerings of champagne and bottled water. The photographer offered Madonna an escape from the barrio through modeling, and under his tutelage she achieved cover girl status. But Madonna desired the younger, more attractive Latino man. And the Latino boyfriend's inconsistent behavior—he alternately embraced, rebuffed, and once literally pushed her away—was a reaction to Madonna's own ambivalence. Ultimately, Madonna chose the multicultural world of her Latino boyfriend. And with "Borderline," Madonna became a pop sensation by pushing the borderlines of Reagan-era standards of respectability.

In the video, the appeal of the multicultural world was conveyed by images, spectacle, and interwoven narratives. The scenes with the photographer were shot in black-and-white, the barrio in full, vibrant color. Madonna's urban, edgy clothing, messy hair, dramatic make up, piles of costume jewelry, and a punk studded belt signified her connectedness to the multicultural world. The Latino boyfriend and his posse were likewise decked out in urban street fashion, including studded belts, track suits, and bandanas; the photographer

1

wore a neutral palette. In one scene, Madonna sported a denim jacket with "boy toy" emblazoned on the back, the self-applied label an ironic contrast to the world of modeling that she ultimately rejected by trashing the photographer's studio, notably spray-painting X's over the genitals of his nude male statues. Thus Madonna countered the photographer, and spectator, with the "possibility of a female sexuality that was independent of patriarchal control, a sexuality that defied rather than rejected the male gaze."[2]

Via the song lyrics and Madonna's role as protagonist of the video, spectators were positioned to identify with this independent woman's preference for the working-class Latino lover who was "pushing [her] love over the borderline." After Madonna's dalliance with the photographer, she attempted to return to the Latino, and he initially rejected her. The borderline she sang of, which was perhaps also a euphemism for orgasm, was the borderline of her patience with her Latino lover's inconsistency. His rejection pained her, too. Although the Latino initially pushed her away and could not offer her the capital that the photographer had at his disposal, Madonna wanted the younger man. With this video, Madonna "present[ed] herself both as an alluring sex object and as a transgressor of established boundaries."[3]

The nuanced gender and race politics playing out in the video surfaced in the conditions of its production as well. The song was written and produced by Reggie Lucas and remixed by Madonna's then-boyfriend, John "Jelly Bean" Benitez, who was of Puerto Rican descent. But it was Madonna, an Italian American woman, who received acclaim for—and the lion's share of profit from—"Borderline," which was substantial. That year, the song reached number ten on the Billboard Hot 100 chart,[4] was certified Gold,[5] and in the years since, it has been covered by several artists[6] and continues to chart in "Best of" lists,[7] while Madonna's early work has sparked much interest and debate in the culture at large[8] and among academics.[9]

"Borderline" was significant not only because its then-controversial representation of an interracial relationship and female sexual assertiveness signaled a career-making moment for Madonna, but because the video played out—and played with—struggles over immigration, gender roles, and multiculturalism that were at the forefront of American politics in the 1980s, and continue to shape U.S. politics to this day. How and why those struggles surfaced in all arenas of American culture, from the floor of Congress to MTV, is the focus of this book. Douglas Kellner observes that "media culture is a contest of representations that reproduce existing social struggles and transcode the political discourses of the era."[10] This book will examine many examples taken from TV, film, and print media—alongside the rhetoric of politicians and pundits—which speak to the themes of immigration, gender roles, and multiculturalism, and it will analyze them especially in the context of immigration legislation and congressional debates.

In the United States—the quintessential "nation of immigrants"—pluralism is celebrated as a national value, yet the diversity that immigrants carry over the border has been perceived as a threat to the complexion, economy, and unity of the nation, making immigration a perpetual topic of debate. From the political cartoons and plays of the late nineteenth century to the blockbuster films and blogs of today, tensions over immigration and American identity have surfaced in various media and been hashed out on the congressional floor and in the culture at large. Amid increasing immigration from Latin America, the Caribbean, and Asia in the 1980s, the language and common imagery of immigration debates were transformed. In Reagan's America, the circle of who was considered American seemed to broaden, reflecting democratic gains made by racial minorities and women, and that broadening was increasingly visible in the daily lives of Americans via TV shows, films, and popular news media. Yet that broadening was circumscribed by gendered and race-based discourses, such that immigrants were either feared and censured or welcomed exclusively as laborers. A discordant combination of gatekeeping and welcoming emerged, making immigration crucial to the rising neoliberal project. This book argues that the gender and racial formations that cohered and were contested through 1980s immigration discourses in law and popular culture inaugurated the paradigm for neoliberal immigration, or what I call "neoliberal crossings." As such, 1980s immigration discourses are a crucial but understudied aspect of the development of neoliberalism.

The specifics of these debates are what make them neoliberal. Beginning with his election in 1980, Ronald Reagan, "one of the most popular presidents of the twentieth century,"[11] set out to revolutionize America with deregulation of the economy, privatization, and the Cold War globalization of American capitalist democracy, as well as to placate a polity suspicious of the presidency and government in the aftermath of Vietnam and Watergate. Gender and racial politics were also in flux, with the period seeing a conservative backlash against the gains of feminism and hysteria and homophobia surrounding the AIDS crisis[12]—exemplified by the "family values" movement—as well as reactions to the gains of the civil rights, black power, and Latina/o social movements—exemplified by attacks on affirmative action, opposition to bilingual and multicultural education, and increasing pushes for privatization and its rhetorical correlate, "personal responsibility" (that is, the notion that the individual rather than the state is responsible for meeting even one's most basic human needs, such that failure to do so is the fault of the individual alone rather than the result of structural inequalities such as racism, sexism, and the like). This depoliticized notion of personal responsibility also crystal-ized around "family values." Yet the insights and gains of feminism and the struggles to displace white supremacy could not be ignored: they affected lawmaking and resonated in popular culture, as indicated by the meteoric rise of unconventional, boundary-pushing entertainers like Madonna, Cyndi Lauper, Michael Jackson, and Prince.

While Madonna showed America the pleasures of barrio culture and transgressing borderlines, lawmakers attempted to remedy an undocumented immigration crisis that was attributed primarily to immigrants from Mexico. Soon after the 1980 Mariel Boatlift, involving masses of Cuban refugees, a series of immigration measures were introduced in Congress. But it was only after five years of heated bipartisan debates and numerous joint congressional hearings—highly unusual in immigration debates—that the U.S. Congress passed the Immigration Reform and Control Act (IRCA) of 1986, the first comprehensive immigration reform since 1965. IRCA, sponsored by conser-vative and flagrantly nativist Senator Alan Simpson (R-WY), ushered in new sanctions for employers of undocumented workers, cut welfare, and increased border security, while also including an amnesty program widely praised as a democratic watershed for the undocumented. Thus with the new law, "mul-ticultural" immigrant men and women seemed to be embraced, even as they were disciplined in the same breath. The law delineated the legal paradigm for neoliberal crossings, while concurrently negotiations of neoliberal ideologies were taking shape in popular culture.

As Asia and Latin America, and especially Mexico, came to dominate immigration, a new national narrative was popularized. The quintessential American success story became that of the white ethnic immigrants (Irish and eastern and southern European) who arrived at the turn of the twenti-eth century and in the midst of poverty and discrimination created a better life for their children with nothing but hard work and plucky determination. According to the new "nation of immigrants" narrative, immigrants earned access to American equal opportunity through hard work and adherence to respectable heterosexual "family values." Since these self-reliant immigrants succeeded, so too, the narrative went, could anybody. America was indeed a land of opportunity and abundance, for the personally responsible.

In the popular and media culture of the 1980s, inclusion was framed as multicultural and sometimes feminist, giving rise to a spate of popular new TV shows and films that featured lovable white ethnic immigrant characters such as Italian Americans Sophia Petrillo (*Golden Girls*) and Tony Micelli (*Who's the Boss?*), and Balki Bartokomous, who emigrated to Chicago from the fictional Mediterranean island Mypos (*Perfect Strangers*), along with spectacles like the celebration of America as "mother of exiles" at the Statue of Liberty centennial in 1986. News media also positioned the United States as the exceptional nation where women from patriarchal cultures—often in the "third world"—could be truly empowered and free. White ethnics provided the initial model for this discourse, featuring "empowered" white ethnic women like the "Material Girl" Madonna, who forged a career by shaking up the borderlines of white ethnic "nation of immigrants" discourse and feminine respectability. The 1990s saw the opening of the Ellis Island Museum and the Latinization of American pop culture, epitomized by the rapid rise of stars such as U.S.-born Latinas Selena and Jennifer Lopez, which showed what was available to and for worthy immigrants. While neither Selena nor Lopez is an immigrant, both were sometimes cast as such, and both self-consciously tapped into common salutary immigration discourses and were celebrated along those racialized lines.[13] The circle of inclusion seemed to continue to broaden.

But when immigrants deviated from the dominant value system—like ostensibly fecund, teenaged welfare-abusing Mexican American mothers in the film *Mi Vida Loca* (1994) or criminally inclined Cuban refugees, like the hyperviolent Tony Montana, antihero of the film *Scarface* (1983)—they were rendered undeserving of everything from social services to residence in the United States and even to sympathy itself. Similar images proliferated in news media, with representations of Latino drug smugglers, dealers, and users, and promiscuous, welfare-draining Latina mothers, which tended to conflate important distinctions between, for example, the undocumented immigrant and the native-born American, and contributed to a general sense of an "immigration crisis" that originated south of the U.S.–Mexico border. Meanwhile, recurring stories about immigration indicated that punitive legal action (such as border militarization, welfare restriction, deportation) was not racist or sexist, but necessary to preserve the fiscal and moral health of the nation-state. These two conceptions of immigration—"nation of immigrants" and "immigration emergency"—surfaced repeatedly with various twists, turns, and embellishments in law and media beginning in the Reagan years, and continued to be the dominant modes of thought and expression about immigration until September 11, 2001, brought "terror" to the forefront of immigration politics.

Ultimately the consensus needed to pass IRCA was hard-won, given conflicting interests that crossed party lines and made for strange-bedfellow alliances that have become characteristically neoliberal. Free-market Republicans like Reagan supported amnesty measures for Mexican migrants not for humanitarian reasons, like some Democrats and activists, but because cheap Mexican immigrant labor was profitable. The amnesty provision tied applicants to their employers during a long waiting period, making applicants vulnerable to abuses, and included the Seasonal Agricultural Worker (SAW) program for temporary laborers. This pro-immigrant labor stance was controversial in the context of recession and the highest unemployment rates since the 1930s, as it suggested a lack of concern for native laborers; organized labor opposed amnesty on the basis of labor competition.

But the most urgent fears of an "immigration emergency" pivoted on gender and racial politics. Nativist organizations like the Federation for American Immigration Reform (FAIR) and lawmakers like Simpson argued that family reunification provisions should be cut to curtail waves of "Hispanic" immigrants, because their family configurations and "culture" conflicted with American "family values." "Hispanic," "culture," and "family values" are mystifying terms that erase how power operates through intersecting categories of race, gender, sexuality, and other axes of identity. First, people of Latin American descent—Central or South American, immigrant or native-born U.S. citizen—are lumped into the same general category of "Hispanic" or Latina/o, despite significant differences among these groups. For example, though often associated with immigration in popular discourse, Puerto Ricans are U.S. citizens, and Mexicans, who have historically inhabited the areas that became California and the southwestern U.S. became "immigrants" and then "undocumented" only through a series of territorial appropriations and restrictive immigration laws.

Scholars working at the intersection of Latina/o Studies and Queer Studies have produced important work on this problem of terminology. In 1992, Ana Maria Alonso and Maria Teresa Koreck wrote about how the federal government, alongside Hollywood and multinational corporations, produced and circulated discourses that fashioned a new subject in response to the discovery of a new consumer and voting bloc in the 1970s and 1980s: "Hispanics." Racial/ethnic category definitions on federal tax and census forms also fixed the meaning of "Hispanic" in relation to "black" and "white": white and black persons were "not of Hispanic origin," while "Hispanic" was applied to "persons of Mexican, Puerto Rican, Cuban, Central or South American or other Spanish cultural origin, regardless of race."[14] "Hispanics" were conglomerated, despite the claim of racial differentiation within the description, and defined in terms of their differences from blacks and whites. The term simultaneously homogenized people of Latin American origins as a coherent group, and "whitens" Hispanic identity by linking it to Spanish heritage while erasing African and Indian heritage. Prominent Latina/o Studies scholars continue to problematize the more contemporary term meant to denote

Latin American origins, "Latina/o," which became prevalent in popular culture, media, and marketing in connection with the "Latin Explosion" of the
1990s. Like "Hispanic," the term "Latina/o" continues to "lump all difference
among Latinas/os into an undifferentiated pile," erasing the "different historical and lived experiences"[15] among Latinas/os.[16] Yet it is often the preferred
term that many scholars utilize for the sake of critical clarity in examinations of Latinas/os as a racial formation. The gender distinction, like the term
Latin@s, which is also preferred by some scholars, indicates the importance
of consistent attention to gender difference as a vector of analysis. Alonso
and Koreck also asserted that categories of sexual orientation (homosexual,
heterosexual, and so on) are culturally specific rather than universal; applying them to Mexicans and Chicanos creates silences that have resulted in the
prevalence of AIDS among Mexican men who engage in homosexual behavior.[17] Lionel Cantu, Jr., arguing that sexuality shapes processes of migration
and incorporation and that the socioeconomic transitions of migration shape
the formation of identities, showed how terms such as "gay" and "queer" are
problematic because they are not used by Mexicans as an identity label. He
used such terms only as analytical tools.[18]

Asian American Studies scholars have likewise examined both the dangers and the productive possibilities of a panethnic or diverse national-origins
group identity. On one hand, the lumping together of Americans of Chinese,
Japanese, Filipino, Korean, and Vietnamese origin erases the different histories and experiences among Asian Americans. On the other hand, as Yen Le
Espiritu shows, large-scale group affiliation under the identity "Asian American" has allowed for collective action that has effectively challenged racism.[19]
Like the term "Latina/o," the term "Asian American" is also preferred in many
scholarly analyses of Asian Americans as a racial formation.[20]

Following the work of these scholars, I use terms such as "Latina/o," "Asian
American," "heterosexual," and the like only as analytical tools to denote what
are in fact fluid, unsettled categories, and I tease out the erasures that such
terms accomplish. How and why erasures around Latina/o identities—in
comparison to contemporaneous Asian American and especially white ethnic identities—were part and parcel of the coherence of neoliberal crossings
will be explored throughout this book, which adds a comparative dimension
to Latina/o Studies scholarship on terminology and processes of racialization and sexualization. Moreover, comparative analysis shows how discourses
about migration were central to the erosion of the welfare state and the transformation of multiculturalism to support that process; that is, comparative
analysis reveals how migration was essential to the cohesion of neoliberalism
in the 1980s.

mig'r → neoliberalism

The New Right commitment to "family values" solidified in the 1970s as a response to what is often viewed as "second-wave" feminism[21] and the civil rights movement and was central to the dismantling of the welfare state. The "family values" narrative conflated the patriarchal bread-winning nuclear family, traditional Christian morals, and opposition to abortion with "good" mothering but also with "good" American citizenship. Working women and single mothers—many of whom were of color—and the extended kinship arrangements common among immigrants became un-American, and the AIDS crisis and its early attribution to gay men added a layer of urgency. "Family values" discourse rationalized economic and social policies that appeared to be race-neutral but that actually impoverished people of color and immigrants primarily from Latin America, Asia, and the Caribbean.

The conservative backlash of the 1980s and its cohesion in opposing Mexican immigration was also fueled by the gains of Latina/o social movements in the 1960s and 1970s,[22] including multicultural education and bilingualism. A number of legal victories, such as *Mendez v. Westminster* (1947) and *Brown v. Board of Education* (1954), which overturned legal segregation in schools, and the *Hernandez v. Texas* (1954) ruling, which gave Mexican Americans and other historically subordinated groups equal protection under the Fourteenth Amendment, permitted Latinas/os to gain unprecedented rights. The 1964 Civil Rights Act and 1965 Voting Act allowed Latinas/os to participate directly in politics. Mexicans and other Latinas/os built lobbying organizations such as the League of United Latin American Citizens (LULAC), Mexican American Legal Defense and Education Fund (MALDEF), and United Farm Workers (UFW). Latinas/os participated in mass actions such as the Chicano public school student "Blow Outs" in 1968 (when ten thousand Mexican American students and allies demonstrated for educational equality in Los Angeles), national grape boycotts, and the Chicano Moratorium,[23] a series of protests and marches that called attention to the fact that in the Vietnam War, Chicanos were recruited and died in battle at greater rates than other racial groups. Radical activity also flourished among groups such as Raza Unida, the Puerto Rican Socialist Party, and the Young Lords, as well as in *Areito*, a magazine created by Cuban refugees who aimed to establish relations with Cuba. A model of internal colonialism developed to address the intersections of race and class in the United States, and academic studies on Latina/o politics were published.[24]

Between 1965 and 1975, the Chicano Movement, or El Movimiento, which was initially radical, came to utilize a liberal framework to fight for rights. This often more militant phase of Mexican American political struggle exerted new political influence both through Raza Unida and within the

Democratic Party and formed numerous lobbying and social organizations. Significantly, the most prevalent thread of protest took the form of ethnic nationalism, employing the trope of a traditional heteropatriarchal family, called La Raza ("the race"), in order to unify Mexican Americans. Ethnic nationalism also countered the stereotype of the Mexican "illegal alien." Men and women had prescribed roles in the ethnic nationalism schema: the symbolic mothers of La Raza, women were relegated to the domestic sphere. Alicia Schmidt Camacho has noted that this was heterosexist and drew on Cold War nationalism that viewed as threatening migrants and immigrants from Latin American countries where communist activity was prevalent. The trope was thus more divisive than unifying.[25] While the La Raza trope actually complements "family values" ideology (and highlights the centrality of "family" in debates), Chicano Power and new political clout of Latinas/os alarmed conservatives.

Multicultural education was similarly unpalatable to the Right. Ethnic Studies and Women's Studies classes, programs, and departments developed throughout the civil rights era and into the late twentieth century. Campus activism, the Chicano Movement, and other civil rights and feminist groups were key to this sea change, which sought to empower and enfranchise women and people of color via the education system. Given the new hegemony of civil rights–era liberalism, opponents of multiculturalism argued that their opposition was fueled not by racism, but by a desire to salvage a dangerously fractured national unity. (Ironically, this same argument about harming unity with "difference" is what rationalized the subordination of women and erasure of immigrants within the Chicano Movement.) Opponents averred that national identity needed to be defended against "ethnic and racial pride."[26]

Anti-bilingualism rhetoric was comparable: although Spanish speakers represented only 7.3 percent of the U.S. population in 1985,[27] fears about growing "Hispanic" populations coalesced with lobbies to establish English as the official national language on the grounds that official multilingualism was culturally divisive and detrimental to U.S. national heritage and unity. In 1986, California, which was home to a substantial Spanish-speaking population, was the first state to amend its constitution to "preserve and enhance the use of English" through Proposition 63. Six similar federal bills were proposed in 1987.[28] Importantly, in the early 1980s, English Only/Official English resolutions were part of the first round of legislation that became IRCA. English Only efforts also focused on the alleged divisiveness of "cultural" difference and rhetorically cast non-English speakers or bilingual persons as "foreigners" and un-American. This turned non-English speakers into a highly vulnerable workforce, insofar as their options for employment were severely restricted by English Only rules.

Given these "multicultural" factors, family reunification and immigration threatened to increase the already substantial Latin American immigrant population and increase the political clout of Latinas/os. Otto Santa Ana has shown that dominant metaphors for Latinas/os in mainstream media in the 1990s, casting them as invaders, animals, parasites, and diseases, blurred the lines between Latinas/os and immigrants and framed all as threats to the nation.[29] As I will show, such discourse that treated immigration as a powerful, damaging force became ubiquitous in the 1980s. It is not a coincidence that this attitude developed on the heels of the Chicano Power and Latina/o social movements, as demand for immigrant labor increased and the Latina/o population rose; rather, it responded to these changes.

Concerns that unrestricted family reunification would disrupt the nation were also directly related to changes in global capital. Historically, solicitation of migratory male workers and prevention of marriage lessened the social and biological costs of immigration. In the 1980s, however, more immigrants were women[30] from Latin America and Asia. This change was largely a result of poverty created by U.S. imperialism,[31] as well as increases in domestic and service industry jobs for which immigrant women were preferred. For instance, the late 1960s marked the beginning of a transition to the increased migration and settlement of Mexican women and whole families,[32] which coincided with an economic crisis in Mexico and the growing availability of service jobs.[33] Desire to limit family migration and women's migration is also part of what Claudia Sadowski-Smith calls the "illegality spiral," the series of restrictive immigration laws that began in the nineteenth century and "targeted the non-elite segment of each new immigrant group through differential forms of racialization."[34] Initiated to address Chinese and European immigration, the illegality spiral later transformed Mexicans into the quintessential undocumented immigrants. During World War I, when border crossing cards were introduced for Mexican residents, individuals and families who were previously able to freely migrate for seasonal work were rendered "illegal." During World War II, when Mexicans became the most important source of unskilled labor, the U.S. government recruited Mexican labor through the Bracero Program, and because many did not qualify for the program (which favored single men), undocumented immigration increased; Mexicans were "transformed into quintessential *indocumentados*,"[35] or "wetbacks." Mexico, in an effort to retain citizen workers for the industrialization of agriculture that was simultaneously occurring, supported binational border enforcement and thereby contributed to this transformation. For in-

How is inmis understood through popular disc.

— why have Conser Repub. before Anti-immg + no longer
strong [?]

INTRODUCTION | 11

stance, beginning in 1945, U.S. Border Patrol agents began deporting undocumented Mexicans, and Mexican officials forcibly relocated them, often to
areas of labor shortage. When the Bracero Program was suspended, as in 1949
and 1953, the Mexican government positioned military on the Mexico–U.S.
border to keep Mexican citizens from emigrating.[36] By the 1940s, policymak-
ing in the United States shifted to focus almost exclusively to undocumented
Mexican immigration. This set the stage for the collapsing of people of Latin
American origins—immigrants *and* U.S. citizens—into the "illegal alien" in
the public imagination.

In the late twentieth century, with the increased migration of women and
families and in the context of this older illegality spiral, new efforts to reduce
the social and biological costs of immigration focused on reproduction and
child-rearing, and immigrants were accused of disproportionately high birthrates that drained public resources, thereby threatening the economy, "family
values," Americanism itself. Meanwhile, men of Latin American origins were
stereotyped as criminals. Both constructions drew on the earlier construction
of the Mexican (always already) "illegal alien." The "immigration emergency"
was therefore a gendered as well as racialized affair that made family reunification, welfare cuts, border security, and other punitive measures seem to
be logical and rational—rather than part of ongoing governmental efforts to
control unskilled immigrant labor, and/or arising from rote nativism. These
restrictive measures eventually became "commonsense" matters that conservatives and liberals like President Bill Clinton could get behind.

Sexism and racism were further cloaked by a politics of comparison. As
Philip Kresdemas has noted, in matters of immigration under neoliberal governance, some people are protected and nurtured, while others are "subjected
to disciplinary techniques designed to stimulate maximum productivity, but
with much less concern for the welfare of the individual."[37] In political debates and popular culture, Latin American immigrants were pathologized,
while white ethnic immigrants were romanticized. Tropes of immigration in
the 1980s—ranging from celebratory "nation of immigrants" discourses to
damning accusations of threat from fecundity, lack of respectability, laziness,
and criminality—negotiated not only conflicting positions on immigration,
but also broader economic, gender, and racial upheavals. Regardless of differing relationships to histories of slavery, colonization, and imperialism, and
strides made for women's rights, only those who adhered to the white ethnic
model were deemed worthy of inclusion. As Matthew Jacobson shows, white
ethnicity was formed in response to civil rights movement identity politics
and the social justice gains of people of color;[38] the 1980s iteration of white
ethnic "nation of immigrants" identity/discourse that rendered personal re-

sponsibility heroic continued to respond to those gains in ways that were used to support a nativist agenda without seeming racist or nativist. Comparative politics made devaluation of certain immigrants seem logical.

These differing imaginings of immigration intertwined and supported one another, such that the value system of the "nation of immigrants" was framed as endangered by the "immigration emergency," and represented the fusion of progressive and conservative ideologies that made oppressive neoliberal cultural politics come to seem like "common sense." Neoliberal theory originates in the classical liberalism of the eighteenth century, in which "political ideals of 'liberty' were harnessed to economic ideas of the free market." As agrarian and later industrial manufacturing privileged classes formed, a slave ship captain could proclaim his commitment to "liberty" while selling slaves;[39] the hard work of *free white men* was universalized freedom. The neoliberal nation-state rooted government in free market entrepreneurial values like competiveness, self-interest, and decentralization, according to the theory that "social good will be maximized by maximizing the reach and frequency of market transactions"[40] across the globe. Globalization was imbued with the logic that integrating markets universally increased individual freedom and progress.[41] Yet as immigration polemics and a host of other examples indicate, the ideal of the "the free possessive individual engaging with others through market transactions"[42] circumscribes "freedom" and "liberty" along racialized and gendered lines.

Reagan, the "great communicator" who left office in 1989 with a 70 percent approval rating, facilitated the neoliberal redefinition of American "common sense." Along with deregulation of the economy, privatization, liberalization and integration of global markets, consumerism, and an increase in Cold War defense expenditures,[43] Reagan nurtured a sense of American exceptionalism. His patriotism was based on traditional family values, optimism, economic expansion, and celebratory consumerism. Framing the United States and capitalism as moral and "free" in contrast to the "evil empire" of the Communist Soviet Union, he championed and the notion that the reasonable and capable individual rather than the government was the proper locus of social responsibility.

A complex negotiation of race and gender politics was also central to the Reaganite neoliberalization of "common sense." While Barry Goldwater was the last Republican presidential candidate to run on an overtly anti–civil rights platform, Reagan appropriated civil rights–era antiracist discourses to serve his national narrative of ascendance while enabling endemic racism and sexism. On one hand, race was coded through the language of rights, taxes, crime, drugs, and welfare.[44] On the other hand, some people of color were visibly included or represented in media, various professions, and even the government. The Reagan administration also spearheaded the backlash against second-wave feminism (in its opposition to the Equal Rights Amendment [ERA]), but sexism too was similarly reframed to complement the more inclusive political climate. Thus, while Reagan staunchly opposed the ERA and worked to dismantle affirmative action, he noted that there were several women and people of color in his administration (much as Mitt Romney did when asked about women's equality in the second 2012 presidential debate). Likewise, Reagan nominated black American Clarence Thomas to the Supreme Court. But hiring a few women here, a few black Americans there—tokens—did not add up to the structural equality that feminists and civil rights activists were fighting for, and the tokens themselves sometimes advanced neoconservative agendas. Thomas surely benefited from affirmative action, but like other Reaganites, he was committed to dismantling the welfare state, and as the Anita Hill sexual harassment scandal showed, he was no friend to women. Such tempered neoconservatism became a core of neoliberal projects.

To be clear, neoconservatism here means a combination of the liberal theory of free markets and limited government as ensuring individual liberty with the exercise of state power to support a highly patriotic and traditionally moral national imaginary. One important element in this mix was a post-Vietnam anticommunism characterized by the unilateral use of military power to further national interests. Reagan dramatically increased defense expenditures to protect America from the Soviet Union and international terrorism. The historic high point for U.S. defense spending was in 1987, when it hit $456.5 billion (in projected 2005 dollars)—quite a jump from Reagan's first two years in office ($325.1 billion in 1980 and $339.6 million in 1981). The bulk of the increase was for procurement and research and development programs, including the Strategic Defense Initiative (SDI), the infamous "Star Wars" program.[45] In a restart of the arms race, SDI was meant to protect the country from Soviet nuclear attack with a defensive missile shield based in outer space. Intrusive foreign policy had its domestic parallel in government regulation of the citizenry to protect "public security and traditional morality" in such a way that superseded concern for individual rights,[46] as reflected in the "family values" movement. Early neoconservatives also rendered a harsh critique of the New Deal and civil rights legislation, holding that "at best, society (and government) can offer only opportunity and incentive" and that accordingly, "big government" and especially social services, public programs, and affirmative action bred "dependence and poverty."[47] To advance these neoconservative moves, Reagan, "during his first four months in office, met with members of Congress about 70 times."[48]

Reagan provided an enduring model for U.S. neoliberal projects. Neoliberalism itself first developed after World War II, when European intellectuals critiqued statism and especially social engineering and the welfare state. Freeing the market from governments was framed as the solution to the danger of totalitarianism and what would ameliorate workers' dependence on the state. In the United States, these ideas became part of public debate after President Lyndon Johnson expanded New Deal welfare programs with his War on Poverty; there was a pejorative association of "liberalism" with Franklin Delano Roosevelt's New Deal social welfare policies, which allegedly "intervened in the 'personal liberty' of the contract between equals."[49] "Big government" increasingly came under fire as a cause of rather than a solution to economic and social problems. With the 1980 election of Reagan, theory became practice.

The core aspects of neoliberalism involve modes of government rooted in entrepreneurial values; policies that result in the deregulation of the economy, liberalization of trade, and privatization of state services; and the theory that consumerist free trade will bring unprecedented prosperity to both the "developed" and "developing" world.[50] In Europe this is often considered "liberalism" in contrast to statism, while in the United States it is more directly connected to what is considered "conservativism,"[51] though neoliberalism actually—and necessarily—combines elements of various "isms." More specifically, although neoliberals and neoconservatives shared a commitment to free markets, and while some neoliberals have embraced aspects of neoconservatism such as "family values" and a strong military, for neoliberals, freedom and a "hands-off" attitude were defined by globalism, less intrusion in the lives of the citizenry, and neoliberals were often ostensibly committed to socially progressive values. The linking of conservativism and neoliberalism (which Margaret Thatcher also successfully did in the United Kingdom) emblematizes what Stuart Hall has articulated so well, that ideology works best by connecting contradictions that are often visceral. The linking of free market ideology with conservative attachments to "nation, racial homogeneity, Empire, tradition"[52] worked, and neoliberal ideology appropriated and reframed those attachments so that they seemed progressive, or "necessary," given one crisis or another.

In the United States, Reagan combined neoconservatism with "modern" and seemingly broadminded sensibilities, particularly with consumerism and embrace of celebrity culture. This made him attractive to a wide cross-section of the American public and cultivated a sense of unity even as individualism, self-sufficiency, a "wild west" (laissez-faire, deregulated) Wall Street, and consequent intense consumerism became the new normal. Ironically, FDR's "embedded liberalism" created the stage for Reaganite neoliberalism. The welfare state incorporated the working classes into the economy, which facilitated consumer demand and the increasing commodification of society.[53] This was likely not lost on Reagan, especially given that he idealized FDR even as he attacked "big government." Reagan personified and popularized a sense of national confidence that had been lost in the 1960s and 1970s; he facilitated the conservative reorientation of mainstream America, alongside and within his implementation of neoliberal policies. He was astutely moderate.

Reagan's embrace of consumerism, celebrity culture, and "modern" sensibilities was also a slippery slope. Reagan, a former actor, peppered his speeches with allusions to pop culture, notably referring to the hit movie *Back to the Future* (1985) in a State of the Union address.[54] Reagan and his wife, Nancy, hosted glittering state dinners, inviting many of their old Hollywood friends, and drew scorn for their spending on clothing and new White House china. And Reagan sometimes missed the mark completely, as when in a 1984 campaign speech he heralded Bruce Springsteen as the voice of the new America, even as Springsteen's then hit song "Born in the U.S.A." critiqued Reagan's America. Characterized as the "ferocious cry of an unemployed Vietnam veteran" and as a "working-class howl," it contains lyrics such as

> Down in the shadow of the penitentiary
> Out by the gas fires of the refinery
> I'm ten years burning down the road
> Nowhere to run ain't got nowhere to go.[55]

Reagan embodied the contradiction underscoring neoliberalism: "the capitalism and consumerism he helped unleash threatened to destroy the ideals he seemed to most cherish,"[56] in that selfishness, self-interest, and materialism, rather than altruism and commitment to the common good—the nexus of his patriotism and exceptionalism—were the order of the day. In the 1980s, Americans were spending more on homes, clothes, and food, and increasing media coverage of the wealthy led to more competition and envy; TV shows like *Lifestyles of the Rich and Famous*, and businessmen like Donald Trump and Lee Iacocca became celebrities simply for becoming wealthy.[57] In Reagan's America, consumerism became a value too.

In the 1980s, as the neoliberalization of domestic and foreign policy kicked into high gear with privatization, new free trade agreements, and structural adjustment policies (SAPs) in the global south, and with appropriations of feminist and multicultural discourses blended with Cold War rhetoric of America's exceptional benevolence, America appeared more multicultural and gender-equitable than ever before. Yet as David Harvey notes, "redistributive effects and increasing social inequality have in fact been such a persistent feature of neoliberalization as to be regarded as structural to the whole project."[58] Along similar lines, in an article analyzing the "catastrophic consequences" of neoliberalism following the financial crisis of 2007–2008 in order to make a case for radical rethinking on the Left, Stuart Hall, Doreen Massey, and Michael Rustin point out that the people most harmed by neoliberalism and who have received the burden of solving the crisis are, of course, groups already vulnerable and disenfranchised: working people, the poor, people of color, women, single parents, the disabled and mentally ill, students, and the young unemployed.[59]

Unnamed in this list are immigrants, though the authors do mention that the international migration that neoliberalism engenders provides the new free global workforce.[60] Showing how and why discourses of immigration were at the center of rising neoliberalism—and how and why certain immigrants were, like other marginalized populations, blamed for and expected to fix a host of financial and social ills—is the focus of this project. While some scholars, such as Christina Gerken, zero in on immigration discourses in the 1990s and after as properly neoliberal,[61] the 1980s set not only the stage but also the paradigm for what followed. Hall, Massey, and Rustin define neoliberalism as the system of "global free-market capitalism . . . that has come to dominate the world in the three decades since 1980."[62] I argue that the immigration discourses that took shape in the 1980s were of vital importance to the coherence—and maintenance—of the global hegemony of neoliberalism. In order for the Left to do the radical rethinking that Hall, Massey, and Rustin call for, this piece of the puzzle is necessary, for discourses of immigration that emerged during the Reagan era and held sway until 9/11 constituted a significant but understudied rhetorical force that powerfully masked and/or rationalized the racist and sexist social relations that structure neoliberalism.

Law and culture are not separate but rather interrelated spheres that shape people's lives and relationships to power.[63] A host of 1980s films, TV shows, and commercials participated in the emergent conversation about neoliberal crossings and helped to form its lasting contours. Madonna's early work is particularly relevant. While "Borderline" was not about immigration per se— there is no overt immigration narrative or any signifiers of immigration, as there is in "Like a Virgin"—the video nonetheless engages contemporary debates about immigration, feminism, and multiculturalism, and both "nation of immigrants" and "immigrant emergency" discourses can be traced in it, as can the way that white ethnic identity *responded to* Latina/o identity.

First, the video was filmed in a Los Angeles barrio, visually conveyed by a California license plate on the photographer's car and its urban industrial setting in which the only place of business is a Mexican/Salvadoran restaurant and pool hall boasting a sign in Spanish, where the multicultural crew hung out. Historically and into the present, barrios are the result of specific local, state, and federal plans that have created racial segregation, substandard schooling and housing, and severely limited socioeconomic mobility. At the same time, barrios are important settlement communities for new arrivals and include social and economic networks and resources that often transcend local and national boundaries.[64] The Mexican barrio in Los Angeles was formed in the aftermath of the Mexican-American War and the transformation of Los Angeles into an "Anglo" city via laws and policies that stigmatized Mexican residents and relegated them to barrios in cities and to *colonias* (unincorporated settlements along the U.S.–Mexico border) in rural areas.[65] For many, Los Angeles was ground zero of the immigration crisis, so the video's setting itself is connected to immigration polemics. Yet the mainstream public narratives about Mexican immigrants conveniently failed to consider the history of the Mexican-American War, formation of barrios, and transformation of Mexicans into immigrants. A 1985 *Time* article christened L.A. the "New Ellis Island" and "America's Uneasy Melting Pot" because the city was being "flooded" by Asian and Latin American legal and undocumented immigrants who were not "melting" into the American pot.[66] In the same issue, an article on "Losing Control of the Borders" anxiously reflected on the proposed IRCA bill, given the "flood" of Mexican immigration.[67] Madonna's video is about the relationship between a white woman and Latino man in the new/uneasy Ellis Island/melting pot, and features what many nativists like Alan Simpson feared: a colorful multicultural "nation of immigrants" in which the barrio is favored. It is not just that Madonna rejects the white male photographer in favor of the cooler multicultural entourage, but that he is outnumbered by them.

While some have celebrated Madonna as a radical maverick (which is also the name of the record company she launched in 1992 and sold in 2004[68]), just as many have passionately criticized her.[69] Early in her career, the commotion was about the legibility of her performances as rebellions against the confines of Catholic womanhood.[70] In "Like a Virgin," the title track of her second album, released in 1984,[71] Madonna challenged the pure, virginal ideal of premarital heterosexual womanhood enshrined in mainstream Catholic ethics and overtly deviated from the ultimate ideal of Catholic femininity, her namesake, the Virgin Mary—*the* Madonna. The song reached No. 1 on the 1984 Billboard chart, where it remained for six weeks,[72] and was certified

Gold in 1985;[73] the song and video continue to surface today in "Best of" lists. In the video, Madonna portrays a sexually experienced and assertive young woman pretending to be virginal (hence the "like" in the title) for her own pleasure. The song and video challenge traditional femininity, "family values," and religious ideals with direct recourse to white ethnic immigration: the video features her emigration by boat from New York City to Venice, Italy, where she writhes around in a gondola while sporting crucifix necklaces and romps in a palace wearing a white wedding dress. The Catholic imagery is not subtle, and in the 1980s, this sinfully subversive representation of female sexual agency met with outrage from conservatives, who felt that it promoted premarital sex and pornographically defiled religious imagery.[74] Paul Smith and Lisa Frank, editors of the anthology *Madonnarama: Essays on Sex and Popular Culture*, assert that the "crucial ingredients" of Madonna's 1992 photography book *Sex*—what made it popular—are "sex, race, power, and capital."[75] These ingredients soon became her signature, while in early videos such as "Borderline" and later in "Like a Prayer" (1989), interracial relationships are the vehicle through which Madonna challenged gender norms.

Bell hooks argues that at the start of Madonna's career, she claimed and represented a transgressive whiteness that was "other than, different from the mainstream, more connected to folks marginalized by race or sexual practice. For a time, Madonna seemed to desire to occupy both a space that is different and a space that is familiar."[76] Hooks connects this to "her personal history as a dark ethnic from an immigrant background."[77] The notion of white ethnic identity as "different" from mainstream whiteness is conveyed in "Borderline" through Madonna's identification with and preference for the multicultural entourage, aesthetic, and barrio. It is also part of Madonna's off-screen, off-stage identity.

The descendant of Italian immigrants, Madonna Louise Ciccone has her own "rags-to-riches" story, which was ascendant when "Borderline" was released. According to this story, after growing up in Detroit and briefly attending the University of Michigan on a dance scholarship—in keeping with "nation of immigrants" and neoliberal norms—Madonna landed in New York City in 1977 with just thirty-five dollars and with self-reliance, determination, and hard work, went from struggling dancer to "overnight" success. In reality, however, she studied dance, modeled, and worked low-paying jobs, barely surviving until friends convinced her that she had a good voice. Her experiments with disco and pop caught the ear of a disco DJ who helped land her a deal with Sire Records in 1982. Sire reportedly paid her $5,000 per song for several singles, which found moderate popularity on dance and R&B stations, led many to believe she was a black artist, and convinced the company to finance a full LP.[78] The result of her plucky fortitude and hard work (complex racial politics and confusion notwithstanding), *Madonna* the album made her famous. "Borderline" was thus part of Madonna's personal "nation of immigrants" story at a moment when that story was both navigating and reinventing white privilege in the context of multiculturalism and feminism.

In *Roots Too: White Ethnic Revival in Post–Civil Rights America*, Matthew Jacobson shows that in the 1960s and 1970s, in response to civil rights discourses and victories among people of color, the white "ethnic revival" cast white ethnic immigrants and their descendants as the victims rather than the perpetrators of racism, as well as inaugurating the national narrative of the hardworking Ellis Island immigrants who pulled themselves up by their bootstraps in order to succeed.[79] This immigrant variation of the classic liberal ideal was the blueprint for the 1980s neoliberal version of the "nation of immigrants" trope. The ethnic revival was initially formed in connection with progressive multicultural and feminist projects; as Jacobson demonstrates, second-wave feminism, dominated by white ethnic women, attempted to establish a sense of common struggle with women of color and recent immigrants on the basis of shared patriarchal oppression and the history of white ethnic immigrants' poverty, tenement life, and social marginalization, while also trying to distance white ethnics from the legacy of slavery and racism.[80] "Borderline" (and other popular culture texts that will be addressed in later chapters) took up that notion of commonality by imagining coalitions among immigrants and people of color and white ethnic women and portraying them as allies in parallel struggles for social justice, or at least as fellow travelers in a quest for empowered coolness and sexiness. But this progressive narrative was quickly appropriated by neoconservatives to rationalize privatization and opposition to affirmative action and proved useful in nativist and "colorblind" or ostensibly race-neutral attacks on Latin American, Asian, and Caribbean immigrants as freeloading exploiters of America's welcome to immigrants.

Along these lines, "Borderline" offers spectators an alternative to the status quo: it imagines an interracial romance and valorizes multiracial, working-class urban subculture at a time when nativists were convinced the United States was in the throes of an "immigration emergency" that was pouring over the Mexican border. "Borderline" celebrates what nativists and "family values" proponents feared: a white minority figure happily and willingly immersed in a multicultural and perhaps Spanish-speaking or bilingual working-class majority. Adding insult to injury, that white minority figure is an independent woman who makes her own choices about love and capital, rejecting mainstream values.

At the same time, however, traces of the neoconservative appropriation of ethnic revival discourse and feminism may also have been transcoded in this video. White ethnics were celebrated as the quintessential models of as-similation and self-sufficiency for immigrants and minorities at a moment when people of color were fighting for and gaining rights at unprecedented levels. This formulation occluded the slavery, colonialism, and ongoing dis-enfranchisement that people of color contend with by presenting America as democratic and equal for those willing to work hard enough and made it pos-sible to frame whites as a minority unfairly embattled by multiculturalism in an equal system. Madonna, the white ethnic woman, is the only person in the video with an opportunity to move up; her choice to reject that opportunity and return to the working-class multicultural world is presented as liberating, but what about those who do not have the choice? That the liberating choices were not available to everyone does not register in the video, just as the ways that gender and race circumscribe access to an ostensibly exceptional Ameri-can "freedom" are elided in classic liberal and neoliberal discourses. More-over, it is a white person—white privilege—that renders the barrio "cool," and this too is part of an older history of colonization and white appropriation of the cultures, practices, and spaces of people of color.

There is also the matter of race, gender, and violence. The Latino man shoves Madonna when she returns to him after her dalliance with the pho-tographer; thus the video includes a stereotypical representation of Latino machismo, or exaggerated masculine pride often conveyed in dominance and chauvinism. The stereotype of Latino violence, specifically against a white woman, is not central to the plot nor is it lingered over, but racially inflected machismo is visible. In the context of debates over an immigration emergency that heated up over the issue of immigrant violence following the Mariel Boatlift, and given the concurrent heavy circulation of media images of violent men of color, that brief shove is not something that can or should be ignored.

The stereotype of Latino violence that "Borderline" touches on has long circulated in American cinema. Dramatizations of Mexican male violence toward white women began in silent-era "greaser" films such as *Licking the Greasers* (1910) and *Guns and Greasers* (1918). Later films such as *Bordertown* (1935), *The Lawless* (1949), and *Trial* (1955) were based on accusations of inter-racial rape and/or crimes of passion.[81] Similarly, *West Side Story* (1961), the first major film and play about Puerto Ricans in the United States, established a stereotype of Puerto Rican males as violent gang members.[82]

In *Black Sexual Politics: African Americans, Gender, and the New Racism*, Patricia Hill Collins argues that popular cultural images of black sexuality perpetuated black subordination. These images reimagined racist, sexist stereotypes in ways that complemented (appropriated) civil rights discourses of antiracism.[83] Latinos are also subject to such "controlling images." In the 1980s and 1990s, controlling images of Latinos proliferated with films such as *Scarface* (1984), about the rise and fall of a Cuban immigrant drug dealer, *American Me* (1992), about the rise of the Mexican American mafia in California prisons between the 1950s and 1980s, *Carlito's Way* (1993), about the unsuccessful effort of a Puerto Rican criminal to lead a law-abiding life, and *Fort Apache, the Bronx* (1981), about the struggle of white policemen fighting crime in a Puerto Rican Bronx neighborhood.

"Borderline" is much more playful than these films, and Madonna likely meant to pay homage to Latino urban culture: its multiculturalism and her proximity to it are cool, fun, and sexy. And Madonna's off-screen romances with Latinos continued for decades. Nevertheless, the video not only hints at Latino violence against a white woman, but also does so in such a way as to mitigate some of the feminist punch of the video in that Madonna's allegedly empowered "choice" is that of a violent man.

Recuperation of the status quo is also evident in the video's conditions of production. Madonna received the lion's share of the profit and fame from the video and song, in contrast both to her then-boyfriend, "Jelly Bean" Benitez, who remixed the song, and to the Latino actor in the video. Decades later, it is only Madonna who is a household name. In his study tracing the marginalization of Latinas/os in media industries in the late twentieth and early twenty-first century, Hector Amaya notes that "labor discrimination is one of the most efficient means used in neoliberal governmentality to constitute unequal citizenship experiences."[84] Stratified citizenship experiences within media industries begin at the level of the labor rights of Latinas/os, which have been eroded since the 1970s, when corporations transformed 1960s efforts for labor equality (via the Equal Employment Opportunity and affirmative action [EEO/AA] measures) into the neoliberal standard of self-regulation. For Amaya, a striking example of this change is in the way that diversity came to connote not racial justice but rather profitability.[85] This became common in the 1980s, and Madonna's video celebration of diversity was certainly profitable for her, the white ethnic woman, at a moment when the white ethnic was enshrined as the model American citizen. Thus "subversive play"[86] was not necessarily social intervention, but a commodification of diversity as subversion—turning it, and herself, into a product—that made Madonna a wealthy woman. She was embracing rather than rejecting the consumerism central to Reaganism and rising neoliberal projects.

In this sense, the mainstream backlash against multiculturalism and feminism, along with mainstream racial, gender, and immigration politics, also made their way onto the small screen of the video's narrative, visual codes, and conditions of production. "Borderline" visibly engages Reagan-era immigration debates, as well as broader concerns about feminism, multiculturalism, and the welfare state, and sets up a gendered dialectic between white ethnics and Latinas/os that became increasingly significant in immigration politics. As such, "Borderline" suggests that in the context of neoliberal governance, culture is the politics of immigration by other means.

***

With an interdisciplinary Cultural Studies methodology that draws from critical legal studies, feminist theory, queer theory, comparative critical Race and Ethnic Studies, and Media Studies, I bring to light the previously understudied role of immigration discourses in the 1980s in the hegemonic development of neoliberalism, contribute to an ongoing conversation in American Studies and Cultural Studies about the relationship between law and culture, and offer a fresh perspective on the formation of contemporary American identity. Taking seriously the Cultural Studies axiom that "culture is politics by other means,"[87] I consider overtly political speech and expression in direct conversation with patterns of assumption and logic produced, promoted, consumed, and negotiated in the culture at large. Importantly, given that the connections among public policy, pop culture, and media are uneven and asymmetrical and that neoliberalism is a "complex, contradictory cultural and political project,"[88] this study of law and media discourses is likewise uneven and asymmetrical. As Lisa Duggan observes, "developing analyses of neoliberalism must ask how the many local alliances, cultural projects, nationalist agendas, and economic policies work together, unevenly and often unpredictably, rife with conflict and contradiction, to redistribute the world's resources upward—money, security, healthcare, and mobility; knowledge and access to communication technologies; leisure, recreation, and pleasure; freedom—to procreate or not, to be sexually expressive or not, to work or not; political power—participatory access to democratic public life, and more . . . in short, resources of all kinds."[89]

With close attention to "coexisting, conflicting, shifting relations of power along multiple lines of difference and hierarchy,"[90] I trace recurring tropes, narratives, and images about immigration (or images coded as such) in order to evaluate the development of cultural scripts through which questions of immigration, American identity, and labor are explored in relation to rising U.S. neoliberalism.

Close analysis of the law is essential to this task. In her magisterial article, "Is There a Cultural Studies of Law?," Rosemary Coombe asserts that the law creates and diffuses certain forms of power that "constrain and enable agency in social life"; law is central to the cultural conditions of producing everyday life, and what happens in everyday life—what is usually considered "culture"—impacts the formation of law and legal discourse.[91] Developing Coombe's important project in their introduction to a special issue of *Cultural Studies* titled *Cultural Studies and/of the Law*, which aims to explain "the efficacy of the law despite of [sic] and because of the cultural contradictions of neoliberal capitalism,"[92] editors Jaafar Aksikas and Sean Johnson Andrews note that "culture itself is one of the primary resources of law," and law itself is a cultural phenomenon.[93]

Joining this conversation about culture, the law, and neoliberalism, I look at how and why what counted as American "common sense" in general, and especially in relation to immigration, was intertextually reframed in law and culture, which was rather fitting under the tenure of a president who first achieved national prominence as a film star. The structure and methodology of the book reflects this inseparability of law and culture. Primarily through comparative discourse analysis, I focus on language, tropes, and imagery about immigration in law-making and popular media, which gave authoritative accounts of immigration. Thus my study also further develops a Cultural Studies project that analyzes and situates media as part of larger social, cultural, and economic contexts, including the production, distribution, and consumption of texts.[94]

***

Two theoretical approaches shape my inquiry: Cultural Studies views of media as complex primary sources, and intersectionality. First, I analyze popular media as a primary source alongside the materials that are typically the focus of immigration studies: the congressional record, texts of bills, presidential papers, and immigration records. Benedict Anderson importantly demonstrated that print media is crucial to the formation and reproduction of nationalism or a national imagined community.[95] Since the mid-twentieth century, various kinds of media have been major agents of entertainment, information, and socialization. While today this is even more pervasive, given the Web, smartphones, MP3 players, e-book readers, and so on, in the 1980s more "traditional" media—film, TV, and print media (magazines and newspapers)—permeated daily life, competing with and/or augmenting older social institutions such as the legal system, education system, family, and religion, and thus helping to produce "the fabric of everyday life, dominating leisure time, shaping political views and social behavior, and providing the materials out of which people forge their very identities."[96] As groundbreaking critical discourse analysis (CDA) scholars have shown, text and language in media can powerfully reproduce social domination;[97] "as systems of communication, [media] are better able than other social institutions to produce and circulate images and messages that consumers use to construct knowledge and values."[98]

As Cultural Studies scholars have also noted, media are inherently polysemous sites where battles over meaning and values are fought. Negotiation is fostered by the commercial logic of mass media (it is designed to be popular and "relevant" to consumers);[99] the inevitable disruptions intrinsic to hegemony given that it is produced rather than natural or given; and by the "wild card" of audience reception: stereotyping and marginalization in media may acculturate viewers to the status quo. Media representations may also galvanize members of social groups to protest via boycotts and to take control of media production to create their own images; they may engender a more moderate response; or they may produce some combination of these reactions. Stuart Hall observes that the meaning of media is always somewhat circumscribed, since its production structure results in an encoded text that is decoded by audiences.[100] That is, what consumers see is shaped by who writes, produces, and distributes media, and given that most media receive revenues from advertising, what consumers see is also shaped by what sells. So the economic and ideological location of media often results in a "preferred reading" that reproduces the dominant values of a society.[101] More recently and in the context of the kind of media monopoly that Ben Bagdikian warned against in 1983,[102] Hall, Massey, and Rustin argue that "Corporate ownership of the dominant sectors of the media gives capital sway over the means and strategies of representation. . . . [Corporate interests] function as the primary definers of reality. Contrary views have a more fleeting visibility."[103] Consequently, "neoliberal ideas seem to have sedimented into the western imaginary and become embedded in popular 'common sense.' They set the parameters—provide the 'taken-for-granteds'—of public discussion, media debate and popular calculation."[104] The "sedimentation" of neoliberal ideas about immigration discourses is my focus, while I also keep in mind that, as Lawrence Levine argues, the "process of popular culture" must be understood "not as the imposition of texts on passive people who constitute a tabula rasa but as a process of interaction between complex texts that harbor more than monolithic meanings and audiences who embody more than monolithic assemblies of compliant people."[105]

Therefore, while media present particular, industry-supported, and often conservative views of immigration, gender, and race, media also open up spaces for alternatives. The complexity of this is evident in the specific—and uneven—history of media in relation to U.S. immigration. In *Immigration and American Popular Culture: An Introduction*, Rachel Rubin and Jeffrey Melnick note that popular culture "has long been an important collective processing site for questions concerning the politics and ethics of immigration," both given immigrants' involvement in producing as well as consuming popular culture and because popular culture helps to define significant moments in immigration history.[106] Many scholars have shown how popular culture has promoted fear of and panic surrounding immigrants. Film and literature at the turn of the twentieth century were often explicitly xenophobic. Linda Rosa Fregoso, for example, details the maligning of Mexican and Mexican American women as promiscuous criminals in silent film, and others have shown how Asian and white ethnic immigrants were similarly slandered in early twentieth-century popular culture.[107] Fear and panic resurfaced in the "alien invasion" films in the 1980s and 1990s, such as the blockbuster *Alien* (1979) and its three sequels. In *Ecology of Fear: Los Angeles and the Imagination of Disaster*, Mike Davis argues that the prevalent theme of "alien invasion" and filmic representations of disasters in Los Angeles indicate white racial anxiety and fear of dark races.[108] In *The Latino Threat*, Leo Chavez takes up the ongoing currency of that theme and those representations in the media.[109]

Immigrants also produced texts that are considered quintessentially "American," without an explicit trace of immigrant identity; ironically, immigrants have created versions of unadulterated Americanness that nativists held dear. At the turn of the twentieth century, at the height of xenophobia toward eastern and southern European immigrants, immigrant and first-generation Jews formed and headed the major Hollywood production companies such as Universal, Paramount, Metro-Goldwyn-Mayer, Columbia, Warner Brothers, William Fox, and Samuel Goldwyn. The men behind these companies, which created Hollywood, an emblem of American ingenuity and a primary generator of American culture, were Yiddish-speaking immigrants or their sons, who were born into poverty in either Europe or the United States.[110] Thus, not surprisingly, the involvement of Jewish immigrants in early Hollywood production has been a focus of anti-Semitism.[111]

Another example of the immigrant imprint on the formation of a "pure" American identity is the work of Italian American director Frank Capra. In films such as his Depression-era trilogy *Mr. Deeds Goes to Town* (1936), *Mr. Smith Goes to Washington* (1939), and *Meet John Doe* (1941), white male protagonists epitomize an American ideology of individualism, social responsibility, and democratic ideals. Capra himself emphatically wanted to leave his immigrant roots behind. After visiting Italy in 1977, he remarked, "Who the hell cares where you were born? . . . You know that colored guy? That *Roots* thing? He's full of shit. I hate the word roots, people are so proud of their roots it's sickening."[112] Thus, regardless of whether they have embraced it, white ethnic immigrant filmmakers and producers have lived proto–"nation of immigrants" narratives by successfully producing American culture, and in their respective media productions, they have not only reflected but also formulated what counted as American culture.

Other scholars have focused on media as a means for assimilation. Historians have shown that in the early twentieth century, film often helped immigrants acclimate by exposing them to the norms of daily life and showing them how to navigate their liminal position between two cultures,[113] while literary scholars such as Werner Sollors have showed how literature and especially works by immigrant authors have had similar results.[114] The idea of pop culture as an agent of assimilation and negotiation was taken up in some 1980s media such as the sitcom *Perfect Strangers*. Balki (Bronson Pinchot), a white ethnic immigrant who arrives on the Chicago doorstep of his unsuspecting distant cousin, carries knowledge of America based entirely on popular culture. He often flubs his references and their meanings, providing comic relief. For example, Balki expresses admiration of his new country by enthusiastically proclaiming it, "America, home of the Whopper," a mash-up of a Burger King slogan and a line from the national anthem.

Pop culture has also introduced the plight of immigrants to American spectators, and pop cultural texts have critiqued xenophobia and racism. The alternative to *Scarface* came in films such as *El Norte* (1983) and *Born in East L.A.* (1987). The former, a drama directed by Gregory Nava, follows the arduous undocumented migration of two indigenous Guatemalan youths. Seeking relief from ethnic and political persecution during the Guatemalan Civil War, the two are sympathetically depicted as seekers of the freedom that, true to the neoliberal narrative of ascendance, only America can offer. The latter, a comedy directed by and starring Cheech Marin, of Cheech & Chong stoner film fame, follows the repeated attempts of Rudy, a Chicano citizen, to return to his home in East L.A. after being mistaken for an undocumented Mexican and deported. The film's title, an intentional nod to Bruce Springsteen's "Born in the U.S.A.," likewise critiques America—in this case, by showing through comedic satire how Mexican men are unfairly treated as aliens, regardless of citizenship status. These two films are not enduring cultural icons like *Scarface*, but such films do humanize Latin American immigrants and Latinas/os and indicate that the "immigration emergency"—and the dominant "nation of immigrants" narrative—is only part of the story of neoliberalizing America.

Finally, Rubin and Melnick also chronicle how immigrant culture(s) that were imported along with immigrants, as well as those that were formed in the United States when immigrants encountered American culture (such as Zoot Suits among young male Latinos in the 1940s and the development of Jamaican reggae in the South Bronx in the 1970s) have imprinted American culture. Immigrants continue to remake American culture, as indicated by the Latinization of American pop culture in the 1990s. Thus, in any analysis of immigration in the self-proclaimed "nation of immigrants"—especially in the 1980s, when media became integral to daily life—it is necessary to look at popular culture: without it, the picture is incomplete.

My second primary theoretical approach is intersectionality. I follow woman of color feminists' use of intersectionality in order to understand the intertwined and overlapping construction of gender and other components of subjectivity such as race, ethnicity, class, sexuality, age, body size, and nationality, which collectively place individuals in differing positions of power and privilege, oppression and violence. Black feminist legal scholar Kimberle Crenshaw, an early proponent of intersectional analysis in legal studies, interrogated the Anita Hill–Clarence Thomas controversy to demonstrate that "the experiences of women of color are frequently the product of intersecting patterns of racism and sexism, and to show how these discourses tend not to be represented within either feminist or antiracist efforts."[115] As Crenshaw shows, caught between the dominant trope of rape advanced by feminists and the dominant trope of lynching advanced by Thomas's antiracist supporters, the respective race and gender dimensions of Hill's experience were erased. Queer feminists of color have also employed intersectionality to account for erasures that follow when a universal understanding of "woman" or a particular race is the starting point for progressive scholarship and theory. Here, *This Bridge Called My Back: Writings by Radical Women of Color* was path-breaking. Concerned with the erasure of women of color and especially queer women of color in feminism, as well as the invisibility of women in race studies, the 1981 anthology bridged a gap between feminist studies and race studies by considering intersections of race, gender, sexuality, and class in their historical specificity.[116]

Similarly, Latina/o Studies scholarship focuses on the intersectional and specific dimensions of Latina/o experiences. While mine is a comparative racialization project that brings into dialogue Latina/o Studies, Whiteness Studies, and Asian American Studies scholarship, the work of Latina/o Studies scholars such as Elena Garcia, Gina M. Perez, Cecilia Menjivar, Alicia Schmidt Camacho, Rosa Linda Fregoso, Pierette Hondagneu-Sotelo, Patricia Zavella, Arlene Davila, Maria de los Angeles Torres, and Cristina Maria

Garcia, to name only a few, and of scholars of Latinas/os and media, such as Angharad Valdivia, Isabela Molina-Guzman, Leo Chavez, Hector Amaya, and Otto Santa Ana, is vital to analysis of 1980s immigration discourses and thereby foregrounded in my work as well. My comparative approach also contributes to this body of scholarship by showing that several connected gendered racial projects—particularly the politics of comparison between white ethnics and Latinas/os—made immigration key to U.S. neoliberalism.

My method of inquiry, informed by Cultural Studies/Media Studies scholarship and intersectionality, is discourse analysis and the production of authoritative accounts; these necessitate examining "the social practices both in which that production is embedded and which it itself produces."[117] Gillian Rose's approach includes Discourse Analysis I (DAI) and Discourse Analysis II (DAII). DAI interrogates modes of talk and text, and DAII interrogates the social and historical context of texts. Following Rose, I examine the rhetorical and visual structure of tropes in specific legal and media texts, analyzing "how a particular discourse describes things . . . in how it constructs blame and responsibility, in how it constructs accountability, in how it characterizes and particularizes."[118] Additionally, I interrogate "the cultural significance, social practices, and power relations" in which discourses are embedded.[119]

More specifically, I focus on the major tropes of immigration, valuation, and devaluation, inaugurated in the early 1980s under the two broad categories of "nation of immigrants" discourse and "immigrant emergency" discourse, and analyze them dialectically. Using DAI, I examine the specific language and imagery used in laws and law-making processes to value and devalue immigrants. For instance, following the work of scholars such as Teun A. van Dijk, who argue that the way that lawmakers talk about immigration and civil rights can powerfully contribute to negative views of minorities,[120] I ask, how were value and threat defined, implied, negotiated, particularly in terms of gender and race? In direct dialogue with the language of law and law-making processes, I examine popular[121] television shows, films, commercials, and news media that feature immigrants or immigration themes.[122] I consider a text's topic, along with its narrative and visual structure, in relation to its form and format. How are characters linguistically and visually coded as immigrants, citizens, "illegal aliens"? If the story or text is not directly "about" immigration, how is an immigration story signified? Are different narratives told/shown about the value of immigration in relation to the "nation of immigrants"/"immigrant emergency" themes? I also interrogate texts' production. With DAII, I link close analysis of language and imagery with power relations to uncover why texts mobilize discourses of immigrant de/valuation around gender and race.

In sum, the different threads of immigration discourse I bring together, and the unevenness of the connections between legal shifts and popular culture (and the unevenness of neoliberalism itself) in the context of the United States in the late twentieth century[123] necessitates my interdisciplinary Cultural Studies methodology. Such methodology is an intellectual and political commitment to intervene in and transform concrete social conditions.[124]

Chapter 1 begins with a discussion of the 1980 Mariel Boatlift. Media coverage was initially positive, framing President Jimmy Carter's welcoming of Cuban refugees as an example of America's benevolent generosity in stark contrast to the cruelty of a Communist regime. Yet when news broke that the Mariel Boatlift included refugees who had been released from Castro's prisons and mental health facilities—and as refugee numbers grew beyond initial estimates—the media spectacle became alarmist. News media and popular culture, like Brian DePalma's *Scarface* (1983), made it clear that the United States was under siege in an "immigrant emergency" that originated south of the border, manifested itself in gendered ways, and necessitated action. This chapter explores, in conversation with media, the proposed solution, the Immigration Emergency Act (IEA) of 1982, which would have given the president unilateral powers in the face of a vaguely defined "immigration emergency," and situates these developments in immigration history.

Chapter 2 opens with discussion of *The Perez Family* (1990), a romantic comedy film about a group of Mariel refugees who pretend to be a family to increase their chance of remaining in the United States. I then turn to family reunification in the early debates around IRCA. While family reunification has been the primary focus of immigration policy since 1965, in the context of the "immigration emergency," some lawmakers viewed Asian and Latin American immigrant families as threats to American "family values" and the economy. I trace backlash against second-wave feminism as it arose in "family values" rhetoric. Crucial to this facet of neoliberal cultural politics are the sympathetic representations of white ethnic immigrant families and the other dominant trope of neoliberal crossings, the "nation of immigrants" narrative, which I trace in television shows such as *Perfect Strangers* and *The Golden Girls*. Both represented white ethnic immigrants as industrious additions to the nation who overcame poverty with nothing but hard work—that is, according to the typical liberal narrative. Such families were sometimes queer in that they were comprised of a single gender, or were non-nuclear, thereby subverting "family values" in some ways. At the same time these families, which I characterize as "near queer" (if "queer" is understood to mean fluid, progressive, transgressive politics of gender, sexuality, and other intersecting modes of subjectivity and identity), adhered to norms of the white ethnic bootstrap narrative that privileged hard work and heterosexual romantic relationships and tended to erase or gloss over both the racial politics affecting Asians and Latin Americans and the global forces underscoring immigration. As such, near queer families reflected and created a flexible neoliberal narrative of "personal responsibility" that only seemed progressive.

Chapter 3 begins with a discussion of the framing of the Statue of Liberty as the "mother of exiles" during the 1986 centennial celebration of "Liberty Weekend," as a striking example of Reaganite appropriation of multiculturalism. This chapter intervenes in and develops the rich body of leftist feminist scholarship on welfare: I show that that Reagan-era immigration discourse was crucial to the establishment of a neoliberal welfare regime. IRCA welfare cuts and later laws that elaborated upon its precedent minimized the social and economic costs of Latin American and especially Mexican-origin immigrants' reproduction and family formation while exploiting their labor. Pathologizing Latin American immigrant and Latina mothering was at the center of this neoliberal project, as was a politics of comparison. American popular culture delineated a hierarchy of maternity. While films like *Lonestar*, *Mi Familia*, and *Real Women Have Curves* featured condemnatory portrayals of Latina mothering (and such portrayals proliferated in news media), often blatantly imperfect white ethnic immigrant mothers were idealized in shows such as *The Golden Girls*. While representations of Asian immigrants are more difficult to find, films like *Joy Luck Club* exoticized Asian mothers, placing them between white ethnic and Latin American immigrant and Latina mothers and thereby engaging the "model minority" discourse that rationalized the erosion of the welfare state, while bolstering the ostensible inclusivity of the "nation of immigrants" trope. I argue that language and policy about welfare inaugurated in the IRCA debates and in racially coded media representations of immigrant mothers established the paradigm for welfare discourse that was realized in two bastions of neoliberal welfare policy: California's Proposition 187 of 1994 and the U.S. Congress's Personal Responsibility and Work Opportunity Reconciliation Act (PRWORA) of 1996.

Beginning Chapter 4 with analysis of the Genesis song and video for "Illegal Alien," I show how and why Latin American immigrants and Latinas/os were criminalized in media, policy debates, and law, particularly given the simultaneous expansion of the prison-industrial system. The 1983 song, with its refrain of "It's no fun / Being an illegal alien," was supposedly a light satire about the struggles of undocumented immigrants that actually played up every extant stereotype of Mexicans. At the same time, romanticized Italian American mafia families in films like *The Godfather* trilogy and *Goodfellas* provided a sharp contrast to media alarm—the continuation of the "immigrant emergency"—over unmarried Latino gangbangers in films like *Colors* and *Fort Apache, the Bronx*. This was largely accomplished by portraying Latina/o family and gender arrangements as dysfunctional deviations from "family values," which contrasted the romanticization of the white ethnic crime family. Meanwhile, in martial arts films like *Shanghai Noon* and the *Rush Hour* series that made Asians more visible in pop culture, Asian men were cast as exotic and often family-less crime fighters and thus again occupied a place between Latin American immigrants and Latinas/os and white ethnics. Focusing on increased border control and punitive immigration law that functioned increasingly like criminal law, as well as on racialized tropes of immigrant criminals in media, I assert that racially disparate discourses of immigrants and crime produced, justified, and negotiated racist and sexist social relations for neoliberalizing America.

Chapter 5 begins with a discussion of Jennifer Lopez's buttocks—a memorable symbol of the explosion of Latina/o pop culture in the 1990s—and there I link the celebration of Latina/o culture and especially Latina bodies to democratic rhetoric surrounding IRCA's amnesty program and show how they erased the material realities of immigration, sexism, and racism. Nuyorican (New York–born, of Puerto Rican descent) Lopez is not an immigrant (nor were many of the most prominent stars), yet she and other Latina/o stars were rhetorically framed as immigrants in the media in a celebratory manner. Two seemingly contradictory strains of "nation of immigrants" discourse affectively (and thus effectively) portrayed America as the globally exceptional guarantor of democratic rights and equal access to economic mobility. Both race-neutral immigrants and explicitly racialized immigrants who succeed based on hard work were regarded as quintessentially American. With the former strain, "overlooking" race and gender was cast as multicultural and feminist; with the latter, tokens of diversity like Lopez embodied American inclusivity. This neoliberal elaboration on the prototypical immigrant bootstrap story suggests that anyone—specifically, a Latina woman—can be successful if she takes personal responsibility and works hard enough . . . and is sufficiently curvaceous. Much like amnesty, the Latinization of popular culture was steeped in language of enfranchisement. Yet immigrant laborers continued to be exploited, Mexican Americans continued to be disproportionately poor, women were excluded from the amnesty program, the celebration of Latina stars' curves was inseparable from the colonial history of articulating racial difference through the hypersexualization of women, Latina/o stars were rhetorically framed as immigrants—that is, foreigners or outsiders—and gendered anti–Latin American immigrant sentiment increased. And of course the only valuable immigrant was one who took personal responsibility for him- or herself. I argue that with a cosmetic rather than redistributive equality, both "nation of immigrants" strains powerfully masked the exploitation and violence that are constitutive of neoliberalism.

The concluding chapter begins with a discussion of the creative, professional, and advocacy work of Junot Diaz. I then examine the legacy of Reaganite neoliberal crossings and their more recent iterations. I consider white ethnic female pop artists like Gwen Stefani and Lady Gaga, who have continued Madonna's tradition of negotiating racial, gender, and sexual social norms, and establish the ongoing significance of the paradigms inaugurated in the late twentieth century: President George W. Bush's lobby for an amnesty/guest-worker program based on the IRCA model in the midst of post-9/11 restrictions on immigration and civil liberties, Obama administration struggles for immigration reform in relation to labor and terrorism, and overtly racist laws such as Arizona's SB 1070. These collectively show that the issues underscoring Reagan-era immigration have not been resolved, nor have the major tropes been entirely abandoned even as the "War on Terror" following 9/11 altered immigration discourse. Identifying continuities in legislation and media, I aver that nation-based rights are worthless under neoliberalism, given that the system and immigration itself is by definition transnational and unequal, and I make a case for queering immigrant rights in law and culture to obviate the lingering hegemony of de/valuing immigrants on the basis of personal responsibility, hard work, and adherence to conventional gender and sex roles. That is, I make a case for rejecting the paradigm of neoliberal crossings.

***

Curtis Marez observed that "migration is not a marginal, temporary feature of life in the U.S. but rather a permanent part of it."[125] Along similar lines, Chicana poet and novelist Ana Castillo noted, "From the beginning of time, the human being, just like all nature, has migrated to where it could survive. Trying to stop it means one thing only for the species: death."[126] The necessity of migration is also a structural feature of neoliberal projects: both immigration and neoliberalism are by definition transnational. Hannah Arendt famously stated, "Sovereignty is nowhere more absolute than in matters of emigration, naturalization, nationality, and expulsion."[127] Taken from *The Origins of Totalitarianism*, which examined Nazism and Stalinism as emblematic cases of governance systems that attempted to control every aspect of public and private life, this statement suggests that immigrants are especially vulnerable to totalitarian exercises of power: they are liminal in a system in which nations grant rights. Arendt wrote prior to the coherence of neoliberalism, but her statement is nonetheless salient: neoliberal projects coerce migration in ways that are always already exploitative and sometimes even deadly, because immigrants lack rights in a system that profits from their surplus labor. Moreover, differential gendered racialization through immigration discourses guarantees that certain groups remain marginal even when rights are granted, and even among native-born citizens. But such sinister aspects are difficult to recognize when Madonna's dance moves, Sophia's Petrillo's quips, and J-Lo's curves made immigration seem fun, cool, sexy, and empowering, whether through seemingly accessible feminine agency and/or upward mobility. And on the other end of the spectrum, when films like *Scarface* and *Mi Vida Loca* made immigration seem like a frightening emergency, restriction and punitive measures make sense. Thoroughly understanding U.S. immigration in the period in which nation crossings became neoliberal necessitates analyzing the variety and ubiquity of immigration discourses. Only by comprehending how the discourse of an "immigration emergency" has been used—and veiled and justified by "nation of immigrants" discourse, from the congressional floor to the Billboard Top 10—is there a chance of fostering a truly democratic project that puts immigrants' human rights at the center of immigration politics.

1

Immigration as Emergency

In the spring of 1980, Americans were transfixed by an international humanitarian crisis unfolding on their TV screens. Cuban President Fidel Castro, after years of restricting emigration, opened the port of Mariel, and thousands of Cubans set out for the Florida coast, on boats and any jerry-rigged contraption that would float. In accord with U.S. policy to provide refuge to persons fleeing Communist nations, as codified in the recently passed Refugee Act, President Jimmy Carter dispatched U.S. Navy and Coast Guard vessels to assist Cuban refugees. As TV cameras captured the poor, exhausted Marielitos coming ashore, news coverage was sympathetic and praised America's exceptional ability to offer these immigrants safe haven, in stark contrast to the oppression of Castro's Cuba.

Two days after Marielitos began arriving, a *Washington Post* article noted that while Key West was "besieged," "swarmed," and "clogged" by the "tide" of Cubans who threatened to exceed Carter's offer to accept 3,500 refugees, the "nation of immigrants" welcomed them. The U.S. Immigration and Naturalization Service (INS) "dutifully" processed immigrants while the Coast Guard organized private boats in small flotillas to rescue refugees travelling without supplies in overloaded, unseaworthy vessels.[1] In 1979, Castro had allowed increased contact between separated families in Cuba and Miami, and by 1980 the hope of family reunification and the promise of America outweighed the risks of the journey.

Nationalist chest-thumping was ubiquitous. The Cuban revolution was a key point of tension in the Cold War because, as Maria de los Angeles Torres notes, "for the international Left, it restored the utopian dream of socialism that had been distorted by Stalinism; for the free world it marked the expansion of the evil empire."[2] Regarding the refugees, *Time* claimed, "All seemed happy to be finally on American soil."[3] Hungry refugees spoke of hardships and repression in Cuba as they "wolfed down" the fried chicken, ham, and Cokes they were given at a local chamber of commerce. In describing America's offer of refuge, news media showed that U.S. capitalist democracy was—in contrast to Castro's Communism—humane, free, and abundant. The endeavor was accordingly christened the "Freedom Flotilla" and seemed a continuation of Cold War policies that welcomed Cubans as refugees from communism.[4]

But the media spectacle quickly became alarmist. Refugees numbered approximately 125,000, rather than the 3,500 President Carter agreed to accept.[5] In addition, after the port of Mariel was opened, prisoners and inmates of mental institutions (including some homosexuals, then considered mentally ill in Cuba) were deliberately released and put on boats. One article noted, "Although no reliable figure exists for the full wave of refugees, half of a group of 220 single men interrogated by police recently admitted having criminal pasts. 'We're looking at everything from robbery to drug trafficking, to murder, and those are only the people who admitted to their crimes or who were identified to us by other refugees,' . . . a spokesman for the Dade County sheriff's office, said."[6] Domestic fears supplanted Cold War chest-thumping, and this disquieting revision of the Mariel story became the dominant and enduring one. For instance, the *New York Times* published a series of articles with headlines like "Miami Homicide Rate 5 Times above Usual among Cuban Exiles" and "Cuban Ties Boatlift to Drug Trade," which included speculations that some Marielitos were spies.[7] Media and soon congressional discussions about Florida's inability to handle the deluge of needy refugees—and especially that state's alleged inability to adequately protect resident Americans from the refugee criminal element—proliferated.

The lives of many Marielitos, who were mostly men between the ages of eighteen and twenty-six, were indeed difficult. Many, already traumatized under an oppressive regime, arrived homeless and without any organized resettlement plans in place;[8] they also spoke no English and had minimal marketable skills,[9] as was often the case with immigrants. Mirta Ojito's 2005 memoir, *Finding Mañana: A Memoir of a Cuban Exodus*, shows that most involved in Mariel "endured a wrenching family affair that had nothing to do with their sexual persuasion or criminal tendencies."[10] In fact, crime rates were rising in Miami before Mariel, and in fact, only 350 felons and 1,306 persons accused of lesser crimes entered, comprising 1.4 percent of the arrivals.[11] Nonetheless, Marielitos quickly became identified with crime and disease as Florida struggled to cope with the socioeconomic strains the new residents created.

The Carter administration dealt with the boatlift under the 1980 Refugee Act, which offered asylum and assistance to persons subject to persecution in other nations, raised the annual ceiling of refugees, and created a uniform procedure for admittance, resettlement, and absorption. It attempted to deal with refugees from Communism, a salient issue in the 1970s with Vietnamese "boat people"—thousands of men, women, and children (not only Vietnamese, but primarily so) who fled the Indochinese peninsula after Saigon fell in 1975. The ensuing international humanitarian crisis involved the United Nations and numerous governments.

Between 1975 and 1980, the United States admitted 400,000 Southeast Asians, under ten ad hoc refugee programs, as existing immigration legislation (passed in 1965) had envisioned only 17,400 refugees per year. The Refugee Act set the annual refugee limit at a more realistic 50,000 and included the first systematic framework for admittance and resettlement. The law seemed to incorporate human rights into foreign policy, a first in American history. In accordance with language the United Nations began using in 1967, the law defined a refugee as "any person who is outside any country of his nationality or in the case of any person having no nationality, is outside of any country in which he last habitually resided, and who is unable or unwilling to avail himself of the protection of that country because of persecution, or a well-founded fear of persecution, on account of race, religion, nationality, membership of a particular social group, or political opinion." The law also created "asylees," refugees who applied for status while already in the United States. Both could become legal resident aliens after one year and begin the five-year naturalization process.[12]

While welcoming Communist refugees "proved" that America's capitalist democracy was more appealing and humane, humanitarian claims, in the absence of certain political conditions, were not a basis for admittance to the country. Haitian "boat people," who arrived in South Florida during the years 1957–1986, were considered "economic migrants" from a "friendly" government, though many were fleeing political persecution (and extreme poverty) under François "Papa Doc" and Jean-Claude "Baby Doc" Duvalier. Thus at the same time the United States welcomed Marielitos, it turned away 25,000 Haitians.[13]

Observers attributed this to racism, as Haitian migrants were black, poor, and affiliated with disease at a time when full-on panic over AIDS was taking shape. A 1981 *Newsweek* article noted, "Many . . . [Haitian refugees] suffer from venereal disease, tuberculosis and other ailments."[14] Until 1981, Haitian "boat people" were detained in Florida and quickly repatriated. Widely criticized for this, the Carter administration created a vague category for undocumented Haitians that granted minimal refugee rights. Still, from 1981 to 1991, only twenty-eight of the 22,000 Haitian "boat people" intercepted by the Coast Guard were granted asylum.[15]

The differing status of refugees shows how issues of immigration, race, and politics played out in popular culture as *a part of* public policy. As Rosemary Coombe observes, the cultural study of law considers local complexities in relations between power and meaning in daily life—how law shapes everyday life,[16] and how everyday life surfaces in public policy debate. Cultural study of the law also includes examining how "the law engages the aesthetic strategies of narrative in the service of an authoritative version of the cultural identity of a nation, and to that extent, enshrines ethical and political values."[17] Law and culture are entwined and mutually constitutive, particularly in the neoliberal context when an ideological rationale is needed to justify legal changes that do not have a material correlate to inspire consent to them (unlike the economic incorporation of the working classes with New Deal policies).

Racist stereotypes of Haitians were, not surprisingly, replete in 1980s pop culture. In horror movies and thrillers, representations of Haitians were reified, as those of Marielitos would be. Haitians were portrayed as Voodoo doctors who practiced dark arts and were linked to primitivism and "uncivilized" behavior. Voodoo, a religion practiced mostly in Haiti and in the Haitian diaspora, originated in the context of eighteenth-century colonialism and testifies to the adaptability and resilience of enslaved Africans, who blended their tribal beliefs with the Christianity forced upon them. Mainstream texts did not explore this syncretism. Rather, films such as *Angel Heart* (1987), *Serpent and the Rainbow* (1988), and *Voodoo Dawn* (1990) sensationalized Voodoo with sordid sex, violence, and even cannibalism and child sacrifice. *The Believers* (1987) similarly sensationalized Santeria, the Latin American syncretic blend of indigenous and pagan beliefs and rituals with Catholicism, also a response to colonization. In Voodoo films, the threating evil in Haiti originated in Africa, and its embodiment was black. Given the connection of racism and white supremacy in spectacles of Voodoo, the xenophobic impetus underscoring policy that greeted Haitians is therefore not hard to see.

Voodoo stereotypes aside, from the perspective of immigrants, or would-be immigrants, the "refugee" label was important. Cecelia Menjivar found in her examination of the role of kinship networks in shaping the experience of Vietnamese, Salvadoran, and Mexican immigrants that U.S. government classification of migrants significantly determines social and economic opportunities. Vietnamese refugees fared better than Salvadorans and Mexicans, who were not granted refugee status. Access to federal aid programs supported the formation strong kinship networks;[18] what Ruben Rumbaut calls a "structure of refuge" made it easier for refugees to adjust.[19] In other words, groups classified as refugees were often in a better position to receive financial help as newcomers.[20] Thus in some respects, as refugees Marielitos were well-positioned as migrants.

But when coverage of Mariel became alarmist, the granting of that privileged immigration status became problematic; the outcomes of Mariel suggested that the Refugee Act was ineffective. Carter was criticized, and calls for refugee restriction and more presidential control over immigration ensued. In fact Reagan's promise to "get tough on Cuba" was an important part of his first election platform.[21] As Carter's term ended, the "immigration emergency" was in full swing, beginning a period when restrictive, punitive legislation came to seem logical and necessary—"common sense." This notion of "common sense" gave rise to policy debates and proposed legislation to handle the "immigration emergency." Given that immigration itself was changing, the emergency manifested itself in racialized and gendered ways. Mariel heightened a sense of crisis that was carried through popular culture, news media, and legislative bodies. "Emergency" bills introduced in Congress shared similar concerns, discourses, tropes, and even sponsors. Thus, the immigration debates and rhetoric of this period can be understood as a legislative process that began with the Mariel Boatlift and culminated in the Immigration Reform and Control Act (IRCA) of 1986.[22]

The changes in this period were profound; the beginnings of neoliberal crossings emerged then. Neoliberalism, based on the notion that consumerist free trade will engender universal prosperity, roots government in entrepreneurial values, pivots on policies that result in deregulation of the economy, liberalization of trade, and privatization of state services,[23] and therefore affects how and why people migrate and how they are received.

Race and Gender: Defining the "Immigration Emergency"

When the Mariel Boatlift ended in October 1980, it continued to have repercussions in an ongoing discussion about immigration in Congress, news media, and popular culture and amplified an existing immigration problem that originated south of the border. Immigration reform that focused on Latin America in general and Mexico especially had been under discussion for the previous decade or so. The U.S. Population Reference Bureau and Leonard F. Chapman, President Richard M. Nixon's commissioner of immigration (1973–1977), claimed that the country was experiencing an undocumented immigration crisis of considerable volume.

But the volume of undocumented immigration had not substantially increased in the 1970s; rather, the volume of non-white immigrants from "Third World" nations had increased.[24] Asian and Latin American nations came to dominate immigration, and Mexico, the top source of legal and illegal immigration, assumed a "singular significance."[25] This was a dramatic change from 1951 to 1960, when 60 percent of undocumented immigrants came from Europe and Canada, while Mexico was only the third largest source.[26]

Moreover, more women from Asian and Latin American countries were migrating, which also affected the trajectory of debates. Historically, most immigrants from nations with substantial non-white populations were male, and the costs of family formation and maintenance were kept low through policies that prevented marriage. For example, during the nineteenth-century construction of the Transcontinental Railroad, when male Chinese laborers were temporarily needed, the 1875 Page Act restricted the immigration of unmarried non-elite Chinese women, involuntary Chinese migrant laborers, and Chinese women suspected of prostitution. It was assumed that without the option to form or reunite with family, Chinese laborers would eventually return to China. In the mid-twentieth century, the U.S. government also solicited male temporary workers through the Bracero Program, which from 1942 to 1964 imported and deported Mexican laborers in accordance with wartime and agricultural needs.

In the late twentieth century, however, more women began to migrate in response to several factors, including the removal of race and gender restrictions in immigration law and increased domestic and service-sector employment opportunities for them. New means of cutting the biological and social costs of immigration were required. To that end, "family values" and welfare restrictions were significant topics of debate amongst policymakers (as further discussed in Chapters 2 and 3). Cuts in welfare were justified in terms of allegations of immigrant women's fecundity and consequent propensity to abuse social services.[27] Thus gender underscored the "immigrant emergency" as it developed in the early 1980s, although debates were not always framed explicitly in such terms. Senator Alan Simpson (R-WY), for example, said that "American people were 'offended' by an immigration and refugee policy that made them the 'sugar daddies of the world.'"[28] He cast immigrants as feminized burdens that drained the masculinized national polity, and while Simpson's phrasing was unique, he was by no means the only pundit who coupled misogyny and immigration policy. Gender was a constant underlying theme, even in debates that were ostensibly over other issues.

In 1978, President Carter convened the Select Commission on Immigration and Refugee Policy (SCIRP) to thoroughly review immigration policy.[29] Chaired by Reverend Theodore Hesburgh, then president of Notre Dame, it was composed of sixteen individuals from the legislative branch (including Simpson, a major player in immigration reform), the executive branch, the cabinet, and the public, including such individuals as Cuban American Joaquin Otero, vice-president of the AFL–CIO Brotherhood of Railway and Airline Clerks and president of the Labor Council for Latin American Advancement. SCIRP was the first to undertake comprehensive examination of immigration policy since the 1907 Dillingham Commission.

In early 1981, the committee delivered its final report to the newly established Reagan administration, which recommended "closing the back door to undocumented/illegal immigration, opening the front door a little more to accommodate legal migration in this country, defining our immigration goals clearly and providing a structure to implement them effectively," and called for establishing efficient, fair procedures.[30] SCIRP proposed modest amnesty, employer sanctions and a system of worker verification, and increased border control, claiming that illegal immigration was the most significant immigration problem facing the United States.

SCIRP also recommended ratifying most reforms passed under the standing Immigration and Nationality Act (INA) of 1965, such as the removal of race-based restrictions and giving preference to family reunification. But not all SCIRP members agreed, which is where the gender and race politics underscoring the "immigration emergency" become clearer. The INA expanded family reunification and made it a focus of immigration policy. Simpson disapproved, since he identified family reunification as a cause of the increasing volume of immigration from Asia and Latin America.[31] His racist and sexist critique of family reunification, which began in SCIRP proceedings, took full shape in the first version of IRCA he sponsored. Unifying heterosexual spouses and families had been a cornerstone of immigration policy since 1921,[32] and given that men were migration pioneers,[33] traditionally more women than men entered under family reunification. In other words, the entrants Simpson sought to restrict were following established patterns, but now came mostly from Asia and Latin America. He was thus calling to restrict the immigration of Asian and Latin American women.

Thus the "immigration emergency" must be understood as including two distinct but interrelated elements. On one hand, the "immigration emergency" was a consequence of changing immigration patterns since 1965. According to the historical pattern, these newer migrants were considered distinct from previous immigrants in this "nation of immigrants." At the same time, the other dominant immigration discourse in the 1980s, the "nation of immigrants" trope, was threaded through "immigration emergency" discourse. The "nation of immigrants" trope offers an idealized version of the history of U.S. immigration as one of logical ascent within an exceptional democratic system that offers the opportunity for a better life to all immigrants who work hard, usually for the sake of family. This immigration version of the classic liberal narrative (which has a specifically neoliberal iteration) of a free person's hard work paying off in a fair system often seemed to mitigate the more flagrant racism and sexism that surfaced in "emergency" discourses, *and* the "nation of immigrants" discourse sometimes rationalized that racism and sexism: the "immigrant emergency" was ostensibly threatening the exceptional "nation of immigrants." Immigration reform was already on the table in the early 1980s, but with the "immigration emergency" trope that circulated in relation to proximate issues such as Haitian "boat people" and Mariel, broader reform issues were often subsumed under alarmist discourses. Immigration policymakers were therefore discussing long-term immigration reform while they debated quick fixes. The Mariel Boatlift had provided pundits and the public with tangible evidence of a gendered, racialized emergency that demanded immediate and decisive action. In this discourse, immigration became the central cause of a crime emergency, a population emergency, an employment emergency, a birth-rate emergency, a welfare emergency, and a loss-of-American-values and culture emergency.

Codifying the "Immigration Emergency"

After SCIRP's recommendations in 1981, the Reagan administration created its own policy review mechanism by establishing the President's Task Force on Immigration and Refugee Policy.[34] An unprecedented five years of congressional and popular debates "driven simultaneously by economic and identity considerations"[35] followed, with the committee's work finally ending with IRCA's passage in 1986. Action moved to Congress, with the House side managed primarily by Romano Mazzoli (D-KY) and the Senate side by Simpson, under the auspices of the Subcommittee on Immigration and Refugee Policy. (Thus in the following pages, "SCIRP" refers to congressional subcommittees, not the Select Commission.) The duo lent their names to a pair of unsuccessful sweeping immigration bills until 1985, when a third version (co-sponsored by Peter Rodino (D-NJ), rather than Mazzoli), passed as IRCA. Until 1985, Mazzoli and Simpson held numerous single-chamber and joint hearings to consider various pieces of proposed legislation. The tropes that circulated as two federal committees and Congress sought to negotiate economic and ethnocentric concerns in this immigration crisis became a core component of Reagan-era nation-building and thus a core component of the rising hegemony of neoliberalism.

In September 1982, Representative Bill McCollum (R-FL) proposed the Immigration Emergency Act (IEA) (H.R. 7234) in reaction to the government's alleged inability to effectively respond to the Mariel Boatlift under the Refugee Act. The proposed law allowed the president to unilaterally declare an "immigration emergency" and utilize vaguely defined powers, including interdiction and indeterminate detention of immigrants, restrictions of citizens' international and domestic travel, and removal of federal jurisdiction to review provisions under the act itself.[36] While Senate and House hearings on several versions—all sponsored by both Republican and Democratic Florida lawmakers—continued into 1983, and while all died in subcommittees, the salient point is that in the context of an "immigration emergency" partisans joined forces to pursue "commonsense" restriction of immigration and expanding executive power. This provides an example of how neoconservative elements blended into the rising neoliberal project in U.S. immigration debates.

In SCIRP hearings on the initial version of IEA, lawmakers, activists, and academics presented reports that epitomize the language, imagery, and contours of the neoliberal "immigration emergency." The bill, written by a committee chaired by the unapologetically nativist Simpson, cited an extraordinary incident, the Mariel Boatlift, as its rationale; civil liberties should be restricted and the president granted unilateral power to protect the nation from an immigrant threat that had already occurred once with Mariel. If both liberal and conservative proponents were correct about "a threatened mass migration of undocumented aliens,"[37] then this extreme measure was "common sense." As political philosopher Giorgio Agamben asserts, "Power no longer has today any forms of legitimation other than emergency. . . . Power is everywhere and continuously refers and appeals to emergency as well as laboring secretly to produce it."[38] Similarly, Jaafar Aksikas and Sean Johnson Andrews point out that retaining the "hegemonic legitimacy of the law as a social, cultural and political force" underscores every official attempt to establish a "state of exception."[39] "Moreover, reified belief in the law as a 'higher' legitimizing social force . . . is a constant feature of the U.S. social formation, but in the neoliberal conjuncture, the law has been assigned a peculiarly central place and given a special form of efficacy and potency. . . . The law itself is seen as superior to other social bonds, especially those based on reciprocity, trust or common cultural belief. It is the central legitimizing ideology."[40]

That discourse of "immigration emergency," which surfaced repeatedly in hearings and would be used over the next decade in connection with immigration, helped the U.S. neoliberal project to cohere. It made neoliberal law seem like *the* "higher order" that would solve socioeconomic immigration-related problems, rather than a force of exploitation and oppression. For instance, in support of IEA, Senator Lawton Chiles (D-FL) averred that Castro used immigrants who wanted to be reunited with their families to invade the United States; Mariel indicated that emigration could be used as a weapon. Chiles argued that the IEA would protect the United States.[41]

Senator Paula Hawkins (R-FL) claimed that one year after the boatlift, "Dade County's population increased by roughly 10 percent, but the increase in serious crimes rose double that, 23 percent."[42] For years after the boatlift, this sense of a crime emergency was repeatedly proclaimed in media and popular culture as well, further legitimizing the sense of emergency and the need to address it in the law.

In 1983, *Scarface*, written by Oliver Stone, made a spectacle of the trope of the criminal Marielito. In the remake of a 1932 film by the same name, Antonio "Tony" Montana (Al Pacino) is a Cuban refugee and bona fide criminal who comes to Florida via Mariel. The graphically violent film chronicles Montana's bloody rise and fall in Miami's drug trafficking underworld, dramatizing the criminal threat for audiences with enduring images of the violence that unregulated immigration from Latin America created. Detained by the INS on (correct) suspicion of criminal activity, Montana is held in a refugee camp, where he earns a green card in exchange for the murder of a former aide to Castro at the behest of fellow Latino Frank Lopez (Robert Loggia), a powerful drug lord. Montana steals Lopez's girlfriend, Elvira Hancock (Michelle Pfeiffer), who as a white, blonde-haired, blue-eyed woman symbolizes his ascent in the crime underworld. White women have historically been the property of white men, so protecting their purity as property and literal reproducers of heirs also meant preventing miscegenation.[43] In the context of Mariel and neoliberalizing shifts, the film updated fear of racialized violence and miscegenation which has persisted from the colonial origins of the United States and is part of a long history of stereotyping Latinas/os in U.S. mainstream film.[44]

Although the film initially received mixed reviews, it grossed $4.6 million its opening weekend and over $45 million total in North America. With this perversion of the American Dream[45] and "nation of immigrants" narrative trope, the stereotype of the violent, criminal Latino—the backbone of the 1980s "immigrant emergency" trope—charted in the box office and eventually became iconic. Pacino was nominated for a Golden Globe award for Best Actor in a Motion Picture Drama, and the film is still recognized on numerous "Best of" lists such as the 2008 American Film Institute's "Ten Top Ten" list of the best ten films in ten "classic" American film genres. Today it is a cult classic.[46]

A similar representation of Latino violence surfaced in *Miami Vice*. The crime drama series, produced by Michael Mann for NBC, ran from 1984 to 1989 and focused on James "Sonny" Crockett (Don Johnson) and Ricardo "Rico" Tubbs (Phillip Michael Thomas), Metro-Dade Police Department undercover detectives. The show was nominated for a litany of awards, taking four Emmys, two People's Choice Awards, two Golden Globe Awards, and three Grammys. It is remembered for its artistic cinematography, soundtrack, unique pastel color scheme, and contributions to 1980s fashion (namely, Don Johnson's iconic blazer with pastel t-shirt and linen pants). *Miami Vice* also stands out for its representations of multiculturalism. Sonny, a white man, and Rico, a black man, are a multiracial crime-fighting team when representations of people of color were only beginning to diversify. And the show featured Latinos doing things other than selling drugs and committing violent crimes, such as fighting crime on the police force and being victims of crime. The Latino and specifically Marielito violent crime stereotype, however, was built into the show's premise. The detectives do after all work undercover in Miami's drug underworld.

For instance, in the series pilot, "My Brother's Keeper" (September 16, 1984), antagonist Trini DeSoto (Martin Ferrero), lieutenant to a Columbia drug kingpin, is a Marielito. After a series of violent acts, DeSoto dresses in drag to murder a former associate who plans to cooperate with law enforcement. Thus like Tony Montana, the Miami Latinos of *Miami Vice* were often violent drug dealers, and DeSoto's turn in drag united the discomfort surrounding the homosexuality of some Marielitos with the stereotype of masculine violence. Episodes frequently end with spectacular gun battles that result in the death of villains, but there are always more criminals to fight, and sometimes the main adversary escapes. The show proffered a sense of the inevitability of violent crime that was frequently coded as Latino.

The neoliberal(ized) stereotype of male Latino violence and its colonial origins will be more fully covered in Chapter 3. Now, I return to the question of why such representations in popular culture matter, especially in relation to law. Traditionally, studies of popular culture and the law either provide accounts of the legal regulation of pop culture or explore popular representations of courtrooms and legal proceedings. Christy Collis and Jason Bainbridge argue that two assumptions should animate analyses of pop culture and the law. First, that law is cultural and thus formed by a set of social practices. Second, "popular culture is not simply a domain in which the law is represented; rather, it is a domain in which law is practiced, negotiated, legitimized, and embodied."[47] As Lieve Gies asserts, legality—a general sense of right and wrong, and how law should manage these categories—is not restricted to courts and courtroom dramas. Individuals and societies possess a "legal consciousness" that affects daily experiences and consumption of popular culture.[48] Moreover, as Rachel Rubin and Jeffrey Melnick observe in their study of immigration and popular culture, "popular culture is an arena where 'Americanness' and 'otherness' are constantly being negotiated."[49] Thus shows like *Miami Vice* and movies like *Scarface*, along with newspaper headlines, shaped and were shaped by wider social and political discussion that included the law-making process. In effect, a sense of "right and wrong" is formed through and nurtured by both the law-making process and in pop culture.

In *The Latino Threat: Constructing Immigrants, Citizens, and the Nation*, Leo R. Chavez examines the "Latino threat" narrative, which posits that Latinas/os are, in contrast to previous immigrant groups who assimilated into American culture, unable and unwilling to become part of the national community and that in the case of Mexicans, they are also clamoring to reconquer formerly Mexican territories in the southwestern United States. The public discourse of the "Latino threat," which includes Latin American immigrants as well as U.S.-born Latinas/os, represents women as fecund and hypersexual burdens on the state, and men as violent criminals. "Latino threat" discourses, abundant in law and popular media, explain and rationalize Latin American immigrants' and Latinas/os' disenfranchisement and exclusion from the national community.[50] Robert Entman and Andrew Rojecki have shown that Americans learn about "difference" not through personal relationships but through what the media shows them.[51] When what people learn from media is negative, restrictive or punitive laws can seem quite reasonable, and likewise beliefs about race can influence the law-making process. Tony Montana and Trini DeSoto certainly fit the description of the "Latino threat."

As noted, most Marielitos were not violent criminals and wanted only to reunite with their families or escape persecution. Yet that is not the story that popular media told in the years after the boatlift, nor is it a story that would garner support for the IEA. The specter and spectacle of Mariel were invoked to rationalize a neoconservative aspect of the neoliberal project that became increasingly familiar over the next decades. As would be the case with the PATRIOT Act of October 2001, IEA legislation supported unilateral presidential power, intrusion on the civil rights of citizens, and aggressive military action, all justified by the need to protect citizens. In the early 1980s, even as the Reagan administration attacked "big government," it supported the IEA. Policy that might seem to be racist or was likely to produce racial profiling, disenfranchisement, and xenophobic nationalism was justified in the name of national security.

During IEA hearings, comprehensive immigration reform was already on the floor, with the 1982 IRCA including provisions that some observers found to be extreme and racist but that proponents framed as reasonable in the context of crisis. The bill included sanctions to deter employers from hiring undocumented immigrants and a worker verification system, increased border security, family reunification restrictions, and a modest amnesty program. While opponents argued that the bill targeted Latin American immigrants and would result in discriminatory hiring practices (that is, employers would not hire persons who looked or sounded foreign), support for a law proposed to resolve the "immigration emergency" was not hard to come by. A 1982

New York Times editorial characterized the proposed law as "Not Nativist, Not Racist, Not Mean," but rather as "a rare piece of legislation: a responsible immigration bill" that was "tough . . . fair . . . and humane."[52] Mazzoli pointed to this article and a litany of similar pieces in his opening statement as chair of the first 1982 IRCA hearing,[53] which was the fifth joint hearing that the two subcommittees on immigration held to create new immigration law.

In the initial IEA hearing, some testified about the volume of undocumented entries from Mexico, with pundits averring that the threat of immigration to the country just happened to be perpetrated by people of color. Likewise, IEA hearing discussion of the Mariel Boatlift and Haitian "boat people" trickled over into IRCA hearings. Although the racism that Haitians grappled with in immigration law was criticized,[54] the "boat people" compounded the "immigration emergency." In the first joint congressional hearings on IRCA (1982), Senator Walter Huddleston (D-KY) spoke of a "refugee emergency."[55] He even suggested that refugees were more privileged than U.S. citizens because the former were given access to assistance programs for three years and to job preferences at a time "when severe national economic problems are forcing the Congress to make draconian cuts in vital domestic assistance programs."[56]

Nonetheless, opposing voices were also heard at the first IEA hearing and IRCA hearings. From the start, opposition to IEA testified to its potential impact upon Latin American immigrants and Latinas/os, and to a lesser extent Haitians, and articulated the connection between an "immigration emergency" and racism, noting that Latin American immigrants—who also happened to be the nation's top source of cheap labor—were devalued. In hearings, pundits argued that the proposed granting of unilateral executive power had a precedent in genocide, internment, and unconstitutionality. Mark J. Miller, political history professor, pointed out that similar legislation in Germany had paved the way for Nazis to legally seize power.[57] Wade Henderson of the American Civil Liberties Union (ACLU) testified that the proposed law was frighteningly similar to Title II provisions of the Internal Security Act of 1950, which allowed for individuals to be held in domestic detention camps without charge, trial, or conviction, as had been the case in the World War II internment of Japanese Americans. Henderson viewed the proposed IEA as being on par with such gross violations of constitutional rights.[58]

Numerous representatives from Latina/o activist groups argued that IEA legislation would be extremely harmful to both immigrants and Latinas/os. The League of United Latin American Citizens (LULAC) declared that the "consequences to human and civil rights, to international relations and major administrative upheavals would not be worth the risks when there are other less drastic and reasonable alternatives available."[59] Arnoldo Torres, LULAC national executive director, cautioned that the language of the IEA could easily be applied to Mexican emigrants given that a few thousand immigrants arriving over the course of a few weeks could be declared an emergency.[60] He also worried that provisions for the restriction of vessels, vehicles, and aircrafts would harm the Mexican and U.S. economies and that the liberal search and seizure provisions would exacerbate extant INS abuses of immigrant rights. He cited the decision by U.S. District Judge Byrne to bar the deportation of 150 aliens, of which Judge Byrne commented, "To say the INS is really interested in the rights of these people is absurd."[61]

Others cited evidence of racism in Florida and especially in the Miami area. On December 17, 1979, six Miami-Dade police officers, all white or Latino, beat Arthur McDuffie, a black man, to death, apprehending him after he fled from them on a motorcycle. The police officers attempted to make it look like an accident. When four officers were acquitted of manslaughter in 1980, Miami's black community rioted for three weeks, and eighteen people died.[62] Accusations of racism and civil rights violations were thus prevalent in Florida and provided powerful points of opposition to the IEA, but so were the assertions on the other side, particularly when pundits pointed out that Mariel constituted a perversion of the "nation of immigrants" mythos that made America exceptional.

The same sort of language was employed in the IEA hearings, and by media, especially pundits. In a 1983 *Christian Science Monitor* article that was ostensibly meant to show that most Marielitos were "hardworking people trying to get ahead"—in other words the kind of immigrant subjects that neoliberalism values—nonetheless reminded readers of the other Marielitos—criminals and those who were unable to care for themselves: "'Those people are extremely violent,' said one Spanish-speaking detective who has interviewed many of the murder suspects. 'They have no morals, and they lie and lie and lie.' He says the problem is growing 'because they are starting to understand our laws. They know they are a hundredfold safer here than in Cuba, because here they have rights.'"[63] While the article closed by reminding readers that many Marielitos worked hard, the "good" immigrant story being told was mixed with caveats about criminal tendencies and a lack of understanding of hard work as the ticket to the American Dream.

The endangered state of the "nation of immigrants" was used in support of "immigrant emergency" discourse, and this rhetorical back-bending allowed neoconservative intrusiveness and militarism to blend into neoliberal ideology about the universalized beneficence of the United States' capitalist democracy. In the first IRCA hearings, Walter Huddleston (D-KY), a Democrat, stated, "All of us understand why they want to come here. America is a nation of immigrants and the children and grandchildren of immigrants who have come here seeking and finding a better life than they could have found anywhere else in the world. We have that tradition to uphold, and we should uphold it proudly. But at the same time, we have an obligation to our own citizens to restrict our immigration to numbers that we can manage both economically and socially."[64]

To likewise prove that America was taking the idea of the "nation of immigrants" too far, to the detriment of its citizens, in an IEA hearing, Simpson evoked Haitian "boat people." He conflated the refugee and criminal and postulated that refugees were more empowered than native citizens: "When [Haitians] come here illegally, it is almost as if the minute they leave their shore, they gather unto themselves more degrees of due process than would have ever been imagined by the average American citizen. . . . You know, that makes me scratch my dome somewhat."[65] Those concerned with human rights and racism were probably scratching their domes after Simpson's statement, especially given that he lacked facts to back it up.[66] In fact in the same hearing, Arthur Helton, director of the Political Asylum Project of the Lawyers Committee for International Human Rights, argued that refugees and especially Haitians already lacked rights and protections and that the IEA would exacerbate this. He quoted from the affidavit of a Haitian man who "voluntarily" abandoned his asylum request and left the United States in 1982: "I fully expect that I may be mistreated or even killed upon my return to Haiti. However, I would rather die in my own country than remain any longer in prison in the United States without any indication that I will ever be released."[67] But Simpson was not alone in his argument; nor was it a partisan issue.

Simpson's nativism would become more overt and baldly racist as the immigration debates went on. He was captain of the ship that became IRCA; he was deeply involved in the formation of the law from its SCIRP days to the final passage of the legislation. His name was on every iteration of it, and to this day he is most closely associated with it. This is not to say that the law is a rote recreation of his restrictionist and nativist politics; his family reunification cuts were vetoed and activist voices were also heard throughout the debates. But this verbatim evidence of his nativism in the IEA debate provides an example of the rather undemocratic intentions underscoring immigration reform in the 1980s.

Importantly, the IEA debates show the emerging "immigration emergency" trope and the rising Reaganite, neoliberal version of the "nation of immigrants" tropes working in tandem, with the latter being pointed to as proof that the United States is an inclusive place despite evidence to the contrary or as a reason to address the former with extreme measures. Likewise, films that cast America on a global stage as an exceptionally egalitarian nation by stressing "nation of immigrants" multiculturalism and abundance in contrast to communism countered the material reality of racism, xenophobia, and inequality underscoring the "immigration emergency." *Moscow on the Hudson* (1984), a comedy-drama film directed by Paul Mazursky and produced by Columbia Pictures, follows Soviet saxophonist Vladimir Ivanoff (Robin Williams), who defects from the Soviet Union while touring New York City with his circus troupe. In tracing Vlad's quest for the American Dream, the film furthers the Reaganite ethos that capitalism is the key to equality, freedom, and happiness for people of all races, articulated via the "nation of immigrants" trope. While in Bloomingdale's, described on the back of the DVD version of the movie as a "temple of Western decadence," Vlad is suddenly overcome with a desire for freedom. Despite the presence of two KGB *apparatchik* traveling with the circus troupe to protect them from the corrupting influence of Western capitalism, no American connections, and the possibility that he will never again see his family, Vlad defects, declaring his independence amid a dazzling array of commodities. The department store strikingly contrasts the film's earlier representation of Soviet Russia, where citizens must stand in endless lines for basic necessities like toilet paper and shoes, and gas is rationed. Corruption and bribery of state officials is endemic, basic freedoms are severely restricted, and dissent is severely punished. Thus the film suggests that capitalist commodities and consumerism signify freedom, abundance, and veracity.

The goodies of American capitalism are also indelibly linked to multiculturalism and the "nation of immigrants" trope, which is part of what makes this text neoliberal. Vlad assimilates with the help of a host of multicultural immigrants and black Americans. His multicultural coalition first coheres in Bloomingdales, a symbol of American consumption and excess that is itself a melting pot: perfume counter worker and Italian immigrant Lucia Lombardo (Maria Conchita Alonso) hides Vlad from the *apparatichiks*, Chinese American reporter Connie Chung covers his defection, immigration lawyer and former Cuban refugee Orlando Ramirez (Alejandro Rey) takes his case, and black American Bloomingdale's security guard Lionel Witherspoon (Levant Derriks) moves Vlad into the apartment he shares with his parents, grandfather, and teenaged sister. Before Vlad's trip, the Ivanoffs had watched television footage of blacks protesting the Ku Klux Klan, and Vlad, a fan of jazz, says blacks are "beautiful people, great musicians." So a link between the oppression of black Americans and the oppression of Soviet citizens is established (and is a retort to Soviet accusations of American racism). This conveys a sense of common struggle and allegiance between immigrants—including white ethnic immigrants (Vlad is a Russian Jew)—and American people of color, and foreshadows the film's major point: America is a place where multiculturalism is a national value and all are free to protest, free to succeed. For the duration of the film, the message of a Reaganite multicultural society that nurtures and protects freedom and the pursuit of a better life is self-evident in the alliances of various nationalities, ethnicities, and immigration statuses (Vlad is then undocumented, Lucia is in the process of naturalizing, Orlando was naturalized, and Lionel is native-born.)

The message that America is an exceptionally desirable destination for immigrants is made unequivocally Reaganite when a man who has been long waiting in the thoroughly multicultural and overcrowded immigration office demands to know who an immigration worker's boss is. The worker, a black woman with a Caribbean accent, replies indignantly, "His name is Ronald Reagan." As with the multicultural community that enthralls and aids Vlad, "diversity" is essential to her boss's vision for and of the land of the free. This point is driven home in Lucia's naturalization ceremony. The speech given by the presiding judge, a black woman (which makes one wonder just how many black female judges there were in 1984), updates historical immigration rituals for a neoliberalizing America.

In *Beyond Ethnicity: Consent and Descent in American Culture*, Werner Sollors describes how the graduation rituals of the Ford Motor Company English School during World War I—in the midst of overt nativism and racism in immigration law—conveyed the rebirth of foreign-born employees as loyal American citizens. In the elaborate ceremony, immigrant worker-graduates disembarked from a ship holding signs that proclaimed their national origins, entered a cauldron marked "Ford English School Melting Pot," then emerged and claimed their new, unhyphenated American identities.[68]

In the *Moscow on the Hudson* naturalization ceremony, the judge similarly stresses that elimination of the ethnic hyphen is the pathway to freedom and the reciprocity of the relationship between citizen and government. But this was not the erasure of ethnicity as in the Ford ceremony, for the camera pans across the visibly multicultural, visibly excited crowd as they recite the citizenship oath. Rather this visceral scene declares to viewers that the United States and its capitalist democracy will make all of everyone's dreams come true.

Notably, the film's conditions of production mirrored this brand of multiculturalism. Mazursky's own immigrant story inspired the storyline: his grandfather was a Jew who fled the Ukraine in the early twentieth century because of anti-Semitism.[69] The film employed actors and actresses of many racial and ethnic backgrounds, and in fact one thousand Russian-born extras appeared in the Moscow crowd scenes, which were shot in Munich.[70] The soundtrack is likewise diverse. Ethnic interchangeability—more of the melting pot theme—is also prevalent. First, the actress playing Lucia is Latina. Second, Williams did not speak a word of Russian nor was he of Russian descent; he was either English or Welsh but could not recall[71] (such a lapsed memory is unavailable to many immigrants and citizens who are marked by racial or linguistic otherness and thus lack the privilege to forget about their ethnicity), though he did learn to speak and write Russian for the film and learned to play the saxophone.[72] While the film, which earned just over $25 million domestically,[73] was panned by some critics for being overly critical of the Soviet Union,[74] others praised Williams for a convincing portrayal of a Soviet ex-pat, and praised Mazurky for effectively conveying the multiculturalism that *is* America, given that, as film critic Roger Ebert put it, the director "populates his movie almost entirely with ethnic and racial minorities. In addition to the black and the Italian, there's a Korean taxi driver, a Cuban lawyer, a Chinese anchorwoman, all of them reminders that all of us, except for American Indians, came from somewhere else."[75]

The use of multiculturalism to establish the superiority of Reagan-era America and capitalism in contrast to the Soviet Union and Communism also surfaces in the 1985 drama film *White Nights*, in which Mikhail Baryshnikov plays Russian ballet dancer Nikolai "Kolya" Rodchenko, a Soviet defector (art imitating life given that that is the dancer's own story) who is forced by the KGB to remain in Russia after his international flight makes an emergency landing there. Although Raymond Greenwood (Gregory Hines), a black American defector to the Soviet Union, is supposed to watch Rodchenko and keep him in line, the two become fast friends, and of course dance together since both men are professional dancers. Greenwood decides to help Rodchenko escape and return to America himself when his wife becomes pregnant; he does not want to raise a child in the corruption and scarcity of the Soviet Union, which of course sets America as its opposite, a place of abundance ideal for raising a family. Thus with multicultural "nation of immigrants" discourses juxtaposed against the harshness, depravity, and restriction of Soviet Communism, both films are propaganda for rising U.S. neoliberalism (much like early press coverage of Mariel). In short, the films exemplify the Reagan era inauguration of the neoliberal focus on both "equal access," often via a rhetoric of multicultural (and, we will see, feminist) material success, *and* colorblind "human rights," which reinforce the notion that the United States is a post-racist, post-sexist nation. As Christina Gerken observes, "this tendency to downplay the importance of race is one of the defining features of neoliberal immigration discourse."[76]

While the multicultural "nation of immigrants" ideal often softened the blow of concurrent "immigrant emergency" discourse, there is another crucial, color-coded piece of the "nation of immigrants" trope in the Reaganite rising neoliberal paradigm: even in the midst of the unemployment, stagflation, and recession that Reagan inherited as president, and despite the racial anxieties fueling the "immigration emergency" before and after Mariel, cheap Latin American and especially Mexican immigrant labor appealed to free market supporters. While the settlement and the permanent incorporation of these immigrants was problematic, their labor was often welcome.[77] Reagan made a rather direct policy statement to that effect in 1981: "We must also recognize that both the United States and Mexico have historically benefited from Mexicans obtaining employment in the United States. A number of our States have special labor needs, and we should take these into account. Illegal immigrants in considerable numbers have become productive members of our society and are a basic part of our work force."[78]

Reagan wanted an amnesty program when Mexicans were the group most visibly singled out in the xenophobic attacks of immigrants in the 1980s.[79] Pundits feared that bilingualism and incorporation would be divisive, with Mexicans outnumbering white European Americans and displacing native laborers, and worried that legalization would burden the welfare state when conservatives were committed to dismantling it. These concerns, in turn, fed into the notion of the "immigration emergency." The presidential task force position encapsulated the tension (and it seems, confusion) between the desire for amnesty and fear of Mexicans. It recommended more moderate reform than that of SCIRP, which allowed for legalization of many workers and a guest laborer program in a way that complemented both the desire for a cheap immigrant labor pool and the idea of "nation of immigrants" inclusivity, since it seemed to welcome eligible immigrant laborers with rights. And the task force cautioned that the volume of Mexican immigration was "changing our population, particularly in the Southwest, where many communities will likely have Hispanic majorities in the next decades,"[80] so that again the specter of an "immigration emergency" was present.

Mae Ngai asserts that racialized immigrant laborers are accepted or tolerated because the threat they pose to ethnocentrism is contained through their minoritization; they are made intelligible as outsiders so that while they reside in the nation and are instrumental to its economic sustenance, they remain "foreign" or "other" in relation to the dominant population. She calls this "alien citizenship."[81] While she focuses on the period 1924–1965, this process continues with rising neoliberalism, although it looks a bit different. From the 1970s and 1980s, when Asian and Latin Americans constituted the largest groups of immigrants, "alienage remain[ed] a conspicuous category of legal, cultural, and political difference,"[82] given the ongoing simultaneous desire for and rejection of low-wage racialized workers codified in legislation. Race was reinvented as "cultural" difference, or differences in language and religion, which were paired with alleged tendencies toward poverty and crime. Thus a system of racial de/ valuation was in place but not obviously at odds with new hegemonic discourse of diversity and pluralism broadly or in "nation of immigrants" iterations.

Although the ERA did not become law, a similar story is apparent with regard to patriarchy in this period. Women had more opportunities and power than ever before after second-wave feminism, but inequities like the wage gap and the relegation of immigrant women of color to domestic labor persisted. Cooptation of difference is a component of neoliberal capitalism; capital accumulation continues to be entwined with racism and sexism as it was under slavery and colonialism (free racialized labor), but because of the rising hegemony of antiracism and multiculturalism and feminism, racism and sexism became subtle, sneaky. Jodie Melamed argues that neoliberalism accomplishes the extraction of surplus value from racialized and gendered bodies with two discourses. On one hand, universalized discourses of value that are detached from race and gender move beyond the notion of equal opportunity for all (or abstract) subjects to the notion of the market itself as the conduit of equality for all subjects. On the other hand, multicultural and often feminist rhetoric is mobilized "as the key to a post-racist world of freedom and opportunity;"[83] codes for racial and gender difference "compose an assimilative multicultural order that makes U.S. global hegemony appear just and fair."[84] Consequently, limited antiracism or multiculturalism (and antisexism or feminism), sutured to claims that the neoliberal system itself is the conduit of equality, obfuscates ongoing structural inequities and produces them. Appropriated versions of multiculturalism and feminism consequently became the governing logic of racism (and sexism) that continue to serve capital in a changing political and economic landscape. While Melamed places "neoliberal multiculturalism" in the 1990s, immigration discourses reveal that it was inaugurated and ascendant in 1980s.

The urgency surrounding IEA legislation, which did not pass, made the reinvention of racism and its gendered undertones evident. A look at the "first wave" of U.S. nativism further elucidates how race and gender politics shaped immigration debates, as well as how the simultaneous prevalence and compatibility of the "nation of immigrants" and "immigration emergency" discourses in the 1980s came to be.

The Old Nativism: A Prehistory of Gendered Racialization

Although historically both white ethnic European and Latin American immigrants have encountered nativism, the outlines of the gendered racial hierarchy that 1980s immigration discourses solidified between the two groups (and that was codified by IRCA) can be traced to the early twentieth century. At that time, influxes of "new immigrants" from eastern and southern Europe often worked for lower wages and under poorer conditions than their native counterparts, provoking fears of labor competition. Nativists and eugenicists were overtly concerned with the racial and cultural threat that new immigrants posed because they were often "darker-skinned, more visibly ethnic"[85] than previous migrants, and were usually practicing Catholics or Jews as opposed to the primarily Protestant American citizenry. A surge of immigration of mostly Catholic and destitute Irish provoked by the Irish Famines of the 1840s had previously resulted in a similarly xenophobic reaction.[86] Paradoxically, in the 1980s the former targets of the movement would become its perpetrators.

The 1924 Johnson-Reed Act instituted a nation-based immigration quota system designed to construct a primarily white, Protestant, northwestern European citizenry.[87] It established national quota ceilings for immigrants based the citizen population in 1890, when it had been comprised mostly of northern and western European Protestants. This guaranteed that white Anglo Saxon Protestants would continue to be the majority.

As historian Martha Gardener notes, "If women gave birth to citizens, then sex mattered."[88] In analyzing how early arguments linked biology, race, and reproduction to position immigrant women's fecundity as a stark and troubling contrast to the declining birth rate of natives, Gardner shows that the Dillingham Commission, which reported in 1911, found that eastern and southern European immigrant reproduction threatened the racial equilibrium of the nation, especially given their alleged fecundity and inclinations toward crime, laziness, and unethical behavior. In other words, they were biologically unfit.[89] Therefore stemming the flow of immigrants by diminishing reproduction was an overlapping project at this phase of nation-building.

Popular media of the 1910s and 1920s weighed in, too, carrying these messages into the everyday lives of Americans. David Roediger points out in his magisterial study of the role of labor in the formation of white ethnic identity that in *Good Housekeeping* magazine President Calvin Coolidge sang the praises of the "Nordics" over all other races.[90] In the *Saturday Evening Post*, eugenics proponents such as Lothrop Stoddard argued that new immigrants posed a biological and evolutionary threat to the nation.[91]

This is not to say that there were not competing tendencies in legal consciousness as also evidenced in popular culture. There were hackneyed representations of the greedy and miserly Jew in early American cinema, like the 1904 silent film, *Cohen's Advertising Scheme*, and similarly negative characterizations of Italian Americans as overly passionate, sensual, violent, and exotic, as buffoonish clowns, or as criminals (though the gangster film did not become prevalent until the talkies of the 1930s). Yet dissenting—if nevertheless stereotypical—visions were also evident. *The Goldbergs*, a popular comedy-drama radio series (1929–1946), provided a sympathetic portrayal of a poor Jewish family (with a neurotic, loving, meddlesome Jewish mother), who lived in in the Bronx and then eventually moved from a tenement into the suburbs. The television adaptation ran from 1949 to 1956. Italian American actor Rudolph Valentino was also wildly popular in 1920s silent films. Legal consciousness in popular culture has long been complex affair.

The unique status of Mexico in the xenophobic context of the early twentieth century was also a matter of gender politics. Eugenics proponents lobbied for restrictions on Western Hemisphere immigration in order to keep Mexican immigrants out, but the Western Hemisphere was exempted from quotas and other restrictions for several reasons. First, the United States needed foreign laborers, given the limitations on immigrants from Europe and Asia. Mexican men filled this need. Second, according to Coolidge, few immigrants came from Mexico and a quota system would harm relations with Latin America and Canada.[92] Third, Mexican laborers rarely settled permanently.[93] Thus many believed that Mexican men were ideal laborers because permanent settlement and family formation were rare. The absence of women migrants further eliminated concern over naturalization and the granting of rights to this low-wage labor force.

These conflicting demands for labor and racial and ethnic purity were taken up in the next major immigration legislation, the 1952 McCarran-Walter Act. Previous to that, the Great Depression exacerbated fears of immigrants as labor competition and as fecund burdens on the state, and many Mexicans were forcibly repatriated. World War II also brought about diversification. To address wartime labor shortages, the Bracero Program was initiated, and women entered the labor force in unprecedented numbers. Following the defeat of the Nazis, there was backlash against eugenics and racism, some Jewish refugees were accepted, and the treatment of Asian Americans and Asian immigrants changed such that while Japanese Americans had been interned in accordance with wartime fears, and although the 1945 War Brides Act allowed the foreign-born wives of American GIs to immigrate, Japanese wives were excluded; on the other hand, since the Chinese were wartime allies, the Chinese Exclusion Act was repealed in 1943.

During the Cold War, and against the backdrop of the Korean War, the McCarran-Walter Act, sponsored by Senator Pat McCarran (D-NV), and Representative Francis Walter (D-PA), formally removed race as a bar to immigration, yet the law continued to treat white ethnics and Mexicans differently, and anti-Semitism was built into it. The quotas of the 1920s remained, continuing to favor nations with predominately white Anglo Saxon citizens. With an annual limit of 270,000 immigrants, first preference was given to highly skilled immigrants and their spouses, followed by immigrants seeking family reunification, and then general immigrants. Refugees comprised the final category. Additionally, in response to mounting Cold War tensions, immigrants deemed subversive could be deported, and subversive visitors denied entry.

The law was an attempt to negotiate conflicting desires for racial and ethnic purity and labor. Despite the preference for skilled workers and a provision that allowed the secretary of labor to exclude laborers who might threaten domestic wages and working conditions—the same tensions negotiated in the 1980s among free market economists, nativists and organized labor—the Western Hemisphere remained exempt from quotas. The Bracero Program and its attendant market for undocumented Mexican laborers continued.

Labor codification was gendered, too. Some women who worked as domestic laborers and as nurses were given visas in the new system, and many who entered were from Mexico and the Caribbean. Yet under the McCarran-Walter Act's preference system, most categories of women's work were considered unskilled, even when women were doing the same work as men. For instance, the Board of Immigration Appeals denied an Italian woman entry because her work as a beauty operative was ruled unworthy of a skilled visa, yet a man who worked as a woman's hair stylist was admitted as a skilled worker.[94]

President Harry Truman vetoed the McCarran-Walter Act as racist, saying that it carried over the "isolationist limits of our 1924 law,"[95] but he was overridden by a 278 to 113 vote in the House and a 57 to 26 vote in the Senate. And much like Simpson years later, McCarran defended the racism of the law with democratic rhetoric and by citing national security. In a prepared statement for the Eighty-Third Congress, "The Background of the McCarran-Walter Act," he explained that while he appreciated the contributions "to our society by people of many races, of varied creeds and colors," there was the matter of "hard core indigestible blocs who have not become integrated into the American way of life but which, on the contrary, are its deadly enemies.

Today as never before untold millions are storming our gates for admission and those states are cracking under the strain [sic]."[96]

Clearly, the multicultural "nation of immigrants" narrative that would soon become hegemonic was some years off. The quotas were in fact designed to minimize eastern and southern European immigration when offering asylum to Jews was also controversial, though McCarran claimed, as he spouted white ethnic xenophobia, that the bill was not anti-Semitic nor anti-Catholic, and while some accused the bill of being anti-Asian, numerous "Orientals" approved of it, as it lifted decades of Asian exclusion by providing them with a quota.[97] He emphasized that the law was meant to safeguard America as an exceptional and *sort of* pluralistic nation.

Too much pluralism, or rather the wrong kind, was akin to the "immigration emergency" of the 1980s. Following World War II and as the Cold War began to heat up, racist immigration restriction was deemed a matter of national security, just as it would be after Mariel in the 1980s and then in the wake of 9/11. As the House and Senate override votes show, consideration of multiculturalism was not yet required. U.S. neoliberal projects, like the IEA, would require a subtler, apparently multiculturalist veneer of racism that was unnecessary in the 1950s.

The changes in the law-making process that reflected the changing race, gender, and international politics of the post–World War II era surfaced in popular culture too. The stereotypes of the stingy Jew, the Italian criminal, and the Italian buffoon were standard by this point, but there were some alternative representations too. The Italian American buffoon stereotype was discernible in a host of popular TV comedies such as *The Jimmy Durante Show* (1954–1956), and in the character Mr. Bacciagalupe (Joe Kirk) on *The Abbot and Costello Show* (1952–1954). "Bacciagalupe" became common slang that is still used to demean Italians. The stereotype of the Italian mobster became prevalent after the trials of Al Capone and his cohort. Villains whose last names ended in vowels were ubiquitous, and mafia plots and themes were so popular that they became their own Hollywood genre. The original 1932 *Scarface* was based on the life of Capone, in which Jewish American actor Paul Muni played the mobster. The ABC crime drama *The Untouchables* (1959–1963) was based on a memoir of the same name by Eliot Ness and Oscar Fraley. The show fictionalized Ness's experiences as a Prohibition Agent in 1930s Chicago and was controversial in mainstream news media because it was violent.[98] Some Italian Americans picketed the studio and boycotted its sponsors. Desilu, the production studio headed by Cuban American Desi Arnaz, agreed to revise their representations of Italian Americans.[99] These examples suggest an interchangeability or connectedness between groups considered "ethnic" in pop culture of the period. Jews and Irish played Italians, an elite Cuban American altered offensive plot lines, and as in the case of *Scarface* and numerous late-twentieth century films discussed later, Italian Americans and Latinas/os played each other.

The Latin lover stereotype was updated to include singers such as Frank Sinatra and Dean Martin (born Dino Paul Crocetti), both of whom became national sex symbols: these American-born sons of Italian immigrants made legions of American women swoon. The radio sitcom *Life with Luigi* (1948–1953) brought a more sympathetic and unthreatening portrait of a hardworking Italian immigrant into the living rooms of many Americans. J. Carrol Naish, an Irish American actor, played Luigi in the show, another point of connection among white ethnic groups. In 1948 it was even adapted into a Broadway play.

In sum, racial and gender discrimination persisted in U.S. immigration policy with a direct correlation to labor, and pop culture engaged in debates. To a large extent the national origins quota system accomplished its goal: by 1965, immigrants from the United Kingdom, Ireland, and Germany were given 108,931 visas (70 percent) out of a total of 158, 503. The remainder of Europe received 40,483 visas and other nations received only 9,089.[100] Half of the visas were for skilled work,[101] and liberal Western Hemisphere immigration continued. In the 1960s, however, the playing field changed once again as overt racism and sexism became socially unacceptable.

Gendered Racialization in Multicultural America

In 1965, Congress passed the Immigration and Nationality Act, an amendment to the McCarran-Walter Act designed to rectify persisting inequities by abolishing the nation-based quota system. While the INA ultimately facilitated the immigration of more women and people of color, these consequences were not intended. In order to make the United States at least appear to be more open and welcoming to multiple cultures, the INA shifted the emphasis in immigration law from work skills to family reunification. While labor continued to be directly addressed under the new law—the INA expanded the McCarran-Walter certification program, and immigrants had to demonstrate available employment to receive a visa—first preferences were given to spouses, children, and siblings of U.S. citizens.

More specifically, the INA replaced national quotas with hemispheric caps: 170,000 for the Eastern Hemisphere, and 120,000 for the Western Hemisphere, with a limit of 20,000 annually from any nation. The law placed an annual total limit of 290,000 on immigration, but as had been the case since

1921, provisions for immigrants authorized outside of numerical limits were included. The INA expanded the categories of family members who could enter without numerical limit while reserving most preference slots for close family members and some for the relatives of permanent resident aliens. The preferences were:

1. Unmarried adult sons and daughters of U.S. citizens;
2. Spouses and children and unmarried sons and daughters of permanent resident aliens;
3. Scientists and artists of exceptional ability;
4. Married children of U.S. citizens;
5. Brothers and sisters of U.S. citizens over age twenty-one;
6. Skilled and unskilled workers in occupations needing labor supply;
7. Refugees assigned conditional entry, mostly from Communist countries and the Middle East.
8. Applicants outside of these preference categories.

Under these provisions, most of the 22.8 million immigrants who entered between 1966 and 2000 were family members of recent immigrants, a phenomenon known as "chain migration."[102] The INA provided more opportunities for immigrants from nations outside northern and western Europe (namely Asia and Latin America), as well as for women, while continuing to limit the entry of certain racial and ethnic groups, place women in vulnerable positions, and value only stereotypical "women's work." The contours of neoliberal gendered racialization began to take recognizable shape with the INA.

For example, the sixth preference category included skilled and unskilled live-in domestic workers. Many women, particularly from the Western Hemisphere and the Caribbean, who were included in the preference system and subjected to an annual limit for the first time, entered under this new category. This gave many Latin American and Caribbean women the option to immigrate independently, outside of patriarchal family structures. But often excluded from other preference categories, women wanting to immigrate were essentially channeled into domestic servitude. And as new entrants whose status depended upon employment in a certain field, they were legally accountable to employers who could easily exploit them.

Additionally, the deliberately selective diversification of the racial allotment under the INA emblematized the reconfiguration of racism both after World War II and in response to the civil rights movement. While the liberal climate of the 1960s underscored the immigration reforms and is often pointed to as their impetus, they are also attributable to changing foreign policy goals: the exclusive bent of earlier immigration policy contradicted the new U.S. interest in global expansion and leadership.[103] Seemingly magnanimous foreign policy served a nation in the process of globalizing—and this was crucial as neoliberalism began to take cohesive shape.

Continuing President John F. Kennedy's commitment to end the quota system,[104] Lyndon B. Johnson proclaimed in his 1965 State of the Union Address, "Let a just nation throw open the city of promise to those in other lands seeking [the] promise of America, through an immigration law based on the work a man can do and not where he was born or how he spells his name."[105] Here was the language of inclusion and equal opportunity for all, a statement of official anti-racism and a prototype for the Reaganite version of the "nation of immigrants" trope. The passage of the INA, along with Johnson's other race reform legislation—the Civil Rights Act of 1964 and the Voting Rights Act of 1965—were also obviously connected to civil rights, but this rhetoric also masked ongoing racial inequalities by disconnecting race from material conditions. That is, invisibility of race in law—"colorblindness"—became shorthand for equality for all subjects, and racism was reframed as an anomaly rather than a systemic problem. As critical race theorists have shown, in response to the civil rights movement's exposure of the structural production and maintenance of white supremacy, the concept of colorblindness became the new dominant conduit of white supremacy; it severed racism from material conditions and reinvented antiracism as individual rights.[106]

Proof of ongoing white supremacy was tangible as proponents explicitly stated that the bill would not diversify the country much. As one sponsor of the bill, Representative Emanuel Celler (D-NY) put it, "There will not be, comparatively, many Asians or Africans entering this country. . . . Since the people of Africa and Asia have very few relatives here, comparatively few could immigrate [sic]from those countries because they have no family ties in the U.S"[107]

The INA was also connected also to the racial politics of the ethnic revival and the reconfiguration of white supremacy that they inaugurated. Matthew Jacobson shows how, in the 1960s and 1970s in response to the civil rights movement, the ethnic revival cast white ethnic immigrants and their descendants as the victims rather than the perpetrators of racism, canonizing a national narrative of hardworking Ellis Island immigrants who pulled themselves up by their bootstraps in order to succeed.[108] This was the prototype for the "nation of immigrants" trope of the 1980s. By allegedly overcoming ubiquitous poverty and racism with nothing but hard work and tenacity, white ethnics became quintessential models of assimilation and self-sufficient upward mobility for immigrants and minorities at a moment when people of color were fighting for and gaining rights at unprecedented levels. Like the ascendant rhetoric of "colorblindness," "diversity," and soon "multicultural-ism," this new narrative of national identity, which borrowed from the group identity politics of the civil rights movement, was deceptive. It occluded the structural racism that non-white minority groups had long been subject to and made success simply a matter of hard work.

Moreover, the economic assimilation of white ethnic immigrants occurred with a substantial amount of government aid. Civil rights politics eclipsed divisions among whites (codified with Johnson-Reed quotas) in a way that would not have occurred without the New Deal–era establishment of what David Roediger called "interimmigrant unities." These unities were furthered in trade unions like the Congress of Industrial Organizations (CIO), and by New Deal mass politics and government aid programs such as welfare and Social Security, especially those that racialized federal aid policies, like a two-tier housing policy that served the working poor according to Jim Crow practices. Simultaneously, popular rhetoric characterized black Americans in need as "feckless" welfare seekers, whereas government support for private housing that "massively and deliberately benefitted white homeowners and white prospective buyers" was not viewed as welfare.[109]

Despite this federal aid given to white ethnic immigrants, turn-of-the cen-tury poverty and social stigmatization rationalized the disavowal of white privilege that characterized the ethnic revival, and legitimated white ethnic favoritism under the INA and later under IRCA. This was emphatically re-flected in and informed by the culture at large. Thus, for example, Nathan Glazer and Patrick Moynihan claimed in *Beyond the Melting Pot: The Negroes, Puerto Ricans, Jews, Italians, and Irish of New York City* (1963) that ethnic groups such as "Negroes" and Puerto Ricans could achieve equal standing through organization and self-help because white ethnic European immi-grants did, despite their failure to fully assimilate or "melt." This assertion that people of color, like white groups, could achieve equality with organization and self-help erased the racial hierarchies of privilege and power that slavery, colonialism, immigration policy, and government aid policy had produced. Along similar lines, in 1971, Michael Novak asserted in *Unmeltable Ethnics: Politics and Culture in American Life* that the most salient quality of white ethnic sensibility was that white ethnics do not have white privilege. In the spirit of civil rights identity politics, he advocated the formation of ethnically specific left coalitions to tackle subjective conditions. In his view, white Anglo Saxon Protestants (WASPs) were the shared enemy of both people of color and white ethnics. He also emphatically opposed modernism, capitalism, and intellectualism. Other similarly themed books such as Andrew Greely's *Why*

Can't They Be Like Us? Facts and Fallacies about Ethnic Differences and Group Conflicts in America (1969) and Richard Gambino's *Blood of My Blood* (1974), which focused exclusively on Italian Americans, were popular at the time.

Despite the initial left leanings of ethnic revival discourse, neoconservatives appropriated it to support the erosion of the welfare state. *Beyond the Melting Pot* and *Unmeltable Ethnics* became foundational texts for neoconservative opposition to affirmative action, and Novak moved to the Right, joining the American Enterprise Institute in 1978. In short, as in the case of INA, an inaccurate understanding of white ethnic self-sufficiency was extolled to justify white privilege. Later, in the 1980s, that same fictive self-sufficiency was invoked to justify the denial of public services to people of color according to the logic that says "they" are poor because they fail to take personal responsibility. Given that white ethnics provided the prototype for the "nation of immigrants" trope, racialized exclusion was built into an allegedly inclusive national narrative.

The INA's connections with the ethnic revival were explicit: lawmakers "intended to redress the grievances of European ethnic groups and to give more than token representation to Asians."[110] President Johnson said that the reforms of 1965 were supposed to amend the wrong done to persons from "southern and eastern Europe" in the 1920s by restrictive quotas.[111] As in earlier legislation, spouses and the children of immigrants were exempted from restrictions, and a new emphasis on kin-based immigration was established with a fifth preference category for adult siblings of U.S. citizens. These updated family reunification provisions favored groups already present—not coincidentally, white groups that had economically assimilated—within a framework that made heterosexual kinship arrangements a conduit of immigrant racial formation. As with the McCarran-Walter Act, it was assumed that Asian Pacific populations would not increase much under this legislation because not many were present given decades of Asian exclusion; they would presumably not have much family to reunify, but white ethnics would.[112] The INA was thus designed to function like the national origins system, encouraging migration among "desirable" racial and ethnic groups while discouraging it among "undesirable" groups.

Although some Irish and eastern and southern European immigrants entered under the INA, the decline in European immigration continued. European countries became immigrant destinations as Europe's economies began to thrive in the 1960s. "Likely to Become a Public Charge" (LPC) and other restrictions along with Cold War controls also kept western and eastern European immigration to a minimum. By the mid-1970s the European family reunification backlog was resolved.[113] Thus by 1980, over four-fifths of legal immigrants came from Latin America or Asia (see figure 1.1).

In part, this can be attributed to chain migration. When siblings' spouses naturalized, they utilized immediate family preferences, and this continued with other immediate family members. Under the INA, overall exempt admissions increased from 50,000 to 150,000 in 1980.[114] Immigrants from non-European countries were more likely to utilize family reunification provisions since their backlog was unresolved. The demographic changes INA engendered hence led to a nativist fixation on family reunification in the 1980s, as can be clearly seen in the SCIRP and IEA debates.

In its final sessions, SCIRP debated family reunification, and family became the center of the first round of IRCA debates and the "immigration emergency" and "nation of immigrants" dance. There was no mistaking that those most impacted by policy would be Asian and Latin American immigrant groups. As Representative Hamilton Fish IV (R-NY) reminded the floor, "So it is going to be China and India and the Philippines and Korea and the Dominican Republic and Mexico and Cuba and Columbia. That is going to be the next generation of immigrants into the United States through our family reunification policy, because people who have been here for 40 or 60 years do not have parents and spouses and children abroad."[115] Many lawmakers were alarmed by this prospect, perhaps none more than Simpson. It is thus no surprise that, as will be described in the next chapter, Simpson proposed several restrictions to family reunification in the first draft of IRCA.

Conclusion

According to IEA proponents especially, the nation was under siege. Increasing the president's power to shut down the borders was thus a necessary response to the immigration threat so clearly embodied in the influx of criminals from the Mariel Boatlift and in the deluge of poor Haitian "boat people." The "immigration emergency" trope, strengthened in popular media and with the backing of and a little buffering from the "nation of immigrants" trope, made depriving immigrants and citizens of rights seem like "common sense." Family reunification was certainly part of the "emergency" for some pundits.

Therefore it may seem hard to recollect that Mariel was initially celebrated as an exemplar of American beneficence and that the story told about it was at least partially about families who were able to reunite and thrive on American soil, in a way that shows how the "nation of immigrants" trope supported neoliberalism. For instance, a 1983 New York Times article noted in the aftermath of Mariel that "crime among adult refugees has not run

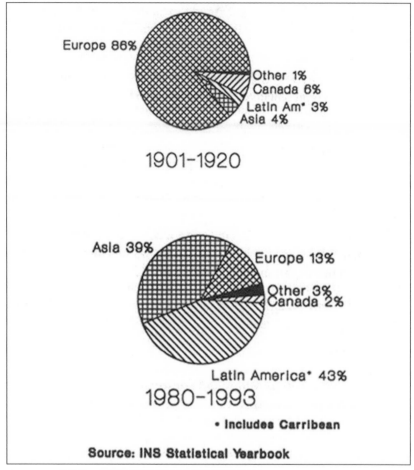

Figure 1.1. Change in Source Countries of Immigrants
Source: "Three Decades of Mass Immigration: The Legacy of the 1965 Immigration Act," *Center for Immigration Studies*, September 1995, http://cis.org/1965ImmigrationAct-MassImmigration.

rampant year in and year out, as many had feared, and crime among juveniles has fallen far short of predictions by a local judge. Work and a pursuit of English have been taken seriously by many, according to workers involved with the refugees."[116] Reporter Reginald Stuart described numerous successful children and a litany of refugees who had won awards, started successful businesses, and overall lived up to the "nation of immigrants" mythos—an outstanding accomplishment, he asserted, given that they contended with so much discrimination.[117]

Moreover, along with the reframing of Cuban émigrés from "Golden Exiles" to threats that encapsulated broader fears about the Latin American and especially Mexican "immigration emergency," a "golden" group of Cuban exiles continued to serve a key symbolic and material function for the Reagan administration. The public image of the unusually hardworking and *highly* successful Cuban American also exemplified the "nation of immigrants" mythos, demonstrated the failure of the Communist revolution, and made racism toward Cubans and people of Latin American origins seem obsolete; inequalities seemed to be the failure of individuals rather than social structures. In other words, the two stereotypes together propped up the image of the United States as a multicultural, humanitarian haven in the global sphere.

As Maria de los Angeles observes, to further its domestic and foreign policy agendas, the Reagan administration deliberately nurtured a group of conservative Cuban exiles and their hardline policies toward Cuba. On the domestic front, this allowed the GOP to appear to incorporate Latinas/os into foreign policy positions within the government[118] and give them a foothold in Florida, which at the time tended to vote Democratic and had a substantial Latina/o population that the Republican Party wanted to court. The Reagan administration also focused on Latinas/os and especially the Cuban community as "its own minority" after having written off the black community as too Democratic. Additionally, since New Right ideology in the 1980s overlapped with many Cuban Americans' conservative foreign policy views, they reciprocally embraced the Reagan administration.[119]

The formation of a lobby of Cuban American businessmen, many of whom were Bay of Pigs veterans, in the Cuban-American National Foundation (CANF) following Reagan's 1980 election is a case in point. This organization of hardline opposition to Castro successfully lobbied for numerous restrictions on trading with Cuba[120] and had a Reaganite structure in which those who paid higher fees had more power. Until 1990 only men served on the board.[121] While the goal of most exiles was to overthrow Castro, there have always been contingents advocating for various iterations of democracy, capitalism, and socialism, even among those who strongly opposed Castro.[122] Yet the hardline position—and its most visible representative, the wealthy, politically savvy businessman—was still prevalent in the Reagan era, in a seemingly dissonant bookend with the Marielito criminal stereotype.

Yet this was not a contradiction. What Maria de los Angeles Torres calls the "Latin Alger" trope was just as useful to rising neoliberalism as the Marielito "immigration emergency" trope. In a 1988 *Nation* article, she deconstructed the myth of "'Horatio Perez'—the Latin Alger," who is "a convenient symbol of the failure of the revolution and the renewal of the American dream, in which nonwhite immigrants pull themselves up by their bootstraps." While Alger-like examples exist (and may be CANF members), "few headlines ever mentioned the signs outside Miami apartment buildings in the 1960s that read, 'No Dogs, No Kids, No Cubans.' The facts show that while many Cubans did make it, many more did not—despite the unprecedented welfare benefits, English-language classes, university and business loans, and covert C.I.A. money that flowed into south Florida."[123] Although Cubans have the highest incorporation rate into the U.S. workforce than any other Latina/o population, family income remains well below the U.S. average.[124] The "Horatio Perez" myth does double if not triple duty in that it appears to indicate the inclusivity of U.S. democratic capitalism, erases the material realities of Cubans, and, when considered in relation to Mariel, makes the "emergency" seem unconnected to racism.

The ways that Cuban exiles in the context of Mariel have been held up simultaneously as examples of the "immigration emergency" and the "nation of immigrants" mythos in a moderately to unusually successful spectrum are symptomatic of neoliberal crossings. Both made neoliberal methods (such as immigration restriction) seem reasonable if not necessary. The uneven racialization of Cuban exiles (and the intersections of gender, sexuality, class, and so on) makes neoliberalism's dissonant promises seem like "common sense."

Nonetheless, the "immigrant emergency" trope has prevailed in legislation and in pop culture—*Scarface* and *Miami Vice* are the enduring cultural icons associated with Mariel. The dominance of the negative and alarmist version of the story is in keeping with much of U.S. immigration history, which is largely a history of response to a perceived threat alongside a quest for cheap labor. Gender has been a pivotal part of this. Although in debates gender politics have often been superseded by a more explicit focus on race and class, the next neoliberalizing wave of nativist fixation on family reunification reveals how "the crossing of national borders routinely serves as an occasion for the policing of sexuality and sexed bodies."[125]

2

The Borderlines of Family Reunification

Fifteen years after the Mariel Boatlift, the event was memorialized as a saga of family reunification in the film *The Perez Family*. The 1995 romantic comedy follows four unrelated Marielitos who share the last name "Perez" and who, upon meeting at a Florida refugee camp, pretend to be a family to better their odds of finding an immigration sponsor. The plot revolves around the "odd couple" romance between refugees Juan Raul Perez (Alfred Molina), an aristocrat and political prisoner, and Dottie Perez (Marisa Tomei), a farm laborer and former sex worker. At Dottie's insistence, Juan pretends to be her husband, and she "adopts" two refugees, a teenage son, who is a petty thief and hustler, and a mentally-ill, mute grandfather, because families rank higher on the sponsorship list.[1] Although the Perez family embodies the "immigration emergency" that in the 1980s motivated nativists to attempt to restrict family reunification, they are sympathetically portrayed in that they embody the hegemonic neoliberal immigration story: committed to hard work and upward mobility for the sake of future generations, they believe in the United States as the exceptional nation that makes dreams of a better life come true. As such, the film provides entry into the contradictions and conflicts of the IRCA family reunification debates, which played a key role in the cohesion of neoliberal crossings.

The Perez Family opens in Cuba as Dottie and Juan prepare to leave. Juan, recently released from prison, hopes to reunite with his wife and daughter. This Marielito "criminal" spent twenty years incarcerated for burning his sugarcane fields rather than turning them over to Castro. His wife, Carmela (Anjelica Huston), and daughter fled to Miami, where they now live the American Dream in a middle-class suburb, supported by Carmela's entrepreneur brother, Angel (Diego Wallraff). Angel, ultimately the villain and laughingstock of the film, embodies the excesses of Reaganism (and lest spectators miss the point, he has a "Time Is Now" Reagan campaign poster in his office): this self-made business man—perhaps a CANF member—is neoconservative in his sexist obsession with security for his sister and niece, and he is flagrantly nativist, disgusted by Marielitos.[2] Dottie quits her job harvesting sugarcane and leaves Cuba. This "hot Latina" gyrates in public, gestures lewdly, and memorably puts on pantyhose on a bus. Her "American dream is to make love with John Wayne."[3] Sponsored by a church, the Perez family embodies what nativists—and proponents of "family values"—most feared: criminals, prostitutes, and mentally-ill "Hispanic" immigrants welcomed and aided by America's generous family reunification provisions.

The film rebukes critics of Marielitos and family reunification. The lack of blood relation among the Perez family, their non-nuclear kinship arrangement formed solely to subvert U.S. immigration law, and each member's complex relation to the law and gender and sexual norms make them appear to be a queer family. To be clear, "queer" points to and encompasses incoherencies in allegedly stable relations between biological sex, gender, and sexual desire and their intersections with other vectors of social identity such as race and ethnicity. Thus a queer family is not simply a family with LGBTQ members; "queer" is a description and identity that is inherently fluid, a zone of endless possibilities that challenges oppressive norms and social institutions.[4] Moreover, kinship too is socially constructed and thus political.[5]

In *The Queer Art of Failure*, Jack Halberstam notes that "success in a heteronormative, capitalist society equates too easily to specific forms of reproductive maturity combined with wealth accumulation,"[6] and he argues that failure may allow us "to escape the punishing norms that discipline behavior and manage human development."[7] Failure can be queer. Following Halberstam, I assert that failure to embrace "family values" and capitalist success—dominant logics about gender, sexuality, race, capital, and so on—could make a family queer. Hence LGBTQ families that uphold traditional paradigms are not queer families, whereas families without LGBTQ members may be queer if they reject traditional paradigms. But while the self-constructed Perez family appears queer (and while the film rebukes nativists), it complements rather than negates prevailing neoliberal logics.

The Perez family quickly becomes legitimate in all the important Reaganite ways, by demonstrating "family values," personal responsibility, and industriousness. Marielitos are romanticized victims of an oppressive regime who want to be free to reunite with or to form families; Communism is cast as anti-family in contrast to the family safe haven of the United States. Juan is desperate to reunite with his family (memories of their life together sustained him throughout his prison sentence), and the docks where Marielitos land are packed with women and children clutching photos of long-lost relatives. Inside the camp, a screen pan covers sleeping mothers and children, settling upon Juan embracing his new son. In addition, an INS official explains to Dottie that sponsors prefer families, as they are viewed as antithetical to the "criminal element from your Cuba: prostitutes, riff raff, AC/DCs." Forming a family allows Dottie and Juan to take the first step toward American respectability; then Dottie creates a roadside flower-selling business, beginning their path to self-sufficiency, and Juan makes an honest woman out of her as they fall in love. While Juan eventually reconnects with Carmela, the two divorce, presumably amicably, as she too has moved on and is happily in love with another man. The film ends with Juan and Dottie embracing as "grandpa" perches in a nearby tree. In the end, the Perez family, which had queer potential, becomes a typical American family.

The film links heterosexual family, freedom, capitalism, and American exceptionalism even as, during the period in which the film is set, nativists worked assiduously in the context of an "immigration emergency" to dismantle family reunification. In the "nation of immigrants," family was linked to freedom (often freedom for the sake of family was the end, with hard work and upward mobility being the means), a freedom that from the congressional floor to news media to pop culture was imagined in stark contrast to Castro's draconian Communist regime. In this sense, the film was part of the U.S. neoliberal project.

As Monisha Das Gupta notes, dominant tropes of immigration—one of which substitutes the heterosexual family for the kind of human life that is considered worthy of inclusion and protection and forms the basis of many contemporary rights claims—create a "powerful national mythology that produces and reproduces the United States as a benign, welcoming space for immigrants. The essential elements of the American immigrant story revolve around the enduring ideology that migrants come to America to seek a better life, and that America makes possible the dream of upward mobility. This hope then justifies the labor exploitation, nativism, and racism that migrants face. The capacity of migrant parents to make sacrifices for their children becomes pinned to their ability to endure these hardships."[8]

Framing the United States as the protector of Cuban "family values" via family reunification, which is how the film recast Mariel, has long contributed a powerful thread to the "nation of immigrants" trope and supported the notion of the United States as a humanitarian haven in contrast to Communism. Maria de los Angeles describes how "ideological and security interests, not children's political and emotional rights, have often defined both U.S. and Cuban government policies that affect Cuban children."[9] Under Operation Pedro Pan, begun in the 1960s, Cuban parents, responding to U.S.-backed propaganda that the Castro government planned to send children to the Soviet Union for indoctrination, sent their children ahead to the United States, where they were processed in camps; parents would immigrate later.[10] Framing U.S. intervention in Cuba as a "family values" issue belies the international interests and domestic ideological work done by a focus on children's welfare, a key part of family reunification rhetoric.

In *Humanitarian Violence: The U.S. Deployment of Diversity*, Neda Atana-soski argues that after the fall of Communism, the fiction of the United States as a multicultural haven conceals the equal brutality of U.S. war-waging and peacemaking in order to spread liberal democracy and free markets. This fiction of exceptional humanitarianism "conceives of parts of the world that are still subject to the violence of U.S. power as being permanently in need of reform because they are homogenous and racially, religiously, and sexually intolerant." Difference is reframed as ideological and cultural rather than directly racial, as in the case of post-socialist and Islamic nations. This "post-socialist imperialism" entangles humanity and atrocity to redefine freedom as multicultural and religious freedom, exceptionally represented by U.S. democracy.[11] The rhetoric of family reunification for refugees from Communism was a precursor to "humanitarian violence."

Therefore, the fact that the immigrant family in *The Perez Family* is "multicultural" further conceals the reality of "nation of immigrants" mythology. The film, directed by Mira Nair and based on Christine Bell's 1990 novel, was part of the brief explosion of Latina/o pop culture in the 1990s, though the film did not do well at the box office or with critics.[12] The presence of Latin big band music (though Dottie demands Elvis upon docking in Florida) and Dottie's occasional paraphrases of Ricky Ricardo, Cuban American actor Desi Arnaz's *I Love Lucy* character, signify along with the storyline that the film is "Latina/o." Racialized gender stereotypes are also prevalent, most obviously in the character of Dottie, who was domesticated through her hard work and heterosexual monogamy. Notably, none of the actors is Cuban; Tomei is Italian American. Like Pacino in *Scarface*, an Italian American stands in for a Marielito.

The film provides—and is still sold as—a neoliberal "nation of immigrants" narrative with a seemingly progressive twist, given that the "multicultural" Perez family is unconventionally formed and the film's critique of nativism. Yet the film flirts with queering immigration, family, and freedom. Thus *The Perez Family*, along with a handful of other popular representations of immigrant families, engages in debates about family reunification going on in Congress and in broader conversations about race and gender politics coded in the language of "family values."

Now I turn to the failed attack on family reunification as the center of immigration policy during early IRCA debates, their connection to backlash against feminism epitomized in the rhetoric and imagery of "family values," and the ways that 1980s racialized concepts of immigrant families supported and sometimes subverted neoliberal projects. As noted, the path to IRCA's passage in 1986 was long. The 1982 version died when the House did not take action at the end of Ninety-Seventh Congress. While the 1984 House bill was less restrictive, the Senate version included the same limits to family reunification and overall restrictions.[13] Both bills died in their respective committees. No cuts to family reunification were included in the final version of IRCA.

While this might seem like a progressive victory, the discourses of both opposition to and support for family reunification were integral to the solidification of neoliberal crossings and established the contemporary prototype for a conflation of "family rights" and human rights that perpetuates inequalities. In other words, the pro-"multicultural" family discourse that circulated in IRCA debates and in pop culture, where it sometimes seemed to queer family, inaugurated a model for making claims for immigrant rights on the basis of adherence to neoliberal work ethic and white heterosexual "family values." As such, multicultural and seemingly queer or near-queer immigrant families furthered neoliberal interests.

While the conflation of immigrant "family rights" and human rights borrowed from and elaborated on long-standing liberal logics, these immigrant family discourses are an important part of what Stuart Hall calls the radical transformation of liberal principles in order to "make them applicable to a modern, global, post-industrial capitalism."[14] Moreover, although in many arenas, the "ethos of the 'free market' is taken to license an increasing disregard for moral standards, and even for the law itself,"[15] with the focus on immigrant "family values," a veneer of morality was ensconced in law, and celebrated and affirmed in news media and popular culture. This placated neoconservatives (though not all, as Simpson's overt racism makes clear) and made cost-cutting and the law itself seem humanitarian. In the neoliberal iteration, family values were turned to in order to account for the market. As Christina Gerken states in the context of 1990s family reunification, "family-sponsored immigrants were described as particularly desirable because the nuclear family unit could function as an informal support network and alleviate the financial responsibilities of federal and state governments. Family-values rhetoric was used to both support and humanize the impersonal economic logic that drove debate."[16]

Family formation also directly impacts immigrants, as shown in much important sociological research on Mexican immigrants. Pierette Hondahneu-Sotelo notes, "It is the immediate context of family and community relations (such as social networks) that shape[s] how people will respond to pressures exerted by structural transformations."[17] In his study of male Mexican migrants who have sex with men, Lionel Cantu, Jr., shows that sexuality shapes and organizes processes of migration and modes of incorporation, just as migration impacts identity formation.[18] Gloria Gonzalez-Lopez asserts that "sex is a family affair": Mexican immigrants' "sex lives were collective, public concerns that took place within the confines of family regulations, expectations, and norms."[19] The family is clearly a significant site of struggle for immigrants and for neoliberalism. Accordingly, the neoliberal position on immigrant family formation, which I argue was delineated in 1980s rather than 1990s immigration discourses, was that immigrant "family values" were a good investment that facilitated immigrants' ability to contribute to the economy. Although these immigrant "family values" appeared to be racially inclusive and morally sound, they worked in accord with a racialized heteronormative ideal.

We Are Not Family

The first version of the Simpson-Mazzoli bill was introduced in an April 1982 joint hearing in the Ninety-Seventh Congress. Senate sponsor Simpson was joined by Charles E. Grassley (R-IA) and Walter D. Huddleston (D-KY), and House sponsor Mazzoli was joined by Robert McClory (R-IL) and Hamilton Fish IV (R-NY.) Ultimately, it failed because of proposed worker identification cards and family reunification cuts.

The proposed restrictions would presumably have cut flows of Asian and Latin American immigrants by curtailing chain migration, opening more visas for skilled immigrants, and prohibiting family reunification among amnesty applicants.[20] Specifically, IRCA 1982, which was the same in the House and Senate (H.R. 5872/S. 2222), proposed to include family reunification for immediate relatives (spouses, parents, or children, exempt from numerical limits since 1924) under a 325,000 overall cap on family reunification. The total for any year would be subtracted from that to determine the limit the following year. Any remaining slots would go to other preferences.[21] Adult unmarried children were removed from the second preference category, and the fifth preference for citizens' siblings over the age of twenty-one was removed.

In the 1982 bill, the new proposed preferences for family reunification were:

1. Unmarried sons and daughters of citizens;
2. Spouses and children of permanent resident aliens;
3. Married sons and daughters of permanent resident aliens;
4. Previous fifth preference who met previous priority date (to resolve backlog and then it would be eliminated).

The proposed annual total was 425,000 and included 100,000 for independent immigration.[22] The new preference categories for independent immigrants were "Aliens with Exceptional Ability" in the arts, sciences, or business, skilled workers, investors, unskilled workers, and non-preference workers.[23] The now standard neoliberal acquisition and nurturing of human capital was the point.

Lawmakers and activists reacted strongly to the proposed family reunification cuts. The arguments on both sides were visceral and seemed to get at the very core of what Americanism was or was not. Ultimately, however, a neoliberal paradigm of "family values" won out. "Family" was thus key to 1980s immigration debates, and Americanism itself, particularly in the context of the ruptures of family engendered by second-wave feminism and multiculturalism, changing immigration patterns, and globalization. Simpson in particular was deeply troubled by the changing colors and shapes of American families. In 1981, he asserted that "family preference categories should be based on the U.S. concept of the nuclear family and not on the definition of such family as expressed in other nations."[24] He made his opposition to "other nations"—as antithetical to Americanism—clearer in a 1982 Senate hearing that addressed the IRCA proposal for changes in numerical limits. Leonel Castillo, representing Immigrant Aid Society, in Houston, Texas, noted that with the largest backlogs, Latin American and Asian groups and especially Mexicans would be most impacted by changes. Simpson replied, "The definition of nuclear family should be ours under legislation and not a definition prescribed by a sending country."[25] Reflecting on IRCA debates in a 1997 interview, Simpson elaborated, "To an American family, reunification is a spouse and minor children. To an Indian-American or to an Asian-American it means brothers and sisters, and adult brothers and sisters, and even aunts and uncles. And that is something that's going to have to be corrected."[26]

His and others' (thinly) coded racial objections were made in terms of population control and protecting resource capital (epitomized by Zero Population Growth [ZPG]), as well as fears of bilingualism. The restrictionist Federation of American Immigration Reform (FAIR) reframed race as language in its support of English Only measures, and Simpson was on board. He said the present immigration situation was distinguished by "the bilingual or black cultural education being used other than as a transitional device; a greater concentration on a single language group if illegal immigration is considered; assuredly a higher tolerance of ethnic diversity; the proximity of Latin America, which is a real issue, which encourages continual contact."[27] Yet he was quick to remind his colleagues that restriction was not about race.[28] In this way, pundits claimed that restricting family reunification (and outlawing bilingualism and what Simpson called "black cultural education") was not racist but rather rooted in beneficent concern for citizens. (Interestingly, Simpson seems aware of the disingenuousness of the argument even as he makes it.)

His racism was also well-documented in popular media both before and after IRCA passed. In the early 1990s, a *Wall Street Journal* reporter compared Simpson to white supremacist David Duke and called him "a xenophobe cum laude;"[29] the *Casper Star-Tribune* published a cartoon of Simpson wearing a button that read, "Never Give a Hispanic an Even Break!";[30] and *Los Angeles Times* cartoonist Robert Conrad turned the American flag into a prison door, with the red stripes dripping blood. Behind the bars were "poor and defenseless" immigrants.[31] While Simpson flippantly dismissed such accusations in his autobiography, the evidence speaks for itself.

Moreover, Simpson was backed by a long history of protecting white—and male—privilege and property in immigration and naturalization law. Whiteness as a prerequisite for citizenship was first explicitly legally protected in the Naturalization Act of 1790. In his important work, George Lipsitz shows that more recently, "racialized space enables the advocates of expressly racist policies to disavow any racial intent. They speak on behalf of whiteness and its accumulated privileges and immunities, but rather than having to speak *as* whites, they represent themselves as racially unmarked homeowners, citizens, and taxpayers whose preferred policies just happen to sustain white privilege and power. One of the privileges of whiteness, as Richard Dyer reminds us, is never having to speak its name."[32] David Theo Goldberg similarly argues that since the civil rights movement, antiracialism (that is, the characterization of race neutrality as antiracist) "saved" racism by making it seem invisible.[33] Simpson was not that subtle.

Sexism, though less obvious, was as salient. In her examination of gender and IRCA debates, Phyllis Pease Chock argues that the category "citizen" entails meanings that implicate gender; it connotes an income-producing worker who is a rational, orderly head of a nuclear family, whereas the non-citizen is dependent, irrational, unproductive, unpaid. In liberal political theory, the former is a male subject and the latter female.[34] Although the gendered meanings of "citizen" are not explicitly named, they too always already shape immigration debates.[35]

Furthermore, Gloria Anzaldua points out in "La Prieta," her visceral, personalized argument for intersectionality (that is, the consideration of how vectors of identity such as race, gender, sexuality, class, nationality, citizenship status, dis/ability, and so on intersect with one another to shape a person's or group's experiences of and relations to power, oppression, and privilege) is necessary to and for social justice. She poignantly describes how her own intersecting social identities—"woman," "Latina," "Mexican," "feminist," "queer," etc.—are inherently entwined. Focusing on only one identity category is violence, as is forcing her to choose from multiple sites of allegiance and oppression.[36] Chock notes that during the IRCA debates, the sometimes overt discourse about race was "curiously uninflected for gender" despite contemporary debates over *Roe v. Wade* and the ERA.[37] Along with race, gender, understood as "not simply a variable to be measured, but a set of social relations that organize immigration patterns,"[38] was clearly implicated in discussions about family and welfare (as in, who will pay for the families in question?).

Simpson's reasoning for family reunification cuts fit into the "family values" discourse of the day (which was about women of color and how they fit into the ascendant neoliberal state). In the 1980s, many tenets of the civil rights and second-wave feminist movements became mainstream; to stay relevant even staunch conservatives had to tolerate at least superficial advances in gender and racial equality. Reagan, ever the crowd-pleaser, did not miss this boat: he often "ritualistically listed all of the women he had appointed to high positions, met with his female appointees regularly, appointed women to recruit more women, and boasted his administration had been better to women than any other." He similarly tokenized people of color.[39] As is common in neoliberal discourse, female and multicultural token individuals are meant to demonstrate inclusion and parity, despite ongoing structural inequalities. Moreover, at the same time, backlash came in opposition to the ERA, affirmative action, and welfare, largely via "family values." Racism and sexism did not disappear; they were rearticulated and appropriated via inclusive discourse, and they were entwined.

The "dramatic diversification" of the American family in the 1970s[40] was jarring at a moment when race and gender equality were still new ideas. Changes included increasing immigrants of color, internal migration of people of color into the suburbs and Sunbelt, and displacement of the male breadwinner paradigm dominant since the 1950s. Concurrently, there were "high rates of divorce, cohabitation, unwed motherhood, the new visibility of same-sex relationships, the (re)emergence of stepfamilies and working mothers, and a sharp rise in the number of single person households where once married-couple households were the norm."[41]

The New Right was born in response to these changes. Neoconservatism imbued social and economic issues with Christian ethics. The lynchpins of the New Right were big business interests concerned with inroads made by foreign companies, and Christian leaders. Galvanized by Barry Goldwater's explicitly anti–civil rights 1964 presidential campaign,[42] neoconservatives averred that big government and welfare threatened personal freedom and domestic and international economic development. At the same time, with the victory of *Roe v. Wade*, more sexual permissiveness, and the nascent gay rights movement,[43] the Christian contingent held that the "breakdown" of the traditional family demonstrated moral decline. In the 1970s the New Right put a positive spin on anti-pluralist morality: they were "pro-family" and "pro-life" champions of wholesome "family values," which meant battling the ERA, abortion, pornography, gay rights, and gun control.[44] Phyllis Schalfly organized STOP ERA in 1972 on the premise that it "dissolved men's obligation to support their wives and children, forced women into the workplace, and relegated children to day-care centers."[45]

Struggles over the meanings of femininity played out on primetime television in the 1980s, in another example of the connectedness of public policy and pop culture in the context of neoliberalism. Julie D'Acci has shown how the television industry, with a profit-driven need to be socially relevant, attempted to court the new "working women's market" with representations that drew on the new feminist consciousness (namely, the mainstream liberal strain dominated by white middle-class women and focused primarily on equal pay and abortion rights), such as *Cagney and Lacey*, *9 to 5*, *Remington Steele*, *Gloria*, and *It Takes Two*. Yet the backlash against feminism mitigated progressive innovations. In *Cagney and Lacey* (1982–1988), a cop drama that followed white female middle- and upper-middle-class detectives, Christine Cagney (Meg Foster/ Sharon Gless) and Mary Beth Lacey (Tyne Daly), solve their own cases, are rarely shown as "women in distress," and are subjects rather than mere objects of sexual desire.[46] Gloria Steinem and *Ms. Magazine* endorsed the show.[47] Yet when critics fixated on the women's appearances and critiqued their aggression and toughness, CBS replaced Foster with Gless, and made both characters more conventionally feminine, less likely to be mistaken for "dykes," as Frank Swertlow put it in *TV Guide*.[48] Positioning texts (as well as people and institutions) as anti-family, as with accusations of homosexuality or queerness, was another way in which the backlash against feminism took coherent shape.

Conservatives also almost seamlessly articulated opposition to civil rights vis-à-vis "family values." As Zillah Eisenstein notes, "definitions of womanhood are simultaneously definitive and reflective of racist images and practices." In the 1980s, language used to talk about family and women such as "single parent" and "welfare mother" was not directly racially coded but "each engendered construction is illustrative of racial categorizations. We need only to speak of one to elicit the other. In official political talk, 'single parents' mean black teenage girls and/or their mothers on welfare."[49] Conservatives contended poverty was a personal failure to embrace the traditional family, rather than being attributable to racism and/or sexism.

So even as Reagan nominated Sandra Day O'Connor as the first female Supreme Court justice and became the first president to consistently include women in his cabinet, and even as gender and racial inequalities were narrowing, the administration inaugurated a paradigm for the neoliberal appropriation of feminism, multiculturalism, and eventually queerness. Tokenism and appeals to protect and nurture the family did the trick; in fact, the latter, I will show, were used by liberals, radicals, and conservatives alike in ways that supported the market-driven values that characterize claims for rights within neoliberal projects.

The attack on family reunification in immigration polemics in the 1980s was an attack on women from Latin America, Asia, and the Caribbean. Historically, family reunification was about women and race: as Donna Gabaccia observes, "assumptions about gender, and about proper familial relations between men and women, have . . . shaped discussions of immigration policy since the nineteenth century."[50] The 1882 Chinese Exclusion Act first privileged marriage in immigration law by allowing wives and children of Chinese merchants and students to enter.[51] Unifying heterosexual spouses and heterosexual families had long been a staple of immigration[52] and in the 1980s, because historically women were rarely migration "pioneers," far more wives and mothers received family reunification visas than husbands and fathers.[53] Moreover, few American women, civilian or military, chose foreign-born spouses, whereas men often did, and even in the 1990s, three quarters of immigrants entering as skilled professionals were male. With the exception of nursing, most "traditionally female occupations" were not considered "skilled."[54] As Gabaccia notes, "a third world woman has a better chance of entering the United States by marrying an emigrated man or an American citizen than she does waiting unmarried, or childless, for a visa allowing her to work as an office cleaner, factory operative, or clerical."[55] Since a woman's best chance for entering the nation was under family reunification provisions, restricting family reunification was in effect restricting women.

This is not to suggest, however, that family reunification was not problematic. Marxist feminists argue that women's subordination serves the interests of capital and the ruling class through unpaid domestic labor and wage gaps that favor men,[56] an argument that is inflected by race, class, and immigration status. By 1980, the number of working women reached 42 million, or over double than the 19.5 million who worked in 1955. For the first time, over half of American women were employed outside the home; only one third were solely "homemakers".[57] Yet national, civic, and political processes constructed the nuclear family as the source of love and security and maintained that reproduction and childrearing were private tasks done by women. Along with the wage gap, women in the workforce contended with the "double day" of attending to professional responsibilities and to primary unpaid household and childcare responsibilities.

Neoliberal immigration policy mitigates these racialized gender role tensions. Ironically, Simpson's ideal nuclear family—American, and thus white—which coerced racialized immigrant women into low-wage domestic labor, enabled many white middle-class women to work outside the home.[58] At the same time, for many immigrants who were earning low-wages, a nuclear household was impossible. Global capital and immigration policy undermined traditional gender roles, and necessitated the formation of non-nuclear families, often compelling overcrowding in apartments and homes.[59] Furthermore, since family reunification makes immigrants dependent upon family members for residency and citizenship, women's abilities to negotiate working conditions tend to be limited: often working for relations who sponsor their immigration, women are bound to the family and/or ethnic community.[60] Thus, family reunification laws solidify migrant women's dependency.[61]

In sum, the neoliberal negotiation of feminism and multiculturalism is discernible in the family reunification polemics of the 1980s. Simpson's attack on "non-U.S." concepts of family made Latin American and Asian immigrant women into scapegoats for shifting social paradigms while both reinforcing women's subordination and heterosexualizing who counts as human. Evermore sneaky and more directly gendered racism surfaced in arguments supporting family reunification as a solid neoliberal investment, even when those arguments appeared to be multicultural. In fact, the establishment of white ethnic families as ideally American and thus "normal" in alignment with neoliberal values was predicated on "family values" that were ostensibly rare among families of color.

Earlier "nation of immigrants" discourses underscored this de/valuation. Take, for example, the *Moynihan Report* (1965), produced by Daniel Patrick Moynihan, a solider in President Lyndon Johnson's "War on Poverty," a sociologist, and eventually a senator (D-NY, elected in 1982, 1988, and 1994). In this document prepared for the Department of Labor Moynihan claimed that black women heading families was the cause of persistent poverty among blacks, despite civil rights gains.[62] He argued for eliminating black dependence on state assistance by reinstating (coercing) traditional gender norms and marriage. In his early articulation of "family values," Moynihan cited a study that showed that white Italian American and Jewish nuclear families had far higher rates of "married-spouse present" homes than their black counterparts and were not impoverished.[63]

Latin American–origin families were pathologized, too. In the 1960s, anthropologist Oscar Lewis attributed poverty and crime among Mexicans and Puerto Ricans to dysfunctional families that failed to properly socialize children to American values.[64] This idea of the Latin American immigrant and Latina/o family predisposing persons to poverty, crime, and deviance is part of the pathologization of Mexican masculinity, and that history of pathologization was rearticulated for post–second-wave feminism through allegations of typical male violence.[65] As late as 2001, American "experts" reflected on the "authoritarianism, fatalism, hypermachismo, Spanish 'tradition of chivalry still here today,' and female passivity and subordination" that they saw characterizing the Mexican family.[66]

The pathologizing of Latin American–origin families, alongside the idealization of white ethnic families, had tangible consequences in other IRCA provisions, such as racialized amnesty provisions. Approximately 70 percent of Seasonal Agricultural Worker (SAW) amnesty applicants were Mexican, and over 20 percent were from Latin America.[67] Under SAW, if parents crossed borders years apart, only one might be eligible to legalize under cutoff deadlines, or a parent might be eligible but a child who crossed later might be excluded. Family reunification for SAW participants was not a priority as SAW was about cheap labor, and as noted, Simpson had lobbied to make all amnesty applicants ineligible for family reunification when amnesty first came up in SCIRP.[68]

Yet late in the legislative process, Representative Brian Donnelly (D-MA) added an amendment allocating 10,000 special non-quota visas for aliens who were natives of European countries disadvantaged under the INA.[69] In the 1980s, unemployment in Ireland had engendered migration and a substantial undocumented U.S. population of at least 136,000.[70] Donnelly and supporters such as Senator Ted Kennedy (D-MA) correctly assumed Irish would benefit most from the program. New York senator Alfonse D'Amato called it "affirmative action" for white Europeans,[71] as those who qualified were free from the red tape that SAW and general amnesty applicants were subjected to. Amnesty for Latin American immigrants and white ethnic immigrants was not at all equal.

Popular culture representations of families were likewise differentiated, with dismissal and denigration of, and outright attacks on, black and Latin American immigrant and Latina/o families being manifest. At the same time, some of the most popular sitcoms of the 1980s focused on unconventional white families including white ethnic characters who were plucky immigrants themselves or who were descended from immigrants and forging ahead on the quest for a better life. Although the latter representations had the potential to be queer families, they too were part of the neoliberal family discourse, which values only families and persons who are net contributors to the economy and who adhere to the heterosexual model. Along with negotiating feminism by "softening" working women characters, the prototypical white ethnic "nation of immigrants" trope mitigated queerness, feminism, and multiculturalism on the small screen.

The ABC sitcom *Who's the Boss?* (1984–1992) family included Angela Bower (Judith Light), her young son, Jonathan (Danny Pintauro), her housekeeper, Tony Micelli (Tony Danza), his teenage daughter, Samantha (Alyssa Milano), and Angela's mother, Mona (Katherine Helmond). Advertising executive Angela has the traditionally male breadwinning role, and is Tony's boss. He fills the traditional "housewife" role as her sensitive housekeeper. While the original title, *You're the Boss*, refers to gender role reversal,[72] the revised version suggests that either might be the boss. The ostensibly queer family—a family of choice that includes deviations from gender norms—was formed when second-generation Italian American Tony moved Samantha from their working-class Brooklyn neighborhood to Angela's wealthy, WASP-y Fairfield, Connecticut suburb, because he wanted Sam to have a better life. The series, created by TV executives Martin Cohan and Blake Hunter, was nominated for over forty awards and won an Emmy, a Golden Globe, and other accolades.[73] Between 1985 and 1988, it ranked in the top ten primetime ratings[74] and is globally syndicated.

The gender role disruption and unconventional kinship arrangement was countered by proper "family values," which might explain the show's popularity in Reagan's America. The eventually consummated (hetero)sexual tension between Angela and Tony is a major driving force of the show. Gender-conventional parenting is stressed, with storylines affirming that in order for Angela to properly mother Jonathan, she needs male advice and help. Tony often "rescues" Angela, re-feminizing her as a damsel in distress. Tony likewise needs Angela's help, as when Samantha needs her first bra. He is sensitive and domestic (a contrast to then-prevalent media stereotypes of often dim-witted macho working-class Italian Americans like Sylvester Stallone's iconic Rocky Balboa and Danza's own previous role as a torpid, good-natured taxi driver on *Taxi*), but he simply cannot mother Sam. His masculinity is also reinforced by his athleticism as a former baseball pro (and bolstered by Danza's former real-life turn as a professional boxer).

The "nation of immigrants" trope in the Micelli's lives also counters the queer and feminist aspects of the sitcom with sentimental celebrations of the rewards that hard work, patriotism, and proper "family values" bring to those seeking a better life. *Who's the Boss?* anticipated the near-queer Marielito Perez family. In "Yankee Doodle Micelli" (Season 5, Episode 4, 1988) Tony flashes back to childhood memories of Grandpa Micelli (played by Danza), who emigrated from Palermo to raise Tony in the United States after his mother passed away. Grandpa Micelli's dream was to become a citizen. In an over-the-top Italian accent, Grandpa Micelli frequently told Tony, "In this a-country you can-a make a-something of-a yourself," parroting the liberal and neoliberalizing promise of exceptional opportunity for immigrants. Grandpa Micelli aced his citizenship test but missed the swearing-in ceremony because he had to get Tony out of trouble for stealing subway signs, and died soon after. In the episode's visceral closing scene, a tearful Tony, acting as proxy, posthumously naturalizes his grandfather. In skipping the ceremony to teach Tony to obey the law, Grandpa Micelli was a good American, (eventually) rewarded with citizenship, his legacy evidenced in the better life that Tony perpetuates with dreams of college for Sam and attending college himself. Moreover, Danza, born Anthony Iadanza, was the Brooklyn-born son of working-class Italian immigrants (his father a garbage man, his mother a bookkeeper).[75] True to white ethnic "nation of immigrants" form, Danza anglicized his name and benefited from his parents' and his hard work, earning a bachelor's degree and becoming a successful entertainer.

Thus despite some queer characteristics and apparently progressive values, the sitcom reenacts conservative "family values." Given the family-driven deployment of the "nation of immigrants" narrative, Tony can be sensitive, have a "feminine" job, and not be the breadwinner without disrupting any dominant values. Likewise Angela can be an empowered/powerful working woman, but she needs a strong man at home. And the respectability essential to the ideal is a given for the white *Who's the Boss?* family. Angela and Tony are more effective parents and more conventionally successful when they form a nuclear unit, but neither is cast as deviant when they are single parents. Such unconventionality was not an option afforded to families of color.

One need only consider the contemporaneous *The Cosby Show* (1984–1992) to see that the ideal was available only to highly respectable people of color. The sitcom was developed from parts of Bill Cosby's stand-up comedy act and focused on the affluent Huxtable family (doctor father, lawyer mother; one child Princeton-educated, and all five children college attendees). The show has been credited with both reviving the sitcom genre[76] and providing a much-needed alternative to most media representations of blacks, who in the 1980s tended to be cast only as criminals, athletes, and entertainers.[77]

But as black feminist sociologist Patricia Hill Collins shows, wife Claire Huxtable (Phylicia Rashad) exemplifies the modern reworking of the

Mammy, or loyal female servant of chattel slavery, as the "Black lady," into a middle- or upper middle-class, beautiful, articulate black woman whose sexuality, ambition, and aggression are controlled and sanitized so that she does not seem threatening to white supremacy. Claire is never shown in her place of employment; her "sexuality was safely contained to domestic space, and within the confines of heterosexual marriage."[78] The respectable middle-class ideal of a heterosexual family is something that white men and women like Tony and Angela can pull off regardless of whether they are romantically involved or who the breadwinner is (and Angela is often shown at her office, particularly when she opens her own agency). Tony can also be both working class and respectable, though of course he becomes more respectable with upward mobility. In contrast, pains were taken to portray the Huxtables as respectable by showing them adhering to traditional gender and sexual norms and enjoying unusual affluence; in fact, "the Huxtables lived far better than the vast majority of Americans of all racial backgrounds" and "drugs, crime, teenage pregnancy, unemployment, discrimination happened to other people. The family itself was immune."[79] Siobhan Somerville argues that the nineteenth-century colonial structures and methodologies that drove dominant ideologies of race also fueled scientific knowledge about the homosexual body—that, in other words, the same forces have historically constructed race and homosexuality. Racial difference rested on proving the sexual difference of black women's bodies.[80] Comparison of *Who's the Boss?* with *The Cosby Show* indicates that such mutual, intersectional construction got a neoliberal update: Reaganite "family values" rather than alternative kinship and progressive gender arrangements were the boss in pop culture as well as in the IRCA family reunification debates.

Arguments against family reunification encapsulated conservative opposition to feminism and multiculturalism, and were anchored in notions of racialized familial respectability. This was reflected in pop culture. Simultaneously, the conservative idea of family was harnessed to argue *for* immigrant rights. This directly, and even with the best intentions, supported oppressive neoliberal ideologies and policies in significant, lasting ways. As *The Perez Family* suggests, familial respectability was a complicated affair, a trope readily evoked in support of both restriction *and* inclusion of immigrants.

We Are Family

In response to Simpson, pundits from some unlikely constituencies argued to uphold and sometimes expand family reunification. Those opposed to family reunification were a congressional minority. The end result was a more multicultural and thus seemingly more inclusive idea of "family" as the cornerstone of rights claims for immigrants, which endures today. This multicultural idea of family rests on the notion that the nation offers exceptional opportunity to those seeking a better life, an idea articulated in a specific way as part of the shift to neoliberalism.

In the 1980s, congressional and popular arguments proposed that immigrants deserve and earn rights because they are uniquely hardworking, possess proper "family values," and sometimes have the discipline and determination that Americans lack. (This is extant in dominant immigrant activist discourses such as the 2006 Immigrant Rights marches and DREAM advocacy.[81]) Key to these arguments is the notion that families facilitate immigrants' self-sufficiency and upward mobility. Immigrants, including those cast as assets, were positioned as owing something to America and required to "earn" rights that are purportedly inalienable. Such logics make or break fitness for citizenship in accordance with market values and a conservative agenda, but this is hard to recognize when even liberals and activists point to respectability and personal responsibility as prerequisites for human rights. Who counts as human is narrowly defined as a self-supporting member of a heterosexual family. This still-dominant logic for immigrant rights cohered in the congressional and popular rebuff to 1980s attacks on family reunification.

To be clear, supporting family reunification ultimately supported neoliberal ideology and policy; neoliberalism shaped opposition and support. Michel Foucault famously explained in *History of Sexuality* that homosexual identity (as opposed to same sex acts) was invented in the nineteenth century in accordance with larger shifts to industrialization and the formation of medicine, science, and law as fields and institutions of state power. The state could enact discipline upon the new homosexual body, but homosexuality also affronted and perhaps challenged dominant ideals of procreative, marital heterosexuality. With this history, Foucault argued that marginal sexual identities are not just victims of operations of power; rather those same relations of power produce them; power creates resistance.[82] Accordingly, hegemonic power relations shaped support for family reunification, even when it came from progressive contingents.

The Reagan administration favored upholding family reunification from 1981[83] and throughout IRCA debates for the sake of diplomatic relations; in fact, the administration was interested in offering more slots to Mexico and Canada,[84] an agenda that can be understood as part of domestic neoliberal reforms. In the 1980s Mexico entered a thirteen-year economic crisis initiated by the government's declaration of a moratorium on debt services. This was due to a significant population increase from post-revolutionary years to the 1960s, the end of egalitarian land reform laws and corn price guarantees enacted in the 1930s, and increasing pressure from international economic agencies located primarily in the United States.[85] The consequent devastating poverty led to a large-scale uprooting of Mexican rural populations. Simultaneously, in 1976, Western Hemisphere nations became subject to annual quota limits of 20,000,[86] which had the effect of transforming legal migrant laborers into illegal aliens. It also made for an inexpensive labor force and surely provoked desire for family reunification on the part of labor migrants who settled in the United States.

As early as 1978, SCIRP advocated promoting national interests by embracing diversity via family reunification and recommending that sibling preferences within numerical limits continue, in recognition of "the closeness of the sibling relationship and the broader concept of family held by many nationalities."[87] Representative Hamilton Fish IV (R-NY) summed it up: "Our Nation, which cherishes family values, must continue to provide reasonable opportunities for our people to be reunited with close relatives."[88]

Support for a "broader concept of family" also formed the crux of the argument for ethnic lobbying groups and activists. In IRCA hearings, spokespeople for the American Committee on Italian Migration, the Immigrant Aid Society, and the Citizens' Committee for Immigration Reform testified in favor of the fifth preference category for the brothers and sisters of U.S. citizens over age twenty-one. Spokespeople for the Mexican American Legal Defense and Educational Fund (MALDEF) and the National Council of LaRaza, a nonprofit, nonpartisan lobbying group for Latinas/os, wanted amnesty and the undocumented included in discussions of family reunification.[89] The Asian American Legal Defense and Education Fund (AALDEF) and the Organization of Chinese Americans argued that the proposed cuts were racist toward Asian Americans.[90] With restrictions on family reunification, immigration from Latin American and Asian nations would continue to be under a quota system, in effect.

These arguments supporting family reunification, antiracism, and multiculturalism also worked for neoliberalism. Norman Lau Kee, chairman of the Immigration and Refugee Policy Task Force at the U.S.-Asia Institute, argued regarding the fifth preference category that siblings help keep each other off welfare and that "family units tend to form strong economic units. They create investment opportunities which would create more employment."[91] Organized labor and business also stressed that hardworking immigrants who were members of families contributed to rather than sapped national resources.

This argument about the economic value of multicultural immigrant families surfaced repeatedly in news media and pop culture, too, solidifying the neoliberal "family values" discourse. The fiftieth anniversary issue of *Newsweek* in February 1983 provides an example of the emerging trend.[92] Featuring a series of stories about five American families set in Springfield, Ohio, which is meant to stand in as "every American town" and thus the families are meant to represent every American,[93] the text was resplendent with classic liberal and neoliberal "nation of immigrants" rhetoric. Well into the twentieth century, Springfield was a hotbed of racial and religious tensions (between early Protestant settlers and later Roman Catholic immigrants), and successfully coping with such tensions while pursuing a better life was crucial to the American stories being celebrated.

Three of the families were white ethnic immigrant (German, Italian, and Austro-Hungarian), one was African American, and one was white Anglo-Saxon Protestant. Each family story was told in cliffhanger chapters, with heartbreaking narratives involving devastation from the Depression, Jim Crow, and the Ku Klux Klan (KKK). In accordance with the "nation of immigrants" bootstrap mythos, in each installment—even for families not descended from recent or voluntary immigrants—their labor and tenacity resulted in a better life for future generations. In this anniversary issue, American history was indeed a progressive narrative, and *Newsweek* exemplified neoliberal appropriation of multiculturalism via "family values."

To the extent to which Simpson attacked anything but the "American nuclear family," the piece was a dissenting voice: family over many generations and in various shades was American, a position echoed in IRCA family reunification polemics. Yet *Newsweek* collapsed multiculturalism and neoliberalization in the same way the pro-immigrant family position did, masking the racism endemic to neoliberalism. The Springfield KKK targeted white ethnic immigrants as well as blacks, but the former had options that the latter lacked. Though harassed by the KKK and called a "dago," an ethnic slur used against Italians, Matteo Capelli (Matt) transcended his immigrant roots because of his white skin and increasing financial success working his way up in a flower-selling business. He was "a passionate believer in the American Dream because he was living it."[94] The black Bacon family, also subject to KKK harassment and violence, could not simply transcend racism through hard work, yet their story was also cast as a "nation of immigrants" ascent. Moreover, framed by the news magazine in the context of neoliberalism, the worth and value of each family were inseparable from their abilities to generate hardworking, self-supporting net contributors to the economy. As on the congressional floor, so in the magazine, multicultural family values had market value, and the "nation of immigrants" trope masked the material realities of racism as a structural part and consequence of (liberal and neoliberal) capitalism.

A story about a hardworking Mexican American family, the Garcias, published in *Newsweek* a few months later, similarly masked the realities of neoliberal "family values." The Garcia brothers were born in the United States to a Mexican mother who deliberately crossed the border to give birth to each of her sons, providing them with dual citizenship. Raised mostly in Mexico on a corn farm, they migrated every summer to work in Texas cotton fields, earning money for college. As adults, the brothers lived on opposite sides of the border. Eloy, the elder, earned degrees in finance and accounting and rose through the ranks of the Mexican treasury department. In Laredo, Texas, Eliud became a vice president of the International Bank of Commerce. Both succeeded because they learned English, worked hard, and maintained family commitments; the family unit again had market value.[95] This portrait, which seemed to dispel the "immigrant emergency" discourse, elided the xenophobic targeting of Mexicans and the poverty, disenfranchisement, and violence Mexicans were disproportionately subjected to. This was accomplished by painting the American system as democratic and accessible to hardworking families of all races, across borders even, and by casting these Mexicans as a "model minority" family.

The Amerasian children provision in the 1982 version of IRCA also appeared to be inclusive. Based on the premise that Vietnamese nationals abandoned biracial children fathered by U.S. servicemen during the Vietnam War and the heteropatriarchal notion that these children needed and deserved a father,[96] the provision received robust support from Asian American lobbying groups, and all but no opposition, even from Simpson. It was rather ironic that this welcoming of non-white children—essentially as refugees from communism—was framed as humanitarian "common sense" given the simultaneous racialized debates over family reunification.

In the end, Simpson's family reunification cuts were rejected; they contradicted the national mythology of benign welcoming refuge to all who sought it, a mythology that was particularly important to bolster in the context of the Cold War. Moreover, the immigrant family unit was profitable and this could be spun as humanitarian. But at the same time, along with the law's literal investment in whiteness (and patriarchy and heterosexuality), arguments for inclusion based on immigrants' respectable "family values" and commitment to hard work rearticulated inequalities. Likewise, in some 1980s sitcoms, the "nation of immigrants" trope intersected with feminism and queer family structures, complicating "family values" so that its neoliberal, disciplining function was especially difficult to recognize.

Are We a Queer Family?

More direct representations of ostensibly queer families and negotiations of gender norms within hardworking, self-supporting immigrant families were quite popular in the 1980s. These too labored for neoliberal ideology under the rubric of the "nation of immigrants" trope. Namely, a handful of representations that seemed to be queer, feminist, and/or multicultural appropriated aspects of feminism and multiculturalism, and defined the value of family in terms of the financial support that even unconventional families foster.

Women's liberation was evoked to legitimate endeavors from the American occupation of Japan to the U.S. invasion of Afghanistan after 9/11, the latter of which, according to Laura Bush, was partially an effort to "liberate Afghani women" from the Taliban. As John Carlos Rowe notes, feminist universalism is "readily adaptable to Western cultural imperialist projects."[97] Similarly, Jodi Melamed argues that the neoliberal appearance of incorporating racial and gender difference makes U.S. global hegemony seem just and fair.[98] In other words, the inclusion of people of color, women, and immigrants makes U.S. neoliberal projects seem democratizing and just despite neoliberalism's dependence on inequalities. Additionally, Matthew Jacobson asserts that second-wave feminists, dominated by white ethnic women who saw feminists as being like legal aliens within churches and the academy, attempted to establish a sense of common struggle with women of color and recent immigrants on the basis of shared patriarchal oppression and a history of white ethnic immigrants' poverty, tenement life, and social marginalization.[99] A richer consideration of how race, ethnicity, and class impact gender was incorporated into mainstream feminism that, along with the invaluable contributions of women of color, diversified and expanded considerations of difference and power.[100]

But establishing commonality between white women and citizens and immigrants of color is a slippery slope, as seen in *Newsweek*'s portrayal of immigrant families and the black Bacon family, as well as in Madonna's preference for the barrio in "Borderline." Second-wave feminism has been criticized for its elision of intersections of race, sexuality, and class; in mainstream feminism "woman" was too often a monolithic category that was by default white and middle to upper class.[101] Halberstam might say such limited formulations of feminism and multiculturalism failed to achieve the queer art of failure. Failures to fail—ineffectively progressive appropriations of feminism, queerness, and multiculturalism—surfaced in popular representations of seemingly queer immigrant families.

In the 1980s, mainstream popular texts such the sitcom *The Golden Girls* imagined immigrants of color and white ethnic women as allies in parallel struggles for social justice, but along with the limits of claims for inclusion and rights on the basis of respectability and personal responsibility, the notion of common struggle made white privilege especially hard to recognize. Narratives of white ethnic ascendance, particularly when grafted onto the bodies of single elderly women, made it seem like the system would work for *any* respectable hard workers. The notion of common struggle and its manifestation in pop culture coalitions fall under the rubric of neoliberalism's assimilative feminism and multiculturalism.

Golden Girls (1985–1992) was contemporaneous with *Who's the Boss?* and *The Cosby Show*. It premiered at No. 1 with approximately forty-four million viewers, stayed in the Top 10 for six consecutive seasons,[102] and won numerous awards, including an Emmy for Outstanding Comedy in 1986 and 1987, three Golden Globe Awards for Best Television Series–Musical or Comedy, and all four female leads won Emmies. It continues to run in syndication on networks marketed to women such as *Lifetime*. Hailed as maverick because it was the first to represent older women as vibrant, active subjects and objects of desire, the show continues to inform and influence popular culture.[103]

In 1984 Paul Junger Witt, Tony Thomas, and Witt's wife, Susan Harris created *Golden Girls*, which follows four white heterosexual middle-class women in their "golden years," when, widowed or divorced, they become roommates in a sprawling Miami home.[104] Brandon Tartikoff, NBC programming chief, was interested in the premise when he learned that "almost 37 percent of Americans were at least 45 in 1984, and there are now [1986] approximately 10 million more people over 50 than there were ten years ago." In 1986, the show's Saturday night time slot helped increase NBC's Saturday night ratings by 36 percent over the prior year.[105] Regardless of the financial impetus for the show, according to the Grey Panthers, a national lobby against age discrimination, the show empowered a group that network television had previously erased or relegated to the background.[106] Like Mona of *Who's the Boss?*, the older women were sexually active, and like Angela, they were self-supporting. The family was potentially queer in that it was non-nuclear and composed of a single gender, and the show dealt with controversial issues such as ageism, anti-Semitism, racism, sexual harassment, homophobia, and immigration. Several episodes took up the theme of coalition building between women and Cuban immigrants.

Each of the four protagonists in this family might be considered white ethnic: Blanche (Rue McClanahan) is a promiscuous Southern belle, Rose (Betty White) is a naïve woman from a midwestern Norwegian immigrant community, Dorothy (Bea Arthur) is an assertive, intellectual, second-generation Italian American raised in Brooklyn, and Sophia (Estelle Getty), Dorothy's mother, is a Sicilian immigrant and the most directly white ethnic. The feisty matriarch dispenses advice with didactic stories about her experience growing up in a poor village in Sicily and as a struggling young immigrant mother in Brooklyn (which she begins by saying, "Picture It: Sicily," or "Brooklyn" followed by the date of the narrated lesson). True to the white ethnic story, this "colorful," romanticized symbol of the "Old World" pulled herself up by her bootstraps to secure a better life for her American-born children. Sophia and Dorothy, the most proper white ethnics, are at the center of the episodes that focused on coalition-building with Latin American immigrants.

In "Dorothy's Prized Pupil" (Season 2, Episode 21, 1987), Dorothy, a substitute teacher, tutors a boy (Mario Lopez) whose prize-winning essay exposes him as an undocumented immigrant from Cuba. She (successfully) fights to prevent his deportation on the grounds that he is a hardworking, patriotic immigrant—according to Dorothy, "what this country is all about"—and has earned his place here. In "Fiddler on the Ropes" (Season 4, Episode 18, 1989), the ever-enterprising Sophia, who frequently devises get-rich schemes (usually predicated on her stereotypical Italian American culinary prowess), tries to cash in on an immigration story. Sophia embezzles the roommates' money to support Pepe (Chick Vennera), a Cuban immigrant boxer she hoped to manipulate because he did not speak English. Sophia and the others rallied to help him, however, when they learn that Pepe, actually a fluent English-speaker, boxes for prize money to pay for Julliard. A violinist, he has an upcoming audition at the prestigious arts school. But having been knocked out in the first few seconds of a fight—in part a strategy the girls devise to minimize his risk of hurting his virtuoso hands—Pepe forgets his piece during his audition. With the girls' prompting, he launches into a "Cuban American Merchant of Venice" monologue, wows the judges, and is accepted as an actor. Sophia, quick with Hispanic jokes throughout the episode (many episodes, actually), has the last word as the other women celebrate his victory: "When," she quips, "was the last time you saw a Cuban Macbeth?" She concludes that Pepe will spend his acting career getting arrested because Latino actors were usually relegated to criminal parts.

With their cleverness, English fluency, commitment to education and the arts (Euro-American high culture!), and of course patriotism and hard work, the Cuban immigrants in these episodes defy negative stereotypes. They are "Latin Algers," symbols of the failure of the Cuban revolution and the renewal of the American Dream in which people of color pull themselves up by their bootstraps.[107] They are also highly respectable and personally responsible, in contrast to perhaps the most enduring representation of the fearsome Cuban migrant, Tony Montana in *Scarface*. Jokes in these episodes of *Golden Girls* reveal the fallacy of stereotyping and suggest that racism inhibited the American Dream. Both episodes made good public relations material for coalitions of white ethnic women and Cuban immigrants and shone light on how feminism and multiculturalism could help America live up to its democratic ideals.

But even as Sophia helps Pepe, their commonality is limited, though Sophia was herself once a racialized, penniless immigrant who did not speak English. (This is a frequent device for humor in the show; she even rationalizes her embezzlement of the roommates' money with exaggeration of her own migration narrative.) Sophia's race and ethnicity would not prevent her from getting a part in a Shakespeare play nor would she be typecast as a criminal (though she is: in one episode, she steels the Pope's ring, and she lies frequently). In "Hey, Look Me Over" (Season 7, Episode 1, 1991), Sophia, fearing she is being bugged by the INS, loudly, repeatedly, and anxiously overstates that she is a patriotic U.S. citizen, the exaggeration suggesting that she is undocumented. Humor comes from the absurdity of the scenario in which this elderly white ethnic woman has all the privileges of citizenship. Her immigrant past is the stuff of quaint "Old World" stories, not something that will likely result in INS detention or deportation, as it could for Dorothy's prized pupil and perhaps Pepe, too, if he were to fail his audition.

Moreover, success in both episodes is defined as assimilation to American respectability through English fluency, artistic talent, education, patriotism, and hard work. Though not shown in connection with their families in these episodes, the immigrants are valuable and praiseworthy because they fit into the typical neoliberal Reaganite "subject of value" discourse. That the human value of immigrants rested on their market value was opaque given that these immigrants were in multicultural bodies; the United States seemed ever more inclusive. Respectability was key. As Lisa Cacho notes, "Arguments for U.S. citizenship as framed by respectability mobilize U.S. American values that are used to discipline, regulate, contain, incarcerate, and deport people of color."[108]

As in Madonna's "Borderline" video, in *Golden Girls*, there is a connection between Latinos and white women, but the white women have more power. On one hand, the message might be that without coalitions, success for immigrants of color is impossible; from this point of view, the episodes might be seen as a critique of racism in neoliberal projects. Further, the women's unconventional family structure is quite queer and arguably feminist; their kinship arrangement does prove to be empowering for them. On the other hand, the message might be one of white supremacy. As older, unmarried women, the "girls" are systemically disempowered, and Sophia's story of immigrant struggle distances her from privilege. But as black American Representative Shirley Chisholm (D-NY), a feminist, long-time advocate for racial justice, immigrant rights, and the first woman of color to run for president, stated in a 1982 House hearing on immigration reform, while white ethnics did work hard and "pull themselves up by their bootstraps," they, like "Matt" Capelli, "had always had the passport to American society, and the passport was a white skin, even though you may have some color."[109] This is a point Jacobson makes, too.[110] Additionally, the episodes portray Cuban immigrants as reliant on white ethnic women, whereas the women do not need their help . . . even though the Pepe episode opens with the girls' decision to invest money to attempt to get ahead on monthly bills, and other episodes are often about their difficulties getting by as mature divorced and widowed women. As Cacho notes, because "poor people of color are legally disempowered, they are positioned by law as having to rely on those whom the law empowers—those who, consequently, take it upon themselves to evaluate whether marginalized groups deserve the rights, recognition, or resources their members are requesting."[111] Representational politics are also unequal. The privileged status of whiteness is itself power, in that whites have more room to be at least superficially feminist, queer, and imperfect without being marginalized or relegated to deviance or criminality.

Another example of the flexibility afforded to white ethnics in accordance with the neoliberal "nation of immigrants" trope occurs in the sitcom *Perfect Strangers*. Running for eight seasons (1986–1993), the ABC show focused on a family comprised of midwestern American Larry Appleton (Mark Linn-Baker) and Balki Bartokomous (Bronson Pinchot), his distant white ethnic immigrant cousin from the fictional eastern Mediterranean island of Mypos. The premise of the show is a "nation of immigrants"/culture clash twist on the "odd couple" format. Neurotic, shy, white heterosexual Wisconsin native Larry has just moved into his first apartment in Chicago, excited to be on his own. Balki, a previously unknown fresh-off-the-boat heterosexual cousin from Mypos, who brings with him a plethora of often incorrect and decontextualized knowledge of America gleaned from American pop culture, arrives on Larry's doorstep. Larry reluctantly takes him in and sets out to teach him about the United States, though often Larry needs Balki's help as well. The two men are an unconventional and potentially queer family.

But in ways that resonate with neoliberal projects, the "nation of immigrants" theme is intentional and explicit in the sitcom's production and delivery. It was developed by Dale McRaven and for its entire run produced by

Tom Miller and Robert Boyett in association with Lorimar Television. Miller said the show's inspiration came from the "patriotic fervor" and embrace of people from all over the world in Los Angeles when the city hosted the 1984 Olympics. Although Miller noted in an interview, "What we didn't expect was the day after [the Olympics] all ended, everybody said 'Get these Olympic banners down, and get all those people out of here,'" the producers wanted to capture "the feeling of the wonder of someone coming to America and seeing this wonderful country for the first time" and were confident it was "something people would like."[112]

They were right. The show was a top-twenty hit when it premiered in 1986, the year IRCA finally passed, and early reviews were favorable.[113] In subsequent seasons it frequently placed among the Nielson top 40.[114] It still has a cult following: "P.S. I Love You—Perfect Strangers Online," is a fan web site and Facebook page run by Linda Kay that is updated frequently,[115] and in accordance with the fact that Balki always refers to Larry as "cousin" or "Cousin Larry," Kay addresses fans as "cousins," too.[116]

The show, originally titled *The Greenhorn*, was more explicitly "nation of immigrants" than any other at the time. To ensure that viewers got the point, the title sequence for Seasons 1 and 2 shows the contrast between Larry and Balki's individual journeys to Chicago and ends with them meeting in the middle of a formerly split screen, indicating how they unite as an unconventional family. First, Larry says goodbye to his big white family in an affluent suburb of Wisconsin and departs in an old red Mustang packed to the roof with his belongings. Next, Balki rolls away on the back of a horse cart next to a box labeled, "America or Burst" after saying his farewells in Mypos. Balki's iconic first glimpse of the Statue of Liberty from a steamboat approaching New York City follows. In later seasons, the title sequence shows Balki as a happily assimilating American enjoying quintessentially American activities such as going with Larry to a Chicago Cubs game at Wrigley Field.

Balki's background and character fit squarely with subtly exclusive Reagan-era "nation of immigrants" race politics. Pinchot envisioned Balki as Greek, but producers wanted Balki to be "universal,"[117] which meant making him indeterminately white ethnic. Pinchot said in a 1987 interview that the accent came from memories of growing up with his Italian mother, Russian father, and aunts and uncles who never quite melted into the American pot.[118]

The "patriotic fervor" that inspired the show's creation is conveyed in the contrast between Mypos, the "universal" Old World European agricultural country that adheres to traditional customs with just a smattering of American conveniences and commodities, and the United States. Mypos is comically backwards and strange, as in the custom of men choosing their brides through "dimbodega dabodega," a game akin to "eenie meenie miney moe." Presenting the "Old World" as primitive and unrefined—a characterization frequently accomplished through gender traditions that reified women as objects—makes America seem especially sophisticated and enlightened.

As an immigrant learning English, Balki's tendency toward malapropism, the unintentional misuse of a word through confusion with a similar-sounding word, also provides much patriotic humor on the show. In the pilot episode, Balki twists the American idiom, "Land of the free, home of the brave," into "Land of my dreams, home of the Whopper." His mixture of a line from the national anthem and an advertising slogan for Burger King is a striking teachable moment about what *is* "American" in the 1980s: consumption, nutritionally bankrupt fast food, the suturing of nationalism to products, and the conflating of purchasing power with ethics. But this moment and others like it fail to become a pointed critique of America and Reaganite "common sense," and instead focus on the humor of Balki's "greenhorn" mistakes.

Moreover, Balki's assimilation into the American workforce shows him as hardworking and committed to self-sufficiency, and as immediately and literally indebted to the nation that offers him exceptional opportunity for a better life. In the pilot, "Knock, Knock, Who's There?" (Season 1, episode 1, 1986), he earns his first job with Larry's employer, the abrasive and greedy Mr. Twinkasetti, owner of a used goods/antique shop, by fixing a long-broken radio. But Balki undersells items and turns the radio volume so loud it shatters all the glass items in the store. After Twinkasetti fires both cousins, Balki convinces him to give them another chance by promising to work off the losses. When Larry tells Balki he is in debt, Balki beams and says, "I am a true American!" Larry thanks him for getting their jobs back, and Balki replies, "Where I come from, family sticks together." Rather than a critique of the employer's greed and desire to exploit the immigrant within an already exploitative system— Twinkasetti makes out that minimum wage is a generous starting salary—the prevalent theme of the episode is that "family values" and neoliberal values are one and the same. The industrious cousins are financially stronger as a family unit, making the immigrant better able to pay off his debt (a point stressed by ethnic lobbying groups to support family reunification), and, Balki hopes, to put his whole family through college, which he plans to do with his salary. In this example pop culture and the congressional argument in favor of family reunification are directly aligned.

In the same vein, in "Check This" (Season 1, episode 5, 1986), Balki opens his first bank account and promptly substantially overdraws it by purchasing new furniture for the apartment. But rather than critique a financial system that not only allows but encourages debt accrual, the episode spoofs Balki's naïveté about U.S. culture, and as with the pilot episode, frames his debt accumulation as humorous and easily resolved with the help of his family (Larry). Incidentally, in 1986, when the episode aired, 32.4 million were below the poverty rate, and the overall poverty rate was 13.6 percent.[119] Within that group, 9.4 percent of families were white, 26.5 percent Latina/o, and a whopping 29.7 percent black.[120] This suggests that many Americans—most of whom were of color—did not have enough funds to even open a checking account, let alone overdraw it. This is not at all visible, even as Balki gets himself into debt. *Perfect Strangers* is no scalding or even lukewarm critique of the status quo.

Yet the show is queer to an extent. The queerness of Mypos and Balki himself, achieved by troubling gender norms, is a consistent source of laughs, and sometimes rewards. Balki, a shepherd on Mypos, is fiercely attached to Dmitri, his stuffed sheep, because the sheep's live namesake saved Balki's life by pushing him out of the way of a runaway cart. There is thus a link to non-normative sexual practices (not only a stuffed animal; the live sheep Dimitri was male) that some queer theorists like Pat Califia might appreciate. Twinkasetti mocks Balki as effeminate; meanwhile women find him charming. Moreover, Pinchot was then known for playing the flamboyant homosexual character Serge in the popular action-comedy *Beverly Hills Cop* (1984), and both Serge and Balki speak with an accent (with varying degrees of feminine affect) stereotypically associated with gay men. Given that in the 1980s, homosexual characters were barely visible as anything other than AIDS victims or criminals (as on *Miami Vice*), these potentially queer aspects are complex; Pinchot made gender and sexual variance a bit more visible and at times loveable in popular culture, yet he did so by exploiting stereotypes about gay men.

Furthermore, the *Perfect Strangers* family is not the nuclear family that Simpson prized but rather one comprised of two distant male cousins. But race, heterosexuality (episodes frequently focus on each man's love life and each ultimately marries), the reduction of queerness to a joke (also the case in *Beverly Hills Cop*), and the affirmation of "nation of immigrants" respectability mitigate the queerness of the family. And the "other" culture in the "clash of cultures" theme of the show is white ethnic, which in the cultural milieu of the 1980s became the new quintessentially American identity, the ideal base for the neoliberal subject of value.

Judith Butler asserts that arguments for same-sex marriage tend to intensify normalization. She defines kinship as a set of practices that make relationships of various kinds to negotiate reproduction of life and the demands of death and to address fundamental forms of human dependency like birth, child-rearing, emotional attachment, illness, dying, and death. She shows that most arguments for same-sex marriage do not so much disrupt patriarchal

assumptions of kinship as they further pathologize alternative forms of kinship such as polyamorous relationships, thereby damaging radical projects to
support sexual practices outside of marriage and sexual variation.[121] In short,
like immigrant rights' claims based on respectability, arguments for same-sex
marriage tend to draw on conservative investments in forms of relationships
(monogamous, nuclear families) that the state privileges. (And "investment"
is a strikingly apropos word given that corporations literally invested in the
case that led to the federal passage of so-called "marriage equality" in 2015.)

In the 1980s, Balki and Larry's alternative kinship arrangement required
heterosexual members (as in *The Golden Girls*). Moreover, even the show's
gender variation was mitigated by the patriotic theme of the sitcom in ways
that supported the Reaganite status quo. The show cast America as the exceptional place that allowed for and encouraged a whitewashed diversity, as in
Balki's successful blending of "multicultural" aspects with American norms.

Finally, like his plucky white ethnic immigrant sitcom peers, Sophia, Dorothy, and the Micellis, Balki anticipates the strand of respectability rhetoric
that recent immigrant rights advocates and sympathizers have taken up to
mitigate the view of undocumented immigrants as criminals. DREAM activists assert that the immigrant is uniquely patriotic, hardworking, and capable,
perhaps even more so than the native-born American, and other advocates
emphasize immigrants' "commendable commitments to their families" as the
grounds for rights claims.[122] (In its original timeslot, *Perfect Strangers* aired
on Tuesday night after *Who's the Boss?* so spectators received a double dose
of "nation of immigrants" propaganda.) In their supportive family of two,
the heterosexual cousins become increasingly successful, indicating that hard
work in the context of a family—even a pre-marriage family—eventually pays
off (Larry realizes his dream to become a photojournalist, Balki makes a living off of his "nation of immigrants" heritage writing a weekly comic strip
based on [the stuffed] Dmitri, and both fall in love with and settle down with
women.) Like *Golden Girls* and *Who's the Boss?*, *Perfect Strangers* rearticulated
the Reaganite neoliberal "common sense" that excluded and disenfranchised
people of color, reiterated gender and sexual conventions, and made human
value dependent on contributing to the economy. But like the other shows, it
did so in ways made palatable by featuring funny, seemingly inclusive, near-
queer affirmations of the availability of the American dream of a better life.

Conclusion

Two overlapping assertions that support neoliberal advancement formed the
crux of the pro-family reunification argument on the congressional floor and

in the culture at large. First, pundits, news media, and TV shows stressed the immigrant commitment to family given that "family values" were "common sense" in Reagan's America. Second, they emphasized that commitment to family among immigrants was economically beneficial, and from this followed the notion that the immigrant as a member of a hardworking family earned rights and inclusion. This argument for immigrant rights as family rights, which still dominates immigrant activism, is, as Cacho argues, a dangerous recourse for communities of color: "Both undocumented Latinas/os and un[der]employed African American citizens are required to provide evidence that their intimate relationships are proper embodiments of heteronormativity and domesticity. This, then, narrows the focus of rights-based struggles, making them seem synonymous with securing family rights within U.S. law. Moreover, the focus on family rights can sometimes distract us from critiquing the structural conditions of global capital and neoliberal reforms that create, perpetuate, and aggravate hyperexploitability and legal vulnerability."[123]

A focus on family rights is likewise dangerous for queer communities. As Butler observes, claiming normalcy upholds the status quo. And although crucial to political intelligibility, legitimation through the state affirms the power of the state, not the group that becomes intelligible.[124] Under the Obama administration, queerness became rather explicitly appropriated by neoliberalism. In 2011, then–Secretary of State Hillary Clinton said that gay rights were human rights.[125] Obama, the first president to support same-sex marriage, stated in 2012 that family—his own young daughters' and their friends' respectable same-sex families—influenced his endorsement.[126] The new significance of LGBTQ rights has also been evoked to rationalize military interventions in Muslim nations,[127] in a way that exemplifies the "humanitarian violence" Atanasoski describes. International violence is justified and domestic state power is smoothly reiterated by and in the appropriation of same-sex (as well as multicultural, for the Obamas are a highly respectable black family) inclusivity.

The absorptive powers of "family values" and utility of same-sex marriage to U.S. exceptionalism and neoliberalism were especially striking with the June 26, 2015, federal legalization of marriage equality. *Newsweek*'s July 10, 2015 cover story, "The Love Vote: How Corporations Propelled Same Sex Marriage," noted that key support of *Obergefell v. Hodges*, the case that effectively legalized same-sex marriage nationwide, came from 379 large corporations such as Walmart, JP Morgan, and the New England Patriots. The article ends with homage to Milton Friedman's notion that free markets working their ways on society is a social good.[128] The framing of marriage equality as proof of America's progressiveness was also ubiquitous on social media, and corporations embraced it enthusiastically with tweets and ads that featured rainbows, the symbol of LGBTQ pride and social movements, or images of same-sex married life.[129] The White House was even lit up with the colors of the rainbow. In-depth exploration of how and why marriage equality came to dominate LGBTQ rights efforts despite the movement's history of more expansive and more radical agendas are beyond the scope of this analysis. Suffice it to say that the commodification and corporatization of LGBTQ Pride (which commemorates the June 28, 1969, Stonewall Riot for gay rights) and same-sex marriage are striking examples of how neoliberalism incorporates difference into existing norms (here same-sex monogamy, "family values," and consumerism). As with other stigmatized groups, gaining rights, increasing power as a market demographic, and attaining visibility in pop culture are framed as success; "equality" has ostensibly been achieved. Yet the structures that create inequality, such as the legal system and capitalism, remain intact, and ongoing inequality and violence are thereby rendered an anomaly in America's fair, progressive system.[130]

Earlier, the case for immigrant inclusion (in this case, for mostly Latin American and Asian immigrants) was made on the basis of marketized "family values," which in uneven and complex ways were explored in news media and pop culture into the 1990s and continue to surface in activism. And while the families in question in IRCA debates deviated from the conservative ideal to the extent that they included brothers and sisters and were of color, they were nonetheless (assumed or expected to be) heterosexual and adherent to dominant notions of success, as were the (valued) multicultural families in news media. Any deviations from the "family values" ideal were offset with the other piece of the respectability argument: these immigrant families were assets as hardworking contributors to the economy. They earned their access to the American Dream by repaying a debt to the "nation of immigrants." Thus "family values" circumscribed what counted as human *across party lines* by insinuating that if immigrants of color wanted rights, they owed the nation financial contribution along with proper "family values." Pop culture indicated that white ethnic immigrants should do the same, but there was considerably more wiggle room for them, as in the near-queer kinship arrangements featured in 1980s sitcoms. America appeared to be an exceptional nation that, in line with the gains of feminism and the civil rights movement, offered all incomparable opportunity in a way that erased the inherent racialized, gendered, and economic violence of neoliberalism and its market-based determination of human value and left a dearth of space for truly queer families.

***

Although general family reunification cuts and limits did not pass, the definition of family codified in IRCA for amnesty recipients did in fact narrow the
definition of family to reflect a heterosexual, near-nuclear ideal: "The family
group shall include the spouse, unmarried minor children under 18 years of
age who are not members of some other household, and parents who reside
regularly in the household of the family group."[131] Policies and discourses that
would "regulate the influx of brown bodies"[132] were therefore also delineated
in the family reunification debates. For instance, Patricia Zavella has shown
that while with amnesty IRCA did provide opportunities for mostly Mexican undocumented immigrants, its complex legalization criteria and cut-off
dates have created "migrant family formations," which "include suspended,
reunited, separated and mixed-status families and occasionally these types
overlap."[133] In these "migrant family formations," members struggle with the
material, logistical, and emotional challenges of disparities based on immigration status.[134] This does not add up to the inclusive pro-family rhetoric
that prevailed in the IRCA debates, and is certainly not queer. The IRCA
debates also shaped subsequent family reunification legislation such as the
1990 Immigration Act (IMMACT), which significantly increased the total
level of immigration to 700,000 and increased available visas by 40 percent.
Although Simpson continued to lobby for a nuclear definition of family, family reunification and the preference system remained, and the law more than
doubled employment-related immigration.[135] It also increased admission of
immigrants from "underrepresented" countries, and removed homosexuality as grounds for exclusion. While the Defense of Marriage Act (DOMA) of
1996 barred the migration of same-sex couples, IMMACT seemed to expand
the multiculturally inclusive aspects of the IRCA family reunification debates.
But the dominant pro-family discourse of IRCA debates established a paradigm for making claims for immigrant rights on the basis of adherence to a
neoliberal work ethic and white heterosexual "family values." That paradigm
continues to suture claims for immigrant rights to a neoliberal rule of law and
a narrow, racialized, heteronormative definition of family, and does so flagrantly in relation to welfare and motherhood, the topic of the next chapter.

3

Exiled Mothers and Mothers of Exiles

In July 1986, a four-day "Liberty Weekend" celebrated the restoration and centenary of the Statue of Liberty, America's iconic mother of exiles. This "case study of the Reagan-era mythos at work" wedded "commercialism and national symbolism, thereby mythologizing itself as an intrinsic part of the American vision."[1] The four-day televised spectacle began with speeches by President Reagan and other American and French dignitaries.[2] Neil Diamond performed "Coming to America," his 1981 ebullient pop song glorifying the promise of freedom and success that entices immigrants from "everywhere around the world . . . every time the flag unfurls." On July 4, after a naval revue on the Hudson River,[3] Reagan pressed a button shooting a laser beam across the harbor to symbolically reignite Lady Liberty's torch. The largest fireworks display to date followed, set to "Stars and Stripes Forever," and Chief Justice Warren Burger swore in newly naturalized citizens at Ellis Island while four simultaneous ceremonies took place nationwide.[4]

But Lady Liberty was presented as the mother of exiles only with the aid of historical amnesia, in a way that strikingly paralleled the erasures and fictions surrounding the Reagan administration's efforts to eliminate welfare for immigrant mothers (and mothers of color), which was a core but understudied part of rising neoliberalism. The appearance of multiculturalism was key to the overpriced celebration, with a "mini-world's fair in lower Manhattan" including a "40-man American Samoan Dance Ensemble, Olatunji's African Flaming Drums of Passion, [and] the Odessa Balalaikas from Los Angeles," who "transform[ed] the city's financial district into an ethnic Disneyland."[5] The "Medal of Liberty," an "ersatz award" born of "private enterprise," was given to a dozen naturalized citizens,[6] some of whom were members of racial or ethnic groups once restricted or excluded, like Holocaust survivor Elie Wiesel, and composer Itzhak Perelman, both Jews of Eastern European heritage, and Chinese American architect I. M. Pei. The "nation of immigrants" mythos erased a past and present of racial exclusion, a fact that did not go entirely unnoticed. When a "brouhaha developed over the fact that none of the winners [were] Italian or Irish," New York Mayor Ed Koch, "ever ready to leap to the defense of ethnicity, denounced the awards as 'idiotic' and promptly decided to give out 87 medals of his own."[7]

Nevertheless Koch's attempted inclusivity maintained the white ethnic bias of the "nation of immigrants" trope and, like Liberty Weekend, complemented the Reaganite exaltation of consumerist individualism.[8] Contemporary commentators did criticize Liberty Weekend for its excesses, including its $32 million price, and glitzy, self-congratulatory TV coverage.[9] "Keep the Torch Lit," the restoration fundraising slogan, like Reagan's reelection slogan, "Morning in America," framed consumption as national restoration that "could maintain the economic momentum of Reagan's first term," and "warned of darkness, should restoration funds and spending on products fail to materialize."[10] *Time*'s sardonic piece remarked on the prevalence of liberty-themed commodities such as dry-roasted peanuts and tobacco, and pricey festivities like a waterfront restaurant table at $400 per person.[11] Another critic exposed the incongruities between the exclusive event and the inscription on the Statue, taken from "The New Colossus," an 1883 poem by Sephardic Jew Emma Lazarus, noting "While the masses huddle free along the shoreline, 3,000 specially chosen Liberty Weekenders will have prime views of the Statue of Liberty's unveiling . . . for a mere $5,000 a seat."[12]

The poem, which named Lady Liberty the "mother of exiles," was inspired by Lazarus's work with European Jewish refugees who fled pogroms following the 1881 assassination of Russian Tsar Alexander II.[13] In the popular imagination it soon "identified the statue's mission—and by extension that of America—as the provision of refuge for the oppressed."[14] Lazarus wrote:

> Not like the brazen giant of Greek fame,
> With conquering limbs astride from land to land;
> Here at our sea-washed, sunset gates shall stand
> A mighty woman with a torch, whose flame
> Is the imprisoned lighting, and her name
> Mother of Exiles. From her beacon-hand
> Glows world-wide welcome; her mild eyes command
> The air-bridged harbor that twin cities frame.
> "Keep, ancient lands, your storied pomp!" cries she
> With silent lips. "Give me your tired, your poor,
> Your huddled masses yearning to breathe free,
> The wretched refuse of your teeming shore.
> Send these, the homeless, tempest-tost to me,
> I lift my lamp beside the golden door!"[15]

With the poem, the statue "originally intended as a monument to the principles of international republicanism" became "a welcoming mother, a symbol of hope to the outcasts and downtrodden of the world,"[16] although the maternal embrace Lazarus described has always been selectively open in practice, as Lazarus herself realized.[17] In fact, at the original October 28, 1886, dedication ceremony, suffragettes protested "the unveiling of the figure of a woman as Liberty in a State where women [are] not free."[18] When Lazarus's sonnet was placed on a plaque on the Lady Liberty pedestal in 1904,[19] nativists and immigration restrictionists were targeting white ethnics and immigrants of color.

Thus from its dedication, Lady Liberty was a contested site, the rhetoric and imagery around her cloaking stark inequalities. In 1986, participants played along. White ethnics (like first-generation Italian American Lido Anthony "Lee" Iacocca, the Liberty–Ellis Island Foundation president who worked his way up in the automobile industry to achieve wealth and success) and exceptionally successful immigrants of color (like Pei) were imagined as the quintessential "exiles" that the Statue of Liberty mothered, with the implication that she was prepared to mother continuing waves of immigrants. But for most immigrants, the Statue of Liberty mothered exclusively. This time, the waves of immigrants who were only selectively welcome were from Latin America and Asia, and Mexican immigrants were especially and ironically attacked in terms of maternity and mothering.

Racialized attacks on immigrant women and mothers were nothing new, as seen in the 1875 Page Law, which banned convicts, involuntary Chinese migrant laborers, and Chinese women suspected of prostitution, and "Likely to Become a Public Charge" (LPC) provisions, which since 1882 were used to identify and prohibit the entry of immigrants deemed unlikely to support themselves due to mental or physical disability,[20] and were first used to restrict the immigration of white ethnic women; while white ethnic immigrant women were considered useful as inexpensive factory laborers and domestic servants, nativists viewed them as racially inferior, fecund burdens on the state.[21]). In the 1980s, immigration policy updated this paradigm for neoliberalism with IRCA welfare restrictions and later laws meant to cut the costs of reproduction and child-rearing among immigrant women from Latin America and Asia. As in the restrictionist era, immigrants were considered threatening to the economy and "family values" because of allegedly high birth rates and welfare dependence, and as in the conflation of braceros and wetbacks in the World War II era (discussed in Chapter 4), women of Latin-American origins—immigrants and Latinas—were folded into the specter of the "illegal alien," making them synonymous in the public imaginary. While proposed family reunification cuts failed, IRCA welfare restrictions directly tackled the tensions provoked by women's immigration in the late twentieth century.

Throughout the IRCA debates, pundits voiced fears that immigrants would strain the welfare state, especially given that legalization might give applicants easy access to public services. Unlike most of the other provisions, welfare restriction met little opposition. Simultaneously, the Reagan administration pushed general welfare cuts. This chapter shows that Reagan-era immigration and welfare policies and discourses inaugurated a neoliberal welfare regime that has continued to racially stratify women. Expanding on the rich existing literature on welfare by feminist scholars and in dialogue with Latina/o Studies scholars, I argue that Reagan-era discourses about immigrant mothers and immigrant family formation were key to the neoliberalization of welfare policy.

Obliterating the welfare state was central to the neoliberal project, as Stuart Hall explains:

> According to the neoliberal narrative, the welfare state (propelled by working class reaction to the Depression of the 1930s and the popular mobilization of World War Two) mistakenly saw its task as intervening in the economy, re-distributing wealth, universalising life-chances, attacking unemployment, protecting the socially vulnerable, ameliorating the condition of oppressed or marginalised groups and addressing social injustice. . . . But its do-gooding, utopian sentimentality enervated the nation's moral fibre, and eroded personal responsibility and the over-riding duty of the poor to work. It imposed social purposes on an economy rooted in individual greed and self interest.[22]

Reagan spearheaded this narrative in law and ideology, and citizen *and* immigrant mothers of color were at the center of this thread of the U.S. neoliberal project. The relationship between cutting immigrant welfare and general welfare is clear. Reagan addressed welfare in a February 1986 State of the Union address, in the midst of the final round of IRCA debates. (IRCA would be passed with its own welfare restrictions in about nine months.) Reagan claimed that welfare dependency, a rather transparent code for "black female degeneracy," undermined the "family values" at the heart of "the great American comeback."[23]

The "welfare queen" was born during his 1976 presidential campaign when he relentlessly told the story of a woman arrested for welfare fraud.[24] The perpetrator, black Chicago resident Linda Taylor, became "the symbolic embodiment of welfare fraud for legislative conservatives who were trying to reduce welfare costs." Reagan, exaggerating her gains, did not mention her name or race in speeches, but her picture was well publicized.[25] Given also the prevailing "family values" rhetoric, poor women of color were effectively demonized.

Hence in the 1986 State of the Union address, welfare reform was cast as an economic *and moral* necessity:

> As we work to make the American dream real for all, we must also look to the condition of America's families. . . . In the welfare culture, the breakdown of the family, the most basic support system, has reached crisis proportions—in female and child poverty, child abandonment, horrible crimes, and deteriorating schools. . . . The waste in dollars and cents pales before the most tragic loss: the sinful waste of human spirit and potential. . . . As Franklin Roosevelt warned 51 years ago, standing before this Chamber, he said, "Welfare is a narcotic, a subtle destroyer of the human spirit." And we must now escape the spider's web of dependency.[26]

Reagan's war on welfare targeted mothers of color and immigrant mothers. And with recourse to the "welfare queen," a plethora of negative news media and pop culture representations of mothers of color, and simultaneous moves to cut welfare to immigrant mothers, Americans were reminded that these mothers were economically and morally unfit. Welfare discourses about immigrant mothers—key to a neoliberal welfare regime that criminalizes women of color and channels them into low-wage work—guaranteed that immigrant women and their children would be what Rachel Ida Buff calls "denizens," persons who do not benefit from the protections and rights of citizenship: denizens "inhabit a nation, sometimes for generations, without the benefit of political representation or cultural recognition."[27]

My comparative analysis of the racialization of white ethnic, Asian, and Latin American immigrant mothers in public policy, news media, and pop culture illuminates this important strand of neoliberal welfare discourse. Along with the pathologization of Latin American immigrant and Latina mothering—the formation of "matriphobic racialization"—a politics of comparison in immigration debates reshaped welfare policy to suit neoliberalism. White ethnic immigrant "family values" were idealized, while "model minority" Asian immigrant mothers were often imagined as in the middle, on a continuum between white ethnics and denizen Latin American immigrant and Latina mothers. In this asymmetrical process, whereas the neoliberal racialization of white ethnic mothers was occurring primarily through popular cultural texts (policy pieces had mostly solidified in earlier immigration law), and whereas racialization of Asian immigrant mothers occurred mostly in various media, the racialization of Latin American immigrant mothers and Latinas was explicit in the law and various media. Before turning to a detailed analysis of the role of immigration discourses in the formation of a neoliberal welfare regime and to contextualize my contribution, I briefly review the rich body of leftist feminist scholarship. Immigration is an important part of welfare history, though it is not always considered as such.

***

Welfare, the subject of feminist analysis for some time, cohered as a field of inquiry in the 1980s. The first phase of feminist scholarship on welfare focused on the discriminatory character of welfare and how it reinforced sexist arrangements in women's domestic and public lives; a second phase of scholarship developed structural critiques of welfare as a form of social control, focusing, for instance, on a public or state patriarchy as opposed to private familial patriarchy, and on capitalism; and a third phase of early scholarship examined women's political activism and involvement in shaping the welfare system.[28] But while white women's welfarist strategies, which prevailed in mainstream discourse and activity, tended to rely on political influence, economic resources, and social mobility, women of color, often lacking such influence and resources, combined welfare and civil rights activity. Black women and especially mothers were also more likely to be employed than white, and women of color tended to hold different jobs than whites. Therefore, women of color activists often sought programs that would support women's and mother's long-term employment, such as those that included child care.[29]

The 1990 anthology *Women, the State, and Welfare* was the first collection about women and welfare in the United States and established a road map for subsequent feminist thinking about welfare. Filling in gaps left by prior scholarship, it addressed how welfare policy reinforces gender norms; the role of race and class in welfare policy; and the role of feminists and activists and especially women of color in the formation and reform of welfare programs.

Feminist scholars have continued to expand upon these strains of inquiry, with race-conscious structural critique,[30] legal critique,[31] critique of the bipartisan character of neoliberal welfare policy,[32] and consideration of pop culture, given the ubiquity of media images of mothers of color allegedly using and abusing welfare.[33] Studies of immigration, women, and welfare are fewer, but a handful of scholars have produced important studies.[34] Elena Gutierrez's work on the politics of Mexican-origin women's reproduction shows how the stereotype of Mexican women as "hyper-fertile baby machines" who abuse social services became a central issue in U.S. politics in the late twentieth century, both manifesting and providing a rationale for fears of the increasing numbers and consequent increasing political and market clout of Latinas/os.[35] There is much work on California's Proposition 187, a harsh restriction of social services for immigrants that targeted Mexican and other Latin American immigrant mothers. Studies make connections between welfare policy and eugenics.[36] I contribute to this body of feminist scholarship by considering law and popular media about immigrant women and welfare in the 1980s and 1990s, when welfare policy was being neoliberalized. As I will show, California's Proposition 187 and the federal law that severely restricted legal and undocumented and citizen women's access to welfare, the Personal Responsibility and Work Opportunity Reconciliation Act (PRWORA), are neoliberal bastions of welfare restriction descended directly from the racialized paradigm delineated by 1980s discourses. My analysis, which is influenced by and in dialogue with feminist genealogies of neoliberal welfare policy, intervenes in and expands upon this work.

Troubling Immigrant Mothers: IRCA Meets Reagan's "Welfare Queen"

Reagan subjected Keynesian-era social programs to neoliberal reform. With the passage of the Family Support Act of 1988, poverty aid programs such as Aid to Families with Dependent Children (AFDC), school lunch programs, and Medicaid were turned over to state governments, and even major entitlement programs such as Social Security and Medicare were subject to market values to augment "competition" and "efficiency."[37] The gender and racial politics underscoring the seemingly colorblind neoliberal anti-welfare stance crystallized with Reagan's frequent recourse to the "welfare queen." And those demonized women of color were often mothers; being a poor mother of color was cast as crime. In a 1986 report, "The Family: Preserving America's Future," Gary L. Bauer, Reagan's domestic policy adviser, averred that welfare programs, in creating "family fragments, households headed by a mother dependent upon public charity," have "become a powerful force for destruction of family life."[38] Good parenting was a moralized economic issue, and a breadwinning father was necessary to preserve America's future. Women, characterized as dependent, were then criticized for dependency if they looked to the state for support rather than to a father. Women of color implicitly headed the valueless families.

Retrenchment of AFDC, the primary welfare expenditure, highlights the racialized and gendered character of neoliberal reform, but welfare has always been gendered and racialized. The 1911 Illinois Mothers' Pension program, the first statewide mothers pension program, was designed and administered to aid white widows.[39] Similar state programs proliferated then declined with the Great Depression. Mother's pension programs reemerged as the prototype for the 1935 Social Security Act's AFDC program.[40] AFDC, founded on the principle that men should support women and children,[41] literally put women at a disadvantage: in the context of a substantial wage gap, mothers' monthly entitlement was half that of other public assistance recipients.[42] Since child-care was unpaid work that many women did, AFDC mothers could be cast as malingering, and single status—and any female-headed household—might be interpreted as a threatening sexual freedom.[43] Moreover, industries in which blacks were disproportionately employed were excluded from benefit eligibility,[44] and southern congressmen, in accord with business interests that wanted a supply of cheap black labor, demanded state authority and administration of programs.[45] In 1943 in Louisiana, the first state to adopt "employable mother" laws, all AFDC families with children ages seven and older were denied assistance if the mother was deemed to be employable in agriculture.[46] Since blacks almost wholly did seasonal labor, the restrictions targeted them. Thus these differing demands for female home and market labor at a time when white women often remained in the home to reproduce and care for the labor force while women of color and poor women did domestic and service sector low-wage labor,[47] were resolved with patriarchal and racist poverty policies that cast white women as "fit" mothers and black women as better suited for low-wage labor than motherhood.

In the 1960s and 1970s, when welfare activism was combined with civil rights activism, organizations such as the National Welfare Rights Organization (NWRO), which had a largely black female membership, successfully pressured state and federal authorities for a living income for a mother and her children, particularly through increasing the accessibility of AFDC. While the number of welfare recipients rose by 50 percent from 1970 to 1973, the disintegration of NWRO in a subsequent economic slump left poor women without a strong national organization to challenge the assault on the welfare state, which began in the 1970s[48] and picked up steam in the 1980s and 1990s.

In the 1980s and 1990s, welfare reform efforts that focused on getting recipients to work—"workfare," which imposed labor discipline—were embedded in gendered and racialized notions, updated for neoliberalism, of who was worthy/unworthy of aid. Although research indicates that most poor black families were poor before an event such as a divorce, separation, death, or birth of an out-of-wedlock child made them female-headed,[49] conservatives and often liberals blamed single-parent—that is, single-mother—households as an effect of welfare and the cause of poverty. The remedy, the Family Support Act, was developed by Senator Daniel Patrick Moynihan (D-NY), famous for his pathologization of the black family in the *Moynihan Report*, and was co-sponsored by more than forty senators, including liberals such as Senator Ted Kennedy (D-MA). AFDC was amended to emphasize work, child support, and family benefits and created the Job Opportunities and Basic Skills Training (JOBS) program, a welfare-to-work program that supplanted the Work Incentive program (WIN). The Family Support Act multiplied eligibility requirements and added incentives—which in the 1990s became imperatives—for women to work. Financial responsibility for the family was placed upon individuals rather than the state, and only those who worked "deserved" benefits. Thus the ostensibly race-neutral neoliberal focus on "personal responsibility" was codified in law and rhetoric about welfare and parenting.

In the post–civil rights era, the stigmatizing image of the "welfare mother" rationalized the reduction of the cost of sustaining black families (by encouraging poor and working-class women to have fewer children, often via punitive population control policies). Underscoring efforts to control black women's reproduction was the notion that black children, who during slavery were valued as a source of free labor for whites, were superfluous as a labor pool and therefore burdened the state. Furthermore, the "welfare mother" stereotype surfaced just as black women were challenging racist welfare policies.[50] "The underlying belief [underscoring the stereotype] is that these women are looking for a free ride at the expense of the American taxpayer."[51] Reagan's "welfare queen," who was quickly imagined as a Latina as well as a black woman[52] and connected to undocumented Mexican women,[52] was a powerful and enduring signifier. In 1992, ABC's *Primetime Live with Diane Sawyer* investigated welfare fraud. Most welfare recipients featured, who were likened to bank robbers and called "cheats," were black and Latina, even though one investigator noted that most welfare defrauders were from white middle-class families.[54]

Furthermore, dominant discourses erased the fact that welfare was a crucial source of income for single mothers whose options were restricted by the racism and sexism shaping economic opportunity and by cuts in social services and health care while wages and employee benefits stagnated. By the 1980s, as right-wing "family values" discourses were mainstreamed and corporations that had lost profits in the declining economy of the 1970s lobbied for labor discipline via privatization and deregulation, AFDC and the families who used it were villainized for failing to work hard and eschewing personal responsibility, which in turn led to the passage of the "common-sense" Family Support Act and concordant attacks on immigrant mothers' use of welfare. In short, neoliberalism creates the need for welfare among poor and working-class people of color, and then damns those populations for needing assistance.

***

Officially, IRCA welfare restrictions responded to fears that amnesty—explicitly designed to address Mexican illegality—would burden the already beleaguered welfare state.[55] Under the "Legalization" provision, part (h), newly legalized aliens were disqualified for five years from need-based federal programs. Food stamps, some Medicaid, and programs that provided assistance to families with dependent children were also cut. Immigrants were, however, eligible for emergency services and services for pregnant women under section B (ii).[56] The customary "Likely to Become a Public Charge" (LPC) provision was also expanded. While the earlier LPC test required demonstration only of current self-sufficiency, the new test scrutinized immigrants' recent pasts and required a detailed history of employment without prior public aid.[57] These reforms, shifting responsibility to each individual immigrant rather than the state, developed an "actuarial system" to evaluate if immigrants could become good neoliberal subjects (that is, self-supporting).[58]

The characterization of Latin American and especially Mexican immigrant women as excessively fertile that underscored these new restrictions became ubiquitous in the 1980s. Gutierrez has shown that the "greening of hate" in the environmental movement, which linked population growth, immigration, and nativism, began in the 1970s with the one of the oldest, largest, and most aggressive population control lobbies, Zero Population Growth (ZPG). Chain migration and excessive reproduction on the part of Mexican immigrants, population experts averred, were depleting national resources. In the 1980s Latin American immigration restriction was called for as a corrective.[59] Gutierrez also shows that the production of social scientific knowledge about the "unusually high" fertility of Mexican-origin women in the 1980s is part of a legacy that was "informed by the racialized assumptions of assimilation and modernization."[60] Leo Chavez calls the pathologization of Latina's sexuality via such cultural determination the "Latina Threat" stereotype: women of Latin American origins are cast as "hot" and hypersexual seductresses or, given the predominance of Catholicism among people of Latin American origins, as pure virginal girls/married obedient wives and mothers.[61] The merging of those two images produces a notion of uncontrolled fertility that the state pays for and has material consequences for Latin American–origin women, mothers, and children—although, as Gloria Gonzalez-Lopez has shown, the sex lives of Mexican immigrants—their "erotic journeys"—are far more complex and fluid than the stereotypes allow.[62]

The argument to bar immigrants from welfare was that unusually fertile Latin American and especially Mexican immigrants would burden the system, especially if amnesty was granted. This provided the precursor to the "anchor baby" thesis that became prevalent in the 1990s. For example, in the October 1986 Senate session that culminated with the passage of IRCA, lawmakers argued that Mexican immigrant mothers were straining U.S. resources. Paul Simon (D-IL), an organized labor advocate, said that Mexico's population was excessive because of Mexican women's high birthrates and that Mexico must be the explicit focus of immigration policy given that "the main problems [with border control] are from Mexico." "If, by the end of this century, Mexico reaches a status where one female produces one female—I am not trying to be sexist, but that is the way demographers talk about zero population growth—Mexico will taper off with a population of 175 million people."[63] Lloyd Bentsen (D-TX) feared that economic instability in Mexico would draw "20 million over the border in a hurry," burdening the already beleaguered welfare state.[64] Jesse Helms (R-NC) postulated that amnesty would increase illegal flows and the unemployment rate, since immigrants "often cut in on the livelihood of local people and arouse hostility," and "lean heavily on the public purse."[65]

These same concerns were voiced by nativist organizations such as the Federation for American Immigration Reform (FAIR), which had links to ZPG and eugenics research. (Incidentally, Helms referred to FAIR in his statement.) FAIR receives support from the Pioneer Fund, which since its 1937 founding "promoted the eugenics movement and funded research aimed at proving the biological inferiority of minorities."[66] In 1985, the Pioneer Fund's mission was to "conduct or aid in conducting study and research into the problems of heredity and eugenics in the human race generally."[67] That Latin American immigrant mothers were the targets of such organizations was made explicit. John Tanton, former president of ZPG, founder of FAIR, and English Only proponent, published a 1988 memorandum on the "Latin onslaught." He asked, "Will the present majority peaceably hand over its political power to a group that is simply more fertile?"[68] The links between the demonization of immigrant mothers and eugenics—a staple of American immigration history—increased into the 1990s based on the precedent IRCA polemics set.

As Jaafar Aksikas and Sean Johnson Andrews observe, neoliberal "crisis-based arguments for privatizing social security, Medicare, public education or other massive social programmes are more cultural than material. They rely on generating a hegemonic understanding of the problem in order to suggest a neoliberal solution."[69] Pierette Hondagneu-Sotello has noted that undocumented immigrants pay into the kinds of state aid they might receive, such as Social Security and AFDC, yet only 2 to 3 percent of undocumented immigrants actually receive assistance.[70] In the absence of empirical evidence, "constructing Mexicans as parasitic construes Mexican mothers and children as undeserving of education and medical care."[71] In the 1990s, several films provided "commonsense" support for the criticisms of Latin American immigrant and Latina mothers underscoring welfare cuts. Latin American immigrant and Latina mothers, unable to accomplish the essential tasks of childrearing, were cast as unfit.

Deborah Paredez has shown that the recurring trope of the absent or dead Latina mother in pop culture texts about young Latina aspirations produced since the 1990s "Latin Explosion" exposes anxieties about Latinas/os' increasing numbers and recognition as an important voting bloc, market base, and labor pool.[72] Representations of unfit Latina mothers in the late twentieth century likewise functioned as an index of contemporary concerns about Latin American immigrants and Latinas/os that crystalized around reproduction. In *Mi Familia* (1995) María (Jennifer Lopez), a young mother and U.S. citizen, is rounded up in a raid and illegally deported to Mexico. Her disappearance has long-lasting negative effects on her family. In *Fearless* (1993), another young Latina mother, Carla Rodrigo (Rosie Perez), is consumed with guilt because she survived a plane crash and her baby did not. One of the texts Paredez examines, the film *Real Women Have Curves* (2002), an adaptation of Josefina Lopez's 1994 play, was critically praised as a positive representation of a working-class Latina. The Mexican American protagonist, Ana (America Ferrera), dreams of college but her mother believes it is her daughter's vocation to work in her sister's dress store in near-sweatshop conditions. In this case, the mother's gender-based traditionalism makes her "bad" or unfit, inhibiting Ana's access to the American Dream. Thus the film casts the United States a place where women are uniquely free and empowered, in contrast to the backward Mexican tradition that the mother represents.

The earlier film *Mi Vida Loca* (1994) provides a somewhat sympathetic portrayal of Chicana women and created space for working-class Latina subjectivity in mainstream film, yet it entwines Latina motherhood and sexuality with crime. The Alison Anders film is set in 1990s Echo Park, then a Los Angeles barrio, and depicts teenaged Chicana mothers/gang members who form a female support network. Initially the film centers on the resolution of rivalry between childhood best friends Sad Girl (Angel Aviles) and Mousie (Seidy Lopez), both of whom were impregnated by Ernesto (Jacob Vargas), a drug dealer and fellow gang member. Their nonmarital teenage pregnancies and mutual betrayal reiterate hackneyed imaginings of Latina promiscuity; their initial desires to harm one another (the two scream at and threaten each other while each pushes her own child—half-siblings—in a stroller) validate stereotypes of a Latina propensity for violence and bad mothering; their reliance on welfare and illegal economies for subsistence corroborate allegations that Latinas are welfare drains, lazy, and again, bad mothers. Yet the women reconcile and join with local girls to support one another rather than hold out for unreliable men. Like *pachucas*, rebellious urban teenaged Chicanas in the 1950s and 1960s, the women of *Mi Vida Loca* depart from the prescriptive Chicana familial femininity that anchors women to a male provider and the home and reserves sexuality for marital procreation.[73]

One might argue, however, that the women of the film step outside of the confines of domesticity as young single mothers who are part of a female network only because they lack men to support them and because they are lazy. The girls are incredulous when Giggles (Marlo Marron), an older gang member recently released from prison, says she plans to get a job; they prefer male bread-winning, drug-dealing, and/or welfare to working. Unable to get a job with her criminal record and lack of work experience, Giggles ultimately returns to the gang lifestyle. In this way, the film illuminates the material reality of neoliberalism—namely, that poor populations of color are trapped by gendered, racialized neoliberal norms; it is difficult for the women to join the workforce as unskilled, underage single Latina mothers, particularly with criminal records. Yet when the film was released in 1994, proponents of California's Proposition 187 cast Latin American immigrant women, and especially Mexican-origin women, as hypersexual, reproductively irresponsible, welfare-draining cheats. Given this backdrop, the film likely confirmed stereotypes for mainstream audiences.[74]

Another complex picture of Latina mothers was presented onscreen by *Lonestar*. In the 1996 film, writer/ director John Sayles troubled traditional and official notions of U.S. history and presented a biracial woman (half white, half Mexican American) as the emblem of the new multicultural order he envisions. As Ann McClintock observes, "nations are frequently figured through the iconography of familial and domestic space,"[75] and that figuration is racialized in *Lonestar* much as it was in mainstream discourses at that time. As Rosa Linda Fregoso notes, Sayles not only imagines U.S. history as a resolved white oedipal drama—history is about fathers and sons—that is juxtaposed against a fractured, dysfunctional Latina mother-daughter subnarrative, but also imagines white male access to multiculturalism through the bodies of women of color.[76] As such, this text supported the neoliberal status quo, perpetuating the stereotype of "bad" Latina mothering in its figuration of the United States.

Oedipal conflict drives not only Sayles's notion of history, but also the film's plot.[77] According to local legend, former sheriff Buddy Deeds (Matthew McConaughey) murdered his predecessor, the corrupt and racist Charlie Wade (Kris Kristofferson). When Wade's skeleton is discovered, Buddy's son and current sheriff, Sam (Chris Cooper), who had a troubled relationship with the deceased Buddy, investigates the murder. The process exposes complex race relations in Rio County, a stand-in for Texas and the United States. Sam also reconnects with his former forbidden love, Chicana history teacher Pilar Cruz (Elizabeth Pena), only to learn that Buddy had a secret affair with her mother, Mercedes (Miriam Colon), and fathered Pilar. Sam resolves his issues with his father through his investigation, and he and Pilar decide to continue their romantic relationship. They choose to "Forget the Alamo."[78] This choice to forget limited and limiting history and move forward as a couple despite sexual and racial taboos encapsulates Sayles's new multicultural vision. Sayles's dramatization of border life is more nuanced than typical colonialist filmic renderings of the border as a place of "absolute alterity" whose inhabitants are "coded as outcasts, degenerates, sexually hungry subalterns and outlaws,"[79] and he argues for dissolving borders by showing that all people are limited and restricted by living in the past.[80]

But Pilar and her mother remain estranged, and the depiction of Mercedes resonates with the stigmatizing image of the "bad black mother." She is the unmarried owner of a successful business, a public official, and lover. Yet in relation to Pilar, Mercedes is static, consistently argumentative, and critical, particularly of Pilar's lovers; the two cannot connect in any meaningful way. She is also a race and class traitor, unsympathetic because for most of the film she attempts to claim Spanish (that is, white) heritage rather than her actual heritage as an undocumented Mexican and is proudly assimilated in the Anglo community. She insists that her Mexican immigrant employees speak English, refuses to visit Mexico with Pilar, treats her immigrant employees harshly, and calls border patrol when she sees "wetbacks" running through her backyard.

Sayles's critique of assimilation is developed when Mercedes reconnects with her history as an undocumented Mexican migrant, which in turn catalyzes her into aiding the undocumented fiancé of Enrique, an employee. While Mercedes reprimands him for helping Mexicans cross because "either they get on welfare, or they become criminals," she does assist them.

The implication that economic mobility is what has distanced Mercedes from the minority history that Sayles valorizes contrasts with economically couched attacks on Latina mothers. And Pilar too is single, economically independent, and successful. In the case of Mercedes, upward mobility is even problematized because it includes disavowal of her roots. Pilar's economic stability is idealized because she embraces her Mexican roots and minority versions of history, as well as radical sexual behavior. Capitalism and white hegemony are critiqued through the critical portrayal of Mercedes's assimilation, and she is redeemed on this count only when she recognizes her history by helping Enrique and his fiancé.

However, the unspoken message of the film—a reimagining of history as a resolved white Oedipal drama, as Fregoso argues—is that there is no resolution within mother-daughter relations for women of color. The more sympathetic portrayal of Mercedes does not extend to her mothering of Pilar. Their relationship remains contentious and therefore Mercedes remains villainized as a mother; she is unfit. Moreover, Pilar, the emblem of the new multicultural nation, must be barren because procreation within incestuous relationships is taboo. The film suggests that Latina mothers will continue to be a problem for the nation. Thus *Lonestar* complemented the matriphobic racialization arguments underscoring welfare-restricting legislation.

What was lost on the congressional floor and in these films was that IRCA and subsequent immigration law and popular discourse *made* undocumented Latin American women into "bad mothers." That is, it was all but impossible for immigrant mothers, like poor and working class citizen mothers of color, to achieve the family ideal woven into all aspects of mainstream U.S. culture. Along with neoliberal economic restraints that made it difficult for mothers and especially single mothers to support their children, the 1996 Illegal Immigration Reform and Immigrant Responsibility Act (IIRIRA), which made immigration law far more punitive and akin to criminal law, prohibited immigrants, including those who would be otherwise eligible for permanent resident status, from reentering the United States for up to ten years if ever they overstayed a visa or lived in the country unlawfully for over a year. For undocumented mothers with citizen children, immigration law thus hindered rather than facilitated the maintenance of a stable, co-located family, particularly in a labor market that frequently necessitated national border crossing. Consequently, as Laura Flanders writes, "The sick 'Sophie's Choice' for undocumented women is to leave their family for a decade for a chance to apply for legal status or to stay illegally and raise their kids in fear."[81] In a similar vein, Cecilia Menjivar and Leisy J. Abrego argue, on the basis of interviews conducted with immigrant mothers from Guatemala, El Salvador, and Mexico, 1998–2000, that U.S. immigration law functions as "legal violence": by separating families and denying much needed social services, it inhibits legal or legalizing and undocumented immigrant women's ability to parent their children, and causes much suffering.[82] And, as Patricia Zavella further notes, "Even when the unauthorized do have rights, such as to prenatal care, often they are uninformed about them or they worry that presenting themselves in public may jeopardize their stay in the United States and subject them to removal."[83]

Undocumented immigrant mothers are always already cast as unfit mothers because of their unlawful status, *and* according to the "family values" ideal, undocumented women are deserving of censure when separated from their children, and if they need state aid to support their families. Yet punitive immigration policies turn them into absentee parents, and inadequate wages and lack of health care benefits make it very difficult for undocumented immigrant women to support their children and even acquire proper medical care for them. This neoliberal reality is a far cry from the pro-multicultural family reunification rhetoric prevalent in the early congressional debates over IRCA.

Not surprisingly in this context, a compelling and oftentimes the only recourse for undocumented mothers seeking what should be basic human rights was to make the "family rights" as human rights argument that dominated IRCA family reunification polemics and continues to do so in recent rights activism. The "family rights" argument folds women back into traditional gender roles and devalues individuals who are not blood-related parents and children. But for undocumented mothers at the mercy of the state and sometimes also abusive citizen or legal resident partners, the only grounds upon which to argue for human rights is to appeal to "family values" and family rights, to be "good" mothers according to patriarchal assumptions.

Efforts to secure rights by casting Latin American immigrants as taxpayers also reaffirmed oppressive neoliberal ideology. In her prepared statement for the first Senate hearing for IRCA 1984, Mexican American Legal Defense and Educational Fund (MALDEF) spokesperson Antonia Hernandez argued that those granted temporary status (with exceptions only for old age, blindness, disability, or illness, at the discretion of the attorney general) "contribute to the tax base which finances these programs and should therefore be entitled to benefits if they meet the established eligibility requirements."[84] While Hernandez's aim was clearly to secure access to benefits, her argument was as neoliberal—and thus as rights-denying—as the arguments against welfare access for immigrants. As with the "family rights" argument that gelled with "family values," the currency for human worth in the neoliberalizing "nation of immigrants" was monetary contribution to federal and state governments; immigrants were objectified as burdens, legal subjects, and piggy banks.

Furthermore, it was necessary to refute the argument that immigrants burden the welfare state even though, as mentioned above, statistics reveal (again and again) that immigrants do not drain public resources,[85] especially given that the "Latina threat" stereotype provided a powerful rationale for the liberal application of welfare cuts. Although public assistance for U.S.-born children of undocumented parents is perfectly legal under *jus soli* (that is, the right of any person born in the United States to citizenship, which was ratified under the Fourteenth Amendment), the INS, entirely responsible for implementation of assistance, used the new restrictions to reject undocumented Latin American mothers' amnesty applications. In the 1988 *Zambrano v. INS* case a group of Latin American immigrant women with dependents argued that implementation of amnesty and welfare restrictions adversely affected undocumented mothers. The suit was dismissed in 1998 when the IIRIRA limited the ability of courts to review issues of legalization. But the underlying facts cannot be dismissed: 70 percent of amnesty participants were Mexican, and over 20 percent were from Central America and the Caribbean. Of accepted amnesty applicants, over 68 percent were male.[86] There is no question that these provisions had the most negative impact on undocumented Latin American women.

In its execution of IRCA, the INS perpetuated what Grace Chang calls the "feminization of poverty among undocumented immigrants."[87] That implementation has "continued to fill the historical role of the state in using immigration and welfare policies to maintain women of color as a super-exploitable, low-wage labor force" by coercing Asian and Latin American immigrant women—Mexican women in particular—into the secondary labor force, private household work, and institutional service work.[88] The expansion of producer services from the 1970s and 1980s, which created a polarized occupational and income structure in the United States, and the simultaneous large-scale entrance of elite and educated women into the work force dramatically increased demand for domestic services,[89] just as immigration quotas were placed on the Western Hemisphere, and Latin American nations fell into economic depressions largely induced by U.S. polices, as in Mexico. Prior to IRCA, legal and undocumented Latin American immigrant women were disproportionately employed in the service sector and in operative and labor jobs: 26.9 percent of Mexican women and 20.2 percent of South American women were in service, and 18.5 percent and 35.8 percent, respectively, were in operative/labor. Only 7.6 percent of Mexican immigrant women and 11.5 percent of South American immigrant women were employed in the professional sector.[90] IRCA implementation ensured that undocumented women trying to legalize would be channeled into often "under the table" secondary sector employment and all but forced to tolerate exploitative working conditions. Moreover, undocumented women in the secondary labor force often earn wages below the poverty level but rarely utilize public assistance due to fears that doing so will jeopardize applications to legalize.[91]

The INS implementation of welfare restrictions worked much like the "employable mother" laws. Policy execution implied that non-white immigrant mothers were especially employable, alongside a prevalent cultural notion—emphatically stressed by the Reagan administration's trumpeting of "family values," references to the "welfare queen," and evocation of the "model minority stereotype"—that a fit mother had a breadwinning husband/father to her children so that she was presumably available to mother properly and in no danger of needing public assistance. Latin American immigrant mothers and especially the undocumented were therefore trapped, simultaneously cast as women who can, should, and often had to work outside of the home *and* denigrated as unfit mothers.

Not All Welfare Recipients Are Equal: Asian "Model Minority" Mothers

Not all minority mothers were viewed as unfit. Asian immigrants—and implicitly, Asian-origin mothers—were often imagined as upholders of the neoliberal state. Like the white ethnic immigrant story of plucky self-sufficiency, the "model minority" thesis proved the system was equal. Robert Lee argues that the image of Asian Americans mitigates three Cold War specters: "the red menace of communism, the black menace of racial integration, and the white menace of homosexuality. In place of radical critique calling for structural changes in American political economy, the model minority mythology substituted a narrative of national modernization and ethnic assimilation through heterosexuality, familialism, and consumption."[92]

What is "model" about the "model minority"—a term coined by sociologist William Peterson in the 1966 *New York Times Magazine* article "Success Story: Japanese American Style"—is self-sufficient economic success and a strong family ethic. Peterson claimed that an unrivaled emphasis on education and respect for one's parents enabled Japanese Americans to avoid becoming a "problem minority" despite the discrimination they suffered as recently as World War II. He concluded, "By any criterion of good citizenship we choose, the Japanese Americans are better than any other group in our society including native-born white." A contemporaneous article with comparable claims about Chinese Americans was published in *U.S. News & World Report*.[93] This liberal discourse suggested that racism was surmountable and that the Asian family "embodie[d] the nation's hope for a return to hegemony in the global marketplace through discipline, obedience, and return to family values."[94]

The stereotyping of Asian women as "quiet, delicate, and submissive, especially to men's desires,"[95] undergirds the idealization of the Asian family. Images of Asian women's sexual availability from the geisha to the mail-order bride are standard, and since the 1946 expansion of the 1945 War Brides Act, which allowed members of the U.S. military to bring Asian wives and foreign-born children into the country as non-quota immigrants, Asian women have been imagined as ideal wives because of their alleged docility. What Lee calls "Orientalism domesticated" transformed Asian women, cast as sexual deviants at the turn of the twentieth century, into "symbol[s] of domesticity and stalwart[s] of a restored postwar patriarchy."[96] In accordance with this transformation, feminist theorists have argued, "of all women of color, Asian women are perceived as the closest to the stereotype of true womanhood [which is white], but with the discriminating marker of sexual availability."[97]

The Asian American–style entwinement of economic success and "family values" was especially poignant in the context of the Reaganite fashioning of the individual as the nexus of social responsibility in the process of expanding liberal discourse to suit neoliberalism. During his 1984 presidential campaign, Reagan frequently cited statistics indicating that Asians' median income surpassed the national average, and many popular news magazines made similar claims. A 1982 *Newsweek* article on "Asian Americans: The Model Minority" stated that the average family income of Asian Americans exceeded that of the rest of the U.S. population: $22,075 in comparison to $20,840. Similarly themed articles abounded,[98] so it seemed like the system did not discriminate against but rather embraced all self-sufficient individuals.

But being cast as a "model minority" is as harmful as being cast as a "problem minority." The longstanding view of people from the Near and Far East as exotic and fundamentally different from Westerners[99] is rearticulated with notions of Asian American economic and intellectual advantage; this new "yellow peril" essentializes Asians and produces new forms of racialized discrimination such as employment segregation and anti-Asian quotas in college admissions.[100] Furthermore, the "model minority" thesis completely occludes and/or condemns Asians who do not fit the stereotype, including refugees and asylum seekers, who are by definition displaced and often impoverished by war and various forms of persecution. Also erased were the Asian immigrant women disenfranchised by neoliberal immigration policy, such as large numbers of Southeast Asian refugee women in the service sector, and Filipina nurses who since the 1970s have been imported and given only minimal rights.[101]

The story of Hue Cao, a twelve-year-old Vietnamese refugee, disrupts the myth of monolithic Asian success but was manipulated to support the U.S. neoliberal master narrative of opportunity and ascent for the worthy. Cao won the Hawaii "What the Statue of Liberty Means to Me" essay contest (held nationwide in conjunction with Liberty Weekend), but had to decline the prize, a new car, because her family, which fled Vietnam in a small fishing boat in 1979, would then have more than $1,500 in resources and thus be disqualified from receiving the public assistance they depended on. Americans, in the thrall of Reaganite patriotism and anti-communism, were galvanized by the story of this welfare family. The Hawaii essay committee auctioned the car and put the proceeds into a scholarship fund for Cao, President Reagan made a congratulatory phone call to her, an anonymous donor purchased a car worth just under $1,500 for the family, and the family received an all-expenses-paid trip to New York City for Liberty Weekend so that Cao could read her essay at the Statue of Liberty rededication ceremony.[102]

While the white ethnic and "model minority" narratives hold that all immigrants should be able to succeed on their own without public assistance, as Erica Rand observes, the Cao story shows that, despite IRCA's restriction of welfare later that year, immigrants sometimes need public assistance, as well as demonstrating that that all Asian Americans are not rich and all welfare recipients are not lazy cheats. Yet the story was framed to illuminate individual generosity, a kind president, and a nation being exceptionally benevolent to *one* patriotic Asian immigrant family: compelling "evidence" of a just system.[103]

Moreover, characterizing Asian immigrants as good at "Americanness" in terms of "family values" or as occasionally deserving of aid fostered a politics of invidious comparison between Asian American and Latin American immigrants, which crystallized around motherhood. Popular culture located Asian mothers between idealized white ethnic mothers and maligned Latin American immigrant and Latina mothers. In *The Rule of Racialization: Class, Identity, Governance*, Steve Martinot argues that racialization formed white class identities in the United States first through the slavery system and later through practices and structures such as anti-union politics and the criminalization of blacks via racial profiling. Crucial to Martinot's argument is Theodore Allen's notion of the intermediary control stratum.[104] In the colonial South, poorer whites were given dominion over blacks via white bond-labor patrols that enforced slave codes; casting slaves as the common enemy diminished the sense of economic competition between poor and wealthy white farmers. Besides administrative law enforcement, this intermediary control stratum was the primary form of social control and marks the first appearance of class as a sociopolitical and not economic distinction.[105]

Asian immigrant mothers functioned as an intermediary control stratum that affirmed the superior status of white ethnic immigrant mothers and inferior status of Latin American immigrant mothers; a lack of a family ethic and failure to be self-sufficient were the common—and racialized—enemies.

With representations of successful and close-knit Asian families, popular culture popularized the idea that the U.S. system is equitable. But along with pathologizing all who failed to live up to the ideal, the tempered idealization of Asian immigrant mothers affirmed an East/West binary by presenting women's empowerment across generations as something that was only available in the United States.

Amy Tan's *The Joy Luck Club*, a 1989 novel about Chinese American mothers and daughters, and the 1993 film based on it, show that "model" fashioning of Asians resonated with audiences. The novel was on the *New York Times* bestseller list for seventy-five weeks, it was translated into twenty-three languages worldwide, and Hollywood showed interest in a film version before the book was even published.[106] Tan and Ronald Bass wrote the critically acclaimed screenplay. Set in 1980s and 1990s San Francisco, *The Joy Luck Club* follows four sets of Chinese American daughters and their immigrant mothers, who were frequently abused and victimized in China and thus sought to provide better lives for their daughters in America. Racialized gender politics drive home this point that a better life was to be found only in the United States: as is often the case in multigenerational immigrant narratives, the daughters blame the "Old World" Chinese mentality of their mothers for their troubles, but with the help of revelatory flashbacks and by blending some "good" aspects of Chinese culture (food, respecting one's mother, and pre-Communist didactic parables about overcoming difficulty with individual tenacity and moxie) with U.S. culture, the mothers and daughters resolve their conflicts and ascend into the middle class.

The theme of generational conflict, with its representation of the Orientalized Chinese mother bound by patriarchal traditionalism, also appears in other literary texts, which is where most popular cultural representations of Asian Americans can be found in this period; there was a dearth of representations in film and television. Maxine Hong Kingston's award-winning creative nonfiction book *Woman Warrior: Memoirs of a Girlhood among Ghosts* (1975) tells her story of growing up in Stockton, California, as the child of Chinese immigrants. The passionate anger of the book toward the narrator's mother's barbaric "Old World" traditionalism drew critical and popular acclaim and controversy. It remains one of the most widely taught books in universities in a variety of disciplines. Janice Mirikitani, also born in Stockton, California, to Nisei Japanese American farmers, likewise explored with vivid language and raw emotion gender politics and generational conflict in her 1978 poem "Breaking Tradition." The speaker struggles with witnessing and inheriting her mother's Japanese legacy of submissiveness, and emphasizes her desire to "break tradition" for herself and especially her own daughter.[107]

While Mirikitani's poem provides a more comprehensive critique of patriarchy and its racialized specificity, it, too, represents American-born daughters perceiving their immigrant mothers as oppressed and oppressive products of "foreign" patriarchy.[108]

But to a large extent, Asian immigrant mothers are presented to (and perhaps for) American audiences as sympathetic or at least understandable figures who do their best, considering the "Asian" patriarchy they had to contend with before immigrating. In *The Joy Luck Club* and *Woman Warrior* "Asia," rather than a more ubiquitous patriarchy or the mother herself, is blamed for Asian immigrant mothers' failings. Thus, these texts seem to share more in common with Reaganite appropriation of feminism and multiculturalism via "nation of immigrants" nationalism than radical gender and race critique. For instance, in the *Joy Luck Club* film, mother Ying-Ying is an assertive spirited child in China, but loses her "tiger spirit" after marrying an abusive and adulterous man who leaves her for an opera singer. In the midst of depression over her abandonment, she drowns their infant son, and subsequently further loses her sense of self; she is extremely passive in her next marriage and years after immigrating to the United States she continues to be tormented by her past. But she reconnects with her tiger spirit to help daughter Lina, who lacks spirit because Ying-Ying had none to give her. Ying-Ying is thereby symbolically acquitted for the murder (is there any more egregious act of "bad mothering" than infanticide?), and the implication is that she and Lina are free to be independent and strong in the nurturing U.S. environment; that is, the implication is that the United States empowers them to take "personal responsibility."[109] Although all of the American-born daughters resent and rebel against the obedience that their Chinese mothers demand, the daughters eventually realize that their mothers want only to provide their daughters with a better life than is possible in China.

Gender is the conduit of foreignness and Orientalization in these texts,[110] much as Mexico is in *Real Women Have Curves*. In *The Joy Luck Club*, China is a place where women must kill their babies and take other desperate measures (such as An-Mei's mother's suicide in response to the abuse she suffered as a concubine, and Suyuan's involuntary abandonment of her twin babies in wartime). This logic holds that lingering vestiges of that system must be Americanized in order for the mothers and daughters to reconcile. Thus "Americanization and assimilation" are framed "as the 'cure,' as the sign that the disability of [immigrant] culture had been 'overcome.'"[111]

This Orientalist message was also contemporaneously conveyed on the congressional floor with legislation for the "Amerasian" children of American servicemen and Southeast Asian mothers conceived during the Vietnam War.

Responding to the belief that these children—termed *con lai* (half-breed) or *bui doi* (the dust of life) in Vietnamese—were ostracized due to racism in Vietnam and/or that they were abandoned by their mothers,[112] the 1980 Refugee Act and 1987 Amerasian Homecoming Act offered refuge. Southeast Asia (and implicitly Southeast Asian mothers) were thus cast as neglectful and unfit (though the American servicemen who fathered the children were not held accountable). Again America appeared inclusive and progressive, providing ever more "commonsense" support for America's increasing efforts to globalize capitalist democracy as a universally beneficial system via "humanitarian violence," and displacing some blame for mothers onto communism.

The "model minority" thesis suggested that welfare is not necessary for Latinas or blacks because Asians are (usually) so successful. At the same time, Asian patriarchy (and/or racism and/or communism) rather than Asian mothers or mothering was cast as responsible for any "bad" parenting, and the United States was fashioned as liberating. This notion was updated with Amy Chua's 2011 memoir, *Battle Hymn of the Tiger Mother*, which elaborates a strain of the "model minority" stereotype in which Asian parents relentlessly push their children to excel. Chua positing that this is more effective than other forms of mothering drew much criticism,[113] which suggests that even when "model minorities" embody and effectively transmit neoliberal values, they continue to be "foreign."

The Good Mother Is White and Ethnic

Crucial to the simultaneous casting of white ethnics as ideal "nation of immigrants" forbearers was the romanticizing of white ethnic mothers in contrast to Latin American immigrant and Latina mothers. By the 1980s, white ethnic women, who in the early twentieth century were treated as state burdens and threats to the racial order, were reinvented as ideal American mothers; they "proved" that Latin American immigrants and Latinas and blacks were unfit, and that Asian mothers were "foreign." Beginning in the 1920s, restrictions on white ethnic immigrants were eased, and New Deal programs like the Rural Electric Administration (REA) and the Federal Housing Administration (FHA), along with the post–World War II GI Bill—federal welfare—facilitated white ethnic upward mobility. On the heels of the civil rights era, white ethnic identity cohered to challenge the civil rights claims and gains of people of color. White ethnic immigrants were "extolled for their self-reliance," despite the fact that "more than half of public welfare recipients in 1909 were [European] immigrant families, making them three times more likely than native families to depend on public assistance."[114] Regardless, the white ethnic bootstraps narrative was evoked to rationalize cutting affirmative action and welfare. The argument went that if white ethnics could pull themselves up by their bootstraps in the midst of discrimination, so could people of color—and the "model minority" thesis makes the same—equally spurious—argument.

The white ethnic mythos crystallized around "family values," embodied by the canonized white ethnic mother, and was connected to the white ethnic thrust of second-wave feminism. Matthew Jacobson asserts that second-wave feminism, dominated by white ethnic women, displaced patriarchal histories by embracing "foremothers and foresisters" who "supplied both weapons and inspiration for the war against patriarchy." White ethnic "world of our mothers" feminism also attempted to establish a sense of common struggle with women of color and recent immigrants on the basis of shared patriarchal oppression and the white ethnic history of poverty, tenement life, and social marginalization, which was also frequently referred to in order to illustrate white ethnic distance from privilege.[115] Although the intent of this political strategy was pluralistic and inclusive, claiming gendered otherness reinforced white privilege by minimizing or erasing how race and class (and other facets of social identity) intersect to shape women's experiences. In fact, given that white ethnics were never excluded from citizenship as were blacks and Asians, that white ethnic immigrants usually chose to immigrate, that they were paid for their labor, though often meagerly and unfairly, and that New Deal federal aid helped white ethnics become self-sufficient, the white ethnic experience is not at all consonant with the systemic racist impoverishment and disenfranchisement of black Americans via slavery and Jim Crow, Asian Americans via Chinese Exclusion and Japanese internment, or the rearticulation of racism with colorblindness and other neoliberal(izing) strategies.

I return to *Golden Girls* because the show encapsulates the limits of white ethnic feminists' attempts to establish a sense of common struggle with women of color and recent immigrants. Sophia's Italian immigrant heritage makes her an ideal matriarch in a household of mothers. Romanticized Italian American mothers, such as the long-suffering mafia mother in the *Godfather* trilogy, have a long presence in American pop culture. Also prevalent is the comically overbearing, well-intended mother, as in the sitcom *Everybody Loves Raymond*,[116] and the caretaker mother, as in Vinnie Guadagnino's immigrant mother on the reality show *Jersey Shore*.[117] Vinnie's mother happily does her adult son's laundry, spends hours cooking, and serves massive traditional Italian American meals of pasta, sausage and peppers, chicken parmesan, and escarole. These Italian American mothers complement Reaganite neoliberalism with their dependence on men, devotion to their children, and cooking prowess, and while they may not work outside the home, they do not rely on welfare. Not surprisingly, the Italian mother has been used to sell an array of "Italian" food products, as in the Mama Celeste line of pizzas and pasta dishes. These representations are not monolithic, but consistently, the Italian American woman is *all* mother, or at least mother first.

True to this stereotypical form, in the *Golden Girls*, widow Sophia's matriarchal wisdom is drawn from her Sicilian immigrant past and her struggles to make ends meet as a young immigrant mother in Brooklyn. Born in Palermo, Sophia moved to New York after fleeing an arranged marriage. She later married Salvadore Petrillo, with whom she had three children, Dorothy, Gloria, and Phil. Of course, Sophia is an amazing cook. She hints that her family has mafia ties, and most importantly, she frequently dispenses advice with her didactic stories about life in Sicily and Brooklyn and her assiduous efforts to pull herself up by her bootstraps so her children could have a better life.

For example, Sophia exaggerates the difficulty of parenting in Sicily; in "nation of immigrants" format, the United States is presented as far more abundant and comfortable than immigrants' sending nations. While babysitting an infant, the "girls" marvel at technological advances in baby care such as disposable diapers, premade formula, and pop-up disposable wipes. Rose recalls that to change a baby's diaper she used cotton and fish ointment, but Sophia one-ups her, saying, "That's nothing. In Sicily, we used a leaf and the river!" In Sophia's stories, life in Sicily was poor and primitive; the stories demonstrate how skillful she had to be to survive. Similarly, Sophia's numerous get-rich-quick schemes affirm her resourcefulness as she tries to capitalize on stereotypical notions of the Italian mother's cooking aptitude by creating a spaghetti sauce, vending homemade Italian sandwiches, and co-owning a pizza and knish stand. She epitomizes self-sufficiency, wisdom, perseverance, and adaptability, in the context of the abundance that the United States ostensibly offers to immigrants.

Sophia is also caustic and quite imperfect. With biting quips, she regularly mocks Rose for being simpleminded, Blanche for being promiscuous, and Dorothy for being masculine, bookish, unattractive, and without male companionship. She steals from Dorothy, mocks her in public, and favors her other children. Dorothy points out that Sophia emotionally scarred her, as when Sophia, judge of the Little Miss Brooklyn pageant, did not vote for her own daughter. The devout Catholic also gleefully lies and manipulates to get close to the Pope during his Miami visit, and then steals his ring. She regularly steals food, silverware, and linen from restaurants even though she does not need them.

But her venial "sins" do not mar her character nor do they counteract the overall depiction of her as a good, loving white ethnic mother. Her stories always help the "girls," who consistently turn to Sophia for sage advice. (Her name means "wisdom" in Latin.) Her schemes and pranks are the stuff of comic relief, and her feistiness is excused on account of her advanced age, a stroke she suffered, and the hardships she endured as a Sicilian peasant and immigrant, and Dorothy's love for her mother always trumps any resentment she might harbor. Sophia frequently stresses that family matters above all else, for as she says, "If you can't count on family, who the hell can you count on?"

Sophia's feisty resourcefulness expresses the popular cultural register of "world of our mothers" feminism and its neoliberal development, and as such anticipates postfeminism. Media has framed if not explicitly labeled the show as feminist: "The *Golden Girls* valued women and put special emphasis on the importance of women's networks, friendships, and experiences."[118] The show is one of the only popular representations of senior women function-ing as a family, which it refigures in matriarchal terms, especially because it depicts older women as energetic, lively, working, and capable without con-sistent male companionship and financial support. The golden girls are also a near-queer family. While the show may seem to make a case for the United States' incorporation of feminism and increasing inclusion of immigrants and the elderly, what it actually exposes is the ongoing need for feminism and other collective progressive movements. Karen Orr Vered and Sal Humphreys canvassed the extent to which postfeminism is prevalent in media in the neo-liberal conjuncture, which they date as the 1990s and after.[119] As an analytical tool, "postfeminism" "describes the political moment in which the material and ideological gains of second-wave feminism have been accepted and in-corporated into our mainstream values and common ambitions at the same time as neoliberal economics and its associated social policies—including a reduction in social welfare support–have become entrenched." Assuming that equal opportunity, wage equity, and autonomy have been established, agency for change is placed on the individual rather than with collective action or on society; women are "encouraged to concentrate on their private lives and con-sumer expression as the sites for self-expression and agency."[120] While I argue that neoliberalism was becoming entrenched in the 1980s with the Reaganite ethos of personal responsibility, individual freedoms, and consumerism, the gains of second-wave feminism were just beginning to be incorporated. Given its dialogue with feminism and trumpeting of neoliberal economic values, *Golden Girls* could be considered proto-postfeminist. Sophia is especially re-markable as the oldest and pluckiest woman, and her survival skills, updated to suit a neoliberalizing American setting, were acquired through the chal-lenges she faced and overcame on her own as a female immigrant in a nation that was becoming ever more inclusive and hospitable to women. And one of the rewards she receives for her personal responsibility is the ability to purchase modern consumer goods that make the tasks of childrearing easier.

The cultural appeal of the white ethnic mother in the Reagan era is also linked to racism and chauvinism. Michaela di Leonardo showed that WASPs, blacks, and white ethnics were placed in a "Three Bears" analogy in 1970s rhetoric around white ethnicity that made WASPs "too cold" or detached and modern to a fault, blacks "too hot" or primitive and out of control, and white ethnics "just right" because they adhered to the gender, race, and class status quo while possessing ethnic character and flavor. White ethnicity maintained white supremacy when multiculturalism was becoming hegemonic. Idealization of the white ethnic mother was crucial, and thus she was constructed as better than WASP and black mothers.[121] In the 1980s and 1990s, it was Latin American and Asian immigrant mothers that formed the other points of the triangle, but the sentiments and results were similar. White ethnic Sophia is a "good" mother regardless of her shortcomings, Latina mothers such as Lonestar's Mercedes and the teenage girls of Mi Vida Loca are unfit, and the Chinese immigrant mothers of The Joy Luck Club reside between the two, their fallibility blamed on "Asian" patriarchy.

Jacobson observes that the "bootstraps mythology, complete with its striking patterns of self-congratulation and erasure, has become standard fare as white Americans seek 'to define themselves out of the oppressor class.'"[122] Add patriarchy and Sophia's advanced age to the mix, and the myth of white ethnic women's self-sufficient resourcefulness becomes a powerful rationale to deny welfare to women of color and to censure them for any such need. By failing to expose or consider the ways that whiteness—and federal aid—gives some women substantial unearned advantages, while patriarchy continues to be hegemonic, the Golden Girls iteration of "world of our mothers" feminism substantiated "commonsense" gendered racism that justified neoliberal welfare cuts.

Similarly, the alleged victimization of whites by civil rights and antiracism was a point used to support efforts to eliminate social services, and this was done according to the familiar Reaganite brand of multiculturalism: individual rights and responsibility equally for all people. The Reagan administration's staunch anti-affirmative action, pro-privatization stance received potent ideological support from the white ethnic immigrant saga of self-sufficiency in books such as Nathan Glazer's 1976 Affirmative Discrimination: Ethnic Inequality and Public Policy. There, he argued that the civil rights paradigm of group rights was discriminatory, as some racial groups (namely, people of color) were granted more rights than others (namely, whites); policy should thus focus on individual rights.

As the notion of Asian "model minorities" came to be similarly used to rationalize attacks on affirmative action, some Latinas/os joined the fray with their own stories of individual agency rather than collective action as the vehicle for social change. In his 1982 autobiography, *Hunger of Memory: The Education of Richard Rodriguez*, a son of working-class Mexican immigrants described his plucky resolve to learn English as the gateway to his class mobility and belonging. It was also the source of his opposition to bilingual education, which prompted the intellectual Left to dismiss Rodriguez as a "brown Uncle Tom"[123] who sold out his race and ethnicity for a place in the master's home, like *Lonestar*'s Mercedes. The neoliberal immigrant success story is flexible, and can be extended to and advocated by Hispanics.

Thus race and gender shaped the legal treatment and popular representation of immigrants in relation to welfare, which served neoliberalism in complex and uneven ways. The restrictions on federal welfare programs, in concert with IRCA welfare restrictions and media alarm over welfare queens and fecund and costly Latin American undocumented women, set the mold for neoliberal welfare reform. While IRCA welfare restrictions made it necessary for immigrants to work, the Family Support Act's emphasis on individual responsibility both made it more difficult for single mothers of color to support families and punished them when they failed. The next wave of welfare reform aggressively elaborated upon the Reaganite model, and in a way that starkly illustrates how racial politics shape reproductive rights.[124]

The Legacy: Neoliberal Eugenics

Much has been written about matriphobic racialization as the order of the day in the 1990s, yet IRCA is rarely marked as the starting point for the now-standard neoliberal practice of restricting immigrants' access to welfare as part of this larger discourse. Zillah Eisenstein notes that "Presidents Reagan and Bush oversaw and orchestrated the idea that the welfare state is the enemy, because it has wasted our money."[125] Specific ways of talking about and dealing with the costs of insufficient "family values" among people of color and immigrants that coalesced under the Reagan administration continued under the Republican George H. W. Bush administration (1989–1993) and the Democratic Bill Clinton administration (1993–2001). Despite different partisan affiliations and agendas, under each administration and in eerily continuous ways, the government has been rendered responsible for less, individuals and families responsible for more, and "as the state has become more privatized, society has become less equal, and privacy rights have become encoded racially and sexually along economic lines."[126] As the 1980s gave way to the 1990s, Latin American immigrant reproduction became "ground zero in a war not just of words but also public policies and laws."[127] Concerns about the costs of unfit Latin American and especially Mexican immigrant mothers and black mothers crystallized with the Clinton-era Proposition 187 and Personal Responsibility and Work Opportunity Reconciliation Act (PRWORA) of 1996, as well as in media discourses that proliferated simultaneously and helped to frame the issue—controlling the allegedly excessive economic and fiscal reproductive costs of Latin American immigrants and people of color—as "common sense."

Both Bush and Clinton expanded upon and revised Reagan's first wave of neoliberalism in ways that reflected their respective locations on the Right and the Left. Bush supported more liberalized transnational free trade by (unsuccessfully) lobbying for the North American Free Trade Agreement (NAFTA), and during the 1988 and 1992 presidential campaigns, he was the "family values" candidate. His domestic solution to urban poverty was to promote married heterosexual two-parent families, epitomized by the fact that "Murphy Brown, a white upper class TV character who chose to birth a child without a husband, was used by [Vice President Dan] Quayle to invoke a notion of families in crisis."[128] Bush's aggressive interventionist foreign policy and military action in the Middle East, as in the First Iraq War, also distinguished him from Reagan.

Clinton combined neoliberalism with a socially progressive agenda. His commitment to market globalism included moderate social welfare programs, a measure of corporate responsibility, and elimination of neoconservative jingoism, militarism, opposition to multiculturalism, and family values (from which he was personally distanced, given his extramarital indiscretions). He considered "socially conscious market globalism" as key to a global "golden age of technological progress and prosperity."[129] Yet despite his left leanings, the next and more draconian wave of welfare cuts—and eugenicist thinking and policy—occurred under his administration, as did the signing of NAFTA, indicating the bipartisan flexibility of neoliberal governance and its appropriation of multiculturalism and feminism.

An anti-welfare argument that can only be characterized as eugenicist predates both administrations, as does its neoliberal iteration. In the 1980s, in IRCA and broader debates about mothers of color and welfare, pundits argued over who was economically and culturally fit to give birth in the nation; the eugenicist lineage of such thinking became flagrant in the 1990s. Harry Laughlin, the eugenicist employed by Congress, 1920–1931, to provide a "biological" view of immigrants, wanted to restrict eastern and southern European immigration as part of a broad plan to prevent the dilution of the

American (that is, white Anglo Saxon Protestant) race. The first wave of eugenicists, in England and the United States, believed intelligence and personality traits were hereditary, so social problems such as poverty, mental illness, and crime and social policies such as blocking the reproduction of objectionable persons could solve "racial degeneracy."[130] Forced sterilization was a preferred tactic, and several states established involuntary sterilization laws.[131] Immigrant women, as the transmitters of biologized social behaviors or characteristics, were thus the focus of restrictionist endeavors. Scientific racism was abandoned by the time Nazi admiration of U.S. eugenic race policies became known.[132] But in the postwar era, the eradication of racial degeneracy was rearticulated as the sexual conformism of the 1950s and social Darwinism was repackaged as population control and family planning.[133] Forced sterilizations of Latina women in California and New York—population control and family planning—persisted. In the 1970s, working-class Mexican-origin women sued the Women's Hospital at the University of Southern California/ Los Angeles County General Hospital for nonconsensual sterilizations predicated on protecting public health,[134] and in 1975, Dr. Helen Rodrigues-Triad founded the Committee to End Sterilization Abuse in response to similar complaints made by Puerto Rican women in New York City. Such procedures "were supported by federal agencies that began to disperse funds in conjunction with the family planning initiatives of the War on Poverty launched by Johnson in 1964,"[135] the same year that the Civil Rights Acts was passed, supposedly ushering in a national commitment to end racism.

Welfare discourses in public policy debates and media in the 1980s reframed eugenicist efforts in terms of cost-reduction to complement neoliberalism, and laws passed in the 1990s carried that torch to new extremes. Christina Gerken notes that "proper neoliberal citizenship was contingent on not only economic contributions but also a certain type of fertility."[136] That is, "since financial stability was commonly accepted as the ultimate goal in a neoliberal society, poor people were expected to delay or even abandon their desire to have children if they aspired to escape their poverty."[137] Carried out in terms of race and gender, fertility and birth control were framed in terms of cost. Consequently, the 1990s strands of neoliberal discourse about reproduction directly reframed eugenics to fit into an allegedly humanitarian multicultural nation, and the rhetoric had material results in public policy.

Proposition 187, for instance, was about Latin American and especially Mexican immigrant fertility. Passed in California in 1994, but quickly placed under injunction as its constitutionality was reviewed, the law made undocumented immigrants ineligible for all public social services, all public health care services other than emergency services, and public school. State and local agencies were also required to report suspected undocumented immigrants to the California Attorney General and to the INS.[138] The law developed out of the 1993 Save Our State initiative created by ten Californians,[139] including immigration reformers such as Alan Nelson, Reagan's INS commissioner, and other INS officials.[140] White middle-class Californians supported Prop 187 because the state was in recession and racial demographics were shifting; from 1980 to 1995, when approximately 15 million Latin Americans and Asians immigrated, about one third of all legal and one-half of all undocumented immigrants entered California.[141] Supporters claimed Prop 187 would reduce the allegedly high costs of educating, incarcerating, and providing social services for the state's substantial undocumented immigrant population. According to the 2000 census, Hispanics comprised 32.4 percent of the population in 2000, the highest state percentiles in the country.[142] The numbers were likely higher, given the number of undocumented immigrants who were not counted in the census.

Governor Pete Wilson, facing difficult reelection prospects, made the cost of undocumented immigration the centerpiece of his campaign. He requested a federal $2.3 billion reimbursement to cover California's undocumented immigration expenses, reduced to $760 million the following year, and filed three lawsuits against the federal government to receive funds. Wilson and other proponents claimed that social services rather than jobs drew immigrants and used this as a rationale for the restriction of aid.[143]

Wilson's 1993 "Open Letter to the President of the United States on Behalf of the State of California," published in the New York Times during his reelection campaign, laid out the "anchor baby" thesis, which showed that Latin American immigrant reproduction rather than "colorblind" expense was at the center of debates: "Why does the U.S. government reward illegal immigrants who successfully violate the law and manage to have a child born on U.S. soil? Rather than penalizing it, we reward their illegal act: we pay for delivery and confer U.S. citizenship on the baby. Why does the United States reward illegal immigrants by requiring states to pay for the exploding costs of their health care, education, and other benefits?"[144]

Save Our State member Bette Hammond unabashedly asserted that Mexican immigrants "come here, they have their babies and after that they become citizens and all those children use social services."[145] Despite evidence to the contrary, a legislative analyst on Wilson's staff found that AFDC dependence for Latinas was 23 percent higher than for all other women.[146] FAIR claimed that allowing the reproduction of Third World immigrant women was "race suicide."[147]

The "anchor baby" thesis posits that undocumented women have babies in the United States to acquire citizenship through the child, exercise family reunification preferences, and avoid the costs of childrearing by using welfare and public services since *jus soli* grants all American-born children and their parents these rights.[148] There is also the assumption that "pregnant aliens" do this frequently enough to necessitate government intervention.[149] This is a rather convoluted and unlikely scenario, since a baby born to an undocumented mother cannot use family reunification options for twenty-one years; the process for legalization and family reunification is itself extensive and has a sizable backlog; despite the findings of Wilson's staff, undocumented women continued to under-use public services and welfare because they fear detection;[150] and as *Zambrano v. INS* indicates, women who did use services were denied opportunities to legalize.

Following his reelection, Wilson's first act was to order all state and local agencies to discontinue immunizations and prenatal care for pregnant women. And this, as Lisa Lowe puts it, "marks the degree to which this proposition [was] directed at immigrant women; anti-immigrant discourse proliferate[d] images of racialized reproduction and feminized or infantilized bodily need as part of its campaign."[151] Dorothy Roberts and Eithne Luibheid explicitly characterize Prop 187 as a modern-day eugenicist measure.[152] Roberts asserts that "at best, Prop 187 . . . deter[s] undocumented immigrants from having children in the U.S. At worst, it . . . lead[s] to a rise in maternal and infant deaths."[153] And, she adds, "modern-day advocates of these anti-immigrant policies may not espouse eugenicist theory, but, like the former eugenicists, they fear 'not only the immigrants themselves, but also their descendants.'"[154]

What I would also call eugenic thinking was prevalent in the media, too. Kent Ono and John Sloop, examining mainstream and "outlaw" media discourses (that is, non-mainstream voices that are too often silenced), show how the targeting of Latin American immigrants—the racial and gendered aspects underscoring Prop 187—were part of a legacy of right-wing policy and rhetoric from the 1980s.[155] Moreover, Otto Santa Ana has demonstrated how mainstream news media discourses that likened undocumented immigrants to animals justified Prop 187, noting that such framing was indicative of a public opinion that dehumanizes immigrant laborers.[156]

Although the Supreme Court barred enforcement of most of Prop 187, the law quickly and profoundly harmed immigrant communities and Latinas/os in California. It "rekindled the vigilante spirit of the old Wild West"[157] for it "implicitly legitimized discrimination against all Latinos and Asians"[158] *and their children*. Some "outlaw" opinions surfaced. For instance former education secretary William Bennett characterized the Prop 187 anti-immigrant sentiment as "poison in a democracy."[159] News media reported on criticism of the law as a racist violation of human rights.[160] But demonizing and denying rights to undocumented immigrant mothers of color and their children were dominant. Mirroring neoliberal capital itself, the hallmark of racism under neoliberalism is flexibility. It might be (and was) argued that the law was simply about money despite unequivocal evidence to the contrary, and despite evidence that immigrants were not fiscal drains but in fact the opposite: immigrants create jobs because of their need for housing, and undocumented labor keeps prices of food and other goods and services low, while immigrant need for consumer goods both creates more jobs and increases demand. Furthermore, immigrants made Los Angeles the busiest customs district in the country, given that immigrants from Asia and Latin America have language skills, cultural sensitivity, and international connections that allow for trade to be conducted with Asian and Latin American nations.[161] And, for his own part, Wilson supported legalization for undocumented workers and authored IRCA's Seasonal Agricultural Worker program when he was U.S. senator. He also personally benefited from undocumented immigrant labor by employing an undocumented Mexican immigrant as maid.[162]

Such seeming contradictions make sense within neoliberalism. As Lisa Cacho writes, "Supporters of 187 requested that mothers give birth in the streets, that people die from curable diseases, and that families go hungry. But they did *not* ask that undocumented workers stop working. They did *not* ask that employers of undocumented workers be reprimanded. . . . This measure was never about deterring workers from immigrating; it was about capitalizing upon the work of immigrants."[163] While the United States has a need for immigrant labor, there is also a long historical precedent of implementing policies that worsen the living conditions of immigrants along racial lines and that function as a form of labor and social discipline. Like earlier versions of labor and social control, the neoliberal form mitigates racial anxieties and allows for ongoing labor exploitation, though now in an ostensibly multicultural, feminist into "postfeminist" democratic society.

What is most disturbing is that despite protests, widespread allegations of racism, and evidence disproving immigrant mothers' welfare abuse, attempts to save money by managing Latin American immigrant's reproduction soon gained *federal* backing when Clinton signed the Personal Responsibility and Work Opportunity Reconciliation Act (PRWORA) in 1996, at which point eugenicist thinking was federally reframed to complement the U.S. neoliberal project. The so-called Personal Responsibility Act severely limited access to public benefits for documented immigrants, unwed teenage mothers, and children born to mothers on welfare, and it replaced AFDC with Temporary Assistance to Needy Families (TANF). TANF gave states control of most welfare determination and administration, limited lifetime receipt of welfare to five years, and required most adult recipients to work after two years.[164] Family caps, illegitimacy bonuses, and sterilization incentives for the poor and abstinence education were included. The family cap denied additional benefits for the children of women already on welfare[165] and the "illegitimacy bonus" provided $20 to $25 billion per year for three years to the five states that lowered non-marital birthrates the most without increasing abortion rates above 1995 levels. Congress also provided $250 million for states with "abstinence only" programs in public schools.[166]

Family cap legislation, which relies on economic disincentives to discourage women who are framed as "profit-maximizers" from having more children, is, as political theorist Anna Marie Smith observes, "precisely tailored to punish the welfare mother when she gives birth," and "it is indifferent on virtually every other aspect of her sexual practices and intimate behavior."[167] It is not about intervention and rehabilitation, as proponents averred; it is about discipline, and it is a eugenicist measure. TANF does more than pressure poor single mothers to become low-wage workers; "it also presses them to become *childless* workers"[168] via workfare, paternity requirements, family caps, abstinence education, family planning, and incentives to give up children for adoption. Childless workers are more efficient given their increased availability for shift work, overtime, work in toxic or dangerous environments, and relocation.[169]

Kathalene Razzano argues that paternity testing mandated under PRWORA is a new form of controlling women; the question underscoring the search for paternity is "Will women be dependent on the state or on the father?" rather than "What is best for the child?" or woman, for that matter. Women and children might receive needed financial support, but either way women are constituted as dependent, and women's sexual behavior is surveilled and regulated by the state.[170] And while easily moralized, such "family values," from the perspective of the state, are about finding the father to return money to welfare.[171]

Additionally, PRWORA banned state and local governments from providing all services except for emergency care to undocumented immigrants, including prenatal care. Half of the $54 billion savings PRWORA accrued came from the continued restriction of aid to undocumented immigrants, as well as from restrictions on food stamps and supplemental security income (SSI) for documented immigrants.[172] This marked the "first time in U.S history that [federal] government benefits were denied to naturalized citizens because they were not born in the U.S., thus establishing a two-tiered or segmented structure for citizenship."[173]

PRWORA was passed after congressional debates that marked a shift to Republican control of the House and the ascendance of Newt Gingrich. This too points to the overlap of economic and identity-based concerns. *Time* magazine observed in 1994 that "House Republicans have come roaring into Washington promising not just to remake welfare but to pull down the whole edifice of federal poverty programs."[174] And they did, though it was not necessary. In the 1990s, the economy was in decent shape in terms of inflation rates, growth rates, and unemployment rates, but conservatives tapped into and exploited middle-class fears of economic instability by claiming that welfare recipients beleaguered the nation-state. Some of the Democrats' more liberal reform proposals, such as Clinton's plan to provide employment to welfare recipients after aid termination, were rejected.

Simultaneously, alarm over immigration did not abate. In 1996, conservatives criticized Democrats and Clinton for being too lenient with immigration and welfare. They pushed for a federal Prop 187, although just a year later the National Research Council (NRC) found that immigrants' socioeconomic status usually rose and that immigration led to net economic *gains* for the U.S. population as a whole.[175] In addition to the cuts PRWORA enacted, Republicans' initial immigration proposal included denying automatic citizenship to the U.S.-born children of undocumented immigrants.[176] That did not pass but the other restrictions for both legal and illegal immigrants and citizens did. In the tradition of Reagan, the affable Clinton declared in his 1996 State of the Union address that "the era of big government is over,"[177] and in the same year, just before the election, Clinton signed PRWORA.

PRWORA, like Prop 187, epitomizes the ways welfare restriction, immigration restriction, and eugenicist thinking constelled gender and race in service of neoliberal accumulation. "In a society in which people of color are massively overrepresented among the poor, welfare reform sexual regulation is essentially targeting those Americans who were once openly designated by . . . the eugenicists as the 'unfit.'"[178] Reagan's "welfare queen" was invoked in the 1990s to legitimize not only welfare cuts but also moves to reduce black women's fertility,[179] and as noted, half of PRWORA savings came from restricting aid to undocumented immigrants, who were disproportionately Mexican and Latin American. Roberts asserts that in this period, "conservatives today, as during the eugenics movement, propose policies to limit immigrants' reproduction in tandem with policies designed to discourage dispossessed, predominantly minority citizens from having children."[180] The legacy of forced and coerced sterilization and abstinence that eugenicists relied on at the turn of the twentieth century, which morphed into family planning and population control after World War II, were the precursors to these policies. In short, a modern rearticulation of eugenics via matriphobic racialization was part of cost-cutting initiatives that not only Reagan and George H. W. Bush, but also *both* Clintons advocated.

Then-First Lady Hilary Rodham Clinton's support for PRWORA exemplifies another, more mature iteration of neoliberal feminism (along with the "world of our mothers" and "model minority" iterations). Angela McRobbie describes the neoliberal "disarticulation of feminism" in British culture, in which feminism has been reshaped into an individualistic discourse that reestablishes traditional ideas about women and as such combats the formation of a new women's movement. Women must consent to this individualistic, traditionalist discourse about gender in order for the discourse to reproduce itself.[181] The supplanting of collective political engagement with discourses of individual empowerment that reestablish traditional ideas about women is linked to postfeminism, and such postfeminism and "neoliberal feminism," which have different iterations but essentially the same end—more inequality and violence for most women and especially women of color, under the auspices of individual freedoms—persist today.[182] In the United States, the mainstream "neoliberal feminist" position embraces "family values"; in supporting critiques of welfare by pundits as (supposedly) varied as Newt Gingrich and Bill Clinton, Hilary Clinton and other neoliberal feminists advocated sexual conservatism, monogamy, and personal responsibility. In viewing PRWORA as "a historic opportunity to change a system oriented toward dependence to one that encouraged independence,"[183] she reframed this draconian, eugenicist law as empowering for women, giving them choices and options. Economic independence rather than women's rights—human rights—motivated support for PRWORA within a neoliberal system that equates dependence with a lack of morality and frames economic independence at whatever cost (pun intended) as liberation. Race is effectively and emphatically erased, even among liberals, as is any true sexual equality and any connection to actual feminist efforts for social justice.

And within American pop culture, eugenicist theories that attacked black women and Latin American immigrants propelled two nonfiction books onto the bestseller list. *The Bell Curve* (1994), underwritten by the Pioneer Fund, argued that the government should eliminate welfare policies that allegedly encouraged poor women to have babies because hereditarily low IQs doom the poor; welfare leads to dysgenesis, the reproduction of the genetically inferior, which is race suicide.[184] The following year, Peter Brimelow argued in his best-seller, *Alien Nation: Common Sense about America's Immigration Disaster*, that "great waves" of fecund poor and working-class non-white immigrants were invading the nation and destroying its culture, economy, and complexion, especially with their dearth of "family values"—a point brought home by his assertion that groups such as Mexican Americans have out-of-wedlock births at twice the rate of whites.[185]

Themes of alien invasion and impregnation, which paralleled Brimelow's concerns, proliferated in news media, film, and television, casting Mexicans as especially unwilling or incapable of integrating and thereby returning to the *reconquista* narrative that figured Mexicans as an invading force intent on reclaiming formerly Mexican territory in the U.S. Southwest.[186] A 1985 *U.S. News and World Report* cover story, "The Disappearing Border: Will the Mexican Migration Create a New Nation?" points to the prevalence of the *reconquista* narrative in U.S. culture at large. The television show *Alien Nation* (1989–1990), which was first a film in 1988, depicted outer space alien slave "newcomers" created and bred for difficult menial labor. Mirroring Mexican immigration patterns, the aliens live in an L.A. barrio, and although their labor is wanted, their full participation in society is problematic; they struggle to assimilate. This show, the popular *Alien* film series that featured terrifying images of outer space alien impregnation, and *Independence Day* (1996), which dramatizes a hostile alien invasion of earth, show how "immigration and invasion, in a paranoid register, became synonyms."[187] The cover of the April 9, 1990, issue of *Time* ran with the headline "What Will the U.S. Be Like When Whites Are No Longer the Majority?" accompanied by a reconfigured American flag: black, brown, and yellow stripes replaced the white stripes. In the article "Beyond the Melting Pot," writer William Henry stressed that white Americans would soon be a minority because of immigration and high birth rates. Fretting about the difficulty of governing a "truly multiracial society,"[188] he fostered alarm that resonated with eugenicist thinking.

Although the evocation of Darwinian biological determinism in the *Bell Curve* was much criticized,[189] and although scholars and activists denounced Brimelow's racist xenophobia,[190] the eugenicist logic that complemented and served neoliberal projects successfully registered in the PRWORA. The best-seller list, the popularity of alien-themed TV shows and films, and the preponderance of popular news media articles that circulated the *reconquista* thesis indicate that a good-sized chunk of the American public bought it (pun intended). It also has a legacy in contemporary California.[191]

Conclusion

Early in the 2012 presidential race, the "welfare queen" reappeared to support privatization and social service cuts. The message remained much the same as in the 1980s—people of color were abusing the welfare state—and the theme was reiterated clearly in attacks on then-reelection candidate Barack Obama from the three leading Republican candidates, Newt Gingrich, Mitt Romney, and Rick Santorum. Gingrich christened Obama the "food stamp president," Santorum said while campaigning in Iowa, "I don't want to make black people's lives better by giving them somebody else's money," and Romney said repeatedly that under Obama, "America is moving towards an 'entitlement society.'"[192]

The prototype for the demonization of welfare recipients (and for the casting of the first black president, who in many ways forged on with the U.S. neoliberal project in the tradition of his predecessors, as the champion of welfare recipients who were explicitly assumed to be black) was delineated in Reagan-era anti-welfare rhetoric, of which immigration was a critical part. Welfare cuts and discourses about the costs of a lack of "family values," fecundity, and "anchor babies" channeled mostly Latin American and Asian immigrant women into low wage employment. Though not as dominant in public discourse, "model minority" and romanticized, self-sufficient white ethnic immigrant mothers who appeared mostly in popular culture, helped to rationalize and prop up allegedly race-neutral discourses of "family values" and cost-cutting policies that engendered the impoverishment and minoritization of Latin American immigrant women and especially undocumented mothers. These discourses and policies functioned eugenically by inhibiting immigrants' family formation and ability to care for their children. In the 1990s and 2000s, this pattern was echoed and amplified, turning women and children in need into denizens regardless of citizenship status. Gendered, racialized Reagan-era immigration discourses helped to inaugurate the neoliberal erosion of the welfare state and are thus crucial to feminist welfare analysis.

4

Inaugurating Neoliberal Crimmigration

The single "Illegal Alien," from popular British rock band Genesis's eponymously titled 1983 album,[1] satirized the struggles of undocumented immigrants in the United States, as suggested by its chorus, "It's no fun / Being an illegal alien." The song has, however, been criticized and rarely played on radio because it—and the video—explicitly capitalizes on nearly every extant racist, sexist stereotype of Mexican criminality.[2] The lyrics, delivered by white vocalist Phil Collins in a Mexican accent, describe Mexican laziness, drinking (tequila, of course), smoking, use of illegal economies for documentation, and sordid women. In the video, set in a barrio in Mexico, Collins and his white bandmates are coded as Mexican, with black wigs, large moustaches, oversized sombreros, and serapes; they drink, oversleep, play Mariachi music, fight at the passport office, and commit crimes such as passport fraud.

In the final stanza, the speaker appeals directly to "nation of immigrants" ideology, though his plea for compassion for a striving immigrant is delegitimized by his criminal tendencies:

> Consideration for your fellow man
> Would not hurt anybody, it sure fits in with my plan
> Over the border, there lies the promised land
> Where everything comes easy, you just hold out your hand
> Keep your suspicions, I've seen that look before
> But I ain't done nothing wrong now, is that such a surprise
> But I've got a sister who'd be willing to oblige
> She will do anything now to help me get to the outside

There is the promise of crime if this immigrant makes it into the promised land. His assumption that America will take care of him is a proxy for nativist fears that the undocumented exploit the welfare system, and the couplet about exchanging his sister's sexual favors for passage over the border proved so controversial that it was edited out of the song.[3] Collins's Mexican is obviously the wrong kind of immigrant for the "nation of immigrants."

"Illegal Alien" emblematizes the trap that neoliberalism creates with the racialized, gendered criminalization of immigrants—a trap that, I argue, was first set in the 1980s and continues to increase in size, scope, and severity. The stakes in the song are far higher than offensive stereotypes. The song baldly dramatizes what Lisa Cacho calls a "de facto status crime," meaning that being of color and connected to a certain space makes one a criminal regardless of whether or not one has committed a criminal act. Under neoliberalism, race and racialized spaces make certain actions legible as crimes, so a person's status is itself the offense, and includes an assumption of future illegal activity.[4] Mexicans occupy a de facto "illegal" status; even the term "alien" connotes non-human status since it is usually used for beings from outer space.[5] In terms of incorporation of undocumented immigrants into the American polity, only exceptions can be made, like IRCA amnesty for undocumented immigrants who met specific criteria, but as with the DREAM Act, the fundamental problem of immigration law, the creation of rightless status, remains.[6] This rightless status, which materialized in law and was rationalized in news media and pop culture, arises from affixing race, gender, space, and so on, to devalued categories such as "criminal" and "alien," which in turn justify why a person or group is the target of state violence, disenfranchisement, and abandonment.

Steve Martinot asserts that in the post–civil rights era, "Generalization, racialization, and criminalization are interwoven and inseparable in an endless reconstruction of whiteness and white supremacy," and these processes shape class divisions, as well.[7] In the 1980s and 1990s, Latin American immigrants and particularly Mexicans were portrayed and persecuted as quintessential illegal aliens and immigrant criminals along gendered lines. While neoliberal projects are often characterized by a "hands-off" approach to governance as well as the market, the neoconservative policing of the personal lives of citizens and utilization of government funds for security were incorporated into neoliberal advancement because criminalization creates and justifies ongoing racial stratification, which is profitable. Cultural Studies scholars from Stuart Hall until the present have reflected upon the power of the law alongside and in conjunction with what is more often considered "culture" to enforce and create ideology and thus social norms through the production and punishment of the "deviant." Producing and punishing the "deviant" is also connected to capital, in the form of property that an individual or group or corporation owns: "crisis in relation to the law is always a crisis about the law as a site of hegemonic struggle, where contending hegemonic blocs fight over the definition of what should be right and what should be wrong, and, one might add, of what should be property and what should be crime."[8]

This chapter interrogates discourses of immigrant criminality that took shape in the 1980s in accordance with neoliberalization. Legal scholar Teresa

Miller argues that "immigration control is increasingly adopting the practices and priorities of the criminal justice system"[9] in a process that scholars refer to as "crimmigration."[10] As I will show, as the Reagan administration created and reproduced the inevitably "criminal" Latin American immigrant (and "criminal" Latina/o) through militarization of the U.S.-Mexico border and evermore punitive law and procedures, racially disparate representations of immigrant crime in popular culture affirmed that certain immigrant bodies were more "criminal" than others, even when committing the same acts. This chapter focuses on how adherence to or deviation from gender norms made the racialized immigrant criminal legible for neoliberalism.

The Invention of the Illegal Alien

While the term "illegal alien" was not used until the 1970s and has since then been coded as Mexican, what Claudia Sadowski-Smith calls a "spiral of illegality"[11] began in the nineteenth century; by differentially racializing each new non-elite immigrant group, restrictive immigration laws functioned as labor discipline. Systems of indenture, once common among immigrants, were criticized at a time when Africans were preferred for slavery[12] and against the backdrop of national democratic ideology that fetishized the freedom of non-slaves to work for wages. Because inexpensive immigrant labor served and supported national expansion, law attempted to conceal the similarities between unskilled migrant labor and slavery by inventing immigrant illegality, as in the first federal immigration law, the 1819 Steerage Act. This act limited incoming ship passengers in order to curtail the entrance of impoverished European immigrants, who usually came through unskilled labor migration networks.[13]

The first federal immigration law to explicitly convey concerns about women's sexual morality, the 1875 Page Law, banned convicts, involuntary Chinese migrant laborers, and Chinese women suspected of prostitution. The 1882 Chinese Exclusion Act barred the entry of Chinese laborers, allegedly out of concern for civic order, though with the Transcontinental Railway nearing completion, they were threatening to native laborers in the post–Civil War economy.[14] Naturalization for all Chinese was prohibited, and Chinese immigrants used false documentation to claim exempt status, becoming "paper sons" or "paper daughters."[15] Chinese immigrants thereby developed a "criminal" system *in response to restrictive legislation*. At Angel Island, the West Coast processing and detainment facility for Asians from 1910 to 1940, immigrants were subjected to invasive and humiliating medical and psychological exams and imprisonment. This "powerfully influenced Americans' perceptions of Chinese Americans as permanent foreigners,"[16] making the Chinese precursors to Mexicans in terms of the archetype of the illegal alien.

Although they were not excluded from naturalization, restrictive immigration laws also criminalized white Europeans, the most prevalent immigrant labor pool following Chinese restriction. The 1882 Immigration Act established a head tax on all entering through seaports and deemed excludable immigrants "likely to become a public charge" (LPC). Diseases, felony convictions, or crimes involving moral turpitude, polygamy, or the failure to pay for one's own ticket were grounds for exclusion or deportation. The LPC laws also targeted immigrant women specifically. At the moment when suffragettes were challenging assumptions about women's dependence and disenfranchisement, women who attempted to immigrate without connection to a male provider were penalized. Under the moral turpitude clause, pre- and/or extramarital sex and suspicion of prostitution were grounds for women's exclusion, whereas adulterous and bigamous men and men who visited sex workers were "rarely, if ever, subject to deportation on grounds of moral turpitude."[17] The first federal immigration agency, the Bureau of Immigration, formed in 1891,[18] fixated on regulating prostitution among European immigrant women, yet prostitution among Mexican immigrant women was ignored: sexually satisfied migrant male Mexican laborers would presumably not need to bring wives and families across the border to settle. European immigrant women, "viewed as future citizens,"[19] were treated more harshly.

These nineteenth-century laws (and the 1885 Anti-Alien Contract Labor Law that outlawed the use of foreign contract labor), which were passed before Mexicans were considered immigrants, created immigrant illegality in accordance with labor needs. Thus like the category "citizen," which implicates gender even when it is invisible,[20] the category "illegal" implicated gender, race, and capital from the moment of its invention.

Making Illegality Mexican

Casting Mexicans as threats to law and order has been profitable since the U.S.-Mexican War. Under the terms of the Treaty of Guadalupe Hidalgo (1848), the United States annexed Mexican territory in parts of what are now the states of California and Texas, and granted Mexicans citizenship even though they did not appear to be white. The treaty also overrode the 1790 "free white persons" law that made white racial status a requirement for citizenship. This dissonance between racial appearance and racialized citizenship rights exemplifies the legal creation of racial status in accordance with politics rather than innate biological difference; race was no more "natural" than national borders. Therefore, to secure this new political land border and the minoritization of Mexican-origin citizens, Mexicans were discursively cast as a "degraded race" of "mixed blood" because of their indigenous, European, and African ancestry.[21] By the late nineteenth century, as Laura Ann Stoler notes, "Technologies of sex were most fully mobilized around issues of race with the pseudo-scientific theory of degeneracy at their core. . . . The theory of degeneracy secured the relationship between racism and sexuality."[22] Policing and criminalization helped to secure that relationship between racism and sexuality. To protect settlers' interests in the Gold Rush, settlers uprooted Mexicans,[23] and the federal government exercised gendered force,[24] as in the case of the Texas Rangers, who lynched and slaughtered Mexicans and Chicanas/os[25] and raped and abused women.[26] Likewise, laws such as California's anti-vagrancy Greaser Act (1855) allowed police and local militias to terrorize Mexicans, confiscate their property, and lynch with impunity any suspected vagabond, or "a person identified by the term 'Greaser' and, generally, all people of Spanish or Indian blood." (The derogatory term, applied to Mexicans by U.S. troops during the Mexican–American War, referred to men who greased mule cart axels, a lowly occupation typically held by Mexicans.)[27]

The gender politics underscoring this "border panic"—which David Magill defines as spatial, racial, and psychic strategies that assuage fears engendered by the permeability of a border that is only political[28]—were likewise transparent in film, as Latina/o Media Studies scholars have documented.[29] In silent film, stereotypes of the Mexican dark lady/seductress, the bandito/greaser, and the buffoon prevailed. Rosa Linda Fregoso has shown how Mexican women were depicted as degenerate and sexually threatening subjects through "exotic costuming, flamboyant gestures, and immoral behavior," as in *Red Girl* (1908), in which a "Mexican Jezebel" (as she is called in the film's intertitles) steals a white woman's gold and the husband of the American Indian woman who helped her hide from the white woman.[30] The Mexican woman's sexuality is cast as aberrant and depraved in its disrespect for the marital bond and racial boundaries; she is the enemy of *all* women, whites' property, and law and order.

In *Impossible Subjects: Illegal Aliens and the Making of Modern America*, Mae Ngai argues that immigration legislation between 1924 and 1965 cast Asians and Mexicans as permanently foreign and "alien" even when they were U.S.-born and possessed formal citizenship, in order to secure an economical and dispensable labor force.[31] According to Ngai, the 1924 Johnson-Reed Act, in making undocumented immigration a federal crime, created illegal aliens who were "impossible subjects" because "inclusion in the nation was at once a social reality and a legal impossibility."[32] Many immigrants who were already in the United States were therefore suddenly rendered "illegal" (that is, the law turned them into criminals), and many immigrants had to break the new federal law in order to enter the nation at all (especially given new restrictions under Johnson-Reed, such as the establishment of nation-based quotas that were meant to minimize the immigration of eastern and southern Europeans). However, the illegal alien and alien citizen were created with the first restrictive immigration laws and the criminalization of Mexicans, which date back to the U.S.–Mexican War. The creation of "impossible subjects" was bolstered by the 1924 law, and this was a gendered process.

The Border Patrol, formed under the Johnson–Reed Act, was a compromise between eugenicist and southwestern agricultural interests (the former wanted to ban Mexican immigration; the latter wanted Mexicans for cheap seasonal labor[33]), which guaranteed the existence of Mexican "impossible subjects." The first officers were white men and one Mexican American. Although the agency was charged with enforcing civil rather than criminal law, officers carried firearms, often emulated the Texas Rangers, and focused on criminal pursuit and apprehension.[34] Such violence seemed logical when criminologists argued that Mexicans were predisposed to crime, as did "experts" at a 1924 crime symposium, where they used spurious intelligence test scores to assert that Mexican criminality was the result of defective heredity.[35]

During the Great Depression, over 400,000 Mexicans, irrespective of citizenship status, were repatriated, another instance of targeting immigrants in times of economic downturn.[36] Sixty percent were children or native citizens by birth, and relief workers often pressured citizens to return to Mexico.[37] Repatriations were motivated by fears of labor competition and beliefs that Mexican women were excessively reproducing at public expense.[38] Yet during the Great Depression, while much of the country used social welfare programs, Mexican women who remained in the United States did not; fearing visibility, they picked crops and did odd jobs to make ends meet.[39]

When the Immigration and Naturalization Sercice (INS) was established in 1933 as a single organization, the model of patrolman as a cowboy/ranger was supplanted by an ideal of patriarchal benevolence, which was underscored by eugenicist efforts to control immigration to "guarantee the proper racial boundaries of the nation and the intactness of the white American family."[40] According to INS commissioner I. F. Wixon, if an alien (presumed to be male) entered, married, and had children and was then apprehended and deported, he would be abandoning his family, who would then need public benefits to survive.[41] With this logic (like "family values" logic), undocumented immigrants violated both the law and gendered moral and economic rules, and it was the state's role to punish transgressors.

Although exempt from numerical quotas like white ethnic immigrants and not racially excluded from citizenship like Asians, Mexicans were marginalized until immigration laws restricting their entry were passed. Meanwhile, Asian immigration followed a different trajectory. As discussed earlier, Chinese exclusion was repealed in 1943, and the 1952 McCarran-Walter Act removed all formal racial barriers from immigration law. As Communism became U.S. public enemy number one, Asian immigrants became the "model minority," and white ethnics were becoming the ideal immigrants. The ongoing criminalization of Mexicans was accomplished comparatively, by and for the sake of ongoing labor importation.

Importing Colonialism Is Importing Criminals

Even as Mexicans were criminalized, their labor was desirable in particular contexts. Hence, the competing and equally prevalent narratives of Mexicans as criminals and as pliant laborers persisted.[42] The concurrent construction of the bracero, or legal temporary Mexican laborer, and the "wetback," or illegal Mexican laborer, perhaps best illustrates how the gendered, racialized criminalization of Mexicans mitigated social and economic tensions generated by transnational labor flows. The simultaneous construction of the bracero and wetback also set the stage for the conflation of Latinas/os and "illegal aliens," which became ubiquitous in the 1970s and 1980s and included processes of gendered racialization on the congressional floor, in policing, and in media; Latin American immigrants and Latinas/os were folded into the "illegal alien" in an enduring way. The Bracero Program (1942–1964), a wartime contract labor program for Mexican men, was the prototype for neoliberal Mexican labor importation. It was terminated in response to pressure from organized labor and the prevalence of civil rights discourse: contract labor came to be commonly perceived as a form of what Ngai calls "imported colonialism"; that is, laborers of color were brought into the United States and denied the protections and privileges of citizenship, like colonial subjects displaced by a colonizing nation's domination of the resources, labor, and market of a colonized territory.

The political and cultural economies of the U.S. West and Southwest practiced imported colonialism by creating a migratory agricultural proletariat of Mexicans who were outside of the polity,[43] by exploiting workers, and by expelling them when they were no longer needed, as when the demand for foreign labor declined after the Korean War or through repatriation under Operation Wetback.[44] Ideologically, colonialism is based on ethnocentric patriarchal beliefs that colonizers are superior to the colonized. This logic characterized the Bracero Program but criminalization rather than flagrant legal racism or religion resolved ethical or political contradictions. Employers often resorted to illegal means to secure the cheapest labor, so the Bracero Program had the effect of producing the "wetback," or undocumented worker, who was by definition criminal, and consequently deserved poor treatment, marginalization, and violence.

As explored in the last chapter, matriphobic racialization that became prevalent in the 1970s and 1980s also collapsed Latinas and "illegal aliens," and this followed from the concurrent construction of the bracero and wetback. Women in Mexico upheld domestic responsibilities and did the work of migrating male family members. Women were also present at recruitment centers and labor camps as vendors, domestic workers, and sex workers. Female "wetbacks" were considered sexual threats: in the 1940s when Mexican settlement became more common, Mexicana sex work became a concern. Alicia Schmidt Camacho shows that the "wetback" stereotype, which included "destitute females from Mexico [who] cross the line for purposes of prostitution"[45] and conveniently erased the wives and female partners of undocumented laborers who often worked as domestics,[46] reified Mexican women as shamefully and of course illegally sexual, making it easy to devalue their labor, and their humanness.

In American culture at large, the World War II–era criminalization of Mexican-origin men supported state-sanctioned violence toward people of Latin American descent, again regardless of their citizenship status. This can be seen in the Sleepy Lagoon trial and the Zoot Suit Riots. When the body of José Gallardo Diaz was discovered in Sleepy Lagoon, California in 1942, the cause of death was unclear, and there was little evidence about the situation. In a climate in which experts continued to claim that Mexican men were predisposed to criminality because of their mixed race status[47] and the stereotype of illegality always already characterized men of Latin American origins as criminals, the police quickly arrested seventeen Mexican American male youths believed to be *pachucos*—male Mexican American youth who dressed flamboyantly, often in zoot suits, and were affiliated with street gangs—and held them without bail. The zoot suit—high-waisted, wide-legged, tight-cuffed, pegged trousers, worn with a longer coat with wide lapels and wide padded shoulders—was popular among black and Mexican American urban youth in the 1930s and 1940s and considered a signifier of minority gang culture and violence.[48] Mainstream newspaper coverage of the trial condemned the youths, though eventually in response to activism, papers such as the *Los Angeles Daily News* carried more sympathetic stories.[49] When the trial ended in January 1943, nine youths were convicted of second-degree murder, and the rest were convicted of lesser offenses.[50] Another striking instance of state-sanctioned violence against Mexican-origin men, which was justified by the assumption of their criminality, occurred four months later, when the Zoot Suit Riots began. After white servicemen in Los Angeles, primarily sailors, sought out and attacked Latinos in zoot suits, riots between whites and Latinas/os persisted for a week, ending with relative impunity for the servicemen involved, whereas hundreds of Latinas/os were arrested and charged. On the heels of these LA riots, race riots between whites and people of color proliferated nationally.[51] The racial tensions underscoring the Sleepy Lagoon trial and the riots are indicative of the larger national issue of state-sanctioned racism in the context of World War II, which is beyond the scope of this analysis. Suffice it to say that the Sleepy Lagoon case and the Zoot Suit Riots exposed that state-sanctioned racism, and in response to activism on behalf of the Sleepy Lagoon youths,[52] they were released on appeal in 1944. Additionally, the popularity of overtly racialized eugenics soon waned (Chapter 3). But the gendered criminalization of Latin American immigrants and Latinas/os continued.

Zoot Suit, the 1981 filmic adaptation of the Broadway musical of the same name, written and directed by Mexican American Luis Valdez, critiques Latino criminalization. Henry Reyna (Daniel Valdez), inspired by Sleepy Lagoon defendant Hank Leyvas, is arrested along with other *pachuco* gangsters for a murder they did not commit. Narrator El Pachuco (Edward James Olmos), an idealized Zoot Suiter who serves as Henry's conscience, raises ethical questions about racism, crime, and state-sanctioned violence, inviting spectators to raise such questions too. The film comments on racist criminalization at a moment when Latin American immigration was growing and Mexican undocumented immigration was the hot topic in immigration polemics, and implores spectators to be discerning.

Neoliberalizing Imported Colonialism

With IRCA amnesty, a new program for temporary labor importation could be and was dressed up as an example of Reaganite "nation of immigrants" exceptional inclusivity. Yet more thoroughly institutionalized criminalization of immigrants accompanied this iteration of imported colonialism, making it characteristically neoliberal. According to Paul Smith and Lisa Frank, "By definition and design, crises are opportunities to rework ideological and cultural alignments; crises command public attention (public attention is commanded) precisely because they are the events by and which relevant publics will (or will not) be reconstituted."[53] With an economic depression and widespread unemployment in the 1970s, the term "illegal alien" became affixed to Mexicans. It made Mexicans de facto criminals even though it was policy such as the cessation of the Bracero Program, new international trade laws, and new Western Hemisphere immigration quotas passed in 1965 that created undocumented migration from Latin America and cast Mexicans as the quintessential illegal aliens.

Part of neoliberal restructuring is an increasing militarism and securitization at national borders as they become more permeable with transnational flows of capital and labor. Blending the neoconservative penchant for protecting U.S. political and economic interests with border security and the unilateral use of military power with international free trade and transnational labor—a set of practices and policies that will, the story goes, engender democratic returns for all—began under the Reagan administration as did its complement, neoliberal crimmigration. IRCA picked up the issues raised by the specter of an "immigration emergency" to combine recruitment of Mexican labor with increased border security and punitive immigration regulation. The new provisions, which made immigrant laborers evermore vulnerable to exploitation and abuse, required gendered and racialized ways of knowing that reflected the new transnational nature of capital. Pragmatically, punitive measures for immigration-related offenses mitigated objections to amnesty. Along with restriction of immigrant access to welfare, employer sanctions and beefed-up border security appeased organized labor, nativists and, importantly, Reagan's conservative supporters who wanted to "get tough" on crime.

The expansion of the prison system—the logical correlation to "getting tough" on crime—paralleled and overlapped with increasingly harsh immigration law. Media panic over another racialized and gendered crisis, gang violence, was prevalent, and the nation undertook a "War on Drugs" in 1982. Nancy Reagan began the memorable "Just Say No" campaign, urging Americans to simply abstain from drugs, and the Reagans declared a national drug epidemic, presenting international intervention, stricter criminal penalties, and increased incarceration as the cure. In fact, Reagan historian Michael Shaller postulated that "narcoterrorism" replaced Communism as public enemy number one.[54] Reagan approved a 1986 National Security Council directive framing drug trafficking as a threat to the entire Western Hemisphere and fingered Communist governments in Cuba and Nicaragua as the cause of the surge in cocaine trafficking and usage in the United States. These factors explained increased government spending on policing and military intervention south of the border. Under the direction of William French Smith, the Justice Department brought the FBI into the "War on Drugs," and Reagan bolstered the Drug Enforcement Agency (DEA), adding five hundred agents and establishing thirteen regional antidrug task forces that lead to more drug seizures and convictions.[55]

Reaganite backlash against the civil rights movement and feminism cohered around crack cocaine, the domestic centerpiece of the War on Drugs. As Michelle Alexander has shown, with changes in the criminal justice system that began with the War on Drugs, a new racial caste system of mass incarceration that permanently disenfranchised people of color and especially blacks was established. She chronicles how this "new Jim Crow" system was connected to Reagan's racially coded "welfare queen," who stood in for "undeserving" people of color who failed to take personal responsibility for themselves. Although at the time of the War on Drugs, under 2 percent of Americans viewed drugs as the most important issue, "by waging a war on drug users and dealers, Reagan made good on his promise to crack down on the racially defined 'others'—the undeserving."[56] The panic over crack use in inner-city neighborhoods actually preceded crack hitting the streets in 1985 in communities already devastated by deindustrialization and skyrocketing unemployment;[57] crack cocaine was mostly sold and used in black inner-city neighborhoods and approximately half its users were women. When news stories about crack babies began to proliferate in the 1980s, crack mothers were new ammunition for pathologizing black families and especially black women. In thirty states from 1985 to 1995, about two hundred mostly black women were charged with maternal drug use.[58]

Development of the prison-industrial complex was synonymous with the increased incarceration of black men. In 1950, blacks were incarcerated at a ratio of 4 to 1 in comparison to whites; by 1960, 5 to 1; by 1970, 6 to 1; by 1980, 7 to 1.[59] Further, a 2002 study from the Justice Policy Institute found that from 1980 to 2000, the number of black men in prison or jail increased three times as fast as the number of black men in colleges and universities.[60] A rise in gendered and sexualized violence was part and parcel of this process, surfacing in news media with ever-increasing representations of black male violence. This also charted with the figure of the black gangster in rap music and hip hop,[61] and in 1980s and 1990s crime TV shows and films, a disproportionate number of criminals are black men. "Getting tough" on crime was a racialized, gendered project, and one with lasting and far-reaching implications. When Reagan left office, annual spending by federal, state, and local authorities to fight the "War on Drugs" was $15 billion.[62] Today mass incarceration—and its new racial caste system—is a vast industry.[63]

Drugs were a point at which the immigration crisis and crime/gang violence crisis overlapped, particularly in relation to drug smuggling at the Mexican border and drug sales and use in inner-city communities inhabited by immigrants of color, Latinas/os, and blacks. Populations of color were blamed for crime and considered the reason for punitive laws, without discussion of how or why law itself and other policies might have created a crisis—or "criminals"—in the first place. Additionally, in 1983 Reagan established the President's Commission on Organized Crime, which held hearings in 1984 on Chinese, Japanese, and Vietnamese gangs, pegged as emerging organized crime groups. A 1986 hearing held just months before IRCA passed focused on Asian gangs, and Congress began to think of immigration law as a way to make it more difficult for criminals to become citizens.[64]

But it was Latin American immigrants who were the main objects of this thread of the immigration crisis, and as Genesis's "Illegal Alien" shows all too well, Mexicans were the immigrants that lawmakers and mainstream culture-makers had in mind. In 1986, the INS publicized information about a dramatic increase in Mexican illegal entry that was associated with Mexico's declining economy and blamed for an amplification of crime, drugs, and terrorism.[65] Spurious evidence of Mexican culpability was not hard to come by: the Los Angeles County Board of Supervisors asked Reagan to send more troops to the border because of drug-related crime that was ostensibly traceable to illegal aliens,[66] and in 1986, two *Time* articles blamed crime on undocumented immigrants and framed the problem as a battle between good (American) and evil (Mexican) forces.[67]

Border films such as *Touch of Evil* (1958) emphasized Mexican criminal tendencies by portraying the border as an abject space where violence is naturalized.[68] In the 1980s border films neoliberalized the stereotype of Mexican criminality with stereotypes of "*narcotraficantes*/drug dealers, criminals, bandits, gang members, and undocumented workers. Latinas found themselves as prostitutes and *cantineras*."[69] Such films as *The Border* (1982), directed by Tony Richardson,[70] purported to present a more nuanced picture of Mexican undocumented immigration, portraying corruption on both sides of the border. Yet the film rearticulates the long-standing Border Patrol rhetoric of white patriarchal guardianship. Border agent Charlie Smith (Jack Nicholson), who is troubled not so much by his coworkers' drug smuggling as their abduction and smuggling of Mexican babies to white U.S. families, becomes infatuated with a Mexican woman whose baby has been taken and sets out to return (repatriate) her baby to her. While the film suggests that the Mexican woman is better suited to mother her child than a white adoptive couple, thus mitigating the stereotype of the bad Latin American immigrant and Latina mother, the storyline affirms Mexican female dependence on white patriarchal authority and implies that the Mexican baby does not belong in the

United States; heroism, agency, and U.S. citizenship are the exclusive property of a white heterosexual American man.

In films set north of the border, Latinas/os tend to be absent or stereotyped as the help (waiter, maid, bellhop, valet) or as criminal.[71] Clara E. Rodriguez notes that the Hollywood staple of the Latina/o criminal "began with the early bandidos of the silent screen; took voice in the westerns of the subsequent period; moved to urban settings in the 1960s and 1970s with images of juvenile delinquents; and continue[d] in the 1980s and 1990s with gangs, criminals, and drug lords"[72] Following the classic example of Latino criminality in *West Side Story* (1961), films such as *Scarface* (1983), *The Specialist* (1994), *El Mariachi* (1993), *The Mambo Kings* (1992), *American Me* (1992), and *Carlito's Way* (1993) feature drug-dealing and/or drug-using Latino criminals who are often beyond rehabilitation. While many films include Latino drug dealers in incidental roles, Latino drug lords also made frequent appearances in popular 1980s crime drama television shows such as *Miami Vice*, *Hill Street Blues*, *Hunter*, and *Cagney and Lacey*; films with Latino themes such as *La Bamba* (1987), *Stand and Deliver* (1988), *Salsa* (1988), *House of the Spirits* (1993), *I Like It Like That* (1994), *My Family/Mi Familia* (1995), and *A Walk in the Clouds* (1995) have plots including crime, drugs, and violence.[73]

In some films Latinas/os are maligned in contrast to white male upholders of law and order, exemplifying how law and its symbols transform Latinas/os and blacks into de facto status criminals. *Colors*, a crime drama directed by Dennis Hopper that ranked No. 15 in 1988 box office earnings,[74] was described favorably by reviewers as a representation of the "poisonous flowering of gang culture amid ghetto life," which captures a "climate of fear"[75] and the "helplessness of the police."[76] Experienced police officer Bob Hodges (Robert Duvall) and novice Danny McGavin (Sean Penn) fight gang-related crimes in LA barrios, and are obvious Reaganite emblems of law and order and "family values." Loving husband and new father Hodges is levelheaded and compassionate, while the single hotheaded McGavin eventually simmers down to fit the image of a benevolent patriarch. The gang members, all black or Latina/o, are economic and moral aliens. Despite a multiracial police force, a racialized "good" and "bad" binary is striking and made especially clear in the final scenes of the film and dissolution of McGavin's romance with a Latina.

A Latino member of the Blood gang who is high on drugs kills Hodges. The shooting is senseless: the police have just apprehended the Bloods without force but the Latino gangbanger opens fire. The gangbanger, who earlier told a reformed gang member that he had no desire to leave the gang life, is a direct affront—and mortal threat—to the "normal" American values of law-abiding, familial responsibility that Hodges embodies. Moreover, without any real effort and certainly without rehabilitation or incarceration, McGavin becomes the new moral compass of the film after Hodges is murdered. One reviewer stated that the film's "painful, unavoidable implication is that nothing can stop the gang mentality from perpetuating itself."[77] Roger Ebert noted that the gang was presented as a perverted family that, given the lack of a traditional family, cared for members and was willing to die for them, yet "the product of their family is, of course, tragic. Their gang deals in drugs, defends its turf and murders to enforce its authority."[78] This framing is always already racialized: whites who commit crimes tend to be judged individually on the basis of their acts, rather than as representatives of an entire race,[79] and like McGavin, they can change for the better, seemingly with ease. But the black and Latina/o gang members in the film—and often those in real life—are cast as intrinsically corrupt and beyond redemption, in accordance with the new War on Drugs discourse.

Similarly, *Colors* casts Latina sexuality as anomalous, dangerous, and criminal. Along with silent-era films like *Red Girl*, pejorative representations of Latinas can be traced to the common portrayal of Chicanas as sex workers in westerns such as *My Darling Clementine* (1946) and *Death of a Gunfighter* (1946) and as promiscuous in more modern films such as *Grease* (1978), where the "easy" Chicana, Cha Cha (Annette Charles) provides the foil for white "good girl" Sandy (Olivia Newton John). There is also the ostensibly more flattering but no less racist stereotype of the sexy "hot-blooded" Latina "spitfire" embodied by actress Lupe Velez in the 1930s, Carmen Miranda in the 1940s and 1950s, Charo in the 1970s and 1980s, and Rosie Perez in the 1990s.[80]

In *Colors*, the romance between McGavin and Chicana female protagonist Luisa (Cuban actress Maria Conchita Alonso, who incidentally played Vlad's Italian American girlfriend in *Moscow on the Hudson*) links Latinas to unredeemable criminality; they are the support systems, sexual objects, and accomplices of male gangbangers. (A Latina woman is, for instance, the driver in the most violent drive-by shooting in the movie.) Initially Luisa dresses modestly and is associated with maternity and middle-class family life: she cuddles the Hodges's baby and has an "honest" job at a local burger joint. But Luisa breaks up with McGavin because she feels they are from different worlds: she says she is "one of them," a "home girl." When McGavin responds to a drive-by call, he stumbles upon Luisa dressing after a tryst with a gangbanger. Luisa's clothing is revealing and she wears excessive makeup. She repeatedly shouts at the hurt and perplexed McGavin, "This is me too, police man!" Again, in the film, a Latina/o's "true colors" reaffirm the gendered color line, indicating that Latinas/os cannot abide by the same rules and laws as "good" Americans.

The 1981 film *Fort Apache, the Bronx* also perpetuates stereotypes of a Latina/o crime crisis. Set in a mostly Puerto Rican, crime-ridden South Bronx neighborhood that includes bombed-out buildings and literally resembles a war zone, the crime drama, directed by Daniel Petrie, had a respectable domestic gross of $29.2 million.[81] Some critics panned it as over-the-top, and Bronx inhabitants threatened to sue the filmmakers for the negative depiction of their home.[82] For Irish American police officer Murphy (Paul Newman) and Italian American police officer Corelli (Ken Wahl), guarding law and morality is near impossible in the face of black and Latina/o criminality. Although the Puerto Rican barrio in New York formed in response to migration and displacement engendered by U.S. agrarian capitalism following colonization of the island in 1898, the island's industrialization program, and state-sanctioned migration programs,[83] the film characterizes the barrio as a foreign space, with foreign inhabitants. That is conveyed by stressing linguistic difference, since few officers are Latino/a or Spanish-speaking yet many residents are one or both, by residents' violent behavior, and by the nickname of the precinct, Fort Apache, which evokes the criminalization of American Indians during U.S. expansion; the original Fort Apache was a military outpost in the West. These films support and anticipate Norman Denzin's argument, drawn from analysis of representations of blacks, Latinos, and Asians in the "hood movies" of the 1990s, that a "cinema of racial violence" helps to produce a post–civil rights era racial discourse that connects people of color to a culture of violence.[84]

In contrast, the 1987 comedy film *Born in East L.A.*, by Chicano actor Cheech Marin (one half of the famous duo Cheech & Chong, comedic marijuana connoisseurs), tackles the fallacious assumption that all Mexicans are criminals and illegal aliens and is among the "creatively self-determined, full-length narrative features—written, directed, and/or produced by Chicanos" that first had wide distribution in the 1980s.[85] The film was not as popular as the *Godfather* or *Rush Hour* series, both discussed below, or even as popular as *Colors*; it earned a domestic gross of only $17,355,263[86] and it was panned by critics.[87] But it does provide an alternative to the de facto criminalization of Latinas/os and especially Mexican immigrants and Chicana/os. Chicano Rudy (Marin) is mistaken for an undocumented immigrant and is "repatriated" to Mexico. The plot is driven by Rudy's numerous attempts to return home; once, Rudy hides in the camper of an elderly white couple who are returning from a vacation in Mexico and are attempting to smuggle marijuana into the country. This representation disrupts the valorization of whites as law-abiding victims of Mexican crime and presents Rudy as harmless. The message that spectators are encouraged to take away is that not all Latinos are drug smugglers and that Latinos may have legitimate reasons for clandes-tinely crossing the border.

The film is based on the song "Born in East L.A.," a parody of Bruce Springsteen's popular rock song, "Born in the U.S.A.," from Cheech & Chong's 1985 album, *Get Out of My Room*. The original Springsteen song praised working-class struggles but was appropriated by others to indicate that non-white "foreigners" do not belong in the United States,[88] and as noted earlier, Reagan took up the song despite its outright critique of Reaganism. Marin provides an alternative portrayal of the barrio and a powerful critique of rac-ism by showing how male Mexican immigrants and Chicanos are unfairly treated as aliens regardless of their citizenship status.

However, women are reified in the film, and other neoliberal norms remain intact. Rudy's mother is a single business owner, yet she also embodies the *marianismo* stereotype. Rudy's love object, Dolores, an independent El Salva-doran woman who works three waitress jobs so she can support herself when she crosses into the States, is suddenly rendered helpless when Rudy helps her and other undocumented Latin American immigrants cross the border; in the final shots of the film she fearfully clings to Rudy as her American Dream begins. Moreover, in Mexico, Rudy's job teaching male Asian would-be aliens English and how to "blend in" as Latinos after crossing the border—a setup that progressively stresses a commonality of struggle among men of color and highlights the absurdity of racial classification by revealing that race is liter-ally a performance—includes teaching the men how to catcall white, blonde American women. As Angela Davis argues, the elision of gender in antira-cist efforts and the elision of race in feminist efforts perpetuates sexism in the former and racism in the latter,[89] so the film's critique is limited. And Latina/o characters like Rudy, his mother, and his love object are rendered sympathetic because of their hard work and self-sufficiency; as elsewhere, the neoliberal subject of value discourse makes the case for Latina/o worthiness. As a whole these films about Latina/o criminals/criminalization indicate that while representations were sometimes complex, the de facto criminalization of Latinas/os was prevalent and profitable in 1980s pop culture.

Latina/o criminalization was also profitable on the congressional floor, as IRCA gave legal form to fears of Latin American immigrant and Latina/o criminality with new punitive provisions, employer sanctions, and increased border militarization. Employer sanctions were highly controversial, opposed by likely contingents such as Latina/o lobbying groups, liberals, and big busi-nesses that profited from undocumented labor; but yet again, neoliberal cross-ings engendered unusual alliances. Support for sanctions came from nativists and less extreme pundits who wanted to combat undocumented immigration, but sanctions were also framed as democratic and equalizing. Generally proponents argued that penalizing employers who hired undocumented immigrants would curtail undocumented immigration since most immigrants come to the country to work. As early 1981, in the SCIRP final report, Simpson outlined the need for employer sanctions, increased enforcement, and an identification system.[90] Simpson and others stressed that employer sanctions would stop an unfair loophole in immigration law, the Texas Proviso, which made it legal for an employer to hire an undocumented worker, although it was illegal for an undocumented worker to take a job. Pundits claimed it functioned as a "tacit invitation for unauthorized foreign workers to enter the U.S. in order to find jobs."[91] Meanwhile, free market supporters and big businesses picked up the "land of opportunity" piece of the "nation of immigrants" trope while forgetting about its immigrant beneficiaries: they countered that the burden of immigration enforcement—the mandate for employers to verify the status of all employees or face sanctions—should not fall on business owners.[92]

But the strongest opposition to sanctions—consistent throughout the five years IRCA debates—came from pundits who argued that employers would be deterred from hiring persons who looked or sounded foreign—that is, persons of color and persons with accents—and that universalized identification was fascist. In a 1982 House hearing before the Subcommittee on Census and Population of the Committee on Post Office and Civil Services, one Democratic lawmaker after another, academics, and Latina/o activists argued that Latinas/os and people of color—both immigrants and citizens—would be excluded from hiring and disproportionately required to prove legality (this iteration of the bill required that workers and potentially all Americans prove legality with documentation) as a result of racist assumptions about their foreignness on the basis of skin color, surname, accent, and the like.

Representative Edward Roybal (D-CA) co-founder of the National Association of Latino Elected and Appointed Officials (NALEO) and a life-long advocate for Latina/o interests, vehemently opposed the provisions. In fact, in 1986, as chair of the Congressional Hispanic Caucus, which he helped found in 1976, he led unsuccessful opposition to IRCA. While proponents of punitive provisions framed sanctions as part of a "jobs bill" for citizens and authorized workers, Roybal pointed out that "an employer will not interview anyone under this bill, if he just appears to be a little Hispanic; only blue-eyed blondes will be interviewed. But that individual would have the prerogative of simply not interviewing anyone and, by so doing, discriminating against any individual who may have a Spanish surname or look Hispanic from getting a job in the United States. That is one of the fears we have in the Hispanic communities of this nation."[93] Roybal also opposed identification cards. Like

Senator Alan Cranston (D-CA), Roybal feared they would engender treatment of Hispanics akin to treatment of Jews in Nazi Germany.[94]

Simpson also made this connection, though in a different light. In a 1981 interview, just before IRCA hearings began, Simpson said that "every time someone talks about the issue [verification beyond signature certification] they flee to the Statue of Liberty. I want to hear alternatives. We'll consider everything but tattoos."[95] This reference to tattoos for identification evoked Nazi methods of tracking Jews in concentration camps. Although Simpson later declared that he was misquoted, no retraction or correction was ever made.[96]

Despite these flagrant connections between racialized genocide, identification cards, and employer/employee verification, concern for human rights was not the only impetus behind opposition. American individualism, private property, and free market values were at play as well. Cranston argued in his prepared statement that the domestic passport was antithetical to democracy because it "infringes upon our respect for individual liberty in the United States best expressed in the Revolutionary War slogan 'Don't Tread On Me' and New Hampshire's State motto, 'Live Free or Die.'"[97] He supported this with the "nation of immigrants" rhetoric that complemented neoliberalism. The undocumented, he said, contributed to the economy and had thus "earned our acceptance."[98] Roybal put forth a similarly neoliberal pro-immigrants argument: immigrants were the "cream of the crop" because they were "hard working individuals who come here because they are in need of employment. They are practically starving in their country of origin, and they come here to the land of opportunity."[99]

Neoliberal rhetoric casts human beings as worthwhile and deserving of rights only if they are hardworking net contributors, do not sap social services, and—though not mentioned in this congressional session but prevalent elsewhere—adhere to respectable gender and family norms. Thus human rights and/or the inherently transnational lives that so many immigrants led *because of* U.S. foreign and domestic policies that impoverished nations on the one hand and criminalized immigrants on the other, were concealed by neoliberal discourse and policy even in discussions of antiracism.

IRCA did include an "Unfair Immigration-Related Employment Practices" provision that made it illegal for employers to discriminate against potential employees on the basis of race. But in practice, sanctions continued to tip the scales of capital in favor of employers and provoked racist criminalization of immigrants and persons who looked or sounded foreign. First, penalties for employers were reduced to civil offenses and a fine of $250 to $2,000 for each undocumented employee;[100] only those who "knowingly" employed unauthorized immigrants were to be penalized. (Criminal law rarely exculpates a perpetrator who "unknowingly" commits an offense, nor does it usually give a criminal the opportunity to prove or stage his or her unknowingness.) Implementation also decriminalized employers. The INS aimed to complete 20,000 inspections in 1988 but completed only 12,000 that year and 12,000 the following year. Second, undocumented immigrants who entered after the 1982 amnesty cut-off date could work under a grandfather clause exempting existing employers from penalization, though it continued to be illegal for all aliens to work.[101] Third, under Section 116 of Title I, "Restricting Warrantless Entry in the case of outdoor agricultural operations," the INS could not enter an outdoor operation without the consent of the owner and a warrant,[102] which gave employers time to conceal undocumented workers. Moreover, the first citation was issued in August 1987, the first "notice of intent to fine" in October 1987, and the first fine was imposed at year's end, at a Wendy's in Washington, D.C. This was odd since the law was created to address undocumented labor in the Southwest, where most illegal employment occurred.[103] In short, employers could continue using undocumented immigrant labor with relative impunity.

Meanwhile, the provisions harmed undocumented immigrants. They were, like Chinese "paper sons" nearly a century before, encouraged by law to commit crimes such as forging documents that, though expensive, were easily detected. This also rendered them especially vulnerable to employers' exploitation and abuse.[104] Sanctions also intensified racism. A 1991 study found that sanctions led to "widespread discrimination against legal but foreign-sounding or foreign-looking workers."[105] Subsequent MALDEF and ACLU studies concurred, and both organizations advocated repeal of the employment verification requirement.[106] As Cacho observes, "Unemployment and illegal status leave people legally vulnerable because of U.S. law, rather than protected by it, because it is all but legal to discriminate against both groups. Hence, because permanently criminalized, rightless statuses are also always already racialized, law ensures that there will always be a population of color rendered permanently rightless in the United States."[107] In contrast, lawbreaking corporate behavior (such as employing undocumented workers) was a civic infraction unrecognizable as criminal and allowed businesses to bypass labor and antidiscrimination laws. IRCA's employer sanctions were a legal invitation for racist exploitation as a way to increase profits in a neoliberalizing context, as was increased border militarization.

Under IRCA, the Border Patrol, the INS, and other federal agencies dealing with border inspection and enforcement were enlarged; the examinations and service activities of border agents were expanded to facilitate more efficient adjudication of petitions and applications for entry and legalization. The new vaguely defined tasks would be carried out with a 50 percent increase in Border Patrol personnel over two years and a $422 million budget in 1987 and $419 million in 1988.[108]

As with the Bracero Program, a hidden gender contract underscored changes: gendering, always key to the criminalization of immigrants, is part and parcel of neoliberal crimmigration.[109] The new criminalizing provisions and their rationales made undocumented female immigrants especially vulnerable to violence and an especially exploitable labor pool. Yet neoliberalism's premium on personal responsibility, competition, and independence ascribe fault to individuals and certain groups of people rather than a fundamentally exploitative capitalist system, and a focus on crime relegates concerns with racism and sexism to the background or trumps them altogether. When *Newsweek* ran a June 25, 1984, cover story, "Closing the Door? The Angry Debate over Illegal Immigration: Crossing the Rio Grande," and *U.S. News and World Report* ran a March 7, 1983, cover story, "Invasion from Mexico: It Just Keeps Growing," each featured photographs of women of Latin American origins being carried over bodies of water into the United States. As the article titles indicate, those crossings were illegal and increasing. The magazines explicitly linked Latina fertility to undocumented immigration in ways that called forth the gendered intricacies of the "Latino threat" *reconquista* narrative. The focus on women suggests "the invasion carried the seeds of future generations"; undocumented Latin American immigrant women and their American-born children would allegedly beleaguer the welfare state, and women would produce "communities of Latinos who would remain linguistically and socially separate and soon would be clamoring for reconquest of the United States."[110]

Simultaneously, neoliberal shifts called for the incorporation of Third World women into wage labor. The United Nation's Woman's Decade (1976–1985) was framed as a feminist and multicultural initiative with international campaigns that circulated the idea that international wage labor would empower women, and there was increased demand for the labor of immigrant women, at the very moment that United States immigrant women were criminalized. Furthermore, the "sexism that devalued the domestic work of women" carried over into women's employment in manufacturing industries and—along with criminalizing laws that guarantee the vulnerability of the targeted population—made women into especially desirable laborers. Sweatshop garment piecework is often seen as an extension of traditional "women's work" in the home, and women were also wanted for assembly-line work because they are perceived as easy to control.[111]

The reality of immigrant women's experience was far more complicated than either the Woman's Decade or *reconquista* narratives revealed; both rendered labor exploitation and violence against immigrant women invisible. Like the Texas Rangers, the newly beefed-up Border Patrol engaged in gendered brutality and rape. A 1998 Amnesty International study found that women detained by the INS were subjected to degrading vaginal searches by male Border Patrol officers and were frequently sexually abused and assaulted. Women were pressured to remain silent; two women who complained were accused of lying.[112] In reports filed between 1992 and 1997, Human Rights Watch found that sexual abuse was "rampant," but although INS agents were occasionally prosecuted for the rape of undocumented women, the crime was rarely reported.[113]

Anti-prostitution provisions in the Immigration Act of 1990, which linked Latin American immigrant women's sexuality to deviance and crime, further increased women's susceptibility to sexual violence as a mechanism of social and labor control. Along with pro-immigration provisions such as an increasing the number of legal immigrants, relaxing some of the language requirements for naturalization in place since 1906, and revoking the ban on gay and lesbian immigrants, the 1990 law, which was meant to tie up loose ends left by IRCA, made anyone who had engaged in prostitution or "commercialized vice" excludable for ten years.[114] In this case, anti-sex-work provisions could rationalize the systemic disavowal of reports of violence, further discourage survivors from coming forth, and allow employers to utilize with impunity rape and sexual violence to discipline female workers. Rendering the sexuality of Latin American immigrant women and Latinas criminal made punishment of and even violence against undocumented women and Latinas seem logical, and casting women's employment as liberatory made capital exploitation seem impossible.

Selling Porous Borders and Border Security after IRCA

Throughout the 1990s, thanks to the neoliberal paradigms inaugurated by IRCA, militarization, criminalization, racialization, genderization, and labor exploitation continued to be complementary. The 1994 North American Free Trade Agreement (NAFTA) and the 1996 Illegal Immigration Reform and Immigrant Responsibility Act (IIRIRA), two seemingly contradictory laws, developed IRCA's blending of border security and tough immigration law enforcement with the liberalization of international trade and labor. While NAFTA reduced or eliminated tariffs and opened Mexico to imports of U.S. products, including agricultural goods, IIRIRA dramatically increased

penalties for immigration-related offenses and militarization at the U.S.–
Mexico border. As with IRCA, the amplified blend of policing and free trade
rendered women especially vulnerable.

In his support of NAFTA, President Bill Clinton elaborated on prece-
dents established by Reagan. Although Reagan adopted more of a domestic
protectionist stance, as with limiting Japanese auto imports to compel East
Asian economies to open to U.S. agricultural exports, international trade
agreements initiated under his administration were the direct precursor to
NAFTA and other Clinton-era neoliberal initiatives. Along with participat-
ing in General Agreement on Tariffs and Trade (GATT) negotiations to liberalize trade in the agricultural and service sectors, and playing a key role in
setting the agenda for the Uruguay Round, a set of multilateral trade agreements that addressed agriculture, service, and intellectual property rights,
the Reagan administration negotiated the Free Trade Agreement (FTA) with
Canada. Clinton incorporated Mexico in the FTA, expanded GATT and
Uruguay Round negotiations with the new umbrella World Trade Organization (WTO), and generally reduced trade barriers and liberalized certain
industries. Thus, in effect, Clinton solidified neoliberal policies governing an
international economic system.[115] Such policies, which began in the 1970s
and picked up steam under Reagan, are also known as structural adjustment
policies (SAPs) because they literally structurally adjust the laws and economies of nations. That is, in order to receive economic aid, the World Bank
and International Monetary Fund (IMF) required nations, mostly in the
global south, to make their laws and economies compatible with neoliberalism through structural adjustments such as privatization, removing import
restrictions, and lowering the value of local currencies.

Taking and elaborating on a page from the Reagan playbook, the Clinton
administration framed neoliberal measures as democratizing and prosperous
for an increasingly interconnected and interdependent global community.[116]
Yet neoliberal policies benefit the U.S. economy by opening the door for
cheap immigrant labor for service industries and agriculture and protecting
the comparative advantage of the United States in intellectual property, while
causing poverty and migration in sending nations. By requiring Mexico to
cease protectionist agricultural policies that allowed subsistence farmers to
keep their own land, and by allowing the importation of U.S. goods, wages—
and government spending on social services—were simultaneously cut.
Within two years of NAFTA's implementation, more than two million jobs
were lost in Mexico.[117] In turn, widespread poverty led to increased documented and undocumented migration. And while this was also good for the
U.S. economy, creating new consumers and providing an ample cheap labor

pool—part of the reason for the policy in the first place—it also gave rise to more criminalization and securitization of the border in order to assuage nativist objections to the increasing border flexibility neoliberal policies facilitated and to discipline that labor pool.

New securitizing operations demonstrate the seeming incoherence and inconsistency but actual compatibility of neoliberal rhetoric and reality at work. Following IRCA's passage, a steel fence was constructed along the Mexico-U.S. border, large-scale enforcement efforts such as Operation Blockade/Hold the Line (1993) in El Paso, Texas, and Operation Gate Keeper (1994) in San Diego, California were undertaken, more sophisticated technology was implemented, and the INS's budget and personnel were expanded again, with the number of border agents increasing from 3,693 in 1986 to 9,212 in 2000.[118] New "control" efforts generated increasing fear of apprehension and persecution on the part of border-crossers, which was not unfounded, for the number of crossing-related deaths also grew: in 1994, 23 migrants died attempting to cross. After Operation Gatekeeper, there were 61 deaths in 1995, 89 in 1997, and 145 in 1998.[119]

The injustice underscoring securitizing measures was not lost on inhabitants on both sides of the border in El Paso and Cuidad Juarez. Officials in both cities planned a "We are all Fronterizos" celebration that would climax with a "Day of Unity" to celebrate neoliberalism's promise of unity and shared prosperity that was destroyed by Operation Blockade. To apprehend illegal entrants, Operation Blockade literally created a blockade composed of 130 agents on land and air around urban El Paso.[120] This significantly reduced undocumented entries, but the three-week operation, which cost some $250 thousand in overtime—and demanded pulling agents from other duties, like enforcing employer sanctions—merely shifted entries to other areas.[121] These measures, along with the operation's erection of a 1.5-mile steel fence at the border,[122] made the day "Day of Unity" impossible. In fact community leaders on both sides of the border were incensed by the erection of this "Berlin Wall."[123]

While the injustice underscoring this securitizing measure was explicitly acknowledged as a contradiction of the neoliberal metanarrative of multicultural unity, connectivity, and shared prosperity, another injustice, which occurred in Ciudad Juarez and was overtly gendered, was neither criticized nor acknowledged in the mainstream media. Ciudad Juarez, the largest exporting zone on the border, with approximately 350 manufacturing plants located there in the 1990s and about 180,000 workers, most of whom were paid the equivalent of about $23 per week,[124] was also the location of the murders of several hundred Mexican women that began in 1994. By 2005, at least 350 women had been murdered.[125] By 2008, 400 women were murdered, while an estimated 1,000 women had disappeared.[126] Most were poor and dark-skinned and had migrated to the borderlands from southern Mexico and Central America to work in *maquiladoras*, assembly-line factories owned by U.S. companies located in Mexico, which use cheap Mexican labor to produce duty-free and tax-free products: these were one manifestation of the "empowerment" through waged labor promised in the UN's Women's Decade neoliberal rhetoric. At the time of writing, impunity has surrounded the crimes, for the Mexican government has not acknowledged the systematic nature of the murders and has criminalized and blamed the victims. One criminologist asserted that the influence of the United States caused these women to join the workforce earlier than they otherwise might have, leading to promiscuity and other transgressive sexual behavior such as lesbianism and sex work that made them more likely to be victimized.[127] Moreover, as noted earlier, as neoliberal shifts called for the incorporation of Third World women into wage labor, sexism carried over into women's employment in low-skilled jobs. In Mexico young women are recruited for factory work given the assumption that they are naïve and obedient and unlikely to join or form unions.[128] Thus the Ciudad Juarez killers could easily "target members of the urban reserve of wage labor of the *maquiladora* industry, namely a pool of female workers migrating from southern Mexico and Central America and living in the poor surrounding *colonias* [shantytowns] of Juarez."[129]

The securitization of the U.S. side of the border in the midst of increasing border fluidity for capital and goods provided a stark contrast to the impunity surrounding the crimes. The United States secured the border while exploiting the labor of Mexican nationals in *maquiladoras* and of Mexican migrants and immigrants inside the country. The Ciudad Juarez femicide shows with frightening clarity that racialized women workers were truly disposable. Moreover, despite grassroots and nongovernmental organization (NGO) efforts to stop the violence, the criminalization of women's sexuality and the consequent attribution of guilt to victims allowed the Mexican government to avoid responsibility for the security of its female citizens, or in the case of the United States, the security of its female laborers.

The Cuidad Juarez femicide and the increase in border-crossing deaths that corresponded with increased militarization indicated that women workers and the undocumented had much to fear and exposed a slippage between neoliberal rhetoric and neoliberal material reality, which is fundamentally exploitative, harmful, and potentially deadly to populations that are already vulnerable to violence and exploitation—that is, women, people of color, the poor, and the undocumented. In addition, U.S. law made Mexicans and other "illegal aliens" into increasingly dangerous criminals who consequently had no recourse to protections and rights. Anthropologist Roger Lancaster suggests that the production of fear in relation to undocumented immigration rationalizes a spike in punitive laws, for "where fear is the order of the day, protection is the name of the game."[130] This was certainly the case in 1996, when a new Republican Congress (following the "Gingrich revolution" of 1994), passed three punitive laws that directly affected immigrants: the Illegal Immigration Reform and Immigrant Responsibility Act (IIRIRA), the Personal Responsibility and Work Opportunity Reconciliation Act (PRWORA), and the Anti-Terrorist and Effective Death Penalty Act (AEDPA). With this trifecta, legal and undocumented immigrants were stripped of fundamental rights and benefits, such as due process, supplemental security income (SSI), and food stamps, and many immigrants were subject to long-term detention and deportation as a result of past offenses.[131] In essence, IIRIRA made immigration law function more like criminal law, and like Operation Blockade, IIRIRA balanced NAFTA border permeability with punitive action, cementing the gendered criminalization of Latin American immigrants.

More specifically, IIRIRA flagrantly criminalized Latin American immigrants even though undocumented entry, a federal misdemeanor crime since 1924, was usually treated as a civil rather than criminal offense.[132] IIRIRA amplified militarization of the Mexican border again, featured new deportation measures for the undocumented, made allegedly gender neutral economic criteria (that is, evaluation of immigrants' potential to be net contributors) for entry more specific and rigorous, placed income-based restrictions on family reunification, and mandated permanent and obligatory deportation for "aggravated felonies." In 1988, the Anti-Terrorism and Effective Death Penalty Act (AEDPA), another Reagan-era prelude to this increased criminalization, created the category of "aggravated felony" for deportable crimes (those punishable with a sentence of five or more years, including murder and drug and firearm trafficking). IIRIRA added seventeen newly deportable crimes, so that there was no meaningful distinction between murder, shoplifting, assault, and tax evasion. Like Muslims, who were also targeted under this law, "criminal aliens" were framed as a risk group that citizens needed to be protected from. Undefined "crimes of moral turpitude" became grounds for removal, and IIRIRA was also retroactive, applying to convictions prior to its enactment. IIRIRA also contained several seemingly contradictory provisions in terms of state power. On the one hand, one clause expanded the role of local law enforcement in immigration control and reiterated PRWORA's delegation of the authority of states to deny welfare benefits to legal immigrants.[133] On the other hand, other provisions rendered immigration lawyers impotent by making all immigration cases subject to this federal law and the new deportable offenses. Despite the contradictions, all roads led to the draconian restriction of immigrant rights with little recourse for challenge, since immigrant crime was the rationale for such harsh changes. In fact, although Clinton initially opposed many of the measures on humanitarian and foreign relations grounds,[134] and although free market economists worried that IIRIRA would hinder capital accumulation by shrinking the low-wage immigrant workforce, IIRIRA was passed. Moreover, while IIRIRA was revised under allegations of unconstitutionality and cruelty and while many provisions were repealed, undocumented entry was still treated as a civil offense in many cases, and the law did little to decrease immigration and undocumented labor migration.[135] Instead, this law, along with others, secured the systemic reproduction of a criminalized immigrant underclass.

Moreover, in the 1990s there was an increasing use of private actors and individuals to police immigrants (beginning with Prop 187 and its imperative to report suspected undocumented immigrants). This is continuing with laws and initiatives into the 2000s.[136] This privatization complements the neoliberal downsizing of the state and is a literal example of the neoliberal ideology of personal responsibility. Between 2004 and 2008, about three hundred laws were passed in forty-three states requiring government workers and private citizens to verify the legal status of persons and report them if they did not have proper documentation.[137]

Philip Kretsedemas notes that "the mission of immigration enforcement is defined as much by the imperative of labor market regulation as by the imperative of border control."[138] Under neoliberal governance, punitive immigration policies are not conventionally restrictionist because they do not cut back on immigration. Nor does immigration increase the crime rate, as shown by a 1997 National Research Council (NRC) review,[139] and undocumented immigrants are actually more inclined to play by the rules to avoid detection,[140] so this is not the point either. Rather, policies create a climate in which legal status widens the gaps between segments of the U.S. population, such that the unauthorized immigrant becomes "an affront to conventional notions of citizenship, which equate political, social, and civic rights with the criterion of legal residence."[141] Racialized and gendered criminalization—not the actual behavior of immigrants—legitimates the casting of undocumented immigrants as undeserving of rights

Immigrant women of color were harmed in specific ways under IIRIRA. In 1998 Ana Flores, a permanent resident from Guatemala with two citizen children ages nine and eight, faced deportation for defending herself against an abusive husband. Under the expanded definition of "aggravated felony," her act of self-defense was grounds for deportation. Prior to IIRIRA, she could have legally argued before an immigration judge that deportation was "unjustifiably cruel" and this might have ended the deportation proceedings. But IIRIRA reduced judicial discretion in immigration cases so that immigrants convicted of even minor crimes could easily be deported;[142] women could be deported for simply defending themselves. Additionally, almost 75 percent of all H-1B visas are issued to men, and 75 percent of H-4 dependent visas are issued to women. H-4s are ineligible for social security numbers, cannot work legally, and cannot do much of anything—such as open a bank account, rent an apartment—without spousal consent/assistance. This law legally binds female victims of abuse to abusers. Along with the IIRIRA crimmigration provisions, the neoliberal focus on ostensibly gender-neutral economic criteria not only "reinforced heteronormative gender identities and a gendered model of economic activity that portrayed men as economic agents and providers and women as caregivers,"[143] but also directly reinforced immigrant women's vulnerability to violence. And yet, the Immigrant Marriage Fraud Amendment of 1986 (IMFA) indicated that the abuse of immigrant women was an issue that U.S. lawmakers were already well aware of.

The IMFA, passed days after IRCA in 1986, authorized the INS to scrutinize the marriages of immigrants to citizens or legal permanent residents in order to identify and remove immigrants who attempted to obtain legal status through bogus marriage. Under the IMFA, a citizen or legal permanent-resident spouse must file on behalf of his or her immigrant spouse for conditional residence, and the marriage must remain intact for two years in order for the spouse to achieve independent legal status. If this sounds like a trap, it is, because if the immigrant wife is economically and psychologically dependent upon her spouse, her alternatives are limited to the relationship, putting her at an increased risk for domestic violence. Michelle Anderson cites a study that found that 48 percent of Latinas reported that domestic violence against them had increased since they immigrated. In response to these problems, Congress amended the IMFA in 1988 so that wives who had been subject to violence could petition on their own behalf.[144]

Although initiatives such as the United Nation's Women's Decade promised women empowerment through wage work and although neoliberalism was touted as a universally beneficial system, increased efforts to securitize and militarize the border in the midst of border flexibility for goods and labor made immigrant women and especially Latin American immigrant women extremely vulnerable, and thus an extremely cost-effective labor force. This was accomplished by linking Latin American immigrant women with sexual deviance and prostitution and by the erasure of women in securitizing and militarizing initiatives. In short, IRCA repackaged paradigms of gendered Latin American criminality in ways that justified and concealed neoliberalism's inherent violence, creating an easy-sale model of porous borders and border security for later laws such as NAFTA and IIRIRA, and even after 9/11.

Popular Perpetrators

Crimmigration in popular culture was a comparative racialized, gendered operation. While Latinas/os were usually cast as de facto criminals, white ethnic criminals were often romanticized, and Asians were again positioned as an intermediary control stratum, in this case as exotic "model minority" crime fighters.

In U.S. cinema, white ethnics and especially Italian Americans have long been stereotyped as Mafia criminals, but in contrast to Latin American immigrant and Latina/o crime, masculinized white ethnic crime is often glamorized; the genre therefore complements backlash against the civil rights movement and increasing presence and political significance of Latinas/os. Despite comparable Mafia and Latina/o gang violence, such portrayals of the former do not negatively impact the social standing or employment of white ethnics, or a have parallel in contemporary immigration and criminal law. White ethnic gangster films also tend to portray white ethnic women as the victims of their husband's infidelity, dishonesty, and violence or to relegate women to an ancillary role that decriminalizes them. In effect, white ethnic women are not pathologized in the way that Latinas are. The disparity is due to two interlocking factors. First, a commitment to family on the part of gangsters and criminals mitigates criminality. That is, the criminals in question are members of heterosexual families, and often also an intertwined crime *famiglia*, which shows they have relatable and even admirable values: "family values." Second, as noted above, white lawbreakers are legally protected from occupying criminal status since they are usually judged individually on the basis of their particular acts rather than as representatives of the entire race; white ethnicity is not a de facto status crime. Furthermore, white ethnic criminals are often excused (as when they redeem themselves by testifying against their cohorts, then joining witness protection programs, and/or dying tragic deaths) or at least humanized even when their acts are quite horrible; in U.S. film, the same unlawful activity is ascribed different meanings depending on the color of the body committing the act. The "nation of immigrants" trope and its entanglement with the history of discrimination toward white ethnics provided some "commonsense" reasoning for mobster activity, and usually the kind of reasoning Reaganite America understood: the quest for a better life for oneself and one's family.

Likewise, some films about male Irish gang activity and crime romanticized and idealized Irish criminality and did not negatively impact undocumented Irish, who were embraced with the "Legalize the Irish" movement and IRCA's specialized visa program (discussed in Chapter 5). In fact, some pop culture and nonfiction sources alike linked Irish mobsters directly to the "nation of immigrants" mythos, and all but exonerated Irish gangsters. Crime expert T. J. English argues in *Paddy Whacked: The Untold Story of the Irish American Gangster* that the Irish mobster predated the Italian mobster and frames Irish organized crime as a response to the desperation, poverty, and bigotry of the Irish immigrant experience. The jacket copy of the hardcover text describes his book as "a brilliant portrait of a people who fought tooth and nail for a better life from the moment they arrived in America, whether it meant taking charge within the realms of law enforcement and politics—from Tammany Hall to the White House—or capitalizing on what opportunities they could in the darker works beyond the law."[145] Cinematic depictions of Irish criminality in *Boondock Saints* (1999), *Gangs of New York* (2001), *Road to Perdition* (2002), and *The Departed* (2006) were similarly embraced as part of Americans' post–civil rights era love affair with white ethnic "roots."

Sometimes, Irish American crime was downright heroic: *Boondock Saints* features male Irish immigrant fraternal twins (Sean Patrick Flanery and Norman Reedus) who become vigilantes in Boston. The action film, directed and written by Troy Duffy, has a real-life American Dream, "rags-to-riches" parallel: Duffy, a struggling bartender and musician in a rock band, eventually with his brother released the film with Indican Pictures. Although it failed at the box office and was panned by critics, it became a cult classic with its DVD release.[146] The extremely violent protagonists are devout Catholics valiantly purging Boston of the evils of the Russian Mafia. The film aligns working-class Irish immigrant violence with the benevolent white patriarch stereotype fostered by the Border Patrol and *Colors*. Thus *Boondock Saints* configures Irish American male crime as not only excusable—given the title of the film, and its themes, including the brothers' frequent use of prayer and recitation of scriptural passages, the locals' praise of the brothers' efforts, and their commitment and loyalty to one another, to family—but actually constructs these Irish American violent criminals as "saintly." In fact they become vigilantes only after killing Russian Mafia members in self-defense. This decriminalization of Irish crime and its framing as the quest for a better life stand in stark contrast to the legal, social, economic, and pop cultural treatment of Latin American immigrants and Latinas/os as de facto criminal aliens.

The popular fascination with Italian immigrant and Italian American organized crime is a staple of American culture. Mobster films began with titles such as *Little Caesar* (1931) and the original *Scarface* (1932), both released when the Italian American Mafia was quite active, and then underwent a resurgence on the heels of the ethnic revival, when white ethnics were fully enfranchised, with films such as *Once Upon a Time in America* (1984), *The Untouchables* (1987), *Goodfellas* (1990), *Miller's Crossing* (1990), *A Bronx Tale* (1993), *Casino* (1995), *Gotti: The Rise and Fall of a Real Life Mafia Don* (1996), *Donnie Brasco* (1997), and *Mafia!* (1998), a spoof of U.S. mafia films. Perhaps most famous is the classic Frances Ford Coppola trilogy *The Godfather* (1972, 1974, and 1990).[147] The first film, based on the 1967 novel, *The Godfather* by Mario Puzo, follows the Corleones, an Italian immigrant family that assimilated into American culture through violence and organized crime, from 1945 to 1955. The gangsters of *The Godfather* are not the renegade heroes that the Boondock Saints are, and tragedy does result from the men's crimes, but by romanticizing the self-sufficient upward mobility of Italian immigrants via organized crime and by representing them as having traditional "family values" that provide coherence and structure to the crime organizations, these films anticipate and support Reaganite ideology. And even though real Italian Mafiosi such as the Gambino and Gotti crime families were extant, Mafia films did not affect the privileged subject status that Italian Americans earned with "family values," allegedly self-sufficient class mobility, and via the ethnic revival.

In Mafia films, women likewise uphold "family values." Women are generally subordinate to men and are reified as devoutly Catholic, dependent wives and mothers. In Italian mobster classics such as *The Godfather*, *Goodfellas*, and the hit television show *The Sopranos* (1999–2007), women are usually kept ignorant of the family business, deceived, and often cheated on, but stand by their husbands and are committed to their children. Some Mafia wives do challenge gender norms to an extent. In *The Godfather II*, Kay Corleone (Diane Keaton) has an abortion and leaves Michael Corleone (Al Pacino), new head of the Corleone empire, because he fails to legitimize the family business. *The Sopranos* focuses on an Italian American Mafia family in New Jersey and revolves around the efforts of protagonist Tony Soprano (James Gandolfini) to balance his family life and his duties as a Mafia boss. The show won five Golden Globes and twenty-one Emmys[148] and spawned an industry of *Sopranos* merchandise including books, video games, and soundtracks. The series continues to run in syndication and has been credited with transforming television with "dark" and complex characters and story lines; it was called "perhaps the greatest pop culture masterpiece of its day"[149] and the most influential television drama "ever."[150] *TV Guide* ranked it number five in the Top 50 TV Series of All Time.[151] Like Kay, Carmela Soprano (Edie Falco), takes a stand for herself: she leaves Tony after discovering his affairs and toys with infidelity herself. But ultimately both Mafia wives revert to dependence on their breadwinning husbands and chose to maintain the nuclear family, as when Kay reconciles with Michael in *The Godfather III* and Carmela forgives Tony.

In sum, the stories in this genre center on Italian Mafiosi men who began as penniless immigrants or are the privileged children of once-penniless immigrants, and who work hard to provide their families with a better life. While "racialized masculinities of impoverished inner cities serve as the only signifiers for criminal street gangs, white gangs are thought to form for 'ideological' reasons or as a 'business venture'; its members are characterized as purposeful and calculated, even political, but not as ganglike."[152] The Mafia was a business venture; pursuit of the American Dream is usually presented as the raison d'être for Italian American involvement in organized crime; and in the context of neoliberalism, this makes sense.

One might argue that representations of Italian Americans as criminals rearticulate the anti-Italian sentiment that was pervasive at the turn of the twentieth century; after all, even the most celebrated representations such as the *Sopranos* were critiqued as stereotypical.[153] Moreover, as Michaela di Leonardo observes, some popular representations of Italian Americans turned into "permanent condescension and even minstrelsy" in the 1980s: the "glamour and gravitas" of *The Godfather* phenomenon morphed into films like *Moonstruck* (1987), *My Blue Heaven* (1990), and *My Cousin Vinny* (1992), which portrayed working- and upper-class Italian Americans as trashy and tasteless buffoons.[154] Deprecatory portrayals have continued with reality shows such as *Jersey Shore* (2009–2012) and its spin-offs, *Jerseylicious* (2009–2012) and *Mob Wives* (2011–2016). Nonetheless, Italian immigrant criminals (and also Irish) were pardoned, romanticized, and at times celebrated for their criminality both in and outside of the movies, and even while portrayed as "trashy," Italian Americans have not been disenfranchised or treated as alien citizens. For instance, in 2001 and 2007, most respondents to a Fairleigh Dickenson University *Public Mind* survey, which polled 800 randomly selected adults, age eighteen and over, disagreed with the criticism that *Jersey Shore* negatively portrays Italian Americans. Specifically, in 2001, 65 percent disagreed, and in 2007, 61 percent disagreed.[155] Even against the backdrop of an abundance of representations of white ethnic mobsters, white ethnics are not de facto criminals; the privileged legal status of whiteness, which itself has monetary value and legal and social benefits,[156] does not circumscribe potential law-abiding or reify white—including white ethnic—identity.

At the same time, positive filmic representations of Italian American men who transcend or avoid lives of crime—and instead work assiduously to achieve the American Dream—position spectators to root for them, sometimes in contrast to men of color. The Oscar-winning film *Rocky* (1976) and its five sequels provide a striking example. In the popular[157] drama directed by John Avildsen, which was written by and stars Italian American actor Sylvester Stallone, protagonist Rocky Balboa has more than a bit of Italian American machismo (he is a pro boxer, after all), and he is connected to a life of crime in that he is a debt collector for a loan shark. But the *Rocky* films epitomize the white ethnic "underdog" and "rages to riches" mythos frequently used to rationalize racist cuts to welfare and affirmative action: the uneducated Rocky has the opportunity to become the world heavyweight champion, and whether he wins or loses, his most admirable trait is his willingness to work hard to achieve his goal. (Incidentally Rocky's nemesis—who stands between him and achievement of his American Dream—is the black boxer Apollo Creed [Carl Weathers], a fact that points to the ways in which white ethnics came to inhabit the normative white position by way of contrast to people of color, as they do in Glazer and Moynihan's *Beyond the Melting Pot* and Moynihan's *The Moynihan Report*.)

Furthermore, in the 1980s and 1990s, the casting of Italian American actors as Latina/o gangsters and as foils to Latina/o gangsters points to a production-level gendered racial calculus. In the Brian DePalma–directed films *Scarface* and *Carlito's Way*, Al Pacino stars as a Cuban gangster. Although he does not play a Latino character, Sylvester Stallone stars in *The Specialist*, directed by Latino Luis Llosa. Pacino's and Stallone's Italian heritage is relevant, given the dearth of Latino actors playing even stereotypical Latino characters in the 1980s and 1990s despite Latinas/os' increasing numbers in the United States, and given that positive stereotypes of white ethnics were constructed in comparison to negative stereotypes of Latinas/os. In short, films that glamorized white ethnic crime and/or made it heroic, which began to proliferate on the heels of the civil rights movement, could be considered part of the backlash against it, against multiculturalism in general, and against the increasing numbers and significance of Latinas/os as a market and voting bloc.

Meanwhile, in popular culture Asian men were frequently depicted as crime fighters, which not only played into both the exotic foreigner and "model minority" stereotypes, but also indicates the social legitimacy of Asians in relation to criminality; this minority *fights* crime rather than commits it, and is thereby on the "right" side (that is, white middle- to upper-class American as opposed to alien), enforcing laws with "exotic" martial arts skills. Asians were thus "model minorities" in relation to crime, rather than inscrutable criminals, as they were depicted during Chinese exclusion and in accordance with various wars. Nonetheless, more recent portrayals, which elaborate upon the "model minority" thesis, are part of the legacy of gendered criminalization that began in the late nineteenth century, when Asian men were effeminized or at least distanced from "normal" white heterosexual masculinity.[158]

D. W. Griffith's silent film *Broken Blossoms, or The Yellow Man and the Girl* (1919) critiqued the racist assumption of Asian male criminality by recreating the gendered foreignness of an Asian male protagonist. Set in London, the film features an abusive father, Battling Burrows (Donald Crisp), who is outraged when he discovers daughter Lucy (Lillian Gish) has been taken in by Chinese immigrant Cheng Huan (played in "yellow face" by Richard Barthelmess). Even though Cheng, who migrated to London to teach a Buddhist message of peace, loves Lucy and she is happy in his care, Burrows assumes that Cheng is a "heathen," and his "rescue" results in Lucy's death. The racist Burrows is the villain, while Cheng is portrayed as sympathetic, but only because he is desexualized and effeminized—there is no sexual intimacy between him and Lucy. Also, the film implies that everything would have been fine if Cheng had not immigrated: missing China, he loses touch with his religion and begins to smoke opium, and his relationship with Lucy is what leads to her death. The plot does not endorse their interracial relationship or Cheng's ability to assimilate.

The gendered criminalization of Asians in accordance with international relations also provides a precursor to more recent figurations of Asians in relation to crime. For instance, in the midst of Chinese exclusion, Japanese in the United States were treated well because Japan was a rising world power after defeating Russia in the Russo-Japanese War of 1904–1905. The Gentleman's Agreement, a series of notes exchanged between Japan and the United States (1907–1908), stipulated that Japan would issue passports to laborers, and to their parents, wives, and children, only if they had already been to the United States. This had the unintended consequence of significantly increasing Japanese immigration with "picture brides." According to Japanese law, women could marry men they had never met. Japanese laborers took advantage of this to bring brides over to the States, and the Japanese population grew quickly as the Chinese population shrank.[159]

During World War II, the tables turned. Robert Lee observes that although "America's entry into the war against Nazi Germany and Imperial Japan made it increasingly difficult to sustain national policies based on theories of white racial supremacy,"[160] with the bombing of Pearl Harbor Japanese Americans were viewed as threats to national security, and nearly 120,000 Japanese

Americans were interned.[161] Popular culture attempted to tell Americans how to distinguish the now-dangerous Japanese from the now-friendly Chinese (China was allied with the United States against Japan in the war) with a system of racial taxonomy. *Life* magazine published a two-page pictorial that featured photographs of Japanese and Chinese men and both described and *showed* readers the racial differences between the two groups even though physical differences are not really discernible in the photos.[162]

The criminalization of Asian Americans is no longer standard or socially acceptable (and although outside the scope of this book, it is worth noting that the current flagrant fear and criticism surrounding China's rise as a world power and North Korea's nuclear power are socially acceptable). Nonetheless, Asians are still imagined as perpetually foreign in many ways, including in relation to crime and, in conjunction with the "model minority" stereotype, crime fighting. In the 1960s and 1970s, there was a proliferation of Kung Fu and martial arts films such as *Enter the Dragon* (1973), which introduced martial arts legend Bruce Lee to U.S. audiences and was the first in his substantial body of work. The popular genre[163] was predicated on gendered stereotypes of Asian exoticness embodied in martial arts. From the 1980s and on through the 1990s and 2000s, Asian men continued to be exoticized as martial arts gurus, often as crime fighters and warriors and sometimes as otherworldly criminals in films such as *Big Trouble in Little China* (1986). In *Karate Kid* (1984) a Japanese American handyman, Mr. Miyagi (Noriyuki "Pat" Morita), teaches karate to a bullied Italian American teenaged boy Daniel LaRusso (Ralph Macchio). Directed by John Avildsen, who also directed *Rocky*, it is a similar "underdog" story (with a hero played by an Italian American male) that was critically acclaimed,[164] and the film reaffirmed the "model" status of Asians with its Asian–white ethnic coalition. Mr. Miyagi is a father figure to Daniel, teaching him how to be a proper man by defending himself with karate. Yet the film plays up a host of Orientalist stereotypes by depicting Mr. Miyagi as eccentric in ethnicized ways, as when early in the film he attempts to catch flies with chopsticks, and in the premise itself, as he helps Daniel by sharing his mysterious and vast "oriental" wisdom.[165] Martial arts continued to exoticize Asian men as in the popular Jackie Chan action comedy films *Rumble in the Bronx* (1990), *Police Story 1–4* (1984–1996), *Shanghai Knights* (2003), and *The Tuxedo* (2002). Other notable martial arts films include the Academy Award–winning, transnationally produced drama *Crouching Tiger Hidden Dragon* (2001), which featured computer-generated, otherworldly martial arts moves.

"Buddy cop" comedies in which two men of different backgrounds and with conflicting personalities are paired in order to solve a crime, usually depict Asian men both as emblems of the professed inclusivity of the United States and as outsiders who are on the inside or are protecting the inside. In such movies, the Asian men fight with "foreign" techniques—martial arts— which at that time differed from typical "American" masculine crime-fighting techniques such as fisticuffs and firearms. While the "foreign" techniques are effective (and are what draws spectators to the films), their framing distances Asian men from "normal" (that is, white heterosexual) American men and as such repackages gendered Asian foreignness.

Asian male crime fighters are also often quite literally foreigners because they play Asian citizens. In the *Rush Hour* trilogy of action comedy films (1998, 2001, 2007) directed by Brett Ratnor, Jackie Chan plays Detective Lee, a national of Hong Kong. The first film opened at No. 1 in the box office and earned an estimated opening of $31 million,[166] indicating that the martial arts genre continues to enthrall American spectators. The FBI wants to keep Lee, whom they view as an outsider, away from the case—the kidnapping of a Chinese consul's eleven-year-old daughter, Su Yuan, who studied martial arts with Lee in Hong Kong—which he has been brought to the United States to solve. The FBI pawns Lee off on a Los Angeles Police Department detective, black American James Carter (Chris Tucker). Although the two capture the bad guys and save Su Yuan, racism is reaffirmed even as the film self-reflexively jokes about it, as when Carter, assuming that Lee does not speak English, shouts slowly at him. Lee allows Carter to do this for a while, and when Lee does speak in English, fluently, Carter tells him that he "sounds like a Kung Fu movie." The humor in this situation comes from Carter's dramatization of the racist assumption that all Asians in the United States are foreign. But Lee *is* foreign and is represented as such, and Carter's blackness mitigates this thread of racism. *Rush Hour* thereby suggests that an Asian man may be a crime fighter instead of a criminal in popular cinema; but while he may be an ally, he is still always already an alien citizen.

These films also point to the alleged "model" assimilability of most Asian immigrants and Asian Americans. The male heroes of martial arts crime-fighting films are masculinized in narrow ways: they behave and play by American rules, earning a legal and decent living protecting status quo America and American "family values," as in the rescue of Su Yuan. And while there are exceptions, women are also frequently relegated to the background. Martial arts films, in which male fighting scenes tend to dominate, suggest that like crime in mobster films and TV shows, crime fighting is the kind of action that takes place mostly between men. Asians may be models; they are still minorities. As crime fighters in American films, Asian men function as an intermediary control stratum between white ethnics and Latinas/os, neither censured and relegated to de facto criminal status like the latter, nor accorded the full privileges and freedoms white skin grants the former even when they commit crimes.

Thus, pop culture provided "commonsense" representations of certain immigrants and citizens deserving punishment, exclusion, and even violence (that is, people of Latin American origins), while others, even when criminals, are represented as deserving exoneration, forgiveness, glamorization, and praise ("model" Asians, and all variety of white ethnics). On the big screen, small screen, and congressional floor, gendered and racialized crimmigration (or de-crimmigration) indicated who deserved and earned what.

Conclusion

Alicia Schmidt Camacho notes that "the criminalization of the migrant has occurred since the nineteenth century alongside the development of a capitalist economy that actively recruited laborers from Mexico and Latin America. State officials and labor contractors have long colluded to produce the ideal migrant, the temporary worker stripped of labor rights and the entitlements of citizenship."[167] Under neoliberal governance at this time, immigration enforcement was a precondition for expanding the supply of non-citizen labor.[168] Gendered, racialized Reagan-era discourses of immigrant criminality explained why certain immigrants were punished, excluded, and subject to violence, and as such helped to secure an inexpensive, pliable labor pool in the "nation of immigrants." With public ascriptions of gendered and racialized criminality in law, news media, and popular culture, neoliberal crimmigration was Reaganite "common sense," and continues to literally and figuratively make sense. The paradigm of neoliberal crimmigration has proven profitable far beyond its "playful" incarnation in Genesis's "Illegal Alien."

5

Over-Looking Difference

Amnesty and the Rise of Latina/o Pop Culture

"It is better to be looked over than overlooked."
—Mae West in *Belle of the Nineties* (1934)

At the February 1999 Grammy Awards, Ricky Martin's performance of a bilingual Spanish/English song, "La Copa de la Vida," gave rise to "Rickymania" and sparked a wave of media interest in Latin pop music.[1] In May, *Time*'s cover proclaimed, "Latin Music Goes Pop,"[2] while *Rolling Stone*'s cover trumpeted, "La explosion pop Latino," and in a feature story covered Martin, Marc Anthony, Enrique Iglesias, and others.[3] A July *Newsweek* cover featured a photo of Junot Diaz, Shakira, and Oscar de la Hoya, with the headline "Latin U.S.A.: How Young Hispanics Are Changing America."[4] In September, *New York* magazine's cover summed it all up as the "The Latin Explosion" and devoted the entire issue to "Latin culture," especially food and music. For the issue, the magazine changed its cover logo to "Nueva York," included a photo of Jennifer Lopez, and carried a feature on her called "The Star Next Door."[5] Other popular press articles focused on the increasing "Hispanic" population, largely due to immigration, and "Latin" products for these new consumers— everything from beans to cosmetics—flooded the market.

Jennifer Lopez, the New York–born Puerto Rican singer, dancer, actress, reality show host, producer, and creator of multiple clothing lines, perfumes, and home goods, is perhaps the most enduring face of the Latin Explosion as the (then) latest iteration of the American Dream. As Angharad Valdivia notes, "J. Lo is the contemporary signifier for Latinidad and stands alone in a nearly iconic position vis-à-vis other mainstream Latina actresses-cum-entertainers."[6] ("Latinidad" describes a flexible social formation for those who identify as Latina/o in that they may embrace various racial identities such as Latina, American, Chicana, Afro-Cuban, Puerto Rican, and so on, which are shaped by capital [marketing, advertising] and the U.S. Census.[7]) She is a "bona fide star, media mogul, and brand. Moreover, as she has crossed over into mainstream representations, she cannot be contained within an ethnic identity."[8] At the time of writing she has a net worth of $250 million dollars[9]

Figure 5.1. Lopez was frequently racialized as Latina in photographs that highlighted her buttocks, as in this widely circulated image.

and has inspired Latina/o[10] and female "ethnic" entertainers.[11] In 2012, VH1 ranked her No. 16 in its "100 Greatest Women in Music List,"[12] and Forbes ranked her No. 1 in its Celebrity 100 list.[13] From 2010 to 2012 she offered others access to the American Dream as a judge on the hit reality show, *American Idol*. Prominent in the popular press since the early 2000s, she is also the topic of much academic research.[14] But when Lopez was just starting her career in the context of the Latin Explosion, her success as a commodity rode on her derriere and her American Dream story, which looked over and overlooked race and gender in complex ways that, though she is not an immigrant, encapsulate neoliberal crossings.[15]

According to celebrity gossip website, TheInsider.com, Nuyorican (New York–born Puerto Rican) Lopez, who grew up in the Bronx, "is a living embodiment of the 'American Dream': a rags-to-riches story proving that anyone can do great things with hard work, talent and a little luck."[16] In fact, Lopez comes from a comfortable middle-class family. She got her big break as a "fly girl" dancer on *In Living Color*, a 1990s sketch comedy TV show, and then earned acting roles in blockbuster films after her breakout role in *Selena* (1997), the biopic of the popular Mexican American pop singer who was murdered by her manager.[17] With *Out of Sight* (1998), in which Lopez's racial and ethnic identity was undefined, Lopez became the highest paid Latina in Hollywood history. Going on to play a number of racially ambiguous characters, she again played Latina characters only later in her career.[18] She simultaneously launched a successful pop music career,[19] turned herself into an extremely lucrative brand and designer of an array of goods, and in 2013 even launched her own mobile communications retail brand with Verizon.[20]

Lopez's early fame as an actress and pop musician—her rise from "rags to riches"—is inseparable from her Latina identity, and has been articulated most frequently and pointedly in a popular fixation on her buttocks—a fixation extending to rumors that Lopez insured her rear end for millions of dollars.[21] Latina bodies are complex signifiers that both affirm and disrupt the status quo. On one hand, the hypersexualization and exoticization of women of color as a form of social control has a long history, and as Ana Lopez has argued, Hollywood presents some bodies in an ethnographic manner, translating otherness for mainstream audiences.[22] On the other hand, Latina/o Studies scholars have argued that Lopez's celebration of her buttocks resists the marginalization of Latinas/os and overtly challenges white dominance and beauty ideals.[23] In fact Lopez's 2001 debut clothing line of urban sportswear was designed to celebrate curvy and, one might argue, "ethnic" women. Of its debut, Lopez said in the *Puerto Rico Herald*, "I find it is difficult for women who are curvaceous to find clothes in stores that fit. The voluptuous

woman is almost ignored. I want to offer clothes that are wonderfully designed and will fit women of all sizes. Everybody gets to be sexy."[24]

In the mid-2000s, when Lopez's star was rising, this threat to "American
image gatekeepers"[25] was scrutinized in the media as a demanding diva who
cared only about wealth and fame; she, in turn, attempted to redeem herself
by casting herself as a hardworking woman of color who earned everything
she has, in accordance with the neoliberal "nation of immigrants" ideal. Arlene Davila calls sanitized, marketable efforts to show that Latinas/os embody
traditional American values the "Latino spin."[26] As Gina M. Perez, Frank A.
Guridy, and Adrian Burgos, Jr., note in their introduction to *Beyond El Barrio:
Everyday Life in Latina/o America*, although such market discourses "often
emerge as important correctives to negative images of Latina/o communities,
they often do so at the expense of empirical evidence as well as those groups
whose marginal economic and social standing are attributed to individual
failures and moral shortcomings"; the lived experiences of Latinas/os are
erased by these "deeply political constructs."[27] The 2002 song and video for
"Jenny from the Block," from Lopez's third album, *This Is Me . . . Now*, chronicled Lopez's rising star and responded to tabloid criticism with the "Latino
spin." The song, which peaked at No. 8 on the Billboard Hot 100 Chart, begins
with a statement about the necessity of making a living ("Children grow and
women producing, / Men go working, some go stealing, / Everyone's got to
make a living"[28]), and asserts that wealth and fame are not at odds with her
Nuyorican roots. The song thus aligns Lopez's story with the neoliberal "nation of immigrants" trope. (Notably, Puerto Ricans have a distinct relationship to im/migration, with technically full rights as U.S. citizens, albeit these
rights do not quite play out in practice.[29])

Other components of the song and video showcase Lopez's navigation of
race and ethnicity, making this message clearer. The song, blending hip hop
and R&B, features black rappers Jadakiss and Styles P. In the video, which
is shot from the paparazzi's point of view and plays on/with the fallacious
rumors they fueled, Lopez cavorts on a yacht and in other lavish locales
with then-boyfriend Ben Affleck, a white American movie star. Shots of her
rear end abound, a tongue-in-cheek (ahem) acknowledgement of the media
fixation on her buttocks. Against this visual backdrop, lyrics stress Lopez's
hard work and ongoing connection to her ethnic urban roots via an ongoing
association with the Puerto Rican barrio in the Bronx, which was formed
in response to migration and displacement engendered by postcolonial
U.S. agrarian capitalism, the island's industrialization program, and state-
sanctioned migration programs. In the barrio, newcomers found inexpensive
housing, as had previous generations of white ethnic immigrants in other

"ethnic" neighborhoods.[30] In Lopez's case, the barrio is romanticized rather than maligned as it is in *Fort Apache, the Bronx*, though both representations elide or erase empirical reality. The chorus of the song states:

> Don't be fooled by the rocks that I got
> I'm still Jenny from the block
> Used to have a little now I have a lot
> No matter where I go I know where I came from—the Bronx![31]

In a study of how Lopez represents herself and how her marketers and her fans represent her, Tara Lockhart observes that in the song, the "ethnic-American Dream is both fully realized, in terms of her wealth, and authenticated by her allegiance to home and culture."[32] "Jenny from the Block" is as concealing as it is revealing, overlooking a great deal even as it seems to look closely over race and gender and one Latina's achievement of the American Dream. For instance, what kind of fooling (Latino spinning?) were the "rocks" (slang for diamonds) doing? And how might this relate to immigration policy that was literally about overlooking? The neoliberal incorporation of feminism and multiculturalism was striking in the rise of Latina/o popular culture and IRCA amnesty, both of which commodified a variety of things (people, success stories, spaces, policies) while appearing to be democratizing the country. IRCA amnesty was widely praised as a progressive watershed in immigration policy, and just after IRCA passed, the rise of Latina/o pop culture was similarly heralded as an example of American inclusion and diversity.

Considering the rise of Latina/o pop culture in relation to roughly contemporary IRCA amnesty and "nation of immigrants" discourses exposes cultural and legal discomforts with Latinas/os at the moment of their incorporation as desirable, globally commodifiable bodies. In order to show how amnesty and Latina/o pop culture naturalized a causal relationship among citizenship, freedom, and free markets and obscured the inequalities underscoring the U.S. neoliberal project, this chapter traces the "nation of immigrants" tropes circulating in and around amnesty, and in discourses in and about Latina/o pop culture and especially Latina stars.

The etymology of "amnesty" points to the freedom it grants by altering seeing, looking, and remembering. The noun refers to a "'pardon of past offenses,' 1570s, from Fr. *amnestie* 'intentional overlooking,' from L. *amnestia*, from Gk. *amnestia* 'forgetfulness' (of wrong); an amnesty, from *a-*, privative prefix, not + *mnestis* 'remembrance,' related to *mnaomai* 'I remember' (see *mind* [n.]). As a verb, from 1809."[33] In common English usage, "amnesty" describes legislative acts that restore innocence to offenders: amnesty overlooks an offense, obliterating all legal remembrance of it. IRCA amnesty thus connoted liberty in freeing recipients from the dangers, vulnerabilities, and stigma of illegality.

In keeping with the American tradition of turning to law to resolve social issues, amnesty was a promise of freedom and civil rights to the undocumented, an especially powerful promise in the context of 1980s multiculturalism and anti-communism. In terms of the rise of Latina/o pop culture, a variety of "Latin" commodities were sold, and Latina stars who were coded as immigrants such as Selena and Lopez became household names. As the popular media fixated on and celebrated each woman's voluptuous figure and especially her buttocks, both inspired fans with their American Dream stories, which suggested that anyone—including a Latina woman—can be successful and powerful with hard work. So on the heels of the promise of freedom via amnesty, Latinas seemed free to succeed, and Latina/o consumers were free to exercise and express citizenship by consuming a new array of "Latin" products.

The free market economy drove these developments: amnesty secured a cheap immigrant labor pool, and Latina/o pop culture was lucrative for the corporations and producers of Latina/o stars and products and increased Latina/o media representation. Both the market and media made it seem as though the nation offered a level playing field to Latinas/os, but the "nation of immigrants" rhetoric surrounding amnesty and Latina/o pop culture concealed the market-value impetus and attendant racism and sexism behind both changes. As such, amnesty and the rise of Latina/o pop culture worked assiduously for neoliberalism by both overlooking and looking over race and gender.

"Nation of immigrants" discourse enabled this overlooking/looking over in two distinct ways. Under neoliberalism, "ascriptions of value and valuelessness are unevenly detached from overt reference to race, yet their deployment provides for extreme racialized violence."[34] Surplus value is extracted from racialized and gendered bodies with universalized discourses of value (equal opportunity for abstracted subjects, for *every* body, *any* body) *and* through the mobilization of embodied multicultural and feminist rhetoric. On one hand, discourse that welcomed and celebrated an abstracted immigrant subject who was free to succeed (compete) on the basis of individual hard work was coded as the epitome of Americanism. Race and gender were overlooked or erased, much as amnesty overlooked the offense of illegality, and this overlooking was considered antiracist and antisexist. On the other hand, "nation of immigrants" discourse that welcomed and celebrated explicitly racialized and gendered hardworking, successful immigrants was also posited as emblematically American. Tokens of diversity or multiculturalism signified American parity. Race and gender were thus looked over (or overly looked at) as indicators of America's unparalleled commitment to equality and diversity, a commitment best realized through all citizens' access to the free market.

Additionally, "nation of immigrants" discourse that framed citizenship as the conduit of freedom and rights (literally in the case of amnesty, and in terms of wealth and the ability to consume in the case of Latina/o pop culture) concealed and consequently reproduced racialized and gendered violence. Monisha Das Gupta has observed that "full citizenship, which is the goal of civil rights–oriented visions of justice, naturalizes and reinscribes the policing functions of borders that territorialize racialized, ethnicized, and gendered notions of belonging. The civil rights model formulates the lack of or the routine violation of rights of subjects inhabiting a national space as second-class citizenship, a condition that needs to be corrected through struggles for full national belonging." Immigrants whose realities were necessarily transnational and border-crossing are erased: "immigrant rights when framed as civil rights get interpellated by discourses of citizenship."[35] Whether overlooking or looking over race and gender, "nation of immigrants" tropes obscured the transnational realities of immigrants' lives; racialized, gendered labor exploitation; and increasing militarization and violence at the border (which were also rationalized by the "immigration emergency" discourse that circulated simultaneously).

The material consequences of IRCA and its amnesty provisions—namely, women's exclusion, the fracturing of families, bureaucratic red tape that kept applicants dependent upon their employers during a five-year waiting period, and privileging of undocumented Irish—were masked both by the rhetoric of legal inclusion in the "nation of immigrants" and by the "Latin Explosion," which was also enveloped in "nation of immigrants" discourse. My demystification of "nation of immigrants" tropes in connection with amnesty law and pop culture thus further illuminates the relation between public policy and what is more often considered "culture" in shaping the material realities of people's lives.[36] This new immigration legislation was no facilitator of democracy, nor was the success of a few Latina individuals and the marketability of ethnic products. In fact, the "Latin Explosion" was short lived.[37] Neoliberalism combines modernist, Fordist modes of production with "primitive" modes like sweatshops, home work, and undocumented immigrant and child labor. Race and gender support this "one-way globalization."[38] On one hand, the exploitation of a minority labor force seems logical; it is Reaganite "common sense" that a "lesser" population would be poorer, less successful, more inclined to commit crimes, and so on. On the other hand, corporations

market identity in racialized, gendered terms to the increasingly diverse consumer populations that globalization engenders; diverse commodities and the
cultural visibility of difference(s) are framed as evidence of neoliberalism's
"universal" returns.[39] Much like Marx's notion of the capitalist commodity
as a hieroglyph that camouflages alienation and serves "as a stand-in for direct social relations between subjects,"[40] both "nation of immigrants" strains
functioned as neoliberal fetishes that mystified—one might say overlooked—
exploitative social relations.

Forgiving, Forgetting, and Fetishizing Race and Gender

Before IRCA debates began, amnesty was on the table to address the undocumented immigration "crisis" that had begun in the 1970s, when the term
"Latin Explosion" would have had a quite different connotation. Previous
chapters discussed conservative opposition to amnesty. At the center of this
chapter is the humanitarian framing of amnesty: What kind of labor did this
do with and for neoliberalism? What was overlooked and looked over?

From the earliest mentions of amnesty, some pundits used democratic "nation of immigrants" language and imagery to frame it as a humanitarian effort that would provide deserving (that is, self-supporting, net-contributing,
and heterosexual) undocumented immigrants with rights and protections.
Amnesty ostensibly "forgave"—or intentionally overlooked—illegality and rewarded multicultural recipients who earned it with the opportunity to pursue
the "American Dream." This provided pointed support for neoliberalism.

Jodie Melamed proposes that successive formations of multiculturalism
ascribed value and valuelessness to human beings after World War II, when
white supremacy entered a stage of crisis, given the commitment of Western democracies to antiracism, antifascism, and decolonization, and the civil
rights and black power movements exacerbated the crisis. Consequently, different formations of multiculturalism rearticulated racialization as a system of
privilege and stigmatization. Melamed defines "neoliberal multiculturalism"
as a combination of procedure and discourse that portrays multiculturalism
as the "spirit of neoliberalism and posits neoliberal restructuring across the
globe to be the key to a postracist world of freedom and opportunity."[41] While
Melamed's important research distinguishes between liberal multiculturalism
of the 1980s and 1990s and the neoliberal multiculturalism that followed, in
my review of immigration discourses, I show that neoliberal multiculturalism
was already ascendant in the 1980s. Liberal multiculturalism was characterized by the depoliticization of economic arrangements through the establishment of individualism, property rights, and market economies as signifiers

of equality (that is, abstract equality before the law and equal opportunity). Equality was achieved through cultural integration and inclusion of multicultural identities. By privileging individual rights, this system erased the race politics underscoring privatization and the growing gap that deregulation produced. Melamed shows that neoliberal multiculturalism abstracted multiculturalism, coding the free market as the ultimate expression of equality; categories of racial privilege and stigma were rearticulated beyond color lines so that that "neoliberalism's winners" were multicultural global citizens.[42] The reframing of "winners" was underway in the 1980s: abstract equality before the law with the integration and celebration of multicultural identities *and* the abstracted coding of the market as antiracist were inaugurated via "nation of immigrants" rhetoric; the immigrant or the person coded as immigrant provided the prototype for Melamed's "neoliberal winner." Moreover, as argued earlier, the notion that immigrants and especially immigrants of color earned rights through hard work and gendered respectability was also delineated in the Reagan era in a trope that was both a vehicle of and rationale for neoliberalism well beyond Reagan's two terms. Thus, the tone and paradigm for neoliberal multiculturalism and for that matter, neoliberal feminism and/or postfeminism, were established in the 1980s.

Overlap between liberal and neoliberal multiculturalism is evident in the final IRCA Senate session, with abstract "nation of immigrants" rhetoric appearing again. Then-Senator Joe Biden (D-DE) asserted that "immigration has always been in the national interest and the amnesty program in this bill represents the best of that tradition." Amnesty would "move a growing underclass living in the shadows into the daylight of citizenship and opportunity. These individuals must become full partners in government and full participants in our society, not just the object of our concern."[43]

Biden lobbied for inclusion under the law as part of a U.S. tradition of treating citizenship as the pathway to opportunity: with a hint of neoliberal abstracting, his racially neutral underclass of immigrants could become "neoliberal winners" if granted unencumbered access to American equal opportunity. Others looked over race and gender in terms of equal opportunity, which also made neoliberal restructuring look humanitarian. Looking over surfaced as the more prevalent integration and celebration of multicultural identities, and while this version of looking tends to align with liberal multiculturalism, the prototype for neoliberal multiculturalism was evident as well.

In the same session, Gary Hart (D-CO), like Biden, made an impassioned plea for amnesty with direct recourse to racial equality. Hart pointed out that the nation's treatment of undocumented immigrants involved balancing national sovereignty with "the role that America has played as a haven for the oppressed. It is an issue that forces us to reconcile law enforcement needs with our commitment to civil liberties and civil rights." Additionally, Hart opposed earlier versions of IRCA because he feared that employer sanctions were a civil rights issue, as business would surely try to avoid hiring blacks, Hispanics, and Asians.[44]

Similar racialized "nation of immigrants" tropes claims proliferated in the popular press. After IRCA 1984 failed to pass, a *New York Times* article entitled "The Death of a Humane Idea" declared that had the bill passed, its inauguration could have been called "Freedom Day" because "hundreds and thousands of aliens, most of them Hispanic, would have lined up in church basements and country courthouses from Amarillo to Brooklyn, eager to come in from the cold of illegality and accept America's humane offer of amnesty." The article averred that the "loss [of the bill] for Hispanic Americans is monumental," especially since it would have also offered justice to women who had been raped but, fearing deportation, did not report the crime.[45] Focusing on racialized equal opportunity and gender justice, these iterations of "nation of immigrants" discourse in support of amnesty align with liberal multiculturalism.

An article published in the *Times* just after IRCA passed in 1986 also sang its praises as a humanitarian watershed, while emphasizing that Mexican and Latin American undocumented immigrants would *earn* the freedom amnesty promised with hard work and respectability,[46] a neoliberal ideology first articulated in early IRCA debates. In this blend of liberal and neoliberal multiculturalism, the unfettered market was cast as offering freedom for all.

This rhetorical pattern continued the "nation of immigrant" trope that cohered early on in IRCA debates. In the Senate record from September 28, 1982, under a subsection entitled "Nation of Immigrants," Edward Kennedy (D-MA), lifelong immigration proponent, brother of President John F. Kennedy, and co-author of the IRCA special visa program specifically designed to help Irish aliens legalize, worked the trope to challenge restrictionist lobbies. He began by pointing out that "except for native Indian citizens, we are all immigrants or refugees or the descendants of immigrants and refugees."[47] Kennedy averred that Dena Kleman's article "Influx of Immigrants Spices Life of New York," printed in full in the *Congressional Record* and part of a *New York Times* series on "The New Melting Pot" initiated that week, was filled with "overwhelming confidence in America and the opportunities it offers" for industrious immigrants. President Reagan used similar language: pundits on both sides of the partisan divide argued for the national value of "hardworking" immigrants who earned rights.

In her case study of Elmhurst, Queens, "the city's most ethnically diverse neighborhood where 20,000 immigrants from more than 110 countries" live,[48] Kleman noted that a Korean grocer, Argentine butcher, and Colombian baker coexisted and labored harmoniously; saris, mandarin collars, Pakistani pickles, and a variety of other ethnic delicacies, were far more available for purchase in stores than the American dietary staple, the hamburger. While Kleman acknowledged that some immigrants struggled to make ends meet even though they worked hard, rather than dwell on that point and its possible implications, she focused on the victors, on "neoliberalism's winners," like Sarita Ocampo, who, after emigrating from Colombia, worked her way up from being a maid to hiring her own maid following the success of her work in real estate with her husband, also a Latin American immigrant. Ocampo is not the "global multicultural citizen" that Melamed describes; according to Kleman, Ocampo became firmly American with her success. But what enabled that success for her, and the other multicultural immigrants of the article, was the market itself, and of course she literally worked for it.

In sum, the immigrants of these 1980s "nation of immigrants" discourses were not yet fully the global citizens of Melamed's neoliberal multiculturalism in that abstract equality in law and racialized and gendered equal opportunity (overlooking and looking over, respectively) were the dominant tropes, as well as being what made immigrants so useful to Reaganite patriotic chauvinism. But the neoliberal multiculturalism Melamed describes was ascendant in the abstracting of the market as the conduit of universal prosperity and in repeated assertions that immigrants earned their rights and economic opportunities.

The affective power of neoliberalism's multicultural "winners" was perhaps most striking in the rise of Latina/o pop culture. Latinas/os became a target demographic for "Latin American" and "Hispanic" products, and hardworking Latina/o stars exemplified how the "nation of immigrants" trope created multicultural neoliberal winners.

Remembering Race and Gender

Some scholars, like free market economists, view the market as the "great leveler" that facilitates equal representation for all, which is a quintessentially neoliberal position. For instance, Marilyn Halter argues that while historically the market/consumption was a way for immigrants to assimilate, beginning in the late twentieth century the market/consuming goods allowed immigrants and minority groups to *accentuate* cultural differences in becoming American.[49] Halter casts the rise of ethnic marketing as emancipatory, in what might be called "multicultural consumer citizenship." But the marketing of "difference" and marketing to "difference" of/for increasingly diverse consumers epitomizes "neoliberal neoracism, in terms of what Melamed calls the "repressive hypothesis of difference," whereby because difference was repressed historically, not repressing it can be cast as evidence of increasing equality.[50] Representation in mainstream culture thereby becomes a substitute for material equality, so only corporations and perhaps some "different" or "diverse" individuals benefit from increasing visibility in mainstream culture; this mainstream visibility as "evidence" of equality or progress erases the structural genesis and maintenance of inequality and upholds the status quo.

In the early 1980s, the growing Latina/o population was becoming a target market. Studies to determine how to court this new market proliferated; corporations had to avoid offensive stereotypes while selling to various Latina/o markets because research indicated that different nationalities had different purchasing habits. While some scholars map differentiation within Latinidad,[51] in advertising and pop culture, Latinidad is often conveyed in tropes of big families, tropical settings, and "Latin" music and by gendered and racialized physical features such as brown or olive skin color and curvaceousness in women. Linguistic "difference" was considered the most significant overarching feature, so advertisements were often in Spanish, as in Hallmark's revision and expansion of a Hispanic line of greeting cards, Primor, which launched in 1980. Tropes such as tropicalism may seem innocuous enough, as may Gerber's generalized line of Latina/o baby foods and products, Tesoros, or treasures, which featured brightly colored bibs with Spanish phrases and tropical fruits and specialized baby foods like black bean soup.[52] However, as Latina/o Communication Studies scholar Isabel Molina-Guzman has shown, "sexuality plays a central role in the tropicalization of Latinas through the widely circulated narratives of sexual availability, proficiency, and desirability."[53]

Furthermore, as Valdivia has noted, Spanish products and celebrities of Spanish descent such as Penelope Cruz and Antonio Banderas were also collapsed into Latinidad: the "Latina/o boom is often treated as if it referred to an undifferentiated and homogenous group of peoples and cultural traditions." Moreover, the category of Hispanic "executes a far broader and insidious cultural elision" that links authenticity to Latin America, and provides a way to police the borders around the ethnic category.[54] Additionally, neoliberal consumer citizenship reimagines rights as a literalized "purchasing power," which is gendered and racialized, even when the commodities themselves and "purchasing power" appear to be multicultural. For example, while the terms "Latina" and "Latino" refer to a cultural identity that displaces or supersedes national identities to indicate shared ethnicity in an era of globalization, "Latina/o" also describes "a specifically American national currency for economic and political deal-making; a technology to demand and deliver emotions, votes, markets, and resources on the same level as other racialized minorities."[55] "Latina/o" commodities occlude these complexities, as well as the labor involved in their production, distribution, and consumption.

Like "Latin American" commodities such as baby food and greeting cards, in the 1990s stars of various Latin American (and also Spanish) ethnicities were conspicuously celebrated and sold in a complex continuum of looking over and overlooking that affirmed, manipulated, and sometimes challenged tropicalism in connection with the "nation of immigrants" bootstraps/American Dream myths. As in the white ethnic mythos, the visibility of "difference" and upward mobility through individual hard work "proved" that racism and sexism could be overcome, yet inequality persisted. Moreover, the visibility of gender was inseparable from a long history of defining racial difference through the hypersexualization of female body parts.

Numerous Latina/o performers such as Selena, Jennifer Lopez, Gloria Estefan, Shakira, Christina Aguilera, Ricky Martin, Mark Anthony, and Enrique Iglesias became household names in the 1990s, and while the "Latin Explosion" was short lived, these entertainers proved more enduring. Their success hinged upon their convincing performance of stereotypes: they had to be heterosexual, exotic, sexy, bilingual embodiments of otherness who were safely sanitized by wealth, stardom,[56] and, as in the case of Selena and Jennifer Lopez, racially and ethnically flexible embodiments of the "nation of immigrants" and "rags to riches" American Dream story. These stars are neoliberalism's winners.

Selena Quintanilla Perez brought Tejano music, a popular working-class and previously male-dominated Latina/o musical form created in the Texas/Mexico borderlands, into the mainstream. Although Selena is a U.S. citizen by birth and Tejano music is just as "American" as it is "Mexican," the genre was viewed as an immigrant or "foreign" phenomenon. With Selena being frequently "revered as an embodiment of often undervalued aspects of *latinidad*: the *morena* (dark-skinned) and the working class,"[57] her crossover success into the mainstream hinged upon the racialized and gendered fetishization of her body, her simultaneous racial and ethnic flexibility, and the exploitation of her American Dream story.

As with Lopez, media often focused on Selena's full figure and especially her buttocks, so to an extent, Selena's popularity signaled a diversification of concepts of beauty; although she was Chicana, "an ethnicity not associated in the Caribbean popular imagination with big butts," her curvy body type is generally perceived as abject by American standards.[58] But this diversification was quite limited. In the nineteenth century, colonial naturalist Georges Cuvier studied the African woman Saartje Baartman, a.k.a. the Venus Hottentot,

and claimed that her protruding buttocks and large labia evidenced a fundamental difference between Africans and whites. As Siobhan Somerville points
out, "starting with Cuvier, this tradition of comparative anatomy located the
boundaries of race through the sexual and reproductive anatomy of the African female body."[59] Hypersexualization became synonymous with racialization, and women's buttocks became emblems of (always already heterosexual)
racial differentiation. For persons of the Caribbean diaspora, references to the
buttocks are also "a way of speaking about Africa in(side) America."[60] This
extends to the hypersexualization of Latinas.[61]

The commodification of the Latina star and Selena products marketed
to Latinas/os also suggested that anyone can literally buy into the American
Dream with products such as a CD; this too limited Selena's potential as a
challenge to dominant narratives and ideals. After her murder Selena almost
instantly became an icon used both to appeal to the emerging Latina/o market and to reinforce the borders of U.S. identity:[62] "numerous corporate forces
acknowledged Selena's tragedy as a way to inform Latina/os that they could
become American only by becoming consumers."[63] This commodification of
one woman's success erased the disenfranchisement of Latin American immigrants and Latinas/os and offered the rhetoric of transactional freedom in
lieu of systemic empowerment or change, while Selena's marketability was a
tropicalized legacy of the Venus Hottentot. In short, not only Selena products
but Selena herself was a neoliberal commodity fetish.

Furthermore, the micropolitics of choice are also a key feature of postfeminism in terms of presenting consumption as freedom: within an allegedly benevolent, inclusive neoliberal capitalist democracy, a woman's freedom
to choose from among an array of commodities is framed as the conduit to
and fruit of the gains of mainstream second-wave feminism, which emphasized a woman's right to make her own reproductive choices, the "right to
choose." These micropolitics of choice, divorced from history and context,
perpetuate violence against women both nationally and internationally. Karen
Orr Vered and Sal Humphreys observe that in relation to postfeminism, the
theme of gratitude, a theme also inherent to the "nation of immigrants trope"
and its "rags to riches" complement, is linked to the framing of consumption
as freedom. Within the United States, "being grateful [for choices] implies
that women continue to occupy a subjugated role in a power hierarchy that
is indefensible."[64] Moreover, it pitches Western women against women in
other countries by making the modern nation-state that offers (consumptive)
freedoms seem far superior to fundamentalist nations,[65] and, I would add,
Communist nations, or any sending nation really. This casting of the West as
democratically and morally superior because of its vast consumer "freedoms"

for women and people of color was already happening in the 1980s, and is connected to Neda Atananoski's theory of the erasure of U.S. "humanitarian violence" via multiculturalism. Through feminist and multicultural narratives within "nation of immigrants" discourse, the United States is cast as superior in terms of opportunity, freedom, and humanitarian-ness. For instance, Sarita Ocampo's story of working her way up from being a maid to employing her own maid exemplifies how an immigrant woman's mobility within the U.S. labor market and increasing purchasing power, which Ocampo was grateful for, rendered the United States beyond critique.

Ethnic flexibility was also part of the fetishization of Latinas. Interestingly, Lopez had her first taste of mainstream success playing Selena; Lockhart notes, "like Selena, Lopez is celebrated in terms of her adeptness and success in bridging ethnic and racial gaps."[66] And as Molina-Guzman notes, Lopez's successful performance in *Selena* exemplifies the flexibility of Latinidad in that the similarities between the women (body type, skin color, hair, both being U.S.-born to Latina/o parents, neither learning Spanish until later in life) outweighed ethnic differences (Selena was Mexican American/Tejana, Lopez is Puerto Rican). The Arenas Group, an advertising and talent management group focused on the Latina/o market, marketed *Selena* with broad ethnic and racial appeal, and key to the success of this strategy (the film earned a respectable $35.3 million at the box office) was framing Selena's American Dream story in class terms that were not racially specific. That is, Selena was presented as a working-class girl from Texas who made it big, and Lopez's racial and ethnic flexibility was the conduit to the story's broad appeal. Latinas/os and non-Latinas/os would pay to see Latina/o actors,[67] within the context of a universal(ized) American Dream story that had all the components of its most prevalent and visceral iteration, the "nation of immigrants" trope.[68]

The way that Latinidad is signified in the media as panethnic—as not quite white but rarely black, instead occupying a space of racial ambiguity and commodifiable brownness[69]—is applicable to Lopez, but she has also personally and deliberately cultivated a flexible identity that has made her an extremely lucrative commodity (and, arguably, an embodied site of disruption to gendered white ideals). Lopez looks over and overlooks her own racial and ethnic identities in order to fit a particular market. Therefore in a very literal way—not just in her marketing—Lopez herself embodies neoliberal flexible accumulation, the ways that commodities occlude social relations, and the way that marketers flexibly used Latina/o identity. Lopez (and Latina/o media outlets) stressed a Puerto Rican and also generally Latina identity within Latina/o media by highlighting her Nuyorican roots and proudly celebrating her curvaceous body as a signifier of Latina authenticity. Lopez has also played various Latina ethnicities in films, described her music as "Latin,"[70] and verbally emphasized her Latina identity. In addition, she has stressed an affinity with black American urban identity and pop culture by collaborating with black rappers (to which she returned in "Jenny from the Block"), sporting hip hop styles such as cornrows, shooting videos in urban neighborhoods, and in her relationship with black hip hop mogul Sean Combs (Puff Daddy/P. Diddy/Puffy).[71] Beginning with *Out of Sight* in 1998, she began portraying ethnically ambiguous characters that moved her closer to whiteness.[72] Molina-Guzman has shown that the challenge Lopez posed to white dominant ideals with her embrace of her sensuality, particularly through her booty and its connections to Puerto Rican, Latina, and black cultures, was contained via coverage of her as a "diva" during and after her relationship with Affleck (2002–2004), which was part of a continuum of mediascapes that usually cast Puerto Rican women as uneducated and promiscuous.[73]

With "Jenny from the Block," Lopez used the "nation of immigrants" trope as a key part of her rebuff against negative press. But in emphasizing her Nuyorican roots and the hard work that her fame and wealth required, the racial and gendered boundaries of the "nation of immigrants" trope was exposed: as a woman of color dating a white man (that is, white ethnic given that Affleck is Irish American), her economic success—what everyone can and is supposed to strive for in America and what supposedly makes America so exceptional and great—was suspect, excessive, and dangerous. Although mediascapes suggested that diva behavior and dogged pursuit of wealth and fame were what made her deserving of censure, not her race, "the tension between global desire and domestic danger explains the gendering and racialization of Lopez as outside the boundaries of whiteness and middle-class respectability."[74] And Lopez's defense, her hard work via the "nation of immigrants" trope, required embracing the very things that negate what makes Lopez's fame and popularity remarkable, dangerous, and precarious.

Although outside of the scope of this analysis, it is notable that Lopez later gained some respectability by reconnecting with her Latina identity: her sexuality was safely contained in marriage to fellow Nuyorican Marc Anthony in 2005, and she was softened by motherhood,[75] which continues to soften her even after her divorce from Anthony. She returned to playing Latina characters, and for her advocacy on behalf of the Juarez murder victims through the 2006 film *Bordertown*, she received the "Artists of Amnesty" award from Amnesty International.[76] Lopez's adroit performances of race and ethnicity to court different markets have allowed her to take up space as a Latina in the entertainment industry in unprecedented ways and to advocate for others. Lopez, as a symbol or representative of Latinidad, provides points of access to alternative or oppositional narratives and ways of being. But like Selena, the example of Lopez indicates that racism and sexism continue to limit the shape and scope of alternative and oppositional narratives and modes of being.

In the case of Latina stars such as Selena and Lopez, what is fetishized is the prototypical American story of hard work to achieve success and the notion that anyone, including a Latina, can be wealthy and staggeringly successful if only she works hard enough . . . and has a big—but not so big as to cancel out racial fluidity—butt. The alleged visibility of their labor is itself key to the power of the fetish. But there is more to the story. J-Lo's embrace of her buttocks indicates a diversification of beauty ideals and the popularization of an attitude of defiance toward dominant culture: the Latina buttocks are "an invitation to pleasures construed as illicit by puritan ideologies, heteronormativity, and the medical establishment through the three deadly vectors of miscegenation, sodomy, and a high-fat diet. Unlike big breasts, big bottoms have no morals, no symbolic function, and no use in reproduction."[77] Nonetheless, the hyper-heterosexualization of the Venus Hottentot underscores the cultural visibility of the buttocks, and the derriere itself is commodified not for the profit and empowerment of a disenfranchised group, but rather for the profit and empowerment of one Latina woman, the individual success story that was the Reaganite "commonsense" indicator of a fair free market system. And that itself had gendered, racialized limits, as indicated by the discursive disciplining of Lopez as one outside of the boundaries of whiteness and middle-class respectability.

Broadly speaking, the visibility of minority identity is simply not an automatic or even likely path to, or indicator of, socioeconomic equity. The fact that a Latina/o can to an extent manipulate and profit from racist, sexist stereotypes demonstrates the atomizing logic of neoliberal capital and the market value of those stereotypes. This is not to villainize Lopez but rather to show what her story does to and for neoliberalism, and how neoliberalism circumscribes her options. The visibility of Latinas/os in the marketplace did not result in political enfranchisement,[78] and as one executive succinctly put it in a 1993 *Time* article, "None of this [ethnic marketing] would be happening . . . if corporate America wasn't making money."[79] The same is true of "working women" TV shows and most recently the increasing visibility of LGBTQ characters and celebrities, the products marketed to LGBTQ consumers in relation to Pride celebrations, and the passage of same-sex marriage. Indeed, zealous efforts by nativists to pass English Only legislation in the 1980s and 1990s demonstrates that Spanish-language advertising did not "translate" into political empowerment for Latinas/os even as policies seemed to liberalize in some ways, and the fact that the purportedly progressive commodities are heterosexual *women's* butts in a nation that makes sense of race via gender and sexuality cannot be overlooked.

The commodity is a mystification of value that alienates people from themselves and each other. Neoliberal rhetoric compounds that alienation by making the commodities themselves seem to expose (fair, equitable) labor practices and social relations. With Selena and J-Lo products, two-tier alienation happens because the stars themselves and the American Dream mythos surrounding them strongly suggest that the system is fair and accessible to hardworking, curvaceous Latinas (who are also ethnically flexible) and who are thus embodiments of the efficacy of the neoliberal "nation of immigrants" trope.

***

The material realities of the general amnesty program and SAW as humanitarian failures tell a different story. Jaafar Aksikas and Sean Johnson Andrews have analyzed the "neoliberal ideology of the 'free contract'" in which "one side [a corporate entity] has significantly more power in the bargain."[80] This can likely be applied to Latina/o entertainers and the contracts they signed (though such contracts are not my focus here), and can be extended to immigration law and the "free contract" that immigrants and especially immigrant laborers sign (that is, agree to) as legal(izing) U.S. residents. With the Bracero Program such contracts were a matter of rather direct imported colonialism. Under the amnesty program and its neoliberal rhetoric of freedom and progressiveness, it was easy to overlook the imbalanced power dynamic. In extending Aksikas and Andrews's observations, my implication is that under neoliberalism the law functions as a corporate entity given its orientation toward protecting the interests of capital, and the racial and gender politics that that orientation entails. The amnesty provision needed the support of, and thus had to protect, the interests of agribusiness and free market economists in the midst of strong nativist interest in immigration restriction. Though many immigrants did complete the program and legalize, it passed because it protected profits for the propertied rather than immigrants' human rights, and because it did not shake up the status quo. If some encountered some exploitative working conditions along the way or were unable to legalize, neoliberalism had an answer to that too: "individual choices, with those individuals held personally responsible for their actions and the results of those actions. It is not the fault of our employers if we agree to work for no benefits."[81]

Along with the pop cultural fetishization of Latinas/os, the rhetoric of personal responsibility and a "free contract" made systemic exploitation seem impossible. Yet the racism and sexism underscoring the amnesty programs were tangible, exposing that SAW was designed and implemented to secure a cheap racialized, gendered temporary labor pool and that general amnesty was designed and implemented to secure a cheap racialized, gendered legalizing labor pool. The racism and sexism underscoring the INS implementation of amnesty was made clear in the 1988 *Zambrano v. INS* case, and in the data collected in 1986–1988 by the Zapata Canyon Project. The still extant project gathered data from randomly selected undocumented immigrants at the Mexico-U.S. border on transnational labor experiences, the locations and costs of border crossings, reasons for crossings, possible use of smugglers for crossings, and possible INS apprehensions. Its inaugural report found that IRCA's legalization provisions (the general amnesty program and the special visa program), both of which required permanent residency, were designed to favor non-Mexican immigrants. (Non-Mexican Latina/o immigrants tend to have more permanent migration patterns whereas Mexicans tend to be migratory.) On the other hand, researchers concluded that the SAW program channeled Mexicans into low-wage agricultural labor with requirements that complemented Mexican migration patterns and that Mexicans were more likely to fulfill such low-wage positions than any other nationality.[82] Criticism of SAW by Reverend Monsignor Salvador Alvarez, a Catholic deacon who represented Mexican American interests in the church, echoes these findings. He argued that SAW would turn Mexican workers into "slaves" who were used for work and then disposed of. He also asserted that the program was racist because it welcomed Mexican and Latin American immigrants only as cheap laborers and not as citizens.[83]

Like Salvador, some pundits in the IRCA debates did declare that they wanted something more than neoliberal crossings, recognizing and opposing the exploitative nature of immigration and amnesty within a neoliberal system. Senator Edward Roybal (D-CA) was one of the few lawmakers who asserted that the white ethnic bias of "nation of immigrants" rhetoric made IRCA (and the narrative) inherently racist. As early as the 1982 IRCA hearings, Roybal pointed out that no one was concerned with the five million illegal Europeans and especially Irish present; he reminded Congress that raids frequently occurred in Los Angeles, with a substantial Latina/o population, but not Boston, where numerous undocumented Irish resided.[84]

Moreover, in the same 1982 session, Dr. Roy Bryce-Laporte, a researcher at the Smithsonian Institution with his own immigrant story (he spoke with an accent, his family migrated from the Caribbean to Central America, and he then migrated alone to the United States), explained that immigration reform must address the reality that immigrants and refugees respond "to felt or perceived difficulties and dangers in their own countries relative to the United

States and its promises of peace, safety, economic opportunities, freedom and family reconstitution within its borders." Media was crucial to this: "The U.S. media, on one extreme, and very subtle and sometimes forceful U.S. presence, on the other hand, contribute to this promise."[85] He acknowledged that media was also part of a larger network of movement of people and goods, and made a claim that resonates with the labor that Latina celebrities such as J-Lo and Selena did for neoliberalism in embodying the "nation of immigrants" trope. Bryce-Laporte pointed out that immigrants are often "many times outdoing the United States in terms of believing and defending the myths, promises and beliefs of this country."[86] But these voices of dissent were indeed minority voices.

The "nation of immigrants" tropes that circulated in and around amnesty and pop culture labored for neoliberalism as an equitable democratic system in variously gendered and racialized ways. Overlooking race and gender *and* overly looking at race and gender (that is, either the abstracting or highlighting of difference as evidence of inclusion and equal opportunity) proliferated side by side to constitute the deserving neoliberal(izing) citizen as—whether abstracted or overtly marked by race or gender—hard working and respectable. Both strains gelled with utopian neoliberal discourse, for both ways of looking made it easy to overlook the material conditions of Mexican and other Latin American immigrants during the law-making process, amnesty implementation, in its aftermath.

The 1990s were characterized by a national "turn against immigration"[87] that amnesty helped to provoke. As noted, growing nativism was evidenced in amplified punitive measures, in overt expressions of alarm over the volume of Mexican immigration in relation to welfare, crime, and culture from Republican lawmakers such as Simpson and Newt Gingrich,[88] and in opposition among the general public. According to a 2001 Gallup Poll, whereas in 1986, 40 percent of polled citizens wanted decreased immigration, in 1993 and 1995, 65 percent favored decreased immigration.[89] The draconian laws of the 1990s that flagrantly targeted Latin American immigrant women materialized this growing nativism, indicating the humanitarian democratic "nation of immigrants" rhetoric around IRCA amnesty and Latina/o pop culture was merely a fetish that concealed the exploitation, racism, and sexism that undocumented immigrants and Latinas/os were subjected to by and for the changes that allegedly empowered them.

Looking Over the Luck of the Irish Americans

That is, unless the undocumented immigrants in question were lucky enough to be Irish. In the 1980s, domestic issues in Ireland and especially unemployment led to large-scale migration. Combined with previous immigration laws that disadvantaged the Irish, this resulted in a substantial undocumented population of at least 136,000.[90] These "New Irish" overstayed on tourist visas and worked and lived as aliens in Irish American neighborhoods. While they were no less illegal than undocumented Mexican and other Latin American immigrants, Americans rallied to support the New Irish. Undocumented Irish received something of an official hero's welcome from the mayors of Boston and New York City (Ed Koch even established a counseling hotline), and hierarchs of the Catholic Church such as New York's Cardinal John J. O'Connor, the Irish American press, and grassroots organizations publicly labored to provide undocumented Irish a path to legality.[91] As a matter of fact, Simpson pointed out in his autobiography that IRCA 1984 was introduced on St. Patrick's Day, and he put the Irish "O'" prefix in front of his and Mazzoli's names to indicate their solidarity with the Irish. (He further noted that the updated version of IRCA was trying to win one for the Gipper.[92]) During IRCA debates, many members of Congress claimed Irish ancestry. The undocumented Irish had more than luck in Reagan's America; they had widespread support from powerful people. White undocumented immigrants were no "aliens."

The IRCA special visa program—designed by Irish American Representative Brian Donnelly (D-MA) and Senator Kennedy—responded to pro-Irish legalization efforts and the disadvantage that the Irish had been subjected to under the 1965 Immigration Act. (Recall that it increased quotas for Latin America and Asia and gave preference to family reunification, which unintentionally disadvantaged European countries given that their immigration numbers had dramatically decreased, from 70,000 [1956–1965], to just over 10,000 [1976–1985].[93]) Donnelly's clause gave Ireland and the other thirty-six countries disadvantaged by the law 10,000 nonpreferential visas, to be dispersed through first-come, first-serve mailed-in applications received by January 21, 1987.[94] Clearly the law favored white native English-speakers: the application was in English and the eligible were informed by a highly organized and public network of support, as was in place for Irish immigrants, thus putting some countries at an advantage. Irish natives received over 40 percent of "special" visas in the first year. In total, of 1.4 million special visa applications, 3,112 visas went to Ireland, 2,078 to Canada, and 1,181 to Great Britain.[95] Furthermore, while typically immigration laws and records refer to nationality rather than nativity, Donnelly's clause used the term "natives," thereby excluding natives of Third World countries who might be naturalized European citizens.

The clause also established starkly different application processes for European special visa applicants and general amnesty/SAW applicants: general and SAW applicants faced a rigorous and complicated legalization process that made them directly vulnerable to deportation and created immense difficulties for families, whereas specialized applicants simply mailed in applications. Furthermore, labor certification was waived for special visa applicants and was not a factor in eligibility,[96] whereas general amnesty and SAW applicants had to maintain employment for eligibility. Many undocumented Irish also had jobs above entry level,[97] which put them in a different economic class than most undocumented Latin American immigrants.

These disparate amnesty programs indicate that undocumented Irish did not have to *earn* rights to the extent that the mostly Mexican amnesty applicants did, and this difference is attributable to race and racism, though as usual, race went unnamed. As we have seen general/SAW amnesty was framed as a democratizing change alongside increasing hostility toward undocumented Latin American immigrants. Meanwhile unequivocal and widespread support for the Irish prevailed into the 2000s. Throughout, though, the racial and gender politics underscoring the different treatment of the two groups was usually overlooked in policy debate and in the culture at large. The tone for this discrepancy was set in the 1980s with ongoing lobbying and legislation on behalf of the Irish as an unjustly disenfranchised and disadvantaged population (in other words, the prototypical white ethnic discourse of injury and struggle, and success in spite of those odds) and was quite effective, even when organizations or individuals did not intentionally wield it.

The Irish Immigration Reform Movement (IIRM) was formed by Pat Hurley and Sean Minihane, two undocumented immigrants from County Cork, in May 1987 in Queens, New York. The IIRM sought legislative change for the many undocumented Irish, particularly through amnesty. Jennifer Duffy argues that because of their undocumented status, in many regards undocumented working-class Irish immigrants were not, and could not be, invested in the race-conscious and class-dependent values of hard work, loyalty, and family associated with being Irish in the United States (and, incidentally, are exactly what constitute a valued/valuable neoliberal subject). However, in her examination of the IIRM and the Irish Lobby for Immigration Reform (ILIR), in the 1980s and 2000s, respectively, Duffy shows through an ethnographic analysis of ILIR events such as fundraisers and political rallies that when green cards were at stake in an anti-immigrant climate, undocumented Irish immigrants were made, and made themselves, into valuable, respectable neoliberal subjects—what she calls "good Paddies"—with a race-conscious and racist lobbying agenda.[98] As Duffy observes, "Clearly the IIRM sought to represent the self-sufficient, market-oriented Irish against Black welfare recipients and Mexican aliens. . . . Because undocumented immigrants were (and continue to be) demonized as unlawful Mexican border-crossers, emphasis on the Irishness of this undocumented group was a proxy for their white racialness. Only at this specific juncture, when undocumented immigrants were underscored as white, could they be represented as 'risk'-takers and worthy of special treatment under U.S. immigration law."[99]

This claiming of the "nation of immigrants" trope with silent but implied whiteness worked. From 1988 until the implementation of the 1990 Immigration Act, the IIRM helped secure 25,000 visas for Ireland through several extensions of the IRCA special visa program,[100] as for example in the 1988 "Amendment in the Nature of a Substitute for HR 5115," introduced by Peter Rodino (R-NJ) and Mazzoli.[101] Extensions further amended the Donnelly clause to favor the Irish. First, of the 30,000 visas remaining from the 1987 program, a reserve list of 15,000 names, 10,000 of which were Irish, was established, with a second list of 15,000 names to come from the same pool. Second, a new lottery that would randomly provide 20,000 visas over the course of two years was established for "underrepresented" countries, or those with less than 25 percent of visas available the previous year. Of course Ireland was part of that underrepresented group. Third, an extension of temporary H-1 visas for nurses was given until 1989. Irish embassy spokesperson Daragh O'Criordain voiced his approval.[102]

Moreover, grassroots and congressional efforts on behalf of the Irish persisted. The Morrison visa, which was included in the 1990 Immigration Act, was the IIRM's primary legislative victory. Representative Bruce Morrison (D-CT) included a visa program that responded to IIRM lobbying, and greatly benefitted Irish immigrants. The visa allotted 40,000 visas annually for three years for countries disadvantaged by the 1965 Act. Over the course of those three years, Ireland received 48,000 of those visas. In accordance with the IIRM's "all-Ireland" perspective, the visa program also opened the door to more Irish immigrants by including a provision that defined Northern Ireland as a separate state; this allowed thousands from Northern Ireland, who were previously ineligible because they were classified as English, to participate.[103] Matthew Jacobson, who has examined the ways in which Irish undocumented immigrants did not register in media or on the congressional floor as "aliens," notes that "the popular story of Irish victimization *was* the Irish immigrants' unfair advantage."[104] White skin, education, English proficiency, and the racial exclusivity of the "nation of immigrants" trope made these lawbreakers perfectly American in a cultural if not legal sense.

The "do it yourself" grassroots ethos of the IIRM, the general stance that the Irish were disadvantaged, and the often invisible presence of white privilege also surfaced in the music and aesthetic of a number of Irish American punk rock bands that came together in the 1980s and early 1990s and formed an enduring part of what might be called the Irishization of American popular culture. This Irishization, roughly contemporary with the Latin Explosion and also short-lived, included the new mainstream success of the openly political Irish rock band U2 (whose success and fame has lasted far longer, given that U2, formed in 1976, is globally one of the best-selling bands of all time, has won twenty-two Grammys, and was inducted into the Rock and Roll Hall of Fame in 2005),[105] the brief popularity of controversial singer Sinead O'Connor (her 1990 single, "Nothing Compares 2 U," reached No. 1 on the U.S. Billboard Hot 100 chart and she was nominated for several Grammys; she was also infamous for her radical politics and open critiques of Catholicism, as when she tore up a picture of Pope John Paul II during a 1993 *Saturday Night Live* performance[106]), and the popularity of the 1991 film *The Commitments*, co-produced by Irish, British, and U.S. companies. The film, about working-class Dubliners who form a soul band, was nominated for a Golden Globe for Best Picture. This pop cultural segment of the "Re-Greening of America" provides another point of contrast between the treatment and characterization of Latin American and Irish immigrants, for there was not a whisper of panic about an Irish invasion, flood, or reconquest, nor was there ubiquitous rhetoric about a crime wave, dependence, or fecundity, though its pop culture figureheads were overtly political and as in the case of O'Connor, sometimes very provocative.

Similarly, Irish punk bands were overtly political, provocative, and agitating, taking up space in ways that Latina/o stars did not, and could not. While the latter tended to sing the praises of the American Dream and were, like J-Lo, disciplined nonetheless, in some cases, Irish punk bands harshly critiqued with impunity the promise of the "nation of immigrants." In fact criticisms of its white ethnic poster children surfaced in the lyrics of some bands, as did statements of allegiance with other immigrant groups and people of color and the working class. True to the antiestablishment, political ethos of punk rock itself, some bands questioned and criticized the state and systemic inequalities. Bands such as Black 47, Flogging Molly, the Dropkick Murphys, and the Pogues combined the fast, stripped down, and hard-edged sound of punk rock with traditional Irish instrumentation and lyrics focused on Irish heritage and political issues in Ireland, American working-class and bootstraps themes, and multicultural coalition and commonality. While these bands are not as visible in the media as J-Lo, nor have they produced Grammy-winning work like U2, some have released numerous albums, played well-attended if not sold out St. Patrick's Day shows, and continue to tour.

Black 47, which is named after the worst year of the nineteenth-century Great Irish Potato Famine, was formed in 1989 by Irish immigrant Larry Kirwan and Irish American Chris Byrne. While the band received mixed reviews throughout its career, it released seventeen albums to date, mostly recently in 2011, continues to tour and perform,[107] and has been recognized as "the premiere Irish-American rock group who paved the way for the current Irish punk/roots explosion."[108] Byrne was a New York City police officer during much of his time with the band, which combines rock music and instrumentation with traditional Irish music and instruments, such as uilleann pipes, bagpipes, and fiddles. The band's lyrics critique injustice and advocate building coalitions across racial, ethnic, and national boundaries. On its Facebook page, the band describes itself as "espous[ing] an unblinkingly political and thoroughly Irish form of rock'n'roll, with songs covering topics from the Northern Ireland conflict to civil rights and urban unrest in contemporary New York."[109] After the release of its first album in 1980, the band was described in *CMJ Music Report* as "a New York-via-Emerald Isle band with a mission, a rollicking good pub band with its heart and eyes focused on the little people stomped by the headlines."[110]

The 1991 song "Livin' in America" was direct about cross-cultural, international coalitions:

> Workin' with the black man, Dominican and Greek
> In the snows of January or the drenchin' August heat
> No sick days or benefits and for Christ sakes don't get hurt
> The quacks over here won't patch you up unless they see the bucks
> upfront.[111]

The song details the systemic oppression that racial and ethnic minorities and Irish face as members of the working class, or working poor, and makes a case for the commonality of systemic oppression among people of all races. A later song, "Born to Be Free" (1994), is about black American singer, actor, and civil rights activist Paul Robeson, who in the FAQ section on the band's website is described as an ally and hero of the band.[112] Thus the band self-consciously and explicitly made links between people of color, fights for rights, and the Irish and Irish Americans. One early song, "Green Card," even critiqued the chauvinism of the New Irish. While the lyrics of this song cannot be found because it was never recorded, it is described by Kirwan on the band's website as "a reggae type number—which had the temerity to suggest that an undocumented Irish girl might marry a Jamaican guy to become legal. Of course, the song was tongue-in-cheek and it wasn't one of my favorites anyway but, to my amazement, I discovered that the 'new Irish' took a dim view about being the subjects of any song which was not self-glorifying."[113]

The 1996 song "5 Points" also directly challenged the fantasy of the "nation of immigrants" American Dream, with the Irish immigrant speaker, Johnny, proclaiming in the chorus:

> I didn't come here to America
> To give up the ghost and die
> I didn't come here to America
> Across the ragin' foam
> To die like a slave in a pigsty
> I came here to find a home
> Where I could live with dignity
> And hold me head up high
> So don't go messin' with me or me family
> Or I'll blow these Five Points to the sky.[114]

On the other hand, Black 47 did tend to take on the mantle of Irish American disadvantage, and claims of commonality between working-class Irish and people of color did not fully flesh out white male privilege. (Imagine if a Latina/o, or Arab American, pop song speaker threatened to "blow these 5 Points to the sky" if anyone messed with his or her family.) But at the same time, Black 47 pointedly critiqued capitalism, the American Dream, and even Irish chauvinism or myopia. In this sense, Black 47 gives the "nation of immigrants" trope a punk rock kick in the pants, though it is a privileged one.

Other Irish American punk bands that formed later in the 1990s, such as the Dropkick Murphys and Flogging Molly, carried on in the tradition of Black 47 (and also the Pogues[115]), and toed the line between uncritically embracing the mainstream discourses of Irish disadvantage and deservingness, and race-blind working-class woes, and undermining them. Flogging Molly, a seven-member Celtic punk band from Los Angeles, California, was formed by Dublin-born Dave King in 1997. Since their debut album in 2000, sales have continued to increase,[116] and the band continues to tour. Lyrics often focus on Ireland, drinking, politics, and love, working-class alienation in the United States, and globally, and hope for change.[117]

The Dropkick Murphys, formed in Boston in 1996, blend punk, Irish folk, rock, and hardcore. After releasing several records with independent labels, the band enjoyed mainstream success.[118] One of their songs was featured in the Academy Award–winning film The Departed (2006), about the Irish mob in Boston, and they were approached to write an anthem for the most quintessentially American (and historically racially exclusive) of sports, baseball.[119] The band has long played St. Patrick's Day shows and continues to tour and record, debuting a 2013 release in the Top 10.[120] As stated on its Facebook page, the band promotes a political message of unity among the working class, though they embrace the more typical "nation of immigrants" neoliberal story line in a more direct, less complicated way: "In addition to hopefully bringing people together for a good time, we hope to share some of our experiences and beliefs in working class solidarity, friendship, loyalty and self-improvement as a means to bettering society (i.e. You can preach till you're blue in the face but if you're lying in the gutter no one's gonna listen. *If you pick yourself up by the bootstraps and live your life to the best of your ability you may set an example that others will follow*)."[121] This race-neutral imperative of personal responsibility—picking oneself up by the bootstraps—is the very neoliberal discourse that has been used again and again to argue against affirmative action and "prove" that people of color rather than systemic inequality are responsible for poverty, crime, immorality, and a host of social ills in the uniquely democratic, inclusive U.S.A.

The racial limits of New Irish legalization efforts surfaced in Irish punk rock as well. The fixation on Irishness, which some music writers alleged was a gimmick bands were exploiting to sell records,[122] might be considered myopic and chauvinistic, playing into rather than challenging the dominance of the discourse of Irish injury that was circulating at the time, to the detriment of Latin American and Asian immigrants who did not have the option to not consider race. All of the bands also seem to play into the stereotype of Irish alcoholism. (In fact, the on-stage drunkenness of Pogues front man Shane McGowan is an expected and almost celebrated part of the Pogues mythos.) Furthermore, as noted in Chapter 2's discussion of the *Golden Girls*, representations of coalitions between white ethnics and Latin American immigrants and Latinas/os or people of color reiterate dominant social relations in more subtle ways if acknowledgement of white privilege falls away. This is an issue that came up as the Legalize the Irish movement persisted into the 2000s.

Additionally, if Latina/o entertainers aggressively critiqued capitalism and the United States, they not only would not be likely to sell very many records, but also would run the risk of being characterized as militants and predisposed to crime and violence and thus be (further) cast as unfit to be Americans. Were they immigrants, they might very well be deported. After all, racist stereotypes are heaped upon Latinas/os and other people of color even when they are not in punk bands because people of color are cast as de facto criminals. But these were not criticisms that Irish American punk bands had to cope with because of their white skin (and, I would argue, their gender—as noted, Sinead O'Connor has been attacked and shamed for her public criticism of the status quo, and women of color like J-Lo are confronted by the intersection of racism and sexism whether they challenge or embrace the status quo); these bands, all headed by and composed mostly of white men, had the freedom to be controversial, rebellious, and critical of the status quo. In fact, some bands like the Pogues openly sympathized with Irish Republicans known for violence and considered terrorists by the Thatcher administration. In Black 47's "5 Points" the speaker of the song threatens to blow up Five Points to protect his family from the American Nightmare that the American Dream was turning into. Irish American punk rock bands and their lyrics are thus complex texts that negotiate looking over and overlooking in ways that both challenge and reaffirm neoliberal discourses.

The overtly critical sentiments that bands like Black 47 voiced, however—looking over American capitalism and racism and making a case for multicultural coalitions among disenfranchised populations, as an alternative to neoliberal projects—have had a more popular foothold in recent years as the discrepancy between legal and popular support for Irish and Latin American immigrants persists. Evidence that racism continues to play a key role in neoliberal crossings is no longer going mostly unnoticed. The Irish Lobby for Immigration Reform (ILIR), formed in 2005, like the IIRM, has subtly used whiteness to its advantage, as when the ILIR held several immigration rallies and two congressional lobby days on behalf of undocumented Irish workers.[123] The organization has a Facebook page with over 3,140 likes, and received support from Congress on both sides of the aisle, including some, like John McCain (R-AZ), who are usually aggressively anti-immigrant, or more precisely aggressively anti–Latin American immigrant. In fact, in 2006 McCain and Ted Kennedy jointly proposed Irish amnesty (a temporary worker visa with a path to U.S. citizenship for undocumented Irish). While these undocumented Irish are, like the estimated twelve million undocumented Latin American immigrants, mostly working-class laborers, only the former have public support from liberal and conservative members of Congress.

In this the legacy of 1980s neoliberal immigration discourses, the racial divide underscoring immigration reform was well documented in the popular press. A 2007 *LA Times* article entitled "Illegal? Better If You're Irish" opens with the provocative statement: "Imagine Hillary Clinton holding up a t-shirt that read: 'Legalize Mexicans.' That's not going to happen, right? Well, last month in Washington, at a rally hosted by the Irish Lobby for Immigration Reform, the leading Democratic candidate for president actually did have her picture taken holding a shirt that read: 'Legalize the Irish.'" The article observes that race shapes immigration debates, for "Latino activists bend over backward trying to cloak undocumented Mexican migrants in the slogan 'We are America,' but their Irish counterparts don't feel similarly obliged."[124] Similarly, a 2010 *New York Times* article noted that upon hearing the forceful language ILIR chairman, Niall O'Dowd uses about Irish legalization, "You can't help wondering how quickly such words would get a Latino banished to the militant fringe."[125] The racism at work was not lost on or ignored by pundits and instead was explicitly addressed in popular public discourse.[126]

But in terms of the legacy of 1980s immigration discourse and making a case for rights, the racially disparate framing and treatment of Irish and Latina/o immigrants are essentially straight-line developments, with perhaps some thickening. That whiteness makes it easier for some to adhere to and excel at the Reaganite ideal of hard-working respectability—*or fall short or even opt out, as in Irish American punk rock*—without being cast as fundamentally alien and foreign, though looked over in the media, continued to be overlooked by politicians and in policy debates.

Family Fetish: Commodifying White Ethnic Immigrant Sexuality at Ellis Island

The commodification of the white ethnic European immigrant saga provides another telling contrast to the concurrent commodification of Latina/o identity (as does the absence of an "Asian-ization" of American culture, for no such parallel exists). Moreover, the commodification of the white ethnic immigration narrative fits with discourses of Irish immigrants as ideal Americans-in-waiting and thus also rationalizes neoliberalism. In 1990, when the Morrison visa program passed and when Irish American punk rock was in its heyday, white ethnic identity was commodified in gendered and sexualized terms with the opening of the Ellis Island Immigrant Museum and gift shop. But in contrast to Latina/o commodification, the white ethnic version did not involve the hypersexualization of white ethnic women, was not a national phenomenon that resulted in development of new marketing techniques and new retail divisions that traversed national borders, and was not undergirded by the socioeconomic minoritization of white ethnics. Rather, Ellis Island commodities lauded and normalized white ethnic immigrant "family values."

In *Ellis Island Snow Globe*, Erica Rand asks how Ellis Island became a place, symbol, and experience that stands in for the American Dream without need for explanation. She ties this development to the Reagan-era canonization and commodification of white ethnic heterosexual identity. The Ellis Island gift shop carries an array of goods such as books, trinkets meant to represent the artisanal crafts of sending nations such as Russian nesting dolls, and typical tourist shop fare such as t-shirts, hats, shot glasses, snow globes, key chains, and thimbles. Many trinkets sport "breeder signs" that construct images and people as heterosexual and procreative. For instance, Rand describes a souvenir golf ball that features a picture of a man, woman, and child that is frequently used to symbolize Ellis Island. The threesome—coded as a family and wearing clothing that references the common "visual vocabulary of turn-of-the-century European immigrants"—faces the Statue of Liberty from a boat in the harbor. This souvenir, along with a host of others, is popular and lucrative because it represents the white nuclear family ideal that on the heels of/in response to the civil rights movement enabled white ethnics to move into the normative American subject position.[127]

For most people of color, the Ellis Island/immigration in pursuit of a better life narrative does not apply: overlooked is the story of black American families descended from slaves, the incarceration of Asian immigrants at Angel Island, persecution of Latin American immigrants at the Mexico–U.S. border, forced sterilization of Mexican and Puerto Rican women, and the colonization and genocide of Native Americans. As Ann DuCille astutely points out, "It is only those who enjoy the privileges of white skin who can hold matters of race at arm's length."[128] The gulf between those with privilege and those without is reproduced, and it is profitable; white, heterosexual privilege in an immigration narrative sells trinkets, and underscores this whole U.S. history museum.

In Irish American punk rock, which often lyrically addresses heterosexual romance but is not necessarily familial or procreative, this privilege likewise goes unexamined even when the "nation of immigrants" trope is critiqued, thereby indicating that a variety of representations of white ethnics are acceptable and "normal." Thus the white ethnic immigrant does not necessarily have to be a family member in order to deserve rights, and Irish American punk bands can aggressively critique the U.S. system without being characterized as militants or terrorists (though for the Irish in Thatcher's United Kingdom, there is a different story). Much as in pop culture and some news media representations of white ethnic near-queer families, white ethnic mothers, and white ethnic criminals, imperfection and variety are permissible and can be overlooked, held at (a white ethnic) arm's length.

The Latina/o sexuality celebrated in the media was definitely not subtle, and it was definitely not familial, unless, that is, the trope of the family was used to sell products or contained within marriage to a fellow Latino, like Lopez and Anthony. And when Latin American immigrant and Latina sexuality was visible as procreative in immigration polemics, it was represented as a virulent threat to the socioeconomic stability of the nation, or at the very least pathologized. Commodified Latina entertainers were not villainized as women of Latin American–origins were in the news media and other pop culture texts, but Latina sexuality was nonetheless constructed as foreign and sometimes dangerous, as the disciplining of Lopez attests, and therefore provided a contrast to the national norm that Ellis Island commodities proffer.

One final example reaffirms the rather striking relevance of Marx's theory of commodity fetishism to immigration. In the 1990s, Bustelo Coffee Company, which was established by Spanish immigrant Giorgio Bustelo in 1928 and targeted Latina/o families,[129] wanted to reach both white and Latina/o consumers. One of its primary campaign commercials featured the classic scene of white ethnic European immigrant families arriving at Ellis Island. The voiceover, which narrates the founding of the company, "is meant to imply that European and Hispanic immigrants are no different in the trajectories with which they have pursued the American dream."[130] Not coincidentally, this was the same sort of erasure used to support racialized amnesty programs. Despite the assertion of commonality, Latina/o and white ethnic commodities were framed in different ways and each group was treated differently under IRCA in Reagan's America (and of course Latinas/os and white ethnics have vastly different relationships to colonization, structural marginalization, and privilege). The assertion of commonality was a fetish, a fantasy.

In sum, the seemingly nonchalant fixation on white ethnic immigrant heterosexuality effaced the "real" story of turn-of-the-twentieth century white ethnic immigration, other immigrant stories, other ways and points of entry such the Middle Passage, Angel Island, and the Mexico–U.S. border, and other immigrants who were not in heteropatriarchal nuclear families. It implied that other points of entry and those who were not anchored to a nuclear family were not as natural, normal, or as American as (white ethnic) Ellis Island immigrants, a notion that the Legalize the Irish movement from the 1980s up to the present day affirms.

Conclusion

Commodity fetishism is by definition "a way of seeing whereby the definite social relations at capitalism's core assume the fantastic form of a relation between things."[131] Amnesty might be considered a neoliberal way of seeing, and IRCA's "revolutionary" program ostensibly overlooked illegality and also difference, since the language of the law was gender- and color-blind, as were Irish legalization efforts and the increasing casting of neoliberalism itself as the conduit of equality and prosperity. The commodification of Latina/o identity also disavowed labor and social relations but in this case under a guise of visibly gendered, racialized American inclusivity and opportunity. Hence the commodification of Latina/o identity looked over difference. All of these ways of seeing, which are steeped in comparable democratic rhetoric, alienated Latinas/os in gendered, (hetero)sexualized terms in order to turn a profit. Individual Latinas/os profited from this, and Latina/o visibility in media increased, but racialized and gendered narratives of individual success and consumption strengthened the inequitable neoliberal system. This alienation was also bolstered by the Legalize the Irish movement, which reframed whiteness and hard-working respectability as the grounds for deservingness, and by Irish American punk rock bands, which sometimes uncritically reiterated the white ethnic bootstraps story as a viable means of empowerment for all people, thereby similarly erasing race and racism.

In addition to erasing the inherently transnational histories of colonialism, imperialism, and forced migration that quite literally made the United States able to consider itself a "nation of immigrants," the "nation of immigrants" rhetoric and the rights-based paradigm it was mobilized to support offered limited enfranchisement given the inherently transnational nature of immigrants' lives. Neoliberalism created "a new global economy in which employers and factories are free to relocate but workers are often constrained by national immigration policy."[132] Free trade agreements ensured the mobility of capital—thus labor also needs to be mobile—yet immigration law constrained the mobility of people. The neoliberalizing state quite literally invested in keeping immigrant labor cheap by denying certain immigrant populations rights that would protect or empower them as workers and as human beings. Although citizenship has often been conceived as the goal of rights struggles for immigrants, citizenship is not an automatic indicator of rights and can often involve a loss of rights for persons who lead transnational lives. Whether overlooking or looking over gender and race, the work that "nation of immigrants" tropes did in relation to/for amnesty and Latina/o pop culture erased the complexity and the often necessarily transnational character of immigrants' lives in order to make American neoliberalism appear to align with, and even facilitate, a more democratic society. In his 1989 Farewell Address, Reagan declared, "Democracy, the profoundly good, is also the profoundly productive."[133] But the material realities of IRCA amnesty and those underscoring Latina/o pop culture show that productivity is no indicator of democracy. This mere appearance of democracy is what neoliberal crossings look like.

Conclusion

Crossing Neoliberalism?

Junot Diaz, an immigrant from the Dominican Republic and author of the Pulitzer Prize–winning novel *The Brief Wondrous Life of Oscar Wao*, might seem like the luminous exemplar of the neoliberal "nation of immigrants" mythos. He grew up in a poor Dominican neighborhood in New Jersey, where his family received food stamps and his siblings were incarcerated. Diaz worked his way through college at Rutgers University with a series of service and manual labor jobs, and earned an M.F.A. at Cornell University.[1] He is currently fiction editor at *Boston Review*, teaches writing at the Massachusetts Institute of Technology, and has won many prestigious awards for his best-selling fiction, including a MacArthur "Genius" Fellowship.[2] He also supports the success of other immigrants, as in his work with Georgia's volunteer-run Freedom University, which provides post-secondary education to undocumented immigrants who are barred from attending five of Georgia's most competitive universities.[3] But Diaz's success has come from pointed critiques of the neoliberal "nation of immigrants" narrative in his fiction, which focuses on the struggles of Dominican immigrants and citizens, and other writing. Diaz has, in his own words, "seen America from the bottom up." Unlike many other beneficiaries, *because* of this he views the hackneyed description of the United States as a land of opportunity as shorthand for "'a vicious unrelenting competition' that overrides society's 'most cherished racisms and prejudices' in order to turn a dollar." Furthermore he notes that while he "may be a success story as an individual," his family's story of two kids in prison and "enormous poverty, of tremendous difficulty"—and the stories of most immigrants—exposes the United States "deranged attachment to some of its myths; its myths of exceptionalism, its unwillingness to look at the immigrant situation, the callous way it exercises military power."[4]

Accordingly, Diaz's fiction is framed by the destitution, corruption, and violence in the Dominican Republic in the aftermath of Rafael Trujillo's bloody dictatorship[5] and the struggles of low-income and poor Dominican immigrants, most of whom are the children of Dominican exiles. Diaz's 1996 story collection *Drown* centers on a teenaged male Dominican immigrant's struggle to adjust to life in New Jersey given his family's poverty and absent father. *Oscar Wao* tells the story of an obese, sci-fi geek Dominican American and his heartbreaking love for a sex worker, which ends in tragedy for him. *This Is How You Lose Her* is about the difficulties of love and loving (and especially fidelity) for Dominicans and Dominican Americans whose lives have been shaped by the demands of global capitalism, racism, and sexism. Diaz's work is by no means monolithic; it features Dominican characters from all walks of life and some that occupy what resembles Diaz's own privileged position. He is attuned to intersectionality, as the character of Oscar Wao indicates. Through Oscar's dearth of "the special reservoir of male privilege," Diaz explores erasures within Dominican American culture; Oscar is exiled among exiles for failing to be the ideal, that is, macho, Dominican boy.[6] Diaz's fiction has been praised by numerous critics in rather familiar "nation of immigrants" language—for humanizing the Latina/o "immigrant experience" and "street life," and bringing to life characters whose options are circumscribed by "prejudice and poverty."[7] While Diaz's fiction might be considered yet another example of the appropriation of multiculturalism that provides white readers with a sanitized method of becoming acquainted with "difference" and "diversity" and substitutes (market) visibility for material equality—and while Diaz himself has been pointed to as an emblem of neoliberal "nation of immigrants" efficacy—his work, words, and activism speak to the actual experiences and needs of current immigrants.

In fact, Diaz has been explicitly critical of neoliberalism. In his essay "Apocalypse: What Disasters Reveal," written in the wake of the 2010 hurricane that ravished already destitute Haiti, Diaz asserted that global neoliberal economic integration was a "new, rapacious stage of capitalism. A cannibal stage where, in order to power the explosion of the super-rich and the ultra-rich, middle classes are being forced to fail, working classes are being re-proletarianized, and the poorest are being pushed beyond the grim limits of subsistence, into a kind of sepulchral half-life."[8]

I have argued that neoliberal crossings, necessary for the United States and the world to reach that rapacious stage of capitalism, were formed and rationalized by discourses and policies first delineated in the Reagan era. In the officially antiracist and antisexist aftermath of the civil rights era, within the tradition of an imperialistic nation that framed itself as the exceptional champion of democracy and equal opportunity, Reagan-era immigration discourses renegotiated the economic and ethnocentric tensions that underscore immigration to guarantee the exploitation and disenfranchisement of Latin American immigrants and Latinas/os. Democratic rhetoric about inclusive freedom and rights and increasing representation in the "nation of immigrants" masked the exploitation and disenfranchisement of Latin American immigrants and Latinas/os, while the exclusion and punishment of—and violence toward—certain immigrants and citizens were cast as a rational response to criminality and immorality that, for women especially, involved violating gender norms and "family values."

If IRCA's champions such as Alan Simpson were to be believed, racism was combated by color- and gender-blind inclusivity under the law, yet racialized, gendered nativist attacks on immigrants and free market desires to secure cheap immigrant labor abounded and had to be appeased in order for the law to pass. And while representation for and of minorities increased, aesthetics were no substitute for material, lived equality. Moreover, mainstream representations either elided or justified the racism and sexism inherent to neoliberalization; the neoliberal "favoring of the yachts over rafts," as Diaz puts it,[9] seems to be the logical and fair economic dividends accrued from "personal responsibility." Reagan-era tropes of immigration including the "immigration emergency," encapsulated by the Immigration Emergency Act as the rational(ized) response to the Mariel Boatlift and immortalized by *Scarface*; the victory of multicultural "family values" with the retention of family reunification provisions and concordant near-queer immigrant "family values" on primetime TV; the racialized hierarchy of immigrant maternity regulated by IRCA welfare restrictions and pop culture representations of immigrant mothers; the crimmigration of Latin American immigrants and a plethora of films to match (and simultaneous decriminalization of white ethnics and Asians); and the overlooking/looking over of IRCA amnesty and Latina/o pop culture as evidence of democratization and parity—all show that immigration discourses were crucial to the rise and hegemony of U.S. neoliberalism. Neoliberalism could appear to be "the magic process that was to deliver the world's poor out of misery and bring untold prosperity to the rest of us"[10] because those immigration discourses concealed or legitimatized the stratification of labor, resources, and power necessary to globalizing free trade capitalism. Those immigration discourses likewise assuaged nativist and often even pro-immigrant contingents and cleared a path for the 1990s framing of neoliberalism as the "utopic endpoint of the evolution of market economies."[11] In short, gendered and racialized Reagan-era immigration discourses that were produced and circulated in complex and uneven ways in public policy, news media, and pop culture inaugurated an enduring paradigm for neoliberal crossings.

Within both the law and the culture at large the pernicious effects of neoliberal crossings continue to reverberate even after 9/11, President Barack Obama's 2008 campaign promises of "change we can believe in," and the 2008

financial crisis. All were ostensible game-changers that might have brought—
but did not—the fundamental violences of neoliberalism into stark relief, in a
way that might have engendered—but did not—meaningful material change
not just in matters of immigration but more, excuse the pun, globally. Rather
IRCA, 1980s immigration discourses, and Reagan were turned to as exemplars, and neoliberal feminism and multiculturalism continue to be updated,
obfuscating and explaining away exploitation and injustice.

Both conservative and liberal administrations have consistently employed
and elaborated upon IRCA's "three-legged stool" model of enhanced border
enforcement, workplace enforcement and some protections for immigrants,
and earned legalization. For instance, President Bill Clinton's INS commissioner, Doris Meissner, urged immigration agents to use prosecutorial discretion in deportation cases and to consider an immigrant's age, health, and
military service record, along with humanitarian matters. Yet Clinton took
a page from the Reagan playbook when he signed PRWORA and IIRIRA in
1996, laws that had more in common with the legacy of slavery, colonialism,
Jim Crow, and eugenic "race betterment" than with providing a safe haven for
huddled masses yearning to breathe free.

The "War on Terror" initiated by the George W. Bush administration
made immigration restriction and internal security seem like a more urgent
"emergency" than ever before. To protect the United States from the terrorist, who was racialized as Muslim and Arab, the Department of Homeland
Security (DHS) was established in 2002 and consolidated under its umbrella
twenty-one federal departments and agencies including U.S. Immigration and
Customs Enforcement (ICE).[12] The Uniting and Strengthening America by
Providing Appropriate Tools Required to Intercept and Obstruct Terrorism
Act of 2001, the so-called Patriot Act, gave law and immigration enforcement
agencies liberal authority to search the records of citizens and immigrants
and to detain and deport immigrants suspected of terrorism-related acts.[13]
As always, this was carried out along racialized lines.[14] Although some provi-
sions were ruled unconstitutional, many basic tenets were renewed under the
Obama administration.[15]

At the same time, freedom and equality were cast as the essence of global
capitalism, moving beyond the Reagan-era multiculturalism of tokenism and
representation to a more abstracted but no less pernicious multiculturalism.
Terrorism also rationalized the second war in Iraq, "Operation Iraqi Freedom," and occupations in the Middle East, while these efforts also drew on
neoliberal utopianism to portray economic rights as human rights. When deregulation, privatization, and free markets are cast as the essence of equality,
opposition can be framed not only as racist and sexist, but now also as "ter-

rorist," and aggressive and deadly intervention can be framed as "humanitarian violence."[16] Divorced from race, gender, sexuality, and all material conditions, freedom and equality were, as in the administration's 2006 document *National Security Strategy*, about "the rights of capital unleashed from the controls, taxes, and regulations established by sovereign nation-states."[17]

Reagan-era paradigms were by no means gone, particularly in immigration discourses. Bush, eager to capture a pool of inexpensive Latin American and especially Mexican immigrant laborers, also supported 2006 reform proposals, including amnesty, which were described as "strikingly similar" to IRCA, though at the time pundits feared that the failings of its predecessor—that is, fraudulent applications, employers continuing "illicit hiring practices," and a surge of illegal immigration—would persist.[18] Defending the IRCA model in a 2006 *Washington Post* op-ed, Mazzoli and Simpson asserted that problems with IRCA can be traced to the fact that all administrations since 1986 had "allocated funding and personnel resources more generously to securing the border than enforcing IRCA in the workplace" since "administrations of both stripes are loathe to disrupt economic activities—i.e. labor supply in factories, farms, and businesses."[19] This latter point is, I think, a correct observation, but rather than open up a space to discuss the exploitative essence of capitalism driving immigration discourse (and the concurrent perversion of human rights as economic rights), the pair made a case for more enforcement.

As it developed from the paradigm of crimmigration set up by IRCA, the rhetoric of terror supports neoliberalism in gendered and racialized ways, with increased neoconservative militarism and securitization alongside efforts to capture an inexpensive and pliable labor force, which, as the lesson of IRCA shows, are complementary. As Alicia Schmidt Camacho observes, "The new imperatives of the U.S. war on terror sanction the violent interdiction of migrants and border residents on a vaster scale, with greater penalties." This change, along with neoliberal development policies in Latin America that result in impoverishment, necessitate indigenous migration, and create a consumer market for drugs, sex, and firearms on the Mexico–U.S. border, "entail violence that is gendered in nature, with severe implications for poor migrants and for women and children in the border cities."[20] The most vulnerable populations become more vulnerable under neoliberal policies that make it all but impossible for people to have any degree of security in terms of housing, education, and employment. Such policies are framed as the arbiters of freedom for all people, while the terrorist emergency imbues immigration control with what seems to be a new sense of urgency. Consequently, not only a cheap labor force and marginalized population, but also the appearance of a fair, rational, humanitarian nation are secured.

With an economic team composed of Clinton-era retreads, Obama has advanced the same kind of neoliberal agenda as his predecessors, and Obama himself along with other highly successful people of color—"neoliberalism's winners"—seems to prove that neoliberalism is universally beneficiary for those who take personal responsibility. Along with more Middle East interventions, Obama's neoliberal agenda includes support of the NAFTA model. Disregarding the lessons of the 2008 financial crisis about the dangers inherent in a free market, these free trade agreements compel signatory countries to deregulate. They also provide extreme foreign investor privileges that promote job-offshoring and essentially raise multinational corporations to the status of sovereign governments, permitting them to directly challenge public interest laws in private tribunals. Obama supported the similarly problematic World Trade Organization's (WTO) Doha Round (a trade negotiation that began in 2001 and aims to lower global trade barriers), and he expanded and completed Bush-initiated negotiations over the Trans-Pacific Partnership (TPP), a free-trade deal co-authored by numerous multinational corporations and including twelve nations. All these trade deals contain the standard weak labor standards that, as recent history indicates, are racialized and gendered regardless of their "neutral" appearance. Despite conservative accusations of a socialist healthcare agenda, Obama has refused to advocate for anything that vaguely resembles actual socialism, such as "Medicare for all" (that is, a single- payer system), and instead signed a bill that effectively enriches and entrenches private insurance companies. Moreover, Obama has met with corporate executives at the White House, signed an $858 billion dollar tax cut, and turned to Reagan's former chief of staff, Ken Duberstein, for economic tips.[21]

The memorialization of what would have been Reagan's one-hundredth birthday in February 2011 makes his ongoing significance—and a resurgence of interest in him—quite clear. Like Clinton, Obama shares more in common with the Old Gipper than one might initially think: the February 7, 2011 cover of *Time* magazine featured a photo-shopped picture of Reagan and Obama with the headline "Why Obama ♥ Reagan: And What He's Learned from Him." In the image, a smiling Reagan has his arm around a broadly grinning Obama. Although analyses of why Reagan still matters at one-hundred-years old do not focus on immigration as a major aspect of his legacy as a "transformational president,"[22] as I have argued, immigration was a central component of the neoliberal changes he initiated, facilitated, enabled, and protected in law and in ideology.

Current immigration debates and policies on the table are familiar, as are the bipartisan tensions impeding passage of immigration reform: free market interests, the interests of domestic labor, and a desire to protect national "culture" and/or national security still prevail in complex and uneven ways in public policy debates, news media, and popular culture. Neoliberalism marches forward not despite clashing humanitarian or civil rights concerns, but because of them. While the Obama administration is largely sympathetic to immigration, the ongoing and flagrant prevalence of racism and nativism is undeniable in some contexts, such as Arizona's 2010 laws, the Support Our Law Enforcement and Safe Neighborhoods Act (SB 1070) and the anti-ethnic education law, AZ 2281, which targeted Latin American immigrants and Latinas/os. The former aligns the state with a federal law that requires immigrants to carry documentation, makes it illegal for the undocumented to work and for employers to hire them, and makes it mandatory for law enforcement to check the legal status of persons suspected of illegality. Like IRCA's punitive provisions and IIRIRA, SB 1070 and its very title make racial profiling and racism seem necessary for the employment, safety, and well-being of citizens, sentiments that are especially salient after 9/11.

Recent nativist attacks and anti-immigrant laws such as SB 1070 have galvanized opposition, bringing concerns about immigrant rights and racism (though not so much gender) to the center of public debates and influencing some pro-immigrant policy moves. The Obama administration censured SB 1070 and impeded its execution,[23] and in 2009 Obama signed the Children's Health Insurance Program (CHIP) Reauthorization Act, providing health care to eleven million children and removing barriers that prevented legal immigrant children from coverage.[24]

Obama has also supported the DREAM Act. First introduced in 2001, it offers conditional permanent residency to aliens who entered the country as minors, have been residents for at least five years, have graduated from a U.S. high school, and attend college or serve in the military. While opponents predictably claim DREAM rewards illegality and crime, pro-immigration advocates have hailed DREAM as a "paradigm shift" that humanizes the undocumented and mitigates the consequences of immigration laws that have become increasingly cruel and punitive.[25] But pernicious aspects of the Reagan-era immigration paradigm linger. As noted earlier, DREAMers are hard workers, students, members of families, sans felony convictions—in short, well-behaved neoliberal subjects. Those who are not are once again rendered undeserving and thus the "commonsense" targets of exclusion, punishment, and violence. Moreover, DREAMers remain vulnerable without a path to citizenship.

And, these pro-immigration moves are occurring against the backdrop—and as part—of Obama's neoliberal agenda. Like Reagan, Obama too treats immigration firstly in terms of economic health rather than human rights,[26] and DREAM's quasi-amnesty was mitigated by increased securitization, just like IRCA amnesty. The 2009 American Recovery and Reinvestment Act provided over $400 million for U.S.–Mexico border security. The proposed Border Security, Economic Opportunity, and Immigration Modernization Act of 2013 included expanded guest laborer provisions and increased interior security with employer verification requirements and DHS tracking of all immigrants; it also had a clause requiring non-citizens to show a "biometric work authorization card" or "biometric green card."[27] This last clause is eerily akin to Simpson's IRCA-era proclamation that he was willing to consider "everything but tattoos"—which Nazis used to track Jews—to verify immigrants' legal status. Significantly, deportations reached record highs under the Obama administration. Since 2009, the annual average is nearly 400,000, approximately double the annual average during George W. Bush's first term.[28] At the time of writing, immigration debate, with familiar Reaganite neoliberal rhetoric, continues to be polemical and has once again been cast as a matter of national security; this latest "immigration emergency" is about ongoing tensions over undocumented immigration from Latin America and Mexico, as well as Islamophobia surrounding refugees from Syria and other countries devastated in and by the War on Terror.

Current immigration policy statements might have been written in the 1980s in that U.S. economic interests remain the centerpiece of reform efforts, the "nation of immigrants" trope lives on in harmony with the privileging of U.S. economic interests and with appeals to law and order and security, and the material practices surrounding immigrants and immigration are also familiar. Obama's very election and his embrace of neoliberal policy show how the neoliberal system is bipartisan and absorbs "valuable" people of color and minorities, cosmetically concealing inherent racism and sexism. Furthermore, Reagan's influence is unmistakable in Obama's "increasing reliance on his predecessor's career as a helpful template for his own."[29] For Reagan, securing cheap immigrant labor and minimizing the costs of sustaining and reproducing that labor force were crucial to revolutionizing America and paving the way for neoliberalism, and Clinton and both Bushes forged onward with his model. In accordance with historical precedent and as justified by the financial crisis, concerns about domestic economic "health" and "security" trump the human needs of immigrants, thereby suggesting that neoliberal immigration policy will continue to produce gendered and racialized inequities that cannot be resolved by revamping prior measures. Even with more lenient measures, immigrants might be compelled to appease agents in order to stay in the country, and the fact is that workers with limited rights remain desirable; women are especially vulnerable to sexualized and gendered violence under prosecutorial discretion. And what are national rights worth, anyway, within the context of a fundamentally transnational economic and political system? What about the transnationality of many immigrants' lives, which neoliberalism coerces and often demands for survival? What about the choice to be transnational and live transnationally? Moreover, what are "rights" worth? What about the U.S. practice of turning to the law as a "higher order," without consideration for the power relations that shape it in the present and that shaped its very establishment in the U.S. post-revolutionary context in which only white propertied men counted as fully human? How can an inherently unequal system engender equality? A true "freedom day for immigrants"—which was how supporters hailed IRCA when it passed—has yet to arrive.

***

In the introduction to the anthology *Queer Migrations: Sexuality, U.S. Citizenship, and Border Crossings*, Eithne Luibheid asserts that "immigration and citizenship controls function in a double sense: as the means to delimit the nation, citizenry, and citizenship, and, conversely, as the loci for contesting and reworking these limits."[30] Media industries "shape the democratic process by influencing the types of knowledge the citizenry has about the political world, thus helping legitimize or put into question the political and legal worlds,"[31] and they continue to engage with and influence issues of immigration and citizenship. In this context, while continuities from the Reagan era are evident, so are discontinuities. Along the lines of Diaz's work, new popular texts that are more sympathetic, inclusive, and diverse seem to be reworking the limits of citizenship. The TV show *Ugly Betty* (2006–2010) and the film *A Better Life* (2011) weigh in on the worth and place of Mexican immigrants, but like most other pro-immigrant efforts, these texts value immigrants in neoliberal terms: the immigrants of value are—you guessed it—hard-working, personally responsible members of families, and diversity in production of these texts (for instance Latina/o actresses and actors, queer characters, pro-immigrant and diversity story lines, and employment of Latinas/os in other production positions) is a corporatist appropriation of diversity that reduces it to new profit opportunities. Hector Amaya describes this reification of diversity as "good capitalism, which substitutes the state as the primary grantor of citizenship rights. This is a perfect example of corporate liberalism, under which diversity becomes morphed from a term rooted in the racial and sexual struggles of the civil rights movement, to an ethnocentric term that is valued because of the benefits it can provide to the majority who identify with our current racial patriarchy."[32] The representations seem more diverse and explicitly critical of immigration law, and there are Latina/o faces involved, but the case for deservingness continues to hinge on conservative "family values" and individual productivity, and tokens of diversity, which amount to a cosmetic equality rather than true material equality, conceal how neoliberalism creates and requires inequalities.

Ugly Betty, based on the popular Colombian *telenovela* that has several iterations worldwide, revolves around a working-class first-generation Mexican American woman, Betty Suarez (America Fererra), and the issues she confronts as an "ugly" girl working at a fashion magazine. Juxtaposing Betty's ugliness against the white bourgeois ideals of the fashion industry, dominant story lines include her sister's struggles as a low-income single mother and the fight to prevent the deportation of their father, who is undocumented. The show features several LGBTQ characters, including Betty's adolescent nephew and coworkers, all of whom both conform to and defy stereotypes. Betty's colleagues include fashionable, effeminate gay men who are "catty" and superficial; her nephew adores show tunes, and he is a loved, respected member of the non-nuclear Suarez family. Regarding this familial inclusiveness, as Gloria Anzaldua observed long ago in "La Prieta," it might be unusual within Mexican immigrant families and communities, who may denounce any deviation from the dominant white heterosexual ideal or demand racial/ethnic allegiance to the detriment of gender and sexual justice.[33]

Producers such as Mexican American actress Salma Hayek identified the show as being about immigration, and within the media industry the show and its network, ABC, were praised as exemplars of diversity because Latinas/os worked both on the creative side and in production. ABC also made efforts to support "diverse" talent with employee programs such as an "African American Heritage Ceremony" and "Hispanic Symposium Multicultural Day."[34] Molina-Guzman notes that *Ugly Betty* complicates and humanizes Mexican Americans, particularly with queer story lines and working-class ethnic femininity, yet it contains difference "through an emphasis on universal deracialized story lines dealing with love, family, beauty, and social acceptance. Thus, *Ugly Betty* illustrates the ways in which Latinas embody media industry efforts to use ethnic difference, racial ambiguity, and multicultural accents to sell products and programming to global audiences."[35]

Amaya also criticizes the show's deracialized universalization of story lines and enumerates the pernicious neoliberal, corporatist use of diversity in the show's production, a pattern that was initiated in the Reagan era with media industry deregulation and management of diversity in compliance with the Civil Rights Act in ways that translated diversity into profit, rather than actual racial justice.[36] *Ugly Betty* is more nuanced than say, *Colors*; it is not mono-lithic, and, with queer characters of color, intersectionality is brought into American living rooms. But the notion of diversity under which the show operates, and which it promotes, is about profit rather than legal and political equality and is thus an updated version of the Reaganite neoliberal model.

A Better Life is also a limited alternative to the neoliberal status quo. Un-documented Mexican landscaper Carlos Galindo (Demián Bichir) is a single father to Luis (Juaquin Cosio) in urban East Los Angeles. At the end of the film, Carlos is deported to Mexico, and Luis remains in the United States. The film, directed by Chris Weitz, did well at the box office[37] and was well-received by critics,[38] and Bichir was nominated for an Oscar for Best Actor. The film shows that being undocumented makes it difficult for Carlos to ef-fectively parent his son, particularly as a single father, and it is one of only a few films that features an almost exclusively Latina/o cast. But as Monisha Das Gupta has asserted, the alternative social story in *A Better Life* (and also *Ugly Betty*) reiterates the notion that "good," deserving, and valuable Mexican immigrants work hard for the sake of their heterosexual families.[39] The same sort of rhetoric circulating in support of DREAMers is what makes these Latin American immigrants valuable and sympathetic, while diversity is a matter of profitability. By contrast, Diaz's voice of dissent is exceptional; in popular media, profit precludes social justice.

Some texts and entertainers reaffirm the normative subject status of white ethnics while appearing more diverse and inclusive, thus providing another example of the corporatist rearticulation of diversity. Carrying on Madon-na's legacy, Italian American female pop artists Gwen Stefani and Lady Gaga transgress boundaries with and through the bodies of people of color, LGBTQ people, and subcultures, but in doing so they recreate rather than dismantle dominant power arrangements; they are near-queer much like the families in *Golden Girls* and *Who's the Boss?*. One striking example of a female white ethnic pop star's exploitation of the bodies of people of color for the pur-poses of transgressing social boundaries can be seen in the dynamics of the Harajuku Girls, the female Japanese backup dancers/entourage Stefani began using in 2004 for what she called a "fun art project" meant to pay homage to the subversive, often home-made fashions of the women of Japan's Harajuku district.[40] Stefani created lucrative clothing and perfume lines based on Ha-rajuku Girls themes. But her "fun art project" included a contract provision that the dancers speak only in Japanese, though one dancer is American and the others speak English fluently; in fact, they rarely speak in interviews. In photographs and in live performances, the Harajuku Girls surround Stefani and bow down to her. The news website *Salon* memorably noted that Stefani "swallowed a subversive youth culture in Japan and barfed up another image of submissive giggling Asian women" so that her "big kiss to the East ends up feeling more like a big Pacific Rim job."[41] Stefani's silenced, inscrutable ornaments epitomize the long-standing racist "China doll" stereotype of Asian women's passivity, mysteriousness, and foreignness, but were revamped as a celebration of gendered globalized diversity—where neoliberal feminism meets neoliberal multiculturalism in a rather explicit way—which disproportionately profits a white ethnic woman, while making it seem like she supports and celebrates diversity. Thus it is easy for this white woman and white audiences to embrace a corporatized version of diversity without giving up racial privilege, or even recognizing that they have it.

Lady Gaga has been a vocal supporter of LGBTQ rights and underdogs and misfits in general, and she is known for her transgressive fashion. But like Madonna and Stefani, she is white, thin, wealthy, and powerful, and she too appropriates "difference" and the language of individual empowerment for personal gain, as in her song "Born This Way," which is meant to celebrate an allegedly inborn LGBTQ identity. The song's model of individualized empowerment gained by embracing one's (essentialized) identity supplants the collective action that underscored Stonewall and radical LGBTQ activism. Thus Gaga, one of the most internationally popular stars of the 2000s and likely the most famous LGBTQ celebrity advocate of the moment (and vocal supporter of same-sex marriage), embodies and epitomizes neoliberal feminism, multiculturalism, and neoliberal near-queer politics. Gaga's songs, delivered in a glittery, aesthetically outrageous package—as when she arrived at the 2011 Grammys in a golden egg and wore a dress made of raw meat, which provoked the ire of animal rights activists—center on representation/visibility, incorporation/inclusion, and individual rather than collective action and empowerment. Once more race, gender, and sexuality are severed from material conditions, and the fact that political, social, economic, and cultural structures, including the law (not the absence of "choices," lack of diverse representation on MTV or YouTube, or a dearth of self-love) create inequality is likewise obscured. Gaga and her audience can embrace diversity while maintaining privilege. Together these white ethnic women seem, like their antecedent Madonna, to be expanding what counts as "cool" and "normal" in the "nation of immigrants." But they too reiterate white supremacy under the guise of feminist, multiculturalist, and near-queer platitudes, and profit enormously from it. In short, they are quintessentially neoliberal.

The sexism, heterosexism, and racism underscoring early neoliberalism, which were evident on the congressional floor and in pop culture, complemented and were complemented by the free market economy in manner that

Figure 6.1. The gendered ethnic spectacle of the Harajuku Girls signifies their submissiveness, in contrast to Stefani.

feminist theorist Riane Eisler calls "ranking" in her research on gender and domination. Patterns of domination that organized ancient societies, such as man over woman, man over man, white over black, king over subjects, and so on,[42] are endemic to the free market economy paradigm that Reagan delineated,[43] and thus endemic to neoliberal capitalism and its cultural forms; it is fundamentally a system of ranking, and its hierarchies continue to be gendered, sexualized, and racialized not *despite* feminist and multicultural rhetoric but *because* of it—because of the ways that neoliberalism appropriates feminism, multiculturalism, and queerness with integration, representation, and token visibility within law, news media, and pop culture. When severed from material conditions, inequity is rendered rational, fair, or resolvable with selective inclusion, visibility, and legislation. Within neoliberalism, ranking was and continues to be the dominant form of social organization in the United States and, as neoliberalism advances, globally as well. As we have seen, incorporation into an always already unequal, exploitative system—even when women and people of color may "rank" among the top occasionally—does not add up to equality. It may appear to level the playing field, and it may be pointed to as evidence of progress (and indeed many might and have convincingly argued that the situation for immigrant women—women in general—and for immigrants and people of color has improved since the 1980s and in some significant regards it has). But the system itself not only continues to be unequal, but also benefits from inequality and relies upon it to maintain itself. Neoliberalism does not and cannot engender equality; social justice cannot be achieved under neoliberalism.

As I have argued, immigration discourses inaugurated in the Reagan era are a key but previously understudied facet of neoliberal hegemony; seemingly inclusive "nation of immigrants" rhetoric made the neoliberalizing nation seem fair and progressive and cast those excluded from the American Dream as having failed to work hard enough and/or having chosen crime and deviance from traditional gender norms and "family values" (a rationale that has proven flexible enough to incorporate people of color and same-sex couples). In pop culture, things look more globally diverse in terms of form and content, and the stakes of debates about U.S. immigration, identity, and inclusivity look more sophisticated, as with DREAM polemics; thus the status quo continues. Some critiques of and alternatives to the neoliberal status quo are visible—and popular. These include Diaz's work, for instance; the creative work of other Latinas/os as chronicled in the anthologies *The Ethnic Eye: Latino Media Arts*, which focuses on Latina/o self-representation,[44] and *Culture across Borders: Mexican Immigration and Popular Culture*, a study of the cultural production of the undocumented, documented, and the Chicanas/os and Mexican artists, writers, political intellectuals, and other members of society who are sensitive to the issues impacting Mexican immigrants;[45] and the 2013 documentary *Documented* by undocumented Filipino American journalist, immigration activist, and filmmaker Jose Antonio Vargas. While representation is no substitute for rights or material equity, as Lawrence Levine reminds us, popular culture is more than an "overriding instrument of hegemony."[46] The contestation and reworking of the limits of nation, citizenry, and citizenship in immigration discourses in law and pop culture—the latter of which makes it into the daily lives of many Americans via not only television, film, media, and music videos, as it did in the 1980s, but now also

YouTube, blogs, Facebook, and Twitter, long before and often in lieu of the law and "official" debate—are not only possible but necessary.

In fact, the significance of popular media as a key contributor to public conversations about citizenship and identity should not be underestimated. As Molina-Guzman succinctly puts it, "Audiences rely on the media to teach them about ethnic and racial communities with whom they do not regularly interact. Consequently, the media behave as a broad and accessible repository of cultural and social knowledge for audiences."[47] I have shown that immigration discourses inaugurated in the 1980s were crucial to the rising neoliberal project because they managed difference in policy, news media, and pop culture; my focus on migration shows how in the 1980s, neoliberalism began to supplant the welfare state and how multiculturalism and feminism were transformed in support of that process. While these neoliberal crossings, which continue to shape debates, often appear to be multicultural, feminist, and queer, the inequalities and violences that neoliberal crossings actually conceal and produce demonstrate the urgent need for a queer, feminist, antiracist, anticapitalist project of change. What is necessary is radical reform of immigration that places human beings rather than net contribution, "family values," and domestic—or international—"security" at the center of debates; this is impossible without pointed, sustained, uncompromised consideration of discourses about and material conditions of race, gender, and sexuality, as well as the formative and fundamental inequalities of U.S. law. This consideration must begin both on the congressional floor *and* within pop culture, where neoliberal crossings are perhaps most frequently consumed, and one hopes, will be contested and reworked by the people who do and will continue to populate the "nation of immigrants."

NOTES

INTRODUCTION

1 "Billboard Hot 100: Week of June 16, 1984," Billboard.com, http://www.billboard.com/charts/hot-100?chartDate=1984-06-16#/charts/hot-100?chartDate=1984-06-16. Epigraph from Kobena Mercer, *Exiles, Diasporas and Strangers* (Cambridge, MA: MIT Press, 2008), 7.

2 Susan Bordo, "'Material Girl': The Effacements of Postmodern Culture," in *Unbearable Weight: Feminism, Western Culture, and the Body* (Berkeley: University of California Press, 2003), 245–276.

3 Douglas Kellner, *Media Culture: Cultural Studies, Identity and Politics between the Modern and the Postmodern* (New York: Routledge, 1995), 271.

4 "Billboard Hot 100: Week of June 16, 1984," Billboard.com, http://www.billboard.com/charts/hot-100?chartDate=1984-06-16#/charts/hot-100?chartDate=1984-06-16.

5 "Recording Industry Association of America: Madonna," Riaa.com, http://www.riaa.com/goldandplatinumdata.php? resultpage=1&table= SEARCH_ RESULTS&action=&title=Borderline&artist=Madonna&format=&debutLP=&category=&sex=&releaseDate=&requestNo=&type=&level=&label=&company=&certificationDate=&awardDescription=&catalogNo=&aSex=&rec_id=&charField=&gold=&platinum=&multiPlat=&level2=&certDate=&album=&id=&after=&before=&startMonth=1&endMonth=1&startYear=1958&endYear=2009&sort=Artist&perPage=25.

6 Allan Raible, "Is Madonna's 'Borderline' the Hip 'It-Song' to Cover? A Review of Recent Renditions by The Flaming Lips and Counting Crows," Abcnews.com, accessed June 1, 2012, http://abcnews.go.com/blogs/entertainment/2009/03/is-madonnas-bor/.

7 Radhika Jones, "All Time 100 Songs," Time.com, October 24, 2011, http://entertainment.time.com/2011/10/24/the-all-time-100-songs/#borderline-madonna.

8 See Robert Hilburn, "Madonna Takes Total Control," *Los Angeles Times*, November 11, 1984, Sun ed., sec. C; Jim Miller and Cathleen McGuigan, "Rock's New Women; Cyndi Lauper and Madonna are Reinventing Pop's Feminine Mystique with Hot Videos and Wild Styles," *Newsweek*, March 4, 1985, 48; Robert Hilburn, "Madonna Makes a Hot Topic," *Los Angeles Times*, April 22, 1985, sec 6, 1.

9 Paul Smith and Lisa Frank, eds., *Madonnarama: Essays on Sex and Popular Culture* (Pittsburgh, PA: Cleis, 1993); Bordo, "'Material Girl'"; bell hooks, *Black Looks: Race and Representation* (Cambridge, MA: South End Press, 1992.)

10 Kellner, *Media Culture*, 56.

11 Michael Schaller, *Reckoning with Reagan: America and Its President in the 1980s* (New York: Oxford University Press, 1992), vii.

12 Lou Cannon, *President Reagan: The Role of a Lifetime* (New York: Public Affairs, 1991), 732–36.

13 Additionally, migration to and from Puerto Rico is related to but distinct from U.S. immigration in general, given Puerto Rico's status as a former colony. The migration of Puerto Ricans to and from Puerto Rico and U.S. cities has been shaped by the state through projects such as the Chardon Plan and Operation Bootstraps, and gender significantly impacts Puerto Ricans' migration experiences. See Gina M. Perez, *The Near Northwest Side Story: Migration, Displacement, and Puerto Rican Families* (Berkeley: University of California Press, 2004).

14 Ana Maria Alonso and Maria Teresa Koreck, "Silences: 'Hispanics,' AIDS, and Sexual Practices," in *The Lesbian and Gay Studies Reader*, ed. Henry Abelove, Michele Aina Barale, and David M. Halperin. (New York: Routledge, 1992), 111.

15 Angharad Valdivia, "Is Penelope to J.Lo as Culture Is to Nature? Eurocentric Approaches to 'Latin' Beauties," in *From Bananas to Buttocks: The Latina Body in Popular Film and Culture*, ed. Myra Mendible (Austin: University of Texas Press, 2007), 132.

16 Arlene Davila, *Latinos Inc.: The Marketing and Making of a People* (New York: New York UniversityPress, 2008), and Juan Flores, *From Bomba to Hip Hop: Puerto Rican Culture and Latino Identity* (New York: Columbia University Press, 2000).

17 Alonso and Koreck, "Silences," 110–14.

18 Lionel Cantu, Jr., in *The Sexuality of Migration: Border Crossings and Mexican Immigrant Men*, eds. Nancy A. Naples and Salvador Vidal-Ortiz (New York: New York University Press, 2009), 21–22.

19 Yen Le Spiritu, *Asian American Panethnicity: Bridging Institutions and Identities* (Philadelphia, PA: Temple University Press, 1993).

20 For an overview of the field of Asian American Studies, see Cathy J. Schuland-Vials, Linda Trinh Vo, and K. Scott Wong, eds., *Keywords in Asian American Cultural Studies* (New York: New York University Press, 2015).

21 Feminist scholars have questioned and sometimes outright rejected as inaccurate and divisive the standard narrative of "waves" of Western feminism, preferring instead a more nuanced and continuous history and narrative. See Jennifer Purvis, "Grrrls and Women Together in the Third Wave: Embracing the Challenges of Intergenerational Feminism(s)," *National Women's Studies Association (NWSA) Journal* 16, no. 3 (2004): 93–123; Clare Hemmings, *Why Stories Matter: The Political Grammar of Feminist Theory* (Durham, NC: Duke University Press, 2011); Dorothy Sue Cobble, Linda Gordon, and Astrid Henry, *Feminism Unfinished: A Short, Surprising History of American Women's Movements* (New York: Liveright, 2014). I use the term "second-wave feminism"

provisionally for critical clarity, given that the notion of a relatively coherent "second-wave feminism" was central to rising neoliberalism in the 1980s.

22 Maria de los Angeles Torres, *In the Land of Mirrors: Cuban Exile Politics* (Ann Arbor: University of Michigan Press, 1999), 17.

23 Otto Santa Ana, *Brown Tide Rising: Metaphors of Latinos in Contemporary Public Discourse* (Austin, TX: University of Texas Press, 2002).

24 De los Angeles Torres, *In the Land of Mirrors*, 17.

25 Alicia Schmidt Camacho, *Migrant Imaginaries: Latino Cultural Politics in the U.S.–Mexico Borderlands* (New York: New York University Press, 2008), 158–69.

26 Arthur Schlesinger, Jr., *The Disuniting of America* (New York: Norton, 1992), 131, and Samuel Huntington, "The Clash of Civilizations?," in *The New Shape of World Politics* (New York: Norton, 1997), 71.

27 Raymond Tatalovich, "Official English as Nativist Backlash," in *Immigrants Out! The New Nativism and the Anti-Immigrant Impulse in the United States*, ed. Juan E. Perea (New York: New York University Press, 1997), 81.

28 Jean Stefanic, "Funding the Nativist Agenda," in *Immigrants Out! The New Nativism and the Anti-Immigrant Impulse in the United States*, ed. Juan E. Perea (New York: New York University Press, 1997), 121–23.

29 See Santa Ana, *Brown Tide Rising*.

30 From World War II through the 1990s, most immigrants were women. Maxine Schwartz Seller, Introduction, in *Immigrant Women*, ed. Maxine Schwartz Seller, rev. 2nd ed. (Albany: State University of New York Press, 1994), 3.

31 Mimi Abramovitz, Foreword to Grace Chang, *Disposable Domestics: Immigrant Women Workers in the Global Economy* (Cambridge, MA: South End Press, 2000), xi.

32 Chang, *Disposable Domestics*, 5, and Pierette Hondagneu-Sotelo, *Gendered Transitions: Mexican Experiences of Immigration* (Berkeley: University of California Press, 1994), 1–2, 24–25.

33 Wayne Cornelius, "From Sojourners to Settlers: The Changing Profile of Mexican Migration to the U.S" (San Diego: Center for U.S.–Mexican Studies, University of California, San Diego, 1990), 17–20.

34 Claudia Sadowski-Smith, "Unskilled Labor Migration and the Illegality Spiral: Chinese, European, and Mexican Indocumentados in the United States, 1882–2007," *American Quarterly*, special issue, David G. Gutierrez and Pierrette Hondagneu-Sotelo, eds., *Nation and Migration: Nation Past and Future* 60, no. 3 (September 2008): 794.

35 Ibid.

36 Ibid., 791–92.

37 Philip Kretsedemas, "Immigration Enforcement and the Complication of National Sovereignty: Understanding Local Enforcement as an Exercise in Neoliberal Governance," *American Quarterly*, special issue, David G. Gutierrez and Pierette Hondagneu-Sotelo, eds., Nation and Migration: *Nation Past and Future*,60, no. 3 (September 2008): 561.

38 Matthew Jacobson, *Whiteness of a Different Color: European Immigrants and the Alchemy of Race* (Cambridge, MA: Harvard University Press, 1998), and *Roots Too: White Ethnic Revival in Post–Civil Rights America* (Cambridge, MA: Harvard University Press, 2005).

39 Stuart Hall, "The Neoliberal Revolution," *Soundings* (13626620) 48 (Summer 2011): 14–15.

40 David Harvey, *A Brief History of Neoliberalism* (New York: Oxford University Press, 2005), 3.

41 Ahiwa Ong, *Neoliberalism as Exception: Mutations in Citizenship and Sovereignty* (Durham, NC: Duke University Press, 2006.)

42 Stuart Hall, Doreen Massey, and Michael Rustin. "After Neoliberalism: Analysing the Present." *Soundings* (13626620) 53 (Spring 2013): 14.

43 Robert C. Rowland and John M. Jones, *Reagan at Westminster: Foreshadowing the End of the Cold War* (College Station: Texas A&M University Press, 2010).

44 Zillah Eisenstein, *The Color of Gender: Reimagining Democracy* (Berkeley: University of California Press, 1994), 45.

45 Greg Schneider and Renae Merle, "Reagan's Defense Buildup Bridged Military Eras: Huge Budgets Brought Life Back to Industry," *Washington Post*, June 9, 2004, E01.

46 Manfred B. Steger and Ravi K. Roy, *Neoliberalism: A Very Short Introduction* (New York: Oxford University Press, 2010), 22–23.

47 Eisenstein, *The Color of Gender*, 4.

48 Schaller, *Reckoning with Reagan*, 43.

49 Jaafar Aksikas and Sean Johnson Andrews, "Neoliberalism, Law and Culture: A Cultural Studies Intervention after 'The Juridical Turn,'" *Cultural Studies*, special issue, Jaafar Aksikas and Sean Johnson Andrews, eds., *Cultural Studies and/of the Law* 28, nos. 5–6 (2014): 745.

50 Steger and Roy, *Neoliberalism*, 11–14, 55; Harvey, *A Brief History of Neoliberalism*, 2–5.

51 See Philip Mirowski, and Dieter Plehwe, eds., *The Road from Mont Pèlerin: The Making of the Neoliberal Thought Collective* (Cambridge, MA: Harvard University Press, 2009).

52 Hall, "The Neoliberal Revolution," 18.

53 See Sam Gindin and Sam Panitch, *The Making of Global Capitalism: The Political Economy of American Empire* (London: Verso, 2012).

54 Ronald Reagan, "Address before a Joint Session of the Congress Reporting on the State of the Union," *Reagan 2020*, February 4, 1986, http://reagan2020.us/speeches/state_of_the_union_1986.asp.

55 Todd Leopold, "Analysis: The Age of Reagan," *CNN Entertainment*, June 16, 2004, http://articles.cnn.com/2004-06-16/entertainment/reagan.80s_1_cosby-show-pop-culture-family-ties?_s=PM:SHOWBIZ; Bruce Springsteen, "Born in the U.S.A.," Columbia Records, 1984.

56 Gil Troy, *The Reagan Revolution: A Very Short Introduction* (New York: Oxford University Press, 2009), 111.

57 Ibid., 112–13.

58 Harvey, *A Brief History of Neoliberalism*, 16.

59 Hall, Massey, and Rustin, "After Neoliberalism," 9–10.

60 Ibid., 14.

61 Christina Gerken, *Model Immigrants and Undesirable Aliens: The Cost of Immigration Reform in the 1990s* (Minneapolis: University of Minnesota Press, 2013), 11.

62 Hall, Massey, and Rustin, "After Neoliberalism," 9. See also Gérard Duménil and Dominique Lévy, *The Crisis of Neoliberalism* (Cambridge, MA: Harvard University Press, 2011).

63 Rosemary Coombe, "Is There a Cultural Studies of Law?," in *A Companion to Cultural Studies*, ed. Toby Miller. (New York: Blackwell, 2001), 36–62.

64 Gina M. Perez, Frank A. Guridy, and Adrian Burgos, Jr., Introduction, in *Beyond El Barrio: Everyday Life in Latina/o America*, ed. Gina M. Perez, Frank A. Guridy, and Adrian Burgos, Jr. (New York: New York University Press, 2010), 3–4.

65 Ibid, 3.

66 "Los Angeles: America's Uneasy Melting Pot," *Time on the Web*, June 13, 1983, http://www.time.com/printout/0,8816, 952000,00.htm.

67 "Losing Control of the Borders," *Time on the Web*, June 13, 1983, http://www.time.com/printout/0,8816, 952000,00.htm.

68 David Teather, "Madonna Ends Her Maverick Era," *Guardian*, June 16, 2004, http://www.guardian.co.uk/business/2004/jun/16/citynews.arts.

69 Laurie Schulze, Anne Barton White, and Jane D. Brown, "A Sacred Monster in Her Prime," in *The Madonna Collection: Representational Politics, Subcultural Identities, and Cultural Theory*, ed. Cathy Schwichtenberg (Boulder, CO: Westview, 1993), 15.

70 Helen Barolini, "Reintroducing the *Dream Book*," in *Chiaroscuro: Essays of Identity*, ed. Helen Barolini (Madison: University of Wisconsin Press, 1999), 159.

71 Also directed by Mary Lambert, who directed "Borderline," and the early Madonna videos "Material Girl," "La Isla Bonita," and "Like a Prayer." In the 1980s, Lambert directed videos for Janet Jackson, Whitney Houston, The Go-Go's, Sting, and other popular performers, as well as several feature films.

72 "Billboard Hot 100 Chart, Week of December 22, 1984," Billboard.com, http://www.billboard.com/#/charts/hot-100?chartDate=1984-12-22.

73 "Madonna—'Like a Virgin': RIAA's Gold and Platinum Program," RIAA.com.

74 Mary Cross, *Madonna: A Biography* (Westport, CT: Greenwood, 2007), 36.

75 Smith and Frank, *Madonnarama*, 13.

76 bell hooks, "Power to the Pussy: We Don't Wanna Be Dicks in Drag," in *Madonnarama: Essays on Sex and Popular Culture*, ed. Paul Smith and Lisa Frank (Pittsburgh, PA: Cleis, 1993), 77.

77 Ibid., 75.

78 Chris Smith, "Madonna: *Like a Virgin* (1984)," *Pop Culture Universe: Icons, Idols, Ideas*, ABC-CLIO, 2016, http://popculture2.abc-clio.com.mutex.gmu.edu/Search/Display/1511549?terms=Madonna+like+virgin.

79 Jacobson, *Roots Too.*

80 Ibid., 246–311.

81 Chon Noriega, "Citizen Chicano: The Trials and Titillations of Ethnicity in the American Cinema, 1935–1962," in *Latin Looks: Images of Latinas and Latinos in the U.S. Media,* ed. Clara E. Rodriguez (Boulder, CO: Westview, 1998), 92.

82 Richie Perez, "From Assimilation to Annihilation: Puerto Rican Images in U.S. Films," in Rodriguez, *Latin Looks,* 142–63.

83 Patricia Hill Collins, *Black Sexual Politics: African Americans, Gender, and the New Racism* (New York: Routledge, 2005.)

84 Hector Amaya, "Citizenship, Diversity, Law and Ugly Betty," *Media, Culture & Society* 32, no. 5 (2010): 804.

85 Ibid., 804–5.

86 Roseann M. Manduzuik, "Feminist Politics and Postmodern Seductions: Madonna and the Struggle for Political Articulation," in *The Madonna Connection: Representational Politics, Subcultural Identities, and Cultural Theory,* ed. Cathy Schwichtenberg (Boulder, CO: Westview, 1993), 167–88.

87 A play on Terry Eagleton's statement that "war is culture by other means," in his *Scholars and Rebels in Nineteenth Century Ireland* (Oxford: Blackwell Publishers, 1999), 35.

88 Lisa Duggan, *The Twilight of Equality: Neoliberalism, Cultural Politics, and the Attack on Democracy* (Boston: Beacon Press, 2003), 70.

89 Ibid., 70–71.

90 Ibid., 70.

91 Rosemary Coombe, "Is There a Cultural Studies of Law?," in *A Companion to Cultural Studies,* ed. Toby Miller (New York: Blackwell, 2001) 36–62, 39.

92 Aksikas and Andrews, "Neoliberalism, Law and Culture," 756.

93 Ibid., 754.

94 John Fiske, *Television Culture* (New York: Routledge, 1987), and *Power Plays, Power Works* (New York: Verso, 1993); Henry Giroux, *Channel Surfing: Racism, the Media, and the Destruction of Today's Youth* (New York: St. Martin's, 1997); Douglas Kellner, "Toward a Critical Media/Cultural Studies," in *Media/Cultural Studies: Critical Approaches,* ed. Rhonda Hammer and Douglas Kellner (New York: Peter Lang, 2009), 5–24; Douglas Kellner and Meenakshi Gigi Durham, "Adventures in Media and Cultural Studies: Introducing the Keyworks," in *Media and Cultural Studies Keyworks,* ed. Meenakshi Gigi Durham and Douglas Kellner (Malden, MA: Blackwell, 2001), 1–26.

95 Benedict Anderson, *Imagined Communities: Reflections on the Origin and Spread of Nationalism* (New York: Verso, 1991).

96 Kellner, *Media Culture,* 1.

97 Norman Fairclough, *Language and Power* (New York: Routledge, 1989); Teun VanDijk, *Communicating Racism: Ethnic Prejudice in Thought and Talk* (New York: Sage, 1987); and Norman K. Denzin's *The Cinematic Society: The Voyeur's Gaze* (New York: Sage, 1995).

98 Mary Celeste Kearney, Introduction, in *The Gender and Media Reader*, ed. Mary Celeste Kearney (New York: Routledge, 2012), 2–3.

99 See John Fiske, *Television Culture* and *Power Plays, Power Works*.

100 Stuart Hall, "Encoding/Decoding," in *Culture, Media, Language: Working Papers in Cultural Studies: 1972–1979*, ed. Stuart Hall, Dorothy Hobson, Andrew Lowe, and Paul Willis (New York: Routledge, 1992), 128–38; 135.

101 Lisbet van Zoonen, "Feminist Perspectives on the Media," in *The Gender and Media Reader*, ed. Mary Celeste Kearney (New York: Routledge, 2012), 35.

102 Ben Bagdikian, *The Media Monopoly* (New York: Beacon, 2004). This now classic text about the dangers of corporate media monopoly is on its twentieth edition.

103 Hall, Massey, and Rustin, "After Neoliberalism," 18.

104 Ibid., 18.

105 Lawrence W. Levine, "The Folklore of Industrial Society: Popular Culture and Its Audiences," *American Historical Review* 97, no. 5 (December 1992): 1,381.

106 Rachel Rubin and Peter Melnick, *Immigration and Popular Culture: An Introduction* (New York: New York University Press, 2007), 1–3.

107 Rosa Linda Fregoso, *MeXicana Encounters: The Making of Social Identities on the Borderlands* (Berkeley: University of California Press, 2003); Lisa Lowe, *Immigrant Acts: On Asian American Cultural Politics* (Durham, NC: Duke University Press, 1996); Matthew Jacobson, *Whiteness of a Different Color: European Immigrants and the Alchemy of Race* (Cambridge, MA: Harvard University Press, 1998).

108 Mike Davis, *Ecology of Fear: Los Angeles and the Imagination of Disaster* (New York: Vintage, 1999).

109 Leo R. Chavez, *The Latino Threat: Constructing Immigrants, Citizens, and the Nation* (Stanford, CA: Stanford University Press, 2008).

110 Kenneth Libo and Michael Skakun, "All That Glitters Is Not Goldwyn: Early Hollywood Moguls," *Center for Jewish History*, http://www.cjh.org/p/52.

111 Neal Gabler, *An Empire of Their Own: How the Jews Invented Hollywood* (New York: Crown, 1988).

112 Joseph McBride, *Frank Capra: The Catastrophe of Success* (New York: Simon & Schuster, 1992), 11.

113 See Lisbeth Cohen, *Making a New Deal: Industrial Workers in Chicago, 1919–1939* (Cambridge, MA: Cambridge University Press, 1990); Miriam Hansen, *Babel and Babylon: Spectatorship in American Silent Film* (Cambridge, MA: Harvard University Press, 1994); Alison Landsberg, *Prosthetic Memory: The Transformation of Remembrance in the Age of Mass Culture* (New York: Columbia University Press, 2004.)

114 See Werner Sollors, *Beyond Ethnicity: Consent and Descent in American Culture* (New York: Oxford University Press, 1986); William Boelhower, *Immigrant Autobiography in the United States: Four Versions of the American Self* (Verona: Essedue Edizione, 1982); Robert J. DiPietro and Edward Ifkovic, *Ethnic*

Perspectives in American Literature (New York: Modern Language Association, 1983.)

115 Kimberle Williams Crenshaw, "Race Reform, Retrenchment: Transformation and Legitimation in Anti-Discrimination Law," *Harvard Law Review* 101, no. 7 (1988): 1331–87.

116 Gloria Anzaldua and Cherrie Moraga, eds., *This Bridge Called My Back: Writings by Radical Women of Color* (Berkeley, CA: Third Woman Press, 1981.)

117 Gillian Rose, *Visual Methodologies: An Introduction to Researching with Visual Materials,* 3rd ed. (Thousand Oaks, CA: Sage, 2012), 197.

118 Ibid., 210.

119 Ibid., xix.

120 Teun VanDijk, *Elite Discourse and Racism* (New York: Sage, 1993).

121 Levine defines "popular culture" as culture that is "widely accessible and widely accessed; widely disseminated, and widely viewed or heard or read" ("The Folklore of Industrial Society," 1373).

122 From the 1980s and even up to the present day, aliens provided a rather straight-forward metaphor for fears of an invasion of illegal immigrants, and not surprisingly several scholars focused on the abundance of alien-themed films and TV shows that began to proliferate in the late 1980s. See Davis, *Ecology of Fear;* Chang, *Disposable Domestics,* 23–24; Chavez, *The Latino Threat.* In contrast, I focus on representations of human beings who are variously coded as illegal aliens, citizens, and immigrants.

123 My focus on the U.S. national scope recognizes that while certain features are characteristically neoliberal throughout the world, neoliberalism has variants that are national. See Hall, "The Neoliberal Revolution," 12.

124 Aksikas and Andrews, "Neoliberalism, Law and Culture," 742–80.

125 Curtis Marez, "Preface," *American Quarterly,* special issue, David G. Gutierrez and Pierette Hondagneau-Sotelo, eds., *Nation and Migration: Nation Past and Future* 60, no. 3 (September 2008): vii.

126 Ana Castillo, *The Guardians* (New York: Random House, 2007), 118.

127 Hannah Arendt, *The Origins of Totalitarianism* (San Francisco: Harvest Books, 1966), 278.

CHAPTER 1: IMMIGRATION AS EMERGENCY

1 Ward Sinclair and Joanne Omang, "U.S. Cracks Down on Refugee Boats," *Washington Post,* Saturday final edition, first section, April 26, 1980.

2 Maria de los Angeles Torres, *In the Land of Mirrors: Cuban Exile Politics in the United States* (Ann Arbor: University of Michigan Press, 1999), 15–16.

3 "Voyage From Cuba: It Is the Thing We Have Prayed for But Never Thought Would Happen," *Time,* May 5, 1980, 42.

4 Cubans migrated in three Cold War waves. The first, 1959–1962, is the "most celebrated." Most of these middle-class professionals received generous support from the federal government. The 1965–1973 "freedom flights" brought 300,000

refugees who were granted government aid and legal status/asylum under the 1966 Cuban Adjustment Act. Mariel was the third wave with approximately 125,000 émigrés. See Maria Cristina Garcia, *Havana USA: Cuban Exiles and Cuban Americans in South Florida, 1959–1994* (Berkeley: University of California Press, 1997).

5 "Cuba Closes Mariel Harbor, Boatlift Ends," *Facts on File World News Digest*, October 3, 1980.

6 Ross Layer, "U.S. Fears Castro Unleashing Criminals, Spies," *Globe and Mail*, May 1, 1990.

7 "Miami Homicide Rate 5 Times above Usual among Cuban Exiles," *New York Times*, June 1, 1980; "Cuban Ties Boatlift to Drug Trade," *New York Times*, May 1, 1983.

8 Charles R. Babcock, "Navy Ships Will Monitor Cuban Boatlift," *New York Times*, May 1, 1980.

9 Reginald Stuart, "3 Years Later, Most Cubans of Boatlift Adjusting to US," *New York Times*, sec. A, May 17, 1983.

10 David Adams, "Remembering Mariel," review of *Finding Mañana: A Memoir of a Cuban Exodus* by Mirta Ojito, *St. Petersburg Times*, April 10, 2005.

11 Ibid. Also see Mirta A. Ojito, *Finding Mañana: A Memoir of a Cuban Exodus* (New York: Penguin Press, 2005).

12 Roger Daniels, *Guarding the Golden Door: American Immigration Policy and Immigrants since 1882* (New York: Hill and Wang, 2004), 202–4.

13 Matthew J. Gibney and Randall Hansen, eds., *Immigration and Asylum: From 1900 to the Present* (Santa Barbara, CA: ABC-CLIO, 2005), 1:283.

14 "Refugees: 6.2 Million Seek a Haven," *Newsweek*, April 28, 1980.

15 Christopher Mitchell, "U.S. Policy toward Haitian Boat People, 1972–93," *ANNALS of the American Academy of Political and Social Science* 534, no. 1 (July 1994): 69–80.

16 Rosemary Coombe, "Is There a Cultural Studies of Law?," in *A Companion to Cultural Studies*, ed. Toby Miller (New York: Blackwell, 2001) 36–62; 55–56.

17 Ibid., 48.

18 Cecelia Menjívar, "Immigrant Kinship Networks: Vietnamese, Salvadorans and Mexicans in Comparative Perspective," *Journal of Comparative Family Studies* 28, no. 1 (Spring 1997): 1–24.

19 Ruben G. Rumbaut, "The Structure of Refuge: South Asian Refugees in the U.S., 1975–1985," *International Review of Comparative Public Policy* 1 (1989): 97–129.

20 Menjívar, "Immigrant Kinship Networks," 11.

21 De los Angeles Torres, *In the Land of Mirrors*, 105.

22 I examine the proposed immigration emergency bills because they—not the Refugee Act—delineated and best encapsulate the neoliberal "immigration emergency." The Reagan era immigration emergency bills were also meant to "fix" the Refugee Act.

23 Manfred B. Steger and Ravi K. Roy, *Neoliberalism: A Very Short Introduction* (New York: Oxford University Press, 2010), 11–14, 55.

24 Daniels, *Guarding the Golden Door*, 219–220.
25 Aristide R. Zolberg, *A Nation by Design: Immigration Policy in the Fashioning of America* (New York: Russell Sage Foundation, 2006), 340.
26 "Migration Information Source," *Immigration Statistics USA*, http:/www. mapsofworld.com/usS/immigration/immigration-statistics-usa.html.
27 Grace Chang, *Disposable Domestics: Immigrant Women Workers in the Global Economy* (Cambridge, MA: South End Press, 2000).
28 Quoted in Daniel J. Tichenor, *Dividing Lines: The Politics of Immigration Control in America* (Princeton, NJ: Princeton University Press, 2002), 254.
29 SCIRP organized seven taskforces, studied fifty briefing and background papers, and held twelve regional hearings that included seven hundred witnesses and twenty-four scholars. In July–November, 1980, members cast straw ballots on seventy-four memoranda, and considered a total of 140 recommendations. Most votes were unanimous, but SCIRP was divided over the use of identification cards for employer sanctions and the fifth preference category, for brothers and sisters of U.S. citizens. Zolberg, *A Nation by Design*, 592, n. 68.
30 United States Select Commission on Immigration and Refugee Policy, *U.S. Immigration Policy and the National Interest*, staff report, April 30, 1981 (Washington, DC: GPO, 1981), 3.
31 Ibid., 7.
32 Daniels, *Guarding the Golden Door*, 224.
33 Donna Gabaccia, *From the Other Side: Women, Gender, and Immigrant Life in the U.S., 1820–1990* (Bloomington: Indiana University Press, 1994), 39.
34 While the president and congress appoint a commission jointly, a taskforce is usually composed of only executive branch officials.
35 Zolberg, *A Nation by Design*, 340.
36 See "H.R. 7234–97th Congress: Immigration Emergency Act," GovTrack.us, 1982, http://www.govtrack.us/ congress/bills /97 /hr7234.
37 U.S. Congress, Senate, Subcommittee on Immigration and Refugee Policy of the Committee on the Judiciary, *Immigration Emergency Powers: Hearing before the Subcommittee on Immigration and Refugee Policy*, 97th Cong., 2nd sess., 1982, 1–2.
38 Giorgio Agamben, *Means without End: Notes on Politics* (Minneapolis: University of Minnesota Press, 2000), 6.
39 Jaafar Aksikas and Sean Johnson Andrews, "Neoliberalism, Law and Culture: A Cultural Studies Intervention after 'The Juridical Turn,'" *Cultural Studies*, special issue, Jaafar Aksikas and Sean Johnson Andrews, eds., *Cultural Studies and/of the Law* 28, nos. 5–6 (2014): 757.
40 Ibid., 15. See also Katherine Lemons and Joshua Takano Chambers-Leston, "Rule of Law: Sharia Panic and the US Constitution in the House of Representatives," *Cultural Studies*, special issue, Jaafar Aksikas and Sean Johnson Andrews, eds., *Cultural Studies and/of the Law* 28, nos. 5–6 (2014): 1048–77.
41 U.S. Congress, Senate, Subcommittee, *Immigration Emergency Powers*, 2–3.
42 Ibid., 39.

43 Rosa Linda Fregoso, *MeXicana Encounters: The Making of Social Identities on the Borderlands* (Berkeley: University of California Press, 2003), 126–47.

44 Charles Ramirez Berg, *Latino Images in Film: Stereotyping, Subversion, and Resistance* (Austin: University of Texas Press, 2002).

45 "AFI'S 10 Top 10: *Scarface,*" *American Film Institute*, 2008, http://www.afi. com/10top10/moreDetail.aspx?id=28&thumb=1.

46 Ibid.

47 Christy Collis and Jason Bainbridge, "Introduction: Popular Cultures and the Law," *Continuum: Journal of Media & Cultural Studies*, special issue, *Popular Cultures and the Law* 19, no. 2 (June 2005): 162.

48 Lieve Gies, "Law as Popular Culture: Cross-Disciplinary Encounters," *Continuum: Journal of Media & Cultural Studies*, special issue, *Popular Cultures and the Law* 19, no. 2 (June 2005): 165–80.

49 Rachel Rubin and Jeffrey Paul Melnick, *Immigration and American Popular Culture: An Introduction* (New York: New York University Press, 2007), 2.

50 Leo Chavez, *The Latino Threat: Constructing Immigrants, Citizens, and the Nation* (Stanford, CA: Stanford University Press, 2008), 2–3, 83–84.

51 Robert Entman and Andrew Rojecki, *The Black Image in the White Mind: Media and Race in America* (Chicago: University of Chicago Press, 2001). The authors demonstrated how white Americans learn about black Americans through the media and that while blacks are represented with regularity and some nuance, media promote racism by depicting a hierarchy of whites over blacks, and creating a sense of difference and tension.

52 "Not Nativist, Not Racist, Not Mean," *New York Times*, March 18, 1982.

53 U.S. Congress, Joint Hearings, Subcommittee on Immigration, Refugees, and International Law of the Committee on the Judiciary House of Representatives and Subcommittee on Immigration and Refugee Policy of the Committee on the Judiciary Senate, *Immigration Reform and Control Act of 1982: Joint Hearings before the Subcommittee on Immigration, Refugees, and International Law And Subcommittee on Immigration and Refugee Policy*, 97th Cong., 2nd sess., 1982, 1–2.

54 Evidence of the racism that Haitians contended with in immigration proceedings was well-documented. For instance, see Arnold H. Lubasch, "Judge, Citing Bias, Orders Release of Eight Haitians," *New York Times*, March 6, 1982.

55 U.S. Congress, Joint Hearings, Subcommittees, *Immigration Reform and Control Act of 1982*, 344.

56 Ibid., 343.

57 U.S. Congress, Senate, Subcommittee, *Immigration Emergency Powers*, 68.

58 Ibid., 93. That emergency act, sponsored by Senator Pat McCarran (D-NV), is also known as the Subversive Activities Control Act, or the McCarran Act. It established detention camps within the United States during the Korean War in order to detain—without due process—persons considered likely to commit future crimes against the state. The law was connected to, as Henderson pointed out, McCarthy-era hysteria around both aliens and citizens in relation to national security. While

the law was criticized as unconstitutional and was vetoed by President Harry S. Truman, Congress overrode the veto (incidentally, this pattern resurfaced with the 1952 McCarran-Walter immigration act; see p. 55–57). The Non-Detention Act of 1971 repealed some of the provisions of the law, but other provisions still stand.

59 Ibid., 75.

60 Ibid., 72.

61 Ibid.

62 Tamara Lush, "Whatever Happened to Redemption?," *Tampa Bay Times*, May 21, 2006.

63 Gil Klein, "Majority of Cuban Refugees Work Hard to Get Ahead, Contradict Bad Image," *Christian Science Monitor*, May 18, 1983.

64 U.S. Congress, Joint Hearings, Subcommittee, *Immigration Reform and Control Act of 1982*, 344.

65 U.S. Congress, Senate, Subcommittee, *Immigration Emergency Powers*, 98.

66 Such fact-free apocrypha surfaced in support of other neoliberal efforts, notably Reagan's frequent reference to a grossly exaggerated "welfare queen" to justify moves to cut social services (see Chapter 3).

67 U.S. Congress, Senate, Subcommittee, *Immigration Emergency Powers*, 86–87.

68 Werner Sollors, *Beyond Ethnicity: Consent and Descent in American Culture* (New York: Oxford University Press, 1986), 89–90.

69 Stephen Farber, "A Night in Hollywood, a Day in Ukraine" *New York Times*, December 31, 2006, http://www.nytimes.com/2006/12/31/movies/31farb.html?_r=1&ref=world&oref=slogin.

70 Judy Klemesrud, "Speaks Russian like Czech: Robin Williams Tells of His Crash Language Course for 'Moscow on the Hudson,'" *Sarasota Herald Tribune*, April 14, 1984.

71 Klemesrud, "Speaks Russian like Czech."

72 Ibid.

73 "Moscow on the Hudson," *Box Office Mojo*, http://www.boxofficemojo.com/movies/?id=moscowonthehudson.htm.

74 Klemesrud, "Speaks Russian like a Czech."

75 Roger Ebert, "Moscow on the Hudson," *Chicago Sun-Times*, January 1, 1984.

76 Christina Gerken, *Model Immigrants and Undesirable Aliens: The Cost of Immigration Reform in the 1990s* (Minneapolis: University of Minnesota Press, 2013), 21.

77 Pierette Hondagneu-Sotelo, *Gendered Transitions: Mexican Experiences of Immigration* (Berkeley: University of California Press, 1994), xv.

78 Ronald Reagan, "Statement on United States Immigration and Refugee Policy, July 30, 1981," in *Public Papers of the Presidents of the United States: Ronald W. Reagan, 1981, Book 1—January 20 to December 31, 1981* (Washington, DC: GPO, 1982), 676–77.

79 Hondagneu-Sotelo, *Gendered Transitions*, xv.

80 Nicolas Laham, *Ronald Reagan and the Politics of Immigration Reform* (Westport, CT: Praeger, 2000), 80–84.

81 Mae M. Ngai, *Impossible Subjects: Illegal Aliens and the Making of Modern America* (Princeton, NJ: Princeton University Press, 2004), 8.

82 Ibid., 269.

83 Jodie Melamed, "Reading Tehran in *Lolita*: Making Racialized Gendered Difference Work for Neoliberal Multiculturalism," in *Strange Affinities: The Gender and Sexual Politics of Comparative Racialization*, ed. Grace Kyunghwon Hong and Roderick Ferguson (Durham, NC: Duke University Press, 2011), 78.

84 Ibid., 82. See also Jodie Melamed, *Represent and Destroy: Rationalizing Violence in the New Racial Capitalism* (Minneapolis: University of Minnesota Press, 2011).

85 Alison Landsberg, *Prosthetic Memory: The Transformation of Remembrance in the Age of Mass Culture* (New York: Columbia University Press, 2004), 52.

86 See Noel Ignatiev, *How the Irish Became White* (New York: Routledge, 1996).

87 Matthew Jacobson, *Whiteness of a Different Color: European Immigrants and the Alchemy of Race* (Cambridge, MA: Harvard University Press, 1998). See also David Roediger, *Working toward Whiteness: How America's Immigrants Became White: The Strange Journey from Ellis Island to the Suburbs* (New York: Basic Books, 2005).

88 Martha Gardener, *The Qualities of a Citizen: Women, Immigration, and Citizenship, 1870–1965* (Princeton: Princeton University Press, 2005), 169.

89 Ibid., 165–66.

90 Roediger, *Working toward Whiteness*, 139.

91 Landsberg, *Prosthetic Memory*, 50–55.

92 Calvin Coolidge's secretary of state, cited in R. A. Divine, *American Immigration Policy, 1924–1952* (New Haven, CT: Yale University Press, 1957), 52–66.

93 Desmond King, *Making Americans: Immigration, Race, and the Origins of the Diverse Democracy* (Cambridge, MA: Harvard University Press, 2000), 233.

94 Gardener, *The Qualities of a Citizen*, 213.

95 Quoted in David Jacobson, *Rights across Borders: Immigration and the Decline of Citizenship* (Baltimore, MD: Johns Hopkins University Press, 1996), 49–50.

96 U.S. Senate, *Congressional Record*, 83rd Cong., 1st sess., 1953, 518.

97 Ibid.

98 Drew Pearson, "'Untouchables' Labeled Top Violent TV," *Palm Beach Post-Times*, July 16, 1961, 8.

99 Jay S. Harris, *TV Guide: The First Twenty-Five Years* (New York: Simon and Schuster, 1978), 53.

100 King, *Making Americans*, 230.

101 E. P. Hutchinson, *Legislative History of American Immigration Policy, 1798–1965* (Philadelphia: University of Pennsylvania Press, 1981), 306–10.

102 Roger Daniels, "The Immigration Act of 1965: Intended and Unintended Consequences," in *Historians on America: Decisions That Made a Difference*, ed. Paul Malamud (Washington, DC: State Department Bureau of International Information Programs, n.d.), 81–82.

103 Ibid., 82.

104 Kennedy, the descendant of Irish immigrants, was committed to liberal immigration policy, particularly for white ethnics. His *Nation of Immigrants* (1965) laid out his vision for a more welcoming, inclusive America.

105 Lyndon B. Johnson quoted in "National Quotas for Immigration to End," *Congressional Quarterly Almanac*, 89th Cong., 1st sess. (Washington, DC: Congressional Quarterly, 1965), 467.

106 Derrick J. Bell, Jr., *And We Are Not Saved: The Elusive Quest for Racial Justice* (San Francisco: Harper San Francisco, 1989); Richard Delgado and Jean Stefanic, eds., *The Derrick Bell Reader* (New York: New York University Press, 2005); Derrick Bell, Jr., "Racial Realism," in *Critical Race Theory: The Key Writings that Formed the Movement*, ed. Kimberle, Neil Gotanda, Gary Peller, and Kendall Thomas (New York: The New Press, 1995), 302–314; Richard Delgado, "The Imperial Scholar: Reflections on a Review of Civil Rights Literature," *University of Pennsylvania Law Review* 132, no. 3 (March 1984): 561–78; and Richard Delgado and Jean Stefanic, eds., *Critical Race Theory: An Introduction* (Philadelphia: Temple University Press, 2001).

107 "Three Decades of Mass Immigration: The Legacy of the 1965 Immigration Act," Center for Immigration Studies, http://www.cis.org/articles/1995/back395.html.

108 Matthew Jacobson, *Roots Too: White Ethnic Revival in Post–Civil Rights America* (Cambridge, MA: Harvard University Press, 2005.)

109 Roediger, *Working toward Whiteness*, 200–25.

110 Daniels, *Guarding the Golden Door*, 139.

111 Lyndon P. Johnson, "Remarks at the Signing of the Immigration Bill, Liberty Island, New York. October 3, 1965," in *Public Papers of the Presidents of the United States: Lyndon Johnson, 1965, Book 2—June 1–December 31, 1965* (Washington, DC: GPO, 1967), 1038.

112 Mike Davis, *Prisoners of the American Dream: Politics and Economy of the U.S. Working Class* (London: Verso, 1986); see also Ted Kennedy, quoted in "Three Decades of Mass Immigration: The Legacy of the 1965 Immigration Act."

113 Zolberg, *A Nation by Design*, 336.

114 United States Select Commission on Immigration and Refugee Policy, *U.S. Immigration Policy and the National Interest*, 28.

115 Ibid., 45.

116 Stuart, "3 Years Later."

117 Ibid.

118 De los Angeles Torres, *In the Land of Mirrors*, 9, 122, 125. Anti-Castro efforts within this hardline community have included interventionist strategies such as the secret paramilitary camps of the 1960s (some CIA-funded); terrorist groups of the 1970s; and the political action committees of the 1980s and 1990s. See Maria Cristina Garcia, "Hardliners v. 'Dialogueros': Cuban Exile Political Groups and United States–Cuba Policy," *Journal of American Ethnic History* 17, no. 4 (Summer 1998).

119 De los Angeles Torres, *In the Land of Mirrors*, 121–22.

120 Garcia, "Hardliners v. 'Dialogueros.'"

121 De los Angeles Torres, *In the Land of Mirrors*, 115.

122 Maria Cristina Garcia, *Havana USA: Cuban Exiles and Cuban Americans in South Florida, 1959–1994* (Berkeley: University of California Press, 1997); Maria de los Angeles Torres, "Working against the Miami Myth," *Nation*, October 24, 1988, 394.

123 De los Angeles Torres, "Working against the Miami Myth" 393.

124 Ibid.

125 Erica Rand, *Ellis Island Snow Globe* (Durham, NC: Duke University Press, 2005), 65.

CHAPTER 2: THE BORDERLINES OF FAMILY REUNIFICATION

1 Under the Federal Refugee Resettlement Program, created with the 1980 Refugee Act, refugees require sponsors who provide some financial support, and families are favored. *"The Refugee Act" Office of Refugee Resettlement: An Office of the Administration for Children and Families*, August 29, 2012, http://www.acf.hhs.gov/programs/orr/resource/the-refugee-act.

2 Mariel endangered the Latina/o "model minority" stereotype engendered by previous waves of Cuban migrants. Angel's xenophobia and aggression highlight the dangerous side of the conservative hardliner Cuban American businessman: for instance, in 1989 the FBI named Miami the capital of U.S. terrorism after eighteen bombs went off in the homes of Cuban exiles working to improve relations with Cuba. Maria de los Angeles Torres, *In the Land of Mirrors: Cuban Exile Politics in the United States* (Ann Arbor: University of Michigan Press, 1999), 12.

3 Dave Kehr, "'Perez' Misses the Boat: 'Family' Saga of Cuban Refugees in Miami Undone by Clichés," *New York Daily News*, May 12, 1995.

4 Anne Marie Jagose, *Queer Theory: An Introduction* (New York: New York University Press, 1996), 1.

5 Kath Weston, *Families We Choose: Lesbians, Gays, Kinship* (New York: Columbia University Press, 1997), 3. Weston defines gay or chosen families as ones that "embrace friends; they may also encompass lovers, coparents, adopted children, children from previous heterosexual relationships, and offspring conceived through alternative insemination."

6 Judith Halberstam, *The Queer Art of Failure* (Durham, NC: Duke University Press, 2011), 2.

7 Ibid., 3.

8 Monisha Das Gupta, "Dearly Deported: Sentimental Politics and Immigrant Rights," American Studies Association annual conference, San Juan, Puerto Rico, November 15–18, 2012.

9 Maria de Los Angeles Torres, "Elián and the Tale of Pedro Pan," *Nation*, March 27, 2000, 21.

10 Seven hundred children whose parents were fighting in the counterrevolutionary underground were meant to participate, but after the failed Bay of Pigs invasion, 13,300 more children were sent in response to CIA-inspired rumors. The operation continued until the 1962 missile crisis, when the U.S. shut its doors to Cuba. Seven thousand children were awaiting the arrival of their parents. Doors did not reopen until 1965. De Los Angeles Torres, "Elián and the Tale of Pedro Pan," 21. See also De los Angeles, *In the Land of Mirrors*, 7.

11 Neda Atanasoski, *Humanitarian Violence: The U.S. Deployment of Diversity* (Minneapolis: University of Minnesota Press, 2013), 3.

12 Kehr, "'Perez' Misses the Boat."

13 Joyce C. Vialet, "Immigration Issues and Legislation in the 98th Congress," Congressional Research Service (Washington, DC: Library of Congress Congressional Research Service, May 12, 1983; updated November 11, 1984), 10–15.

14 Stuart Hall, "The Neoliberal Revolution," *Soundings* (13626620) 48 (Summer 2011): 15–16.

15 Stuart Hall, Doreen Massey, and Michael Rustin. "After Neoliberalism: Analysing the Present." *Soundings* (13626620) 53 (Spring 2013): 18.,

16 Christina Gerken, *Model Immigrants and Undesirable Aliens: The Cost of Immigration Reform in the 1990s* (Minneapolis: University of Minnesota Press, 2013), 111.

17 Pierette Hondagneu-Sotelo, *Gendered Transitions: Mexican Experiences of Immigration* (Berkeley: University of California Press, 1994), 7.

18 Lionel Cantu, Jr., *The Sexuality of Migration: Border Crossings and Mexican Immigrant Men*, ed. Nancy A. Naples and Salvador Vidal-Ortiz (New York: New York University Press, 2009), 21.

19 Gloria Gonzalez-Lopez, *Erotic Journeys: Mexican Immigrants and Their Sex Lives* (Berkeley: University of California Press, 2005), 98–99.

20 Aristide R. Zolberg, *A Nation By Design: Immigration Policy in the Fashioning of America* (Cambridge, MA: Harvard University Press, 2008), 358.

21 U.S. Congress, Joint Hearings, Subcommittee on Immigration, Refugees, and International Law of the Committee on the Judiciary House of Representatives and Subcommittee on Immigration and Refugee Policy of the Committee on the Judiciary United States Senate, *Immigration Reform and Control Act of 1982: Hearing before the Subcommittee on Immigration, Refugees, and International Law and Subcommittee on Immigration and Refugee Policy*, 97th Cong., 2nd sess., 1982, 41.

22 Ibid., 44–45, 125.

23 Ibid., 45–46.

24 Alan Simpson, *Washington Post*, April 28, 1981, quoted in Roger Daniels, *Guarding the Golden Door: American Immigration Policy and Immigrants Since 1882* (New York: Hill and Wang, 2004), 224.

25 U.S. Congress, Senate, Subcommittee on Immigration and Refugee Policy of the Committee on the Judiciary, *Numerical Limits on Immigration to the United States,*

Hearing before the Subcommittee on Immigration and Refugee Policy, 97th Cong., 2nd sess., 1982, 134.

26 Harry Kriesler, "Alan Simpson Interview," *Conversations with History*, September 17, 1997, Institute of International Studies, UC Berkeley.

27 U.S. Congress, Senate, Subcommittee, *Numerical Limits on Immigration to the United States*, 140.

28 Ibid., 141–42.

29 Alan Simpson, *Right in the Old Gazoo: A Lifetime of Scrapping with the Press* (New York: William Morrow, 1997), 73.

30 Ibid., 164.

31 Ibid., 71–72.

32 George Lipsitz, *How Racism Takes Place* (Philadelphia: Temple University Press, 2011), 35.

33 David Theo Goldberg, *The Threat of Race: Reflections on Racial Neoliberalism* (Malden, MA: Blackwell, 2009), 23–24.

34 Phyllis Pease Chock, "No New Women: Gender, 'Alien,' and 'Citizen' in the Congressional Debate on Immigration," *Political and Legal Anthropological Review* (PoLAR) 19, no. 1 (May 1996): 1.

35 Ibid.

36 Gloria Anzaldua, "La Prieta," in *This Bridge Called My Back: Writings by Radical Women of Color*, ed. Cherrie L. Moraga and Gloria Anzaldua (Berkeley, CA: Third Woman Press, 1981), 228.

37 Chock, "No New Women," 1.

38 Hondagneu-Sotelo, *Gendered Transitions*, 3.

39 Gil Troy, *The Reagan Revolution: A Short Introduction* (New York: Oxford University Press, 2009), 83.

40 Stephanie Coontz, Maya Parson, and Gabrielle Raley, Introduction, in *American Families: A Multicultural Reader*, 2nd ed. (New York: Routledge, 2008), 1.

41 Ibid.

42 Thomas Byrne Edsall and Mary D. Edsall, *Chain Reaction: The Impact of Race, Rights, and Taxes on American Politics* (New York: Norton, 1991), 7.

43 "The New Right," *U.S. History: Pre-Columbian to the New Millennium*, 2011, Independence Hall Association, http://www.ushistory.org/us/58e.asp.

44 Allan J. Lichtman, *White Protestant Nation: The Rise of the American Conservative Movement* (New York: Grove Press, 2008), 320.

45 Ibid., 20.

46 Julie D'Acci, "Defining Women: The Case of Cagney and Lacey," in *The Gender and Media Reader*, ed. Mary Celeste Kearney (New York: Routledge, 2012), 68.

47 Ibid., 72.

48 Frank Swertlow, "CBS Alters 'Cagney' Calling It 'Too Women's Lib,'" *TV Guide*, June 12–18, 1981, A-1, quoted in D'Acci, "Defining Women," 73.

49 Zillah Eisenstein, *The Color of Gender: Reimaging Democracy* (Berkeley: University of California Press, 1994), 41.

50 Donna Gabaccia, *From the Other Side: Women, Gender, and Immigrant Life in the U.S., 1820–1990* (Bloomington: Indiana University Press, 1994), 40.

51 Sucheng Chan, *Entry Denied: Exclusion and the Chinese Community in America 1882–1943* (Philadelphia: Temple University Press, 1994) 110–18.

52 Daniels, *Guarding the Golden Door*, 54.

53 Marion F. Houstoun, Roger G. Kramer, and Joan Mackin Barrett, "Female Predominance of Immigration to the United States since 1930: A First Look," *International Migration Review*, special issue, *Women and Migration* 18, no. 4 (Winter 1984): 908–63.

54 Gabaccia, *From the Other Side*, 39.

55 Ibid.

56 Heidi Hartmann, "The Unhappy Marriage of Marxism and Feminism," in *The Second Wave: A Reader in Feminist Theory*, ed. Linda Nicolson (New York: Routledge, 1997), 97–122.

57 Troy, *The Reagan Revolution*, 82.

58 Grace Chang, *Disposable Domestics: Immigrant Women Workers in the Global Economy* (Cambridge, MA: South End Press, 2000), 71.

59 Pia Moller, "Restoring Law and (Racial) Order to the Old Dominion," *Cultural Studies*, special issue, Jaafar Aksikas and Sean Johnson Andrews, eds., *Cultural Studies and/of the Law* 28, nos. 5–6 (2014): 869–910.

60 Laura Ho, Catherine Powell, and Leti Volpp, "(Dis)assembling Women Workers' Rights along the Global Assembly Line: Human Rights and the Garment Industry," *Harvard Civil Rights Civil Liberties Review* 31, no. 2 (Summer 1996): 383–414.

61 Gabaccia, *From the Other Side*, 40.

62 Miriam Thaggert, "Marriage, Moynihan, Mahogany: Success and the Post–Civil Rights Black Female Professional in Film," *American Quarterly* 64, no. 4 (December 2012): 721.

63 Patrick Moynihan, *The Negro Family: The Case for National Action* (Washington, DC: Office of Policy Planning and Research, Department of Labor, March 1965), http://www.dol.gov/oasam/programs/history/webid-meynihan.htm.

64 Oscar Lewis, *The Children of Sanchez: Autobiography of a Mexican Family* (New York: Vintage, 1963); and Oscar Lewis, *La Vida: A Puerto Rican Family in the Culture of Poverty—San Juan and New York* (New York: Vintage, 1966.)

65 Latina/o Studies scholars have long critiqued the pathologization of Chicano families by Anglo scholars. See Lea Ybarra, "Marital Decision-Making and the Role of Machismo in the Chicano Family," *De Colores* 6 (1982): 32–43; Hondagneu-Sotelo, *Gendered Transitions*, 9.

66 Linda Rosa Fregoso, *MeXicana Encounters: The Making of Social Identities on the Borderlands* (Berkeley: University of California Press, 2003), 82. See also Lea Ybarra, "Marital Decision-Making."

67 Daniels, *Guarding the Golden Door*, 229.

68   See U.S. Select Commission on Immigration and Refugee Policy, *U.S. Immigration Policy and the National Interest*, staff report, April 30, 1981 (Washington, DC: GPO, 1981.)

69   *The Immigration Reform and Control Act of 1986*, Public Law 99–603, 100 (1986), http://library.uwb.edu/static/USimmigration/100%20stat%203359.pdf.

70   Ezbieta M. Gozdziak, "Illegal Europeans: Transients between Two Societies," in *Illegal Immigration in America: A Reference Handbook*, ed. David W. Haines and Karen E. Rosenblum (Westport, CT: Greenwood, 1999), 268.

71   Zolberg, *A Nation By Design*, 369.

72   "WTB Questions," *Who's the Boss? Resource Page*, http://www.wtbr.com/faq/.

73   "Awards for 'Who's the Boss?,'" imdb.com, http://www.imdb.com/title/tt0086827/awards.

74   "TV Ratings: Top 30 Shows for Each Year, from 1950–2000," Classictvhits.com, http://www.classictvhits.com/tvratings.

75   "Tony Danza," Biography.com, http://www.biography.com/people/tony-danza-9542599.

76   "The Cosby Show on NBC," TVGuide.com, http://www.tvguide.com/tvshows/cosby/cast/100456.

77   Lisa Schwarzbaum, "'The Cosby Show's' Last Laugh," EW.com, http://www.ew.com/ew/article/0,,310369_2,00.html. While Cosby's fall from grace is beyond the scope of this study, it should be noted that at the time of writing, he has been accused of sexually assaulting or raping dozens of women, and numerous lawsuits have been filed against him. In the 1980s, however, his reputation as the token respectable black family man prevailed.

78   Patricia Hill Collins, *Black Sexual Politics: African Americans, Gender, and the New Racism* (New York: Routledge, 2005), 140.

79   Ibid., 139.

80   Siobhan Somerville, "Scientific Racism and the Invention of the Homosexual Body," in *The Gender and Sexuality Reader: Culture, History, Political Economy*, ed. Roger Lancaster and Micaela di Leonardo (New York: Routledge, 1997), 40–42.

81   Lisa Cacho argues that the recent use of "family rights" as an argument against deportation of the undocumented, as in the Sanctuary Movement, is meant to negate the perception of criminality by emphasizing commitments to families. Lisa Cacho, *Social Death: Racialized Rightlessness and the Criminalization of the Unprotected* (New York: New York University Press, 2012), 117. Similarly, Rachel Buff shows how DREAM activists argue that immigrants who are perceived as assets (hardworking, with the proper "family values," discipline, and determination that are lacking in native-born students) earn basic rights and should thus be decriminalized. Rachel Buff, "Undocumented and Unafraid: Incantations for a Dream," American Studies Association annual conference, San Juan, Puerto Rico, November 15–18, 2012.

82 See Michel Foucault, *History of Sexuality: Volume I: An Introduction* (New York: Random House, 1978), 101.

83 Sharon Mantz, "Preferred Immigrant Admission Status for Brothers and Sisters of U.S. Citizens," (Washington, DC: Congressional Research Services, March 20, 1982), 758.

84 U.S. Congress, Senate, Subcommittee, *Numerical Limits on Immigration to the United States*, 3.

85 Zolberg, *A Nation by Design*, 340–41.

86 Michael B. Katz, Mark J. Stern, and Jamie J. Fader, "The Mexican Immigration Debate: The View from History," *Social Science History* 31, no. 2 (Summer 2007): 166.

87 Mantz, "Preferred Immigrant Admission Status" 757–58.

88 U.S. Congress, Joint Hearings, Subcommittees, *Immigration Reform and Control Act of 1982*, 84.

89 Ibid., 259–60; Vialet, "Immigration Issues and Legislation in the 98th Congress," 185–86.

90 U.S. Congress, Joint Hearings, Subcommittees, *Immigration Reform and Control Act of 1982*, 611, 616.

91 Ibid., 296.

92 See also *Time*'s multiple immigration issues, such as *Hispanic Americans: Soon the Biggest Minority?* October 16, 1978; *The Changing Face of America*, July 8, 1985; *The New Face of America: How Immigrants Are Shaping the World's First Multicultural Society*, December 2, 1993; *Amexica*, June 11, 2001.

93 William Broyles, Jr., "A Celebration of America," *Newsweek 50th Anniversary Issue*, February 21, 1983, 3.

94 Associated Press, "Bulbs Blooming into a Fortune," *Newsweek 50th Anniversary Issue*, February 21, 1983, 35–53.

95 Stryker McGuire, "The Ties That Bind," *Newsweek*, special report, April 11, 1983, 40.

96 Under the terms of the 1980 Refugee Act, unaccompanied minors and families with absent fathers were allowed to immigrate, a policy that would be expanded and codified for this particular group in the 1987 Amerasian Homecoming Act. Robert S. McKelvey, *The Dust of Life: America's Children Abandoned in Vietnam* (Seattle: University of Washington Press, 1999).

97 John Carlos Rowe, "Reading *Reading Lolita in Tehran* in Idaho," *American Quarterly* 59, no. 2 (June 2007): 259.

98 Jodie Melamed, "Reading Tehran in *Lolita*: Making Racialized Gendered Difference Work for Neoliberal Multiculturalism," in *Strange Affinities: The Gender and Sexual Politics of Comparative Racialization*, ed. Grace Kyunghwon Hong and Roderick Ferguson (Durham, NC: Duke University Press, 2011), 82.

99 Matthew Frye Jacobson, *Roots Too: White Ethnic Revival in Post-Civil Rights America* (Cambridge, MA: Harvard University Press, 2006), 246–51.

100 Ibid., 383–84.

101 Combahee River Collective, "The Combahee River Collective Statement," 1977, in *Home Girls: A Black Feminist Anthology*, ed. Barbara Smith (New York: Kitchen Table Women of Color Press, 1983.)

102 Nicolas Fonseca, "'Golden Girls': A 20th Anniversary Oral History," ew.com, April 24, 2009, http://www.ew.com/ew/article/0,,1100651,00.html.

103 Ibid.

104 Ibid.

105 Todd Gold, "Golden Girls in Their Prime," *Saturday Evening Post* 258, no. 5 (1986): 58–61.

106 Ibid., 59.

107 Maria de los Angeles Torres, "Working against the Miami Myth," *Nation*, October 24, 1988, 393.

108 Lisa Cacho, "The Rights of Respectability: Ambivalent Allies, Reluctant Rivals, and Disavowed Deviants," in *Immigrant Rights in the Shadows of Citizenship*, ed. Rachel Ida Buff (New York: New York University Press, 2008), 202.

109 U.S. Congress, House, Subcommittee on Census and Population of the Committee on Post Office and Civil Service, *Immigration Reform and Control Act of 1982: Hearings before the Subcommittee on Census and Population*, 97th Cong., 2nd sess., 1982, 20–21.

110 Jacobson, *Roots Too*.

111 Cacho, *Social Death*, 22.

112 Ann Hodges, "ABC Gets Perfect Comedy from Two *Perfect Strangers*," *Houston Chronicle*, August 3, 1986.

113 John J. O'Connor, "CBS and ABC Present Two Series Premieres," *New York Times*, March 25, 1986.

114 See "Perfect Strangers Episode Guide," P.S. I Love You—Perfect Strangers Online, http://www.perfectstrangers.tv/episodeguide01.htm.

115 See http://www.facebook.com/groups/148827065152897/.

116 See P.S.—I Love You: Perfect Strangers Online, http://www.perfectstrangers.tv/.

117 Bob Remington, "The Oscar and Felix of the 80's," *Hamilton Spectator TV Times*, April 11–18, 1987.

118 O'Connor, "CBS and ABC Present Two Series Premieres."

119 U.S. Bureau of the Census, Current Population Reports, "Poverty in the United States: 1986," Series P-60, No. 60 (Washington, DC: GPO, 1988), 1.

120 Ibid., 5–6.

121 Judith Butler, *Undoing Gender* (New York: Routledge, 2004), 102–30.

122 Cacho, *Social Death*, 117.

123 Ibid., 117–18.

124 Butler, *Undoing Gender*, 117.

125 "Clinton to United Nations: 'Gay Rights Are Human Rights,'" *Amnesty International Human Rights Blog*, December 8, 2011, http://blog.amnestyusa.org/us/clinton-to-united-nations-gay-rights-are-human-rights/.

126 Noreen Malone, "President Obama Invokes Sasha and Malia, Again" *New York Magazine*, May 9, 2012, http://nymag.com/daily/intelligencer/2012/05/president-obama-invokes-sasha-and-malia-again.html.

127 Paul Amar, "Gay Spring and Arab Spring," American Studies Association annual conference, San Juan, Puerto Rico, November 15–18, 2012; John Hudson, "The World Reacts to Clinton's Gay Rights Speech," *Atlantic Wire*, December 11, 2011, http://www.theatlanticwire.com/global/2011/12/world-reacts-clintons-gay-rights-speech/45883/.

128 Emily Cadei, "How Corporate America Propelled Same Sex Marriage," Newsweek.com, July 10, 2015, http://www.newsweek.com/2015/07/10/shift-corporate-america-social-issues-become-good-business-348458.html>.

129 Patrick Kulp, "The Best Reactions by Major Companies to the Historic Gay Marriage Decision," Mashable.com, June 26, 2015, http://mashable.com/2015/06/26/brands-gay-marriage-legalized/>.

130 Ostensible progress with LGBTQ rights also seemed to engender racial amnesia. Also on June 26, 2015, Obama gave a visceral eulogy for the nine black Americans murdered in a racist massacre at a historically black church in Charleston, South Carolina. Within a few days, six black churches in the South were burned. The corporatized, commodified rainbow explosion—the latest version of neoliberal nationalist exceptionalist chest-thumping—largely obscured these dire examples of ongoing racial inequality and violence, which persist despite black Americans' long-standing legal equality and more diverse (respectable) representation in pop culture and the market.

131 *The Immigration Reform and Control Act of 1986*, Public Law 99–603, 100 (1986), http://library.uwb.edu/static/USimmigration/100%20stat%203359.pdf.

132 Ana Maria Alonso and Maria Teresa Koreck, "Silences: 'Hispanics,' AIDS, and Sexual Practices," in *The Lesbian and Gay Studies Reader*, ed. Henry Abelove, Michele Aina Barale, and David M. Halperin (New York: Routledge, 1992), 111–12.

133 Patricia Zavella, "Why Are Immigrant Families Different Now?," (Berkeley: UC Berkeley Center for Latino Policy Research), 2012, 1, http://escholarship.org/uc/item/77k1m0rm.

134 Ibid., 2.

135 Catherine Lee, *Fictive Kinship: Family Reunification and the Meaning of Race and Nation in American Migration* (New York: Russell Sage Foundation, 2013), 106–7.

CHAPTER 3: EXILED MOTHERS AND MOTHERS OF EXILES

1 Simone Davis, "Checking in the Mirror: Liberty Weekend's Patriotic Spectacle," *Journal of American Culture* 19 no. 2 (1996): 61.

2 The Statue of Liberty was a gift from France recognizing the national friendship established during the American Revolution.

3 "Remarks during Operation Sail in New York, New York," July 4, 1986, Ronald Reagan Presidential Library Archives, University of Texas, http://www.reagan.utexas.edu/archives/speeches/1986/70486a.htm.

4 "Liberty Weekend Offers Full Schedule of Events," *Palm Beach Post*, July 3, 1986, 7F.

5 Ibid.

6 Steve Daley, "Journalistic Integrity Takes a Holiday," *Chicago Tribune*, July 10, 1986, http://articles.chicagotribune.com/1986-07-10/features/8602190021_1_liberty-weekend-abc-liberty-centennial.

7 Richard Stengel, Bonnie Angelo, and Cathy Booth, "The Party of the Century: Rockets Will Glare and Bands Blare to Celebrate the Statue," *Time*, July 7, 1986, 18.

8 Mike Wallace, "Hijacking History: Ronald Reagan and the Statue of Liberty," *Radical History Review* 37 (1987): 130.

9 Larry Eichel, Rick Lyman, and Carol Horner, "A Glitzy Closing to Liberty Salute," *Philadelphia Inquirer*, July 7, 1986.

10 Kathy Evertz, "The 1986 Statue of Liberty Centennial: 'Commercialization' and Reaganism," *Journal of Popular Culture* 29, no. 3 (Winter 1995): 210.

11 Stengel, Angelo, and Booth, "The Party of the Century," 18.

12 "July 4: Teeming with Anticipation," *New York Daily News*, March 19, 1986, http://articles.philly.com/1986-03-19/news/26081423_1_aircraft-carrier-liberty-weekend-david-wolper.

13 Esther Schor, *Emma Lazarus* (New York: Random House, 2006), 121–25.

14 Ibid., 191.

15 Emma Lazarus, "The New Colossus," 1883, Liberty State Park.com, http://www.libertystatepark.com/emma.htm.

16 Paul Auster, *Collected Prose: Autobiographical Writings, True Stories, Critical Essays, Prefaces, and Collaborations with Artists* (New York: Picador, 2003), 508.

17 Schor notes that "within days of composing, 'The New Colosuss,' Emma Lazarus recoiled from its generalized vision of American liberty; she seemed to sense that the sonnet had wandered far from its origins" (*Emma Lazarus*, 192).

18 "Early Suffrage Protests. Miss Blake Tells of Meeting at Statue of Liberty 20 Years Ago," *New York Times*, July 11, 1915.

19 Juan F. Perea, "The Statue of Liberty," in *Immigrants Out! The New Nativism and the Anti-Immigrant Impulse in the United States*, ed. Juan E. Perea (New York: New York University Press, 1997), 47–48.

20 E. P. Hutchinson, *Legislative History of Immigration Policy, 1798–1965* (Philadelphia: University of Pennsylvania Press, 1981).

21 Deirdre M. Moloney, "Women's Sexual Morality and Economic Dependency in Early U.S. Deportation Policy," *Journal of Women's History* 18, no. 2 (2006): 95–122.

22 Stuart Hall, "The Neoliberal Revolution," *Soundings* (13626620) 48 (Summer 2011): 11.

23 Ronald Reagan, "State of the Union Address, February 4, 1986," transcript, http://www.reagan.utexas.edu/archives/speeches/1986 /20486a.htm.

24 Lou Cannon, *President Reagan: The Role of a Lifetime* (New York: Public Affairs, 1991), 456–57.

25 Ibid.

26 Reagan, "State of the Union Address."

27 Rachel Ida Buff, "Introduction: Towards a Redefinition of Citizenship Rights," in *Immigrant Rights in the Shadows of Citizenship*, ed. Rachel Ida Buff (New York: New York University Press, 2008), 8–9.

28 Linda Gordon, "The New Feminist Scholarship on the Welfare State," in *Women, the State, and Welfare*, ed. Linda Gordon (Madison: University of Wisconsin Press, 1990), 9–35.

29 Ibid., 9, 24–26.

30 Mimi Abramovitz, *Under Attack, Fighting Back: Women and Welfare in the United States*, 2nd rev. ed. (New York: Monthly Review Press, 2000); Mimi Abramovitz, "Gender Matters: Women, Caregiving and the Neo-Liberal Assault on the Welfare State," in *The Legal Tender of Gender: International Perspectives on Welfare Law, State Policies and the Regulation of Women's Poverty*, ed. Shelley Gavigan and Dorothy E. Chunn (Oxford, UK: Hart Publishing, 2009).

31 Dorothy Roberts, *Shattered Bonds: The Color of Child Welfare* (New York: Civitas Books, 2002).

32 Zillah Eisenstein, *The Color of Gender: Reimagining Democracy* (Berkeley, CA: University of California Press, 1994); Anne-Marie Hancock, *The Politics of Disgust: The Public Identity of the Welfare Queen* (New York: New York University Press, 2004); Anna Marie Smith, *Welfare Reform and Sexual Regulation* (New York: Cambridge University Press, 2007).

33 Patricia Hill Collins, *Black Sexual Politics: African Americans, Gender, and the New Racism* (New York: Routledge, 2004.)

34 Grace Chang, *Disposable Domestics: Immigrant Women Workers in the Global Economy* (Cambridge, MA: South End Press, 2000); Grace Kyungwon Hong, *The Ruptures of American Capital: Woman of Color Feminism and the Culture of Immigrant Labor* (Minneapolis: University of Minnesota Press, 2006); Lisa Sun Hee Park, *Entitled to Nothing: The Struggle for Immigrant Health Care in the Age of Welfare Reform* (New York: New York University Press, 2011).

35 Elena Gutierrez, *Fertile Matters: The Politics of Mexican-Origin Women's Reproduction* (Austin: University of Texas Press, 2008), xi.

36 Dorothy E. Roberts, "Who May Give Birth to Citizens? Reproduction, Eugenics, and Immigration," in *Immigrants Out! The New Nativism and the Anti-Immigrant Impulse in the United States*, ed. Juan E. Perea (New York: New York University Press, 1997); Robin Dale Jacobson, *The New Nativism: Proposition 187 and the Debate over Immigration* (Minneapolis: University of Minnesota Press, 2008); Eithne Luibheid, *Entry Denied: Controlling Sexuality at the Border* (Minneapolis: University of Minnesota Press, 2002).

37 Manfred B. Steger and Ravi K. Roy, *Neoliberalism: A Very Short Introduction* (New York: Oxford University Press, 2010), 34–35.

38 Gary L. Bauer, cited in Cannon, *President Reagan*, 456.

39 Chang, *Disposable Domestics*, 71–72.

40 Mark Leff, "Consensus for Reform: The Mothers' Pension Movement in the Progressive Era," *Social Service Review* 47 (1973): 397–417.

41 Gordon, "The New Feminist Scholarship," 12.

42 Gwendolyn Mink, "The Lady and the Tramp: Gender, Race, and the Origins of the American Welfare State," in *Women, the State, and Welfare*, ed. Linda Gordon (Madison: University of Wisconsin Press, 1990), 112.

43 Gordon, "The New Feminist Scholarship," 11–12.

44 Teresa L. Amott, "Black Women and AFDC: Making Entitlement out of Necessity," in *Women, the State, and Welfare*, ed. Linda Gordon (Madison: University of Wisconsin Press, 1990), 288.

45 Mimi Abramovitz, *Regulating the Lives of Women* (Cambridge, MA: South End Press, 1988), 317.

46 Chang, *Disposable Domestics*, 73–76.

47 Nancy Chodorow, "Mothering, Male Dominance, and Capitalism," in *Capitalist Patriarchy and the Case for Socialist Feminism*, ed. Zillah R. Eisenstein (New York: Monthly Review, 1979), 95–102.

48 Amott, "Black Women and AFDC," 288–89.

49 Mary Jo Bane, "Household Composition and Poverty: Which Comes First?," in *Fighting Poverty: What Works and What Doesn't*, ed. Sheldon H. Danziger and Daniel H. Weinberg (Cambridge, MA: Harvard University Press, 1986.)

50 Collins, *Black Sexual Politics*, 132–33.

51 Karen Seccombe, Delores James, and Kimberly Battle Walters, "They Think You Ain't Much of Nothing: The Social Construction of the Welfare Mother," *Journal of Marriage and the Family* 60, no. 4 (November 1998): 850.

52 Shelley P. Haley, "Sexual Stereotypes," in *The Reader's Companion to Women's History*, ed. Wilma Pearl Mankiller, Gwendolyn Mink, Marysa Navarro, Barbara Smith, and Gloria Steinem (New York: Houghton-Mifflin, 1999), 570–72.

53 Gutierrez, *Fertile Matters*, 80, 90–91.

54 Veena Cabreros-Sud, "Poor Mothers on Crime Spree!" Fair.org, Fairness and Accuracy in Reporting, November/December 1993.

55 U.S. Congress, Joint Hearings, Subcommittee on Immigration, Refugees, and International Law of the Committee on the Judiciary House of Representatives and Subcommittee on Immigration and Refugee Policy of the Committee on the Judiciary United States Senate, *Immigration Reform and Control Act of 1982: Hearing before the Subcommittee on Immigration, Refugees, and International Law and Subcommittee on Immigration and Refugee Policy*, 97th Cong., 2nd sess., 1982.

56 *The Immigration Reform and Control Act of 1986*, Public Law 99–603, (1986), http://library.uwb.edu/static/USimmigration/100%20stat%203359.pdf.

57 Charles Wheeler and Beth Zachovic, "The Public Charge Ground of Exclusion for Legalization Applicants," Interpreter Releases 64 (September 14, 1987): 35.

58 For analysis of the actuarial system in 1990s immigration law, see Christina Gerken, *Model Immigrants and Undesirable Aliens: The Cost of Immigration Reform in the 1990s* (Minneapolis: University of Minnesota Press, 2013).

59 Gutierrez, *Fertile Matters*, 73–74.

60 Ibid., 55–56.

61 Leo R. Chavez, *The Latino Threat: Constructing Immigrants, Citizens, and the Nation* (Stanford, CA: Stanford University Press, 2008), 74–75.

62 Gloria Gonzalez-Lopez, *Erotic Journeys: Mexican Immigrants and their Sex Lives* (Berkeley: University of California Press, 2005).

63 U.S. Congress, Senate, Subcommittee on Immigration and Refugee Policy of the Committee on the Judiciary, *The Immigration Reform and Control Act of 1986: Hearings before the Subcommittee on Immigration and Refugee Policy*, 99th Cong., 2nd sess., 1986, http://web.lexis-nexis.com/congcomp/printdoc.

64 Ibid.

65 Ibid.

66 Jean Stefanic, "Funding the Nativist Agenda," in *Immigrants Out! The New Nativism and the Anti-Immigrant Impulse in the United States*, ed. Juan E. Perea (New York: New York University Press, 1997), 119–35.

67 Jacobson, *The New Nativism*, 113.

68 Tanton, cited in Chavez, *The Latino Threat*, 84; see also Gutierrez, *Fertile Matters*, 73–93.

69 Jaafar Aksikas and Sean Johnson Andrews, "Neoliberalism, Law and Culture: A Cultural Studies Intervention after 'The Juridical Turn,'" *Cultural Studies*, special issue, Jaafar Aksikas and Sean Johnson Andrews, eds., *Cultural Studies and/of the Law* 28, nos.5–6 (2014): 742–80; 772.

70 Pierette Hondagneu-Sotelo, *Gendered Transitions: Mexican Experiences of Immigration* (Berkeley: University of California Press, 1994).

71 Lisa Cacho, "'The People of California Are Suffering': The Ideology of White Injury in Discourses of Immigration," *Cultural Values* 4, no. 4 (October 2000): 389–418.

72 Deborah Paredez, "All about My (Absent) Mother: Young Latina Aspirations in *Real Women Have Curves* and *Ugly Betty*," in *Beyond El Barrio: Everyday Life in Latina/o America*, ed. Gina M. Perez, Frank A. Guridy, and Adrian Burgos, Jr. (New York: New York University Press, 2010), 129–48.

73 Rosa Linda Fregoso, *MeXicana Encounters: The Making of Social Identities on the Borderlands* (Berkeley: University of California Press, 2003), 91–99.

74 Ibid., 189, n.20.

75 Anne McClintock, "No Longer in a Future Heaven: Gender, Race, and Nationalism," in *Dangerous Liaisons: Gender, Nation, and Postcolonial Perspectives*, eds. Anne McClintock, Aamir Mufti, and Ella Shohat (Minneapolis: University of Minnesota Press, 1997), 90.

76 Fregoso, *MeXicana Encounters*, 56–57.

77 Dennis West and Joan M. West, "Borders and Boundaries: An Interview with John Sayles," *Cineaste* 22, no. 3 (Summer 1996): 14–15.

78 This is a Chicana/o/Mexican retort to official, racist versions of Texas history that cast Mexicans, the original inhabitants of the land, as villains. Pilar says these final words of the film to Buddy when they decide to continue their romantic relationship despite the discovery they are half-siblings.

79 Fregoso, *MeXicana Encounters*, 53.

80 West and West, "Borders and Boundaries."

81 Laura Flanders, "Why Immigration Is a Feminist Issue," *Nation*, December 6, 2011, http://www.thenation.com/article/165014/why-immigration-feminist-issue.

82 Cecilia Menjivar and Leisy J. Abrego, "Immigrant Latina Mothers as Targets of Legal Violence," *International Journal of Sociology of the Family* 37, no. 1 (Spring 2011): 9–26.

83 Patricia Zavella, "Why Are Immigrant Families Different Now?," (Berkeley: UC Berkeley: Center for Latino Policy Research, 2012), 2, http://escholarship.org/uc/item/77k1morm; Patricia Zavella, *"I'm Neither Here nor There": Mexicans' Quotidian Struggles with Migration and Poverty* (Durham, NC: Duke University Press, 2011).

84 U.S. Congress, Senate, Subcommittee on Immigration and Refugee Policy of the Committee on the Judiciary, *Immigration Reform and Control Act: Hearings before the Subcommittee on Immigration and Refugee Policy*, 98th Cong., 1st sess., 1983, 186–87.

85 California Health and Welfare Agency, "A Survey of Newly Legalized Persons in California" (San Diego: Comprehensive Adult Student Assessment System, 1989). See also Douglas S. Massey, "The New Immigration and Ethnicity in the U.S," *Population and Development Review* 21, no. 3 (September 1995): 631.

86 Roger Daniels, *Guarding the Golden Door: American Immigration Policy and Immigrants since 1882* (New York: Hill and Wang, 2004), 229.

87 Chang, *Disposable Domestics*, 55–92.

88 Ibid., 59.

89 Hondagneu-Sotelo, *Gendered Transitions*, 27–29.

90 George J. Borjas and Maria Tienda, *Hispanics in the U.S. Economy* (London: Academic Press, 1985), table 8.5.

91 Ibid., 55–61.

92 Robert G. Lee, *Orientals: Asian Americans in Popular Culture* (Philadelphia: Temple University Press, 1999), 10.

93 Andrew Chin, "A Brief History of the 'Model Minority' Stereotype," Modelminority.com.

94 Lee, *Orientals*, 182–183.

95 Haley, "Sexual Stereotypes," 571.

96 Lee, *Orientals*, 162.

97 Haley, "Sexual Stereotypes," 571.

98 Chin, "A Brief History of the 'Model Minority' Stereotype."

99 Edward Said, *Orientalism* (New York: Vintage, 1979).

100 See Mia Tuan, *Forever Foreigners or Honorary Whites? The Asian Ethnic Experience Today* (New Brunswick, NJ: Rutgers University Press, 1998.)

101 Chang, *Disposable Domestics*, 40–41, 131.

102 Moira Mulligan, "Personalities," *Washington Post*, May 27, 1996, B3.

103 Erica Rand, *The Ellis Island Snow Globe* (Durham, NC: Duke University Press, 2005), 124–25.

104 Theodore Allen, *The Invention of the White Race, Volume I: Racial Oppression and Social Control* (London: Verso, 1992), and *The Invention of the White Race, Volume II: The Origin of Oppression in Anglo-America* (London: Verso, 1997).

105 Steve Martinot, *The Rule of Racialization* (Philadelphia: Temple University Press, 2003), 66–68.

106 Andrea Passafiume, "The Joy Luck Club," *Turner Classic Movies*, http://www.tcm.com/this-month/article/196859%7C0/The-Joy-Luck-Club.html.

107 Janice Mirikitani, "Breaking Tradition," in *The Columbia Documentary History of American Women since 1941*, ed. Harriet Sigerman (New York: Columbia University Press, 2003), 664–65.

108 Other portrayals of "Asian" patriarchy may be seen in novels and memoirs such as Yung Wing, *My Life in America* (1909), Jade Snow Wong, *Fifth Chinese Daughter* (1989), and Chang Yu-I and Pang-Mei Natasha Chang, *Bound Feet and Western Dress* (1999), as well as in David Henry Hwang's play *F.O.B.* (1980).

109 The book is slightly less dramatic than the film: Ying-Ying has an abortion and leaves her husband.

110 Frank Chin, "Come All Ye Asian American Writers of the Real and the Fake," in *A Companion to Asian American Studies*, ed. Kent Ono (Malden, MA: Blackwell, 2005), 134–35.

111 Cacho, *Social Death*, 92.

112 Christine Lai, "The Orphans of Vietnam," Dartmouth.edu; "People & Events: American GIs, Vietnamese Women and Children," pbs.org.

113 Isabel Berwick, "Review: Battle Hymn of the Tiger Mother," *Financial Times*, January 17, 2011; Anne Murphy Paul, "Tiger Moms: Is Tough Parenting Really the Answer?," *Time*, January 20, 2011, http://www.time.com/time/magazine/article/0,9171,2043477,00.html.

114 Roberts, "Who May Give Birth?," 206–7.

115 Matthew Jacobson, *Roots Too: White Ethnic Revival in Post–Civil Rights America* (Cambridge, MA: Harvard University Press, 2005), 269.

116 The award-winning sitcom (1996–2005), which continues to run in syndication, starred Italian American comic Ray Romano. Characters were based on Romano's and writer/producer Phil Rosenthal's families and followed the life of Raymond Barone, an Italian American sportswriter, his wife, children, overbearing parents, and brother.

117 The 2009–2012 reality show followed the lives of eight cast members who lived and worked on the Jersey Shore during the summer. Cast members presented themselves as Italian American in ways that resonated with long-standing stereotypes of Italian American buffoonery and machismo. Emily Friedman, "MTV's Jersey Shore Garners Critics Use of Term 'Guido,'" Abcnews.com, December 11, 2009. It was also one of MTV's most-watched series to date. Bill Gorman, "Jersey Shore Season Premiere Draws Record 8.45 Million Viewers; 4.2 Adults, 18–49 Rating," *TV by the Numbers*, January 7, 2011.

118 Dawn Michelle Nill, "The Golden Girls," *Museum of Broadcast Communication*, www.museum.tv/archives/etv/G/htmlG/goldengirls.htm.

119 Karen Orr Vered and Sal Humphreys, "Postfeminist Inflections in Television Studies," *Continuum: Journal of Media & Cultural Studies* 28, no. 2 (2014): 156, 159.

120 Ibid., 157.

121 Michaela di. Leonardo, "White Ethnicities, Identity Politics, and Baby Bear's Chair," *Social Text* 41 (Winter 1994): 177.

122 Jacobson, *Roots Too*, 244–45.

123 Richard Rodriguez, *Hunger of Memory: The Education of Richard Rodriguez* (New York: Bantam, 1982), 4.

124 Gutierrez, *Fertile Matters*.

125 Eisenstein, *The Color of Gender*, 181.

126 Ibid., 173.

127 Chavez, *The Latino Threat*, 71.

128 Eisenstein, *The Color of Gender*, 78.

129 Steger and Roy, *Neoliberalism*, 51.

130 Mark Haller, *Eugenics: Hereditarian Attitudes in American Thought* (New Brunswick, NJ: Rutgers University Press, 1983).

131 Desmond King, *Making Americans: Immigration, Race, and the Origins of the Diverse Democracy* (Cambridge, MA: Harvard University Press, 2002), 167.

132 Stefan Kuhl, *The Nazi Connection: Eugenics, American Racism, and German National Socialism* (New York: Oxford University Press, 1994).

133 Alexandra Minna Stern, *Eugenic Nation: Faults and Frontiers of Better Breeding in Modern America* (Berkeley: University of California Press, 2005), 10.

134 Alexandra Minna Stern, "Sterilized in the Name of Public Health: Race, Immigration, and Reproductive Control in Modern California," *American Journal of Public Health* 95, no. 7 (July 2005): 1128–38, http://www.ncbi/nlm.nih.gov/pmc/articles/PMC1449330/; Alicia Schmidt Camacho, *Migrant Imaginaries: Latino Cultural Politics in the U.S.–Mexico Borderlands* (New York: New York University Press, 2008), 177–78.

135 Stern, *Eugenic Nation*, 200–3.

136 Gerken, *Model Immigrants and Undesirable Aliens*, 241.

137 Ibid., 205.

138 Proposition 187: Text of Proposed Law, 1994, http://www.americanpatrol.com/REFERENCE/prop187text.html.

139 In certain states such as California, citizens can change laws themselves with majority vote, without going through typical legislative channels. With this "direct democracy," ballot campaigns are expensive and require legal consultation, so wealthy citizens and politicians are usually those with the means to propose ballot initiatives. Thus ballots often expand state powers that benefit the elite and harm vulnerable populations, as in the case of ballots that decrease state resources.

140 Daniels, *Guarding the Golden Door*, 242.

141 Cacho, "'The People of California Are Suffering,'" 390.

142 U.S. Census Bureau, *Hispanic or Latino Origin for the United States, Regions, Divisions, States, and for Puerto Rico (PHC-T-10), 2000*, October 22, 2001, http://www.census.gov/population/www/cen2000/briefs/phc-t10/tables/phc-t-10.pdf.

143 Kevin R. Johnson, "Public Benefits and Immigration: The Intersection of Immigration Status, Ethnicity, Gender, and Class," *UCLA Law Review* 42, no. 6 (1995): 1509–75.

144 Pete Wilson, "An Open Letter to the President of the United States on Behalf of the People of California," *New York Times*, August 10 1993, A-11.

145 Quoted in Chavez, *The Latino Threat*, 72.

146 Annie Nakao, "Assessing the Cost of Immigration," *San Francisco Examiner*, December. 1, 1991, B1, 3.

147 Patrick J. McDonnell and Paul Jacobs, "FAIR at the Forefront of Push to Reduce Immigration Population," *Los Angeles Times*, November 24, 1993.

148 Chavez, *The Latino Threat*, 88.

149 Gutierrez, *Fertile Matters*, 115.

150 A 1989 Comprehensive Adult Student Assessment System (CASAS) study, cited by Chang, concluded that newly legalized immigrants used social services and public benefits at low rates—likely lower than rates for the California population as a whole: 87 percent of newly legalized respondents had not needed or were not willing to apply for public assistance. See Chang, *Disposable Domestics*, 67–68.

151 Lisa Lowe, *Immigrant Acts: On Asian American Cultural Politics* (Durham, NC: Duke University Press, 1996), 193, n. 54.

152 Luibheid, *Entry Denied*, 27.

153 Roberts, "Who May Give Birth to Citizens?," 207.

154 Ibid., 212.

155 Kent Ono and John Sloop, *Shifting Borders: Rhetoric, Immigration, and California's Proposition 187* (Philadelphia: Temple University Press, 2002).

156 Otto Santa Ana, "'Like an Animal I was Treated': Anti-Immigrant Metaphor in U.S. Public Discourse," *Discourse & Society* 10, no. 2 (April 1999): 192. See also Otto Santa Ana and Juan Moran, "Awash under a Brown Tide: Immigration Metaphors in California Public and Print Media Discourse" *Aztlan* 23, no. 2 (Fall 1998): 137–76.

157 Daniels, *Guarding the Golden Door*, 243.

158 Luibheid, *Entry Denied*, 56.

159 Andrew Murr, "A Questionable Proposition," *Newsweek*, October 31, 1994, 29.

160 See Maria Puente and Gale Holland, "Deep Vein of Anger in California/Prop 187 Reinforcing Divisions," *USA Today*, November 11, 1994; William Booth, "Latin Leaders Criticize Growing U.S. Nativism; Trend Is Said to Threaten Improving Relations," *Washington Post*, December 10, 1994, A6; Maria Puente, "Prop 187 Firing Up the Voters/Immigration Issue the Talk of California," *USA Today*, November 7, 1994, 3A; Murr, "A Questionable Proposition," 29.

161 Cacho, "'The People of California Are Suffering,'" 391.

162 Robert Gunnison, "Wilson Maid Was Illegal Immigrant," *San Francisco Chronicle*, May 4, 1995, A1.

163 Cacho, "'The People of California Are Suffering,'" 389–90.

164 *The Personal Responsibility and Work Opportunity Reconciliation Act of 1996*, Public Law 104–93, 110 (1996).

165 Non-welfare mothers have a greater economic incentive to have children. Welfare mothers might receive an increase of $90 per month per additional child, while non-welfare working families receive $2,400 in tax credits for the cost of childcare and childrearing. Gregory Acs, "Does Welfare Promote Out-of-Wedlock Childbearing?," in *Welfare Reform: Analysis of the Issues*, ed. Isabel V. Sawhill (Washington, DC: The Urban Institute, 1995), 3.

166 Chang, *Disposable Domestics*, xv.

167 Smith, *Welfare Reform and Sexual Regulation*, 5.

168 Ibid., 77.

169 Ibid., 82–83.

170 Kathalene Razzano, "Dead-Beat Dads and Paternity Fraud: Paternity Policies and Family Formation," Cultural Studies Association annual conference, Columbia College, Chicago, IL, March 24–26, 2011; Katy Razzano, "'In Light of this Demonstration of Crisis in our Nation': Paternity, Responsibility and Welfare," *Cultural Studies*, special issue, Jaafar Aksikas and Sean Johnson Andrews, eds., *Cultural Studies and/of the Law* 28, nos.5–6 (2014): 947–75.

171 Razzano, "Dead-Beat Dads and Paternity Fraud."

172 Chang, *Disposable Domestics*, 8.

173 Leo R. Chavez, "Immigration Reform and Nativism: The Nationalist Response to the Transnationalist Challenge," in *Immigrants Out! The New Nativism and the Anti-Immigrant Impulse in the United States*, ed. Juan E. Perea (New York: New York University Press, 1997), 65.

174 Richard Lacayo, "Down on the Downtrodden," Time.com, December 14, 1994, http://www.time.com/time/magazine/article/0,9171,982006,00.html.

175 Aristede Zolberg, *A Nation By Design: Immigration Policy in the Fashioning of America* (New York: Russell Sage Foundation, 2006), 427.

176 George Thomas Kurian, ed., *The Encyclopedia of the Republican Party* (Armonk, NY: Sharpe Reference, 1997.)

177 Bill Clinton, "State of the Union Address," *CNN News*, January 27, 1996, http://www.cnn.com/US/9601/budget/01-27/clinton_radio/.

178 Smith, *Welfare Reform and Sexual Regulation*, 84.

179 Patricia Hill Collins, "Producing Mothers of the Nation: Race, Class, and Contemporary U.S. Population Policies," in *Women, Citizenship, and Difference*, ed. Nira Yuval-Davis (London: Zed Books, 1999), 118–29.

180 Roberts, "Who May Give Birth to Citizens?," 214.

181 Angela McRobbie, *The Aftermath of Feminism: Gender, Culture, and Social Change* (New York: Sage, 2009).

182 See Orr Vered and Humphreys, "Postfeminist Inflections in Television Studies," and Catherine Rottenberg, "The Rise of Neoliberal Feminism," *Cultural Studies* 28, no. 3 (May 2014): 418–37.

183 Hilary Rodham Clinton, *Living History* (New York: Simon and Schuster, 2003), 369.

184 Richard J. Herrnstein and Charles J. Murray, *The Bell Curve: Intelligence and Class Structure in American Life* (New York: Free Press, 1994.)

185 Peter Brimelow, *Alien Nation: Common Sense about America's Immigration Disaster* (New York: Random House, 1995), 181.

186 Chavez, *The Latino Threat*, 2–3.

187 Mike Davis, *Ecology of Fear: Los Angeles and the Imagining of Disaster* (New York: Henry Holt, 1998), 280–82.

188 William A. Henry III, "Beyond the Melting Pot," time.com, April 9, 1990, http://www.time.com/time/printout/0,8816, 969770, 00.html.

189 See Stephen Jay Gould, *The Mismeasure of Man* (New York: W. W. Norton, 1996).

190 Grace Chang, *Disposable Domestics*, 25–28.

191 In 2004, California passed Proposition 71, approving distribution of $3 billion over the next ten years to support stem cell research. Stern views this as a new wave of eugenics: some fear that poor women, who we already know are disproportionately of color, will be compelled and/or targeted to provide eggs. Stern, *Better Breeding*, 213–14.

192 John Blake, "Return of the 'Welfare Queen,'" CNN.com, January 23, 2012, http://www.cnn.com/2012/01/23/politics/weflare-queen.

CHAPTER 4: INAUGURATING NEOLIBERAL CRIMMIGRATION

1 While the song peaked at No. 46 on the U.K. charts and did not chart in the United States, Genesis, one of the bestselling groups of all time, was at the height of their popularity in 1980s and 1990s. This was their third U.K. No. 1 album; it reached No. 9 in the U.S. Billboard charts; and several tracks continue in rotation on soft rock and light radio stations. Genesis was inducted into Rock and Roll Hall of Fame in 2010. Even "Illegal Alien" is well known enough to surface on blogs, music magazine websites, and YouTube, and it was rated No. 13 in *Blender* magazine's Worst Songs of All Time. "Genesis," *Official Charts*, http://www.officialcharts.com/artist/_/genesis/; Marc Lee, "Final Chapter in the Book of Genesis?," *Telegraph*, June 2, 2008, http://www.telegraph.co.uk. Michael Rutherford, Phil Collins, Tony Banks, "Illegal Alien" (EMI Music Publishing, Imagem U.S. LLC), metrolyrics.com, 2016.

2 Scott Thill, "Genesis' 'Illegal Alien:' Worst Song Ever? Or Worst Video Ever?," Wired.com, May 30, 2008, http://www.wired.com/listening_post/2008/05/genesis-illegal/.

3 Steven Hyden, "It's No Fun Bein' a Really Good, Really Offensive Genesis Song," *A. V. Club Blog*, February 15, 2008, http://www.avclub.com/articles/its-no-fun-bein-a-really-good-really-offensive-gen,9841/.

4   Lisa Cacho, *Social Death: Racialized Rightlessness and the Criminalization of the Unprotected* (New York: New York University Press, 2012), 38–43.

5   Kevin Johnson, "'Aliens" and U.S. Immigration Laws: The Social and Legal Construction of Non-Persons," *Inter-American Law Review* 28, no. 2 (Winter 1996): 272.

6   Cacho, *Social Death*, 5–6.

7   Steve Martinot, *The Rule of Racialization: Class, Identity, Governance* (Philadelphia: Temple University Press, 2003), 175.

8   Jaafar Aksikas and Sean Johnson Andrews, "Neoliberalism, Law and Culture: A Cultural Studies Intervention after 'The Juridical Turn,'" *Cultural Studies*, special issue, Jaafar Aksikas and Sean Johnson Andrews, eds., *Cultural Studies and/of the Law* 28, nos.5–6 (2014): 753.

9   Teresa Miller, "Citizenship & Severity: Recent Immigration Reforms and the New Penology," *Georgetown Immigration Law Journal* 17 (2003): 612.

10 Juliet Stumpf, "The Crimmigration Crisis: Immigrants, Crime, and Sovereign Power," *American University Law Review* 56, no. 2 (2006): 376; Allison S. Hartry, "Commentary Gendering Crimmigration: The Intersection of Gender, Immigration, and the Criminal Justice System," *Berkeley Journal of Gender, Law, and Justice* 27, no. 1 (Winter 2012): 7–14.

11 Claudia Sadowski-Smith, "Unskilled Labor Migration and the Illegality Spiral: Chinese, European, and Mexican Indocumentados in the United States, 1882–2007," *American Quarterly*, special issue, David G. Gutierrez and Pierrette Hondagneu-Sotelo, eds., *Nation Past and Future* 60, no.3 (September 2008): 779–804.

12 Ibid, 783.

13 Ibid.

14 Henry K. Norton, *The Story of California from the Earliest Days to the Present* (Chicago: A.C. McClurg, 1924), 283–96.

15 Erika Lee, *At America's Gates: Chinese Immigration during the Exclusion Era, 1882–1943* (Chapel Hill: University of North Carolina Press, 2003).

16 Mae M. Ngai, *Impossible Subjects: Illegal Aliens and the Making of Modern America* (Princeton, NJ: Princeton University Press, 2004), 202.

17 Deirdre M. Moloney, "Women's Sexual Morality and Economic Dependency in Early U.S. Deportation Policy," *Journal of Women's History* 18, no. 2 (2006): 95–122; 100.

18 "Immigration and Naturalization Service," findfederalagency.com, 2005–2007, http://findfederalagency.com/immigration-naturalization-service-ins#history.

19 Moloney, "Women's Sexual Morality," 105.

20 Judith N. Sklar, *American Citizenship: The Quest for Inclusion* (Cambridge, MA: Harvard University Press, 1991).

21 Rosa Linda Fregoso, *MeXicana Encounters: The Making of Social Identities on the Borderlands* (Berkeley: University of California Press, 2003), 127.

22 Laura Ann Stoler, *Race and the Education of Desire* (Durham, NC: Duke University Press, 1995), 30–31.

23 Marci R. McMahon, "Manifest Domesticity in the Era of Globalized Nation: Alma Lopez's *California Fashion Slaves*," Migration, Border, and Nation-State Conference, Texas Tech University, Lubbock, Texas, April 8–11, 2009.

24 Joseph A. Stout, *Border Conflict: Villistas, Carrancistas, and the Punitive Expedition, 1915–1920* (Fort Worth: Texas Christian University Press, 1999.)

25 Grace Kyungwon Hong, *The Ruptures of American Capital: Woman of Color Feminism and the Culture of Immigrant Labor* (Minneapolis: University of Minnesota Press, 2006), 136.

26 David Montejano, *Anglos and Mexicans in the Making of Texas, 1836–1986* (Austin: University of Texas Press, 1987), 117–20; Alexandra Minna Stern, *Eugenic Nation: Faults and Frontiers of Better Breeding in Modern America* (Berkeley: University of California Press, 2005), 73–74.

27 "Early U.S. Race Laws Designed to Protect White Employment," Voltairenet.org, May 13, 2005, http://www.voltairenet.org/article30264.html.

28 David Magill, "'Border Panic' and the Bounds of Racial Identity," American Studies Association conference, Albuquerque, NM, October 16–19, 2008.

29 Chon A. Noriega, ed., *Chicanos and Film: Essays on Representation and Resistance* (Minneapolis: University of Minnesota Press, 1992); Rosa Linda Fregoso, *The Bronze Screen: Chicana and Chicano Film Culture* (Minneapolis: University of Minnesota Press, 1993); Charles Ramirez Berg, *Latino Images in Film: Stereotypes, Subversion, Resistance* (Austin: University of Texas Press, 2002); Angharad Valdivia, *A Latina in the Land of Hollywood* (Tucson: University of Arizona Press, 2000).

30 Fregoso, *MeXicana Encounters*, 133.

31 Ngai, *Impossible Subjects*, 8–9.

32 Ibid., 57.

33 Stern, *Eugenic Nation*, 74.

34 Hong, *Ruptures of American Capital*, 68.

35 Stern, *Eugenic Nation*, 99.

36 Abraham Hoffman, *Unwanted Mexican Americans in the Great Depression: Repatriation Pressures, 1929–1939* (Tucson: University of Arizona Press, 1974), 86–87.

37 Ibid.

38 George Horace Lortimer, "The Mexican Conquest," *Saturday Evening Post*, June 2, 1929, 26.

39 Vicki L. Ruiz, *From Out of the Shadows: Mexican Women in Twentieth-Century America* (New York: Oxford University Press, 1998), 30.

40 Stern, *Eugenic Nation*, 78.

41 Ibid.

42 Lisa Flores, "Constructing Rhetorical Borders: Peons, Illegal Aliens, and Competing Narratives of Immigration," *Critical Studies in Media Communication* 20, no. 4 (2003): 362–87.

43 Ngai, *Impossible Subjects*, 13.

44 Alicia Schmidt Camacho, *Migrant Imaginaries: Latino Cultural Politics in the U.S.–Mexico Borderlands* (New York: New York University Press, 2008), 109.

45 Ibid., 149.

46 Ibid., 82.

47 Edward Escobar, *Race, Police, and the Making of a Political Identity: Mexican Americans and the Los Angeles Police Department, 1900–1945* (Berkeley: University of California Press, 1999).

48 Laura L. Cummings, *Pachucas and Pachucos in Tucson: Situated Border Lives* (Tucson: University of Arizona Press, 2009).

49 Edward Obregon Pagan, *Sleepy Lagoon: Zoot Suits, Race, and Riots in Wartime L.A.* (Chapel Hill: University of North Carolina Press, 2003), 327–38.

50 George J. Sanchez, *Becoming Mexican American: Ethnicity, Culture, and Identity in Chicano Los Angeles, 1900–1945* (Oxford: Oxford University Press, 1993).

51 Carlos Larralde, "Josefina Fierro and the Sleepy Lagoon Crusade, 1942–1945," *Southern California Quarterly* 92, no. 2 (Summer 2010): 117–60.

52 Pagan, *Sleepy Lagoon*, 138–43.

53 Paul Smith and Lisa Frank, "Introduction: How to Use Your New Madonna," in *Madonnarama: Essays on Sex and Popular Culture*, ed. Paul Smith and Lisa Frank (Pittsburgh: Cleis, 1993), 12.

54 Michael Shaller, *Reckoning with Reagan: America and Its President in the 1980s* (New York: Oxford University Press, 1992), 85.

55 Lou Cannon, *President Reagan: The Role of a Lifetime* (New York: Public Affairs, 1991), 730.

56 Michelle Alexander, *The New Jim Crow: Mass Incarceration in the Age of Colorblindness* (New York: The New Press, 2010), 49.

57 Ibid., 50–51.

58 Patricia Hill Collins, *Black Sexual Politics: African Americans, Gender, and the New Racism* (New York: Routledge, 2005), 131.

59 Jerome G. Miller, *Search and Destroy: African-American Males in the Criminal Justice System* (New York: Cambridge University Press, 1996), 88; Elizabeth Shulte, "The Sick Face of Racism in the U.S.: More Black Men in Jail than College," Socialistworker.org, September 6, 2002, http://socialistworker.org/2002-2/420/420_12_JailsVCollege.shtml.

60 Shulte, "The Sick Face of Racism in the U.S."

61 Collins, *Black Sexual Politics*, 81–82.

62 Shaller, *Reckoning with Reagan*, 85.

63 Alexander, *The New Jim Crow*.

64 Cacho, *Social Death*, 65, referencing Senator William V. Roth (R-DE) before the U.S. Congress, Senate, Subcommittee on Investigations of the Committee on Governmental Affairs, *Emerging Criminal Groups: Hearings before the Permanent Subcommittee on Investigations of the Committee on Governmental Affairs*, 99th Cong., 2nd sess., 1986, 50.

65 Aristide R. Zolberg, "Reforming the Backdoor: The Immigration Reform and Control Act of 1986 in Historical Perspective," in *Immigration Reconsidered: History, Sociology, and Politics*, ed. Virginia Yans-McLaughlin (New York: Oxford University Press, 1990), 329.

66 See *New York Times*, February 15, 1986, and April 29, 1986; *Wall Street Journal*, May 14, 1986.

67 Roger Rosenblatt, "The Enemy Within," *Time*, September. 15, 1986, and "Battle Strategies," *Time*, September 15, 1986.

68 David R. Maciel and Maria Rose Garcia-Acevedo, "The Celluloid Immigrant: The Narrative Films of Mexican Immigration," in *Culture across Borders: Mexican Immigration and Popular Culture*, ed. David R. Maciel and Maria Herrera-Sobek (Tucson: University of Arizona Press, 1998), 149–202.

69 Frank Javier Garcia Berumen, *The Chicano/Hispanic Image in American Film* (New York: Vintage, 1995).

70 The film had a domestic gross of only $6,118, 683. "The Border," Boxofficemojo. com, http://boxofficemojo.com/movies/?id=border.htm.

71 Clara E. Rodriguez, "The Silver Screen: Stories and Stereotypes," in *Latin Looks: Images of Latinas and Latinos in the U.S. Media*, ed. Clara E. Rodriguez (Boulder, CO: Westview, 1998), 78.

72 Clara E. Rodriguez, "Keeping It Reel? Films of the 1980s and 1990s," in *Latin Looks: Images of Latinas and Latinos in the U.S. Media*, ed. Clara E. Rodriguez (Boulder, CO: Westview, 1998), 180–84, 180.

73 Ibid., 180–84.

74 Leonard Klady, "Box Office Champs, Chumps: The Hero of the Bottom Line Was the 46-Year-Old 'Bambi,'" *Los Angeles Times*, January 8, 1989, http://articles. latimes.com/1989-01-08/entertainment/ca-258_1_box-office/2.

75 Janet Maslin, "Colors (1988) Review/Film; Police vs. Street Gangs in Hopper's 'Colors,'" *New York Times*, April 15, 1988, http://movies.nytimes.com/movie/revie w?res=940DE3DD1731F936A25757C0A96E948260.

76 Roger Ebert, "Colors," *Chicago Sun Times*, April 15, 1988, http://rogerebert. suntimes.com/apps/pbcs.dll/article?AID=/19880415/REVIEWS/804150301/1023.

77 Maslin, "Colors."

78 Ebert, "Colors."

79 Cacho, *Social Death*, 23.

80 See Myra Mendible, ed., *From Bananas to Buttocks: The Latina Body in Popular Film and Culture* (Austin: University of Texas Press, 2007).

81 "Fort Apache, The Bronx," *The Numbers: Box Office Data, Movie Stars, Idle Speculation*, http://www.the-numbers.com/movies/1981/0FABR.php.

82 Variety Staff, "Fort Apache, The Bronx," Variety.com, December 31, 1980, http:// www.variety.com/review/VE1117791034/; Roger Ebert, "Fort Apache, The Bronx," *Chicago Sun Times*, January 1, 1981, http://rogerebert.suntimes.com/apps/pbcs.dll/ article?AID=/19810101/REVIEWS/101010327/1023.

83 Gina M. Perez, Frank A. Guridy, and Adrian Burgos, Jr., Introduction, in *Beyond El Barrio: Everyday Life in Latina/o America*, ed. Gina M. Perez, Frank A. Guridy, and Adrian Burgos, Jr. (New York: New York University Press, 2010), 3.

84 Norman Denzin, *Reading Race: Hollywood and the Cinema of Racial Violence* (New York: Sage, 2002), 2.

85 David R. Maciel and Maria Rose Garcia-Acevedo, "The Celluloid Immigrant: The Narrative Films of Mexican Immigration," in *Culture across Borders: Mexican Immigration and Popular Culture*, ed. David R. Maciel and Maria Herrera-Sobek (Tucson: University of Arizona Press, 1998), 185. See also David R. Maciel and Susan Racho, "'Yo soy Chicano': The Turbulent and Heroic Life of Chicanas/os in Cinema and Television," in *Chicano Renaissance: Contemporary Cultural Trends*, ed. David R. Maciel, Isidro D. Ortiz, and Maria Herrera-Sobek (Tucson: University of Arizona Press, 2000), 93–130.

86 "Born in East LA," *Box Office Mojo*, http://boxofficemojo.com/movies/?id=bornineastla.htm.

87 Richard Harrington, "Born in East LA Review," *Washington Post*, August 31, 1987, http://www.webcitation.org/5xI3NQrOn; Caryn James, "Film: 'Born in East L.A.,' Cheech Marin Comedy," *New York Times*, August 24, 1987, http://movies.nytimes.com/movie/review?_r=2&res=9B0DEFDE153AF937A1575BC0A961948260.

88 Fregoso, *The Bronze Screen*, 56.

89 Angela Y. Davis, *Women, Race, and Class* (New York: Vintage, 1983).

90 U.S. Congress, Joint Hearings, Select Commission on Immigration and Refugee Policy of the Senate Committee on the Judiciary and Subcommittee on Immigration, Refugee, and International Law of the House Committee on the Judiciary, *Final Report of the Select Commission on Immigration and Refugee Policy: Joint Hearings before the Subcommittee on Immigration and Refugee Policy and the Subcommittee on Immigration, Refugee, and International Law*, 97th Cong., 1st sess., 1981, 88.

91 U.S. Congress, Senate, *Immigration Reform and Control Act*, 99th Cong., 2nd sess., 1986, http://web.lexis-nexis.com/congcomp/printdoc.

92 Ibid.

93 U.S. Congress, House, Subcommittee on Census and Population of the Committee on Post Office and Civil Service, *Immigration Reform and Control Act of 1982 Hearings before the Subcommittee on Census and Population*, 97th Cong., 2nd sess., 1983, 13.

94 Ibid.,14.

95 Charles R. Babcock, "Migrant Policy Said to Benefit Western Bosses," *Washington Post*, July 19, 1981, A1.

96 Alan Simpson, *Right in the Old Gazoo: A Lifetime of Scrapping with the Press* (New York: William Morrow, 1997), 89–90.

97 U.S. Congress, House, Subcommittee, *Immigration Reform and Control Act of 1982*, 6.

98 Ibid., 2.

99 Ibid., 13.

100 *The Immigration Reform and Control Act of 1986*, Public Law 99–603, 100 (1986), http://library.uwb.edu/static/USimmigration/100%20stat%203359.pdf.

101 Aristide R. Zolberg, *A Nation by Design: Immigration Policy in the Fashioning of America* (Cambridge, MA: Harvard University Press, 2006), 373.

102 *The Immigration Reform and Control Act of 1986.*

103 Zolberg, *A Nation by Design*, 373.

104 Eithne Luibheid, *Entry Denied: Controlling Sexuality at the Border* (Minneapolis: University of Minnesota Press, 2002), 233, n. 20.

105 Michael Fix, ed., *The Paper Curtain: Employer Sanctions' Implementation, Impact, and Reform* (Washington, DC: Urban Institute Press, 1991), 91.

106 Zolberg, *A Nation by Design*, 374.

107 Cacho, *Social Death*, 22–23.

108 *The Immigration Reform and Control Act of 1986.*

109 Hartry, "Commentary Gendering Crimmigration," 20.

110 Leo Chavez, *The Latino Threat: Constructing Immigrants, Citizens, and the Nation* (Stanford, CA: Stanford University Press, 2008), 83–84.

111 Camacho, *Migrant Imaginaries*, 243.

112 Luibheid, *Entry Denied*, 121.

113 Human Rights Watch, *Brutality Unchecked: Human Rights Abuses along the U.S. Border with Mexico* (New York: Human Rights Watch, 1992), 35, cited in Luibheid, *Entry Denied*, 121.

114 *Immigration Act of 1990*, Public Law 101–649, 104 Stat. (1990).

115 Manfred B. Steger and Ravi K. Roy, *Neoliberalism: A Very Short Introduction* (New York: Oxford University Press, 2010), 35–36.

116 Ibid., 55–56.

117 Carlos A. Heredia, "Downward Mobility: Mexican Workers after NAFTA," *North American Congress on Latin America (NACLA)* 30, no. 3 (Novembe/December 1996): 34–40.

118 Joseph Nevins, *Operation Gatekeeper: The Rise of the "Illegal Alien" and the Making of the U.S.–Mexico Boundary* (New York: Routledge, 2002), appendix F.

119 Ibid., 145.

120 Frank D. Bean, Roland Chanove, Robert G. Cushing, Rodolfo de la Garza, Gary P. Freeman, Charles W. Haynes, and David Spener, "Illegal Mexican Migration & the United States/Mexico Border: The Effects of Operation Hold the Line on El Paso/Juarez," Research Paper for the U.S. Commission on Immigration Reform by the Population Research Center, University of Texas at Austin, July 1994, 7–8, http://www.trinity.edu/dspener/publications/imm-jul94.pdf .

121 Ibid.

122 Ibid.

123 Zolberg, *A Nation by Design*, 401.

124 Fregoso, *MeXicana Encounters*, 7.

125 Melissa W. Wright, "Field Note: Ciudad Juarez, Mexico," *Women's Studies Quarterly* 34, no. 1/2 (Spring/Summer 2006): 94–97.

126 Camacho, *Migrant Imaginaries*, 264.

127 Fregoso, *MeXicana Encounters*, 4–5.

128 Camacho, *Migrant Imaginaries*, 243.

129 Fregoso, *MeXicana Encounters*, 8.

130 Roger Lancaster, "Panic Attack: Sex and Terror in the Homeland," *NACLA Report on the Americas* 41, no. 6 (November/Dececember 2008): 31–36.

131 Jean Hardisty, "Rights for Some: The Erosion of Democracy," *Public Eye* 15, no. 2 (July 31, 2001): 1.

132 "Unlawful Entry a Crime since '29," *Rocky Mountain News*, June 11, 2009, http://www.rockymountainnews.com/news/2006/jun/11/unlawful-entry-a-crime-since-29.

133 *Illegal Immigration Reform and Immigrant Responsibility Act of 1996*, Public Law 104–208, 110, (1996), https://www.uscis.gov/iframe/ilink/docView/PUBLAW/HTML/PUBLAW/0-0-0-10948.html.

134 Clinton was not anti-immigration or anti-immigrant despite the draconian laws that were passed during his presidency. He repealed some welfare cuts after 1996, given the economic stability of the nation, and the "Citizenship U.S.A." program, run by Vice President Al Gore, increased naturalization by loosening some requirements such as English and civic tests for persons over sixty-five with twenty years of residence. From October 1995 to September 1996, 1.2 million immigrants were naturalized, eliminating a backlog of 500,000. Zolberg, *A Nation by Design*, 420.

135 Ibid., 418–423.

136 Christina Gerken, *Model Immigrants and Undesirable Aliens: The Cost of Immigration Reform in the 1990s* (Minneapolis: University of Minnesota Press, 2013), 240; see also Pia Moller, "Restoring Law and (Racial) Order to the Old Dominion," *Cultural Studies*, special issue, Jaafar Aksikas and Sean Johnson Andrews, eds., *Cultural Studies and/of the Law* 28, nos.5–6 (2014): 869–910.

137 Philip Kretsedemas cited in Gerken, *Model Immigrants and Undesirable Aliens*, 240.

138 Philip Kretsedemas, "Immigration Enforcement and the Complication of National Sovereignty: Understanding Local Enforcement as an Exercise in Neoliberal Governance," *American Quarterly*, special issue, David G. Guitierrez and Pierette Hondagneau-Sotelo, eds., *Nation and Migration: Past and Future* 60, no. 3 (Sept. 2008): 555.

139 Zolberg, *A Nation by Design*, 426.

140 See Leo Chavez, *Shadowed Lives: Undocumented Immigrants in American Society*, 2nd ed. (New York: Wadsworth, 1998).

141 Kretsedemas, "Immigration Enforcement," 553.

142 Grace Chang, *Disposable Domestics: Immigrant Women Workers in the Global Economy* (Cambridge, MA: South End Press, 2000), 9.

143 Gerken, *Model Immigrants and Undesirable Aliens*, 23.

144 Michelle J. Anderson, "A License to Abuse: The Impact of Conditional Status on Female Immigrants," *Yale Law Journal* 102, no. 6 (1993): 1401–30.

145 T. J. English, *Paddy Whacked: The Untold Story of the Irish American Gangster* (New York: Regan Books, 2005).

146 The documentary *Overnight* chronicles Duffy's meteoric rise and fall, which the film implies may be connected to alcoholism and egoism, and ends with a potential turn- around given the cult success of the film and Duffy's making of a sequel. See Roger Ebert, "Overnight," *Chicago Sun Times*, November 19, 2004, http://rogerebert.suntimes.com/apps/pbcs.dll/article?AID=/20041118/ REVIEWS/41116007/1023.

147 *The Godfather*, directed by Francis Ford Coppola and featuring an all-star cast including Marlon Brando, Al Pacino, James Caan, Diane Keaton, and Robert Duvall, won Academy Awards for Best Picture, Best Actor, and Best Adapted Screenplay, and the American Film Institute ranked it as the second greatest film of all time. "Citizen Kane Stands the Test of Time," *American Film Institute 1967–2007*, June 20, 2007, http://www.afi.com/Docs/about/ press/2007/100movies07.pdf.

148 The Sopranos," *Emmys Award History*, Emmys.com, http://www.emmys.com/ award_history_search?person=&program=sopranos&st art_year=1949&end_year=2012&network=All&web_category=All&winner=All.

149 Peter Biskind, "An American Family," VanityFair.com, April 2007, http://www. vanityfair.com/culture/features/2007/04/sopranos200704?currentPage=1.

150 Maureen Ryan, "The Sopranos Is the Most Influential Television Drama Ever," Popmatters.com, April 23, 2007, http://www.popmatters.com/pm/feature/ the-sopranos-is-the-most-influential-television-drama-ever/>.

151 Associated Press, "TV Guide Names Top 50 Shows," CBSnews.com, February 11, 2009, http://www.cbsnews.com/stories/2002/04/26/entertainment/main507388. shtml.

152 Cacho, *Social Death*, 46–47.

153 Jonathan Schuppe, "Essex Officials Tell 'The Sopranos': Fuhgeddabout Filming around Here," *Star Ledger*, December 16, 2000, http://www.nj.com/sopranos/ ledger/index.ssf?/sopranos/stories/121600essex.html.

154 Micaela di Leonardo, "White Ethnicities, Identity Politics, and Baby Bear's Chair," *Social Text* 41 (Winter 1994): 181–82.

155 "New Jersey and the Sopranos: Perfect Together?," *Public Mind*, August 15, 2001, http://publicmind.fdu.edu/badabing/tab.html; "New Jersey and Nation in Tune with Sopranos," *Public Mind*, 2007, http://publicmind.fdu.edu/intune/tab. html.

156 George Lipsitz, *The Possessive Investment in Whiteness: How White People Profit from Identity Politics* (Philadelphia: Temple University Press, 1998).

157 The film was made on a $1 million budget and earned $117,235,147 domestically and a total of $225,000,000 worldwide. "Rocky," *The Numbers: Box Office Data, Movie Stars, Idle Speculation*, http://www.the-numbers.com/movies/1976/0RKY1.php.

158 While my focus here is on stereotypes of Asian men in relation to crime and crime fighting, as discussed in Chapter 3, Asian women were similarly distanced from "normal" white heterosexual femininity via sexualized stereotypes. In popular culture from the nineteenth century on, and in connection with particular domestic and international politics, Asian women were villainized as seductive, treacherous "dragon ladies," or fetishized as submissive, docile and sexually available "China dolls." See Chapter 3 and the Conclusion for analyses of neoliberal iterations of stereotypes of Asian women.

159 Roger Daniels, *Guarding the Golden Door: American Immigration Policy and Immigrants since 1882* (New York: Hill and Wang, 2004), 40–45.

160 Robert Lee, *Orientals: Asian Americans in Popular Culture* (Philadelphia: Temple University Press, 1999), 146.

161 Roger Daniels, *Prisoners without Trial: Japanese Americans in World War II* (New York: Hill and Wang, 1993).

162 Lee, *Orientals*, 146–47.

163 The martial arts films of the 1970s and especially Lee's body of work have been characterized as deploying a "discourse of macho Chinese nationalism that proved popular with a range of audiences," from Asian audiences to black and white working-class audiences in the United States and Europe. Yvonne Tasker, "Fists of Fury: Discourses of Race and Masculinity in Martial Arts Cinema," in *The Gender and Media Reader*, ed. Mary Celeste Kearney (New York: Routledge, 2008), 504. While this important research points to the popular incorporation of gendered multiculturalism following the civil rights movement (and ethnic nationalism as an appropriate conduit for it given Cold War suspicions about transnationalism), further discussion is beyond the scope of my project.

164 Roger Ebert, "The Karate Kid," *Chicago Sun-Times*, January 1, 1984, http://rogerebert.suntimes.com/apps/pbcs.dll/article?AID=/19840101/REVIEWS/401010351/1023; Janet Maslin, "Screen 'Karate Kid,' Bane of Bullies," *New York Times*, June 22, 1984, http://www.nytimes.com/1984/06/22/movies/screen-karate-kid-bane-of-bullies.html.

165 Maslin, "Screen 'Karate Kid.'"

166 Richard Natale, "What a 'Rush'—Tucker, Chan Fell Fall Records," *Los Angeles Times*, September 21, 1998, http://articles.latimes.com/1998/sep/21/entertainment/ca-24913.

167 Camacho, *Migrant Imaginaries*, 2.

168 Kretsedemas, "Immigration Enforcement," 555.

CHAPTER 5: OVER-LOOKING DIFFERENCE

1 Mireya Navarro, "After a Summer of High-Profile Coverage of Hispanic Culture, Some Wonder If It Will Last," *New York Times*, October 4, 1989, http://www.nytimes.com/1999/10/04/business/media-after-summer-high-profile-coverage-hispanic-culture-some-wonder-if-it-will.html.

2 "Latin Music Goes Pop," *Time*, May 24, 1999, http://www.time.com/time/covers/0,16641,19990524,00.html.

3 Fred Goodman, "La Explosion Pop Latino," *Rolling Stone*, May 13, 1999, http://proxy.library.georgetown.edu/login?url=http://search.proquest.com.databases.library.georgetown.edu/docview/220178482?accountid=11091.

4 *Newsweek*'s archives are not available digitally. See Sharon Waxman, "Jonathan Alter to Barry Diller: Where Are 80 Years of Newsweek Archives? (Updated)," thewrap.com, June 17, 2013, http://www.thewrap.com/media/column-post/jonathan-alter-barry-diller-where-are-80-years-newsweek-archives-97701. Some articles from *Newsweek*'s July 12, 1999, issue are available on the web. See for instance, Brook Larmer, "Latino America," *Newsweek*, July 12, 1999, http://ccat.sas.upenn.edu/romance/spanish/219/13eeuu/newsweek.html; and "Majorities of Young Hispanic Americans More Likely Than Their Elders to Use English Yet 54 Percent Say Their Heritage Very Important," TheFreeLibrary.com, July 3, 1999. Original *Newsweek* cover image available at https://kindle.amazon.com/work/newsweek-latin-u-s-a-junot-shakira/B0037G6ZHQ/B0037G6ZHQ.

5 Nancy Jo Sales, "Vida Lopez," *New York*, September 6, 1999, http://nymag.com/nymetro/news/culture/features/1395/.

6 Angharad Valdivia, "Is Penelope to J.Lo as Culture Is to Nature? Eurocentric Approaches to 'Latin' Beauties," in *From Bananas to Buttocks: The Latina Body in Popular Film and Culture*, ed. Myra Mendible (Austin: University of Texas Press, 2007) 130.

7 See Frances R. Aparicio and Susana Chavez-Silverman, eds., *Tropicalizations: Transcultural Representations of Latinidad* (Hanover, NH: University Press of New England, 1997).

8 Valdivia, "Is Penelope to J.Lo as Culture Is to Nature?," 137.

9 Brian Warner, "Jennifer Lopez Net Worth," Celebritynetworth.com, 2013, http://www.celebritynetworth.com/richest-celebrities/singers/jennifer-lopez/.

10 Robert C. Cotrell, *Icons of American Popular Culture: From P. T. Barnum to Jennifer Lopez* (Armonk, NY: M. E. Sharpe, 2010), 221.

11 Louise Gannon, "Jessica Alba: 'I'd Definitely Go for the Shy, Nerdy Type of Guy,'" *Mail Online*, October 27, 2007, http://www.dailymail.co.uk/home/moslive/article-489884/Jessica-Alba-Id-definitely-shy-nerdy-type-guy.html; Ashley Mott, "Jennifer Lopez Was an Inspiration for Many Women and Girls in the Late 1990s," *Yahoo Voices*, March 2, 2010, http://voices.yahoo.com/jennifer-lopez-was-inspiration-many-women-and-5564127.html.

12 Mark Graham, "The 100 Greatest Women in Music," Vh1.com, February 13, 2012, http://www.vh1.com/music/tuner/2012-02-13/100-greatest-women-in-music/86/.

13 Jennifer Gordreau, "How Jennifer Lopez Climbed to No. 1 on the Forbes Celebrity 100 List," Forbes.com, May 16, 2012, http://www.forbes.com/sites/jennagoudreau/2012/05/16/how-jennifer-lopez-climbed-to-no-1-on-the-forbes-celebrity-100-list/.

14 Mary Beltran, "The Hollywood Latina Body as Site of Social Struggle: Media Constructions of Stardom and Jennifer Lopez's 'Cross-Over Butt,'" *Quarterly*

Review of Film and Video 19, no. 1 (January–March 2002), 71–86; Frances R. Aparicio, "Jennifer as Selena: Rethinking Latinidad in Media and Popular Culture," *Latino Studies* 1, no. 1 (March 2003), 90–105; Isabel Molina-Guzman and Angharad Valdiva, "Brain, Brow, or Bootie: Iconic Latinas in Contemporary Popular Culture," *Communication Review* 7, no. 2 (April–June 2004), 205–21; Isabel Molina-Guzman, *Dangerous Curves: Latina Bodies in the Media* (New York: New York University Press, 2010).

15 Although Lopez is not an immigrant, she and other Latinas/os were coded as such so that their stories fit into the "nation of immigrants" trope. Lopez and other similarly coded entertainers like Selena have also captured the interest of immigrant audiences.

16 "Jennifer Lopez," Insider.com, 2009, CBS Studios, January 29, 2009, http://www.theinsider.com/ celebrities/Jennifer_Lopez.

17 Ibid.

18 "Jennifer Lopez: Biography," Billboard.com, 2013, http://www.billboard.com/artist/304444/jennifer-lopez/biography.

19 Her 1999 debut album, *On the 6*, debuted at No. 8 on the Billboard chart; the single, "If You Had My Love" was a No. 1 hit, and "Waiting for Tonight" peaked at No.8. Bill Lamb, "Jennifer Lopez: The Top 10 Hit Songs," About.com, 2013, http://top40.about.com/od/jenniferlopez/tp/top-10-jennifer-lopez-songs.htm. In 2002, her second album, *J-Lo*, debuted at No. 1, as did her film, *The Wedding Planner*; see "Lopez Bows at No. 1; O-Town, Dream Debut High 5," Billboard.com, January 31, 2001, http://www.billboard.com/articles/news/80647/lopez-bows-at-no-1-o-town-dream-debut-high5.

20 Mark J. Miller, "Jennifer Lopez Launches Movil, Her Own Mobile Retail Brand with Verizon Wireless," *Brand Channel*, May 23, 2013, http://www.brandchannel.com/home/post/2013/05/23/Jennifer-Lopez-Viva-Movil-052313.aspx. While the sales of her 2014 and 2011 albums were low in comparison to her previous albums, she nonetheless continues to sell records and products internationally, and she is still a popular and high-earning celebrity and presence in various media. Hal Banfield, "Jennifer Lopez Album Sales Slump," Guardianlv.com, June 22, 2014, http://guardianlv.com/2014/06/jennifer-lopez-album-sales-slump/.

21 David Emery, "Jennifer Lopez: The Case of the Billion Dollar Booty," About.com, 2009, http://urbanlegends.about.com/cs/celebrities/a/jennifer_lopez.htm.

22 Ana M. Lopez, "Are All Latins from Manhattan? Hollywood, Ethnography, and Cultural Colonialism," in *Unspeakable Images: Ethnicity and the American Cinema*, ed. L. D. Friedman (Urbana: University of Illinois Press, 1991), 404–24. See also Valdivia, "Is Penelope to J.Lo as Culture Is to Nature?," 131–32.

23 Magdalena Barrera, "Hottentot 2000: Jennifer Lopez and Her Butt," in *Sexualities in History: A Reader*, ed. Kim M. Phillips and Barry Reay (New York: Routledge, 2002), 407–20; Beltran, "The Hollywood Latina," 71–86; Frances Negron-Mutaner, "Jennifer's Butt," *Aztlan* 22, no. 2 (1997): 182–95.

24 Sarah Tippit, "Jennifer Lopez, Hilfiger Unveil 'J.Lo' Fashions," *Puerto Rico Herald*, April 26, 2001, http://www.puertorico-herald.org/issues/2001/vol5n19/JLoClothes-en.html.

25 Negron-Mutaner, "Jennifer's Butt," 189.

26 Arlene Davila, *Latino Spin: Public Image and the Whitewashing of Race* (New York: New York University Press, 2008).

27 Gina M. Perez, Frank A. Guridy, and Adrian Burgos, Jr., Introduction, in *Beyond El Barrio: Everyday Life in Latina/o America*, ed. Gina M. Perez, Frank A. Guridy, and Adrian Burgos, Jr. (New York: New York University Press, 2010), 2.

28 Jose Fernando Arbex Miro, Samuel J. Barnes, Andre Nathaniel Devo, Scott La Rock, Jennifer Lopez, Michael Oliver, Troy Oliver, Lawrence Parker, Jason Phillips, and David Styles, *Jenny from the Block* (New York: EMI, 2002).

29 Since the 1917 Jones Act, Puerto Ricans have been U.S. citizens but continue to be cast as "foreign," "immigrant," or "alien citizens." U.S. projects such as the Chardon Plan, the Chicago Plan, and Operation Bootstraps shaped Puerto Rican migration to/from the continental United States. For instance, in the 1950s, Operation Bootstraps courted Puerto Ricans as migrant workers, factory workers, and domestic workers, but when their numbers increased and Puerto Ricans became more politically active in the 1970s, they were linked to blackness, poverty, and crime, and thus cast as threats to the stability of the United States. See Gina M. Perez, *The Near Northwest Side Story: Migration, Displacement, and Puerto Rican Families* (Berkeley: University of California Press, 2004), and Molina-Guzman, *Dangerous Curves*, 85. Therefore, Puerto Ricans share much in common with other Latinas/os and Mexican and Latin American immigrants; however, among important differences is the fact that their status as U.S. citizens and (technically) former colonial subjects places them in a unique place in relation to power, race, and immigration discourses.

30 Perez, Guridy, and Burgos, Jr., Introduction, 3.

31 Arbex Miro, et al, *Jenny from the Block.*

32 Tara Lockhart, "Jennifer Lopez: The New Wave of Border Crossing," in *From Bananas to Buttocks: The Latina Body in Popular Film and Culture*, ed. Myra Mendible (Austin: University of Texas Press, 2007), 153.

33 "Amnesty," *Online Etymology Dictionary*, 2001–2010, http://www.etymonline.com/index.php?term=amnesty.

34 Grace Hong and Roderick Ferguson, Introduction, in *Strange Affinities: The Gender and Sexual Politics of Comparative Racialization*, ed. Grace Hong and Roderick Ferguson (Durham, NC: Duke University Press, 2011), 1–24, 17.

35 Monisha Das Gupta, "Rights in a Transnational Era," in *Immigrant Rights in the Shadows of Citizenship*, ed. Rachel Ida Buff (New York: New York University Press, 2008), 403–4.

36 Rosemary Coombe, "Is There a Cultural Studies of Law?," in *A Companion to Cultural Studies*, ed. Toby Miller (New York: Blackwell, 2001), 36–62.

37 Agustin Gurza, "1999 Was the Year of the Latin Explosion. Ricky. Enrique. J. Lo. But the High-Gloss Boom Went Bust—with Lessons for the Next Wave," *Los Angeles Times*, August 15, 2004, http://articles.latimes.com/2004/aug/15/entertainment/ca-gurza15.

38 John Carlos Rowe, "Reading *Reading Lolita in Tehran* in Idaho," *American Quarterly* 59, no. 2 (June 2007): 253–75.

39 Grace Kyungwon Hong, *The Ruptures of American Capital: Woman of Color Feminism and the Culture of Immigrant Labor* (Minneapolis: University of Minnesota Press, 2006), 108–10.

40 Paul Smith, *Primitive America: The Ideology of Capitalist America* (Minneapolis: University of Minnesota Press, 2007), 43–45.

41 Jodie Melamed, *Represent and Destroy: Rationalizing Violence in the New Racial Capitalism* (Minneapolis: University of Minnesota Press, 2011), 138.

42 Jodie Melamed, "Reading Tehran in *Lolita*: Making Racialized Gendered Difference Work for Neoliberal Multiculturalism," in *Strange Affinities: The Gender and Sexual Politics of Comparative Racialization*, ed. Grace Hong and Roderick Ferguson (Durham, NC: Duke University Press, 2011), 82–87.

43 U.S. Congress, Senate, Subcommittee on Immigration and Refugee Policy of the Committee on the Judiciary, *The Immigration Reform and Control Act of 1986: Hearings before the Subcommittee on Immigration and Refugee Policy*, 99th Cong., 2nd sess., 1986, http://web.lexis-nexis.com/congcomp/printdoc.

44 Ibid.

45 Associated Press, "The Death of a Humane Idea," *New York Times*, October 18, 1984.

46 Robert Reinhold, "Illegal Aliens Hoping to Claim their Dreams," *New York Times*, November 3, 1986, late city final ed., A1.

47 U.S. Congress, *Congressional Record*, 97th Cong., 2nd sess., 1982, 25355.

48 Ibid.

49 Marilyn Halter, *Shopping for Identity: The Marketing of Identity* (New York: Schocken Books, 2000), 193–97.

50 Jodie Melamed, "Minor Differences: Impossible Politics, Interdisciplinarity, and Intersectionality: A Workshop," Cultural Studies Association annual conference, Columbia College, Chicago, IL, March 24–26, 2011.

51 Valdivia, "Is Penelope to J.Lo as Culture Is to Nature?," 136.

52 Halter, *Shopping for Identity*, 142–47. Latin products continue to be popular: consumer research firm Packaged Foods found that in 2013 Hispanic food and beverages were an $8 billion market, which may reach $11 billion dollars by 2017. Additionally, some products such as tortillas now outsell buns for the classic American staples, burgers and hotdogs, and tacos and burritos have become so popular that most people no longer consider them "ethnic." Suzette Laboy and J. M. Hirsch, "Latino, Other Ethnic Influences Changing America's Food Choices," *NBC Latino*, October 17, 2013, http://nbclatino.com/2013/10/17/latino-other-ethnic-influences-changing-americas-food-choices/. While their consideration is

beyond the scope of this project, these changes point to the onoigoing prevalence and profitablity of neoliberal multiculturalism.

53 Molina-Guzman and Valdivia, "Brain, Brow, and Booty," 211.

54 Valdivia, "Is Penelope to J.Lo as Culture Is to Nature?," 137–38.

55 Negrón-Muntaner, "Jennifer's Butt," 184.

56 Ironically, these public(ized) Latina/o identities were often inaccurate or out of sync with how the performers identified themselves. Anthony never intended to be a "Latin" star. He was born and raised in New York, English is his first language, and his first album was in English. Nonetheless, his performance of stereotypical Latino masculinity made him a star. Goodman, "La Explosion Pop Latino." While Martin was rumored to be gay in the 1990s, he came out in 2010; his lengthy silence about his sexual preferences suggests his awareness of the heterosexual bias in the "Latino Explosion."

57 Deborah Paredez, "Remembering Selena, Re-Membering 'Latinidad,'" *Theater Journal* 54, no. 1 (March 2002): 72.

58 Negron-Mutaner, "Jennifer's Butt," 185.

59 Siobhan Somerville, "Scientific Racism and the Invention of the Homosexual Body," in *The Gender and Sexuality Reader: Culture, History, Political Economy*, ed. Roger Lancaster and Micaela di Leonardo (New York: Routledge, 1997), 40–42.

60 Negron-Muntaner, "Jennifer's Butt," 185.

61 Clara E. Rodriguez, ed., *Latin Looks: Images of Latinas and Latinos in the U.S. Media* (Boulder, CO: Westview, 1998), 76.

62 Hector Cantu, "Selena's Death Got Attention of Market," *Houston Chronicle*, March 12, 1998.

63 Paredez, "Remembering Selena," 65.

64 Karen Orr Vered and Sal Humphreys, "Postfeminist Inflections in Television Studies," *Continuum: Journal of Media & Cultural Studies* 28, no. 2 (2014): 161.

65 Ibid.

66 Lockhart, "Jennifer Lopez," 151.

67 Molina-Guzman, *Dangerous Curves*, 60.

68 For a discussion of the film, see Roberto R. Calderon, "All Over the Map: La Onda Tejana and the Making of Selena," in *Chicano Resistance: Contemporary Cultural Trends*, ed. David R. Maciel, Isidro D. Ortiz, and Maria Herrera-Sobek (Tucson: University of Arizona Press, 2000).

69 Molina-Guzman, *Dangerous Curves*, 58–60.

70 Lockhart, "Jennifer Lopez," 155.

71 Molina-Guzman, *Dangerous Curves*, 58–60; Lockhart, "Jennifer Lopez," 158–62.

72 Lockhart, "Jennifer Lopez," 157.

73 Molina-Guzman, *Dangerous Curves*, 68.

74 Ibid., 53.

75 Ibid., 85–86.

76 Associated Press, "Lopez to Receive Award from Human Rights Group for 'Bordertown,'" 7 News, February 5, 2007, http://www.wsvn.com/news/articles/entertainment/MI39066/.

77 Negron-Mutaner, "Jennifer's Butt," 189.

78 Arlene Davila, *Latinos, Inc.: The Marketing and Making of Identity* (Berkeley: University of California Press, 2001).

79 Thomas McCarroll, "It's a Mass Market No More," *Time*, December 2, 1993.

80 Jaafar Aksikas and Sean Johnson Andrews, "Neoliberalism, Law and Culture: A Cultural Studies Intervention after 'The Juridical Turn,'" *Cultural Studies*, special issue, Jaafar Aksikas and Sean Johnson Andrews, eds., *Cultural Studies and/of the Law* 28, nos.5–6 (2014): 742, 744.

81 Ibid., 745.

82 Jorge A. Bustamante, "Undocumented Migration from Mexico to the United States: Preliminary Findings of the Zapata Canyon Project," in *Undocumented Migration to the United States: IRCA and the Experience of the 1980s*, ed. Frank D. Bean, Barry Edmonston, and Jeffrey S. Passel (Santa Monica, CA: RAND Corporation, 1990), 222–25.

83 Alan Simpson, *Right in the Old Gazoo: A Lifetime of Scrapping with the Press* (New York: William Morrow, 1997), 68.

84 U.S. Congress, House, Subcommittee on Census and Population of the Committee on Post Office and Civil Service, *Immigration Reform and Control Act of 1982, Hearings before the Subcommittee on Census and Population*, 97th Cong., 2nd sess., 1982, 16.

85 Ibid., 30.

86 Ibid., 33.

87 David M. Reimers, *Unwelcome Strangers: American Identity and the Turn against Immigration* (New York: Columbia University Press, 1998.)

88 George Thomas Kurian, ed., *The Encyclopedia of the Republican Party* (Armonk, NY: Sharpe Reference, 1997.)

89 Jeffrey Jones, "Americans Have Mixed Views on Immigration," *Gallup News Service*, July 18, 2001, http://www.gallup.com/poll/4693/americans-mixed-opinions-about-immigration.aspx.

90 Ezbieta M. Gozdziak, "Illegal Europeans: Transients between Two Societies," in *Illegal Immigration in America: A Reference Handbook*, ed. David W. Haines and Karen E. Rosenblum (Westport, CT: Greenwood, 1999), 268.

91 Matthew Jacobson, *Roots Too: White Ethnic Revival in Post–Civil Rights America* (Cambridge, MA: Harvard University Press, 2006), 390–91.

92 Simpson, *Right in the Old Gazoo*, 72.

93 Marvie Howe, "Working to Help Irish Immigrants Stay, Legally," *New York Times*, November 27, 1988, http://www.nytimes.com/1988/11/27/nyregion/working-to-help-irish-immigrants-stay-legally.html?src=pm.

94 Ibid.

95 Aristide R. Zolberg, *A Nation by Design: Immigration Policy in the Fashioning of America* (New York: Russell Sage Foundation, 2006), 602, n. 62.

96 *The Immigration Reform and Control Act of 1986*, Public Law 99–603, 100 (1986), http://library.uwb.edu/static/USimmigration/100%20stat%203359.pdf.

97 Roger Daniels, *Guarding the Golden Door: American Immigration Policy and Immigrants since 1882* (New York: Hill and Wang, 2004), 141.

98 Jennifer Duffy, *Who's Your Paddy? Racial Expectations and the Struggle for Irish American Identity* (New York: New York University Press, 2014), 13.

99 Ibid., 215.

100 "Historical/Biographical Note," *Guide to the Irish Immigration Reform Movement Records AIA 016* Tamiment Library and Robert F. Wagner Labor Archives, http://dlib.nyu.edu/findingaids/html/tamwag/aia_iirm_content.html.

101 Howe, "Working to Help Irish Immigrants Stay, Legally."

102 Ibid.

103 "Historical/Biographical Note."

104 Jacobson, *Roots Too*, 392.

105 Matt McGee, "U2's History," @U2.com, February 9, 2016, http://www.atu2.com/band/bio.htm.

106 Associated Press, "O'Connor Draws Criticism, Pity," *Daily News*, October 6, 1992.

107 Black 47's first eponymously titled 1991 album was self-released and earned them a major label contract, and while they released their second and several subsequent albums with a major label, reviews were mixed. Their 2000 album, *Trouble in the Land*, was more consistently well-received. See Laura Hightower, "Black 47," Contemporary Musicians, 2002, Encyclopedia.com, http://www.encyclopedia.com/doc/1G2-3495500015.html.

108 Star Pulse, "Black 47 Campaign for Iraq in 2008," Starpulse.com, January 8, 2008, http://www.starpulse.com/news/index.php/2008/01/08/political_irish_rockers_black_47_campaig_2008.

109 Black 47, "About," http://www.facebook.com/black47/info.

110 "Discography," Black47.com, http://www.thereelbook.com/groups/Black47/albums/Black47Albums.aspx.

111 Laurence T. Kirwan, "Livin in America" (Sony/ATV Music Publishing LLC), metrolyrics.com, 2016, http://www.metrolyrics.com/livin-in-america-lyrics-black-47.html.

112 "Discography," Black47.com.

113 Ibid.

114 Larry Kirwan, "5 Points" St.Lyrics.com, http://www.stlyrics.com/songs/b/black4761056/fivepoints2190060.html.

115 This Celtic punk band, formed in London in 1982, occasionally critiqued the notion of the American Dream but was especially critical of Margaret Thatcher, the United Kingdom's version of Reagan. Conservative Prime Minister Thatcher

(1979–1990), christened the "Iron Lady" for her uncompromising politics and policies, inaugurated numerous neoliberal reforms and shared Reagan's anti-Soviet stance. Her administration also included censorship of media and harsh treatment of Northern Ireland republicans, who provided one of the most direct and aggressive responses to rising neoliberalism and were consequently frequently labeled "terrorists" by the British press and politicians. (While beyond the scope of this book, the U.K. exploitation of and violence toward the Irish also points to the specificities of neoliberal racialization, nativism, and colonization.)

116 Flogging Molly's 2008 album, *Float*, debuted at No. 4 on the Billboard 200 chart. Katie Hasty, "Alan Jackson Bests Janet to Top Billboard 200," Billboard.com, March 12, 2008, http://www.billboard.com/articles/news/1046191/alan-jackson-bests-janet-to-top-billboard-200.

117 While their early work often focused on Ireland, the 2011 album *Speed of Darkness* was about U.S. working-class struggle in the financial crisis of 2008. "Biography," Flogging Molly.com, http://www.floggingmolly.com/index.cfm?page=biography.

118 *The Meanest of Times*, the Dropkick Murphys' 2007 release, reached No. 20 on the Billboard chart, their first release to crack the Top 20. Katie Hasty, "Reba Outmuscles Kanye, 50 to Score First No. 1," Billboard.com, September 26, 2007, http://www.billboard.com/articles/news/1048990/reba-outmuscles-kanye-50-to-score-first-no-1. The numbers have only increased: the band's 2011 release, *Going Out in Style*, debuted on the Billboard 200 Chart at No. 6. James Reed, "Dropkick Murphys Crack Billboard's Top 10," Boston.com, March 10, 2011, http://www.boston.com/ae/music/blog/2011/03/dropkick_murphy_1.html.

119 Hellcat Records, "Bio: Dropkick Murphys," Hellcat.com, http://www.hell-cat.com/artists/artist/26.

120 Chris Martins, "Who Charted? Guitars Rule and Pop Crooners Drool as the Dropkick Murphys Enter the Top 10," Spin.com, January 16, 2013, http://www.spin.com/articles/billboard-chart-dropkick-murphys-chris-tomlin/.

121 Emphasis added. See "About," Dropkick Murphys, http://www.facebook.com/DropkickMurphys/info.

122 Tim O'Rourke, "Irish Eyes Are Smiling: Luck Brings Flogging Molly to the WOW," http://www.floggingmolly.com/index.cfm?page=press&id=10&section=.

123 "About Us," *Irish Lobby for Immigration Reform*, http://www.irishlobbyusa.org/about.php.

124 Gregory Rodriguez, "Illegal? Better If You're Irish," *Los Angeles Times*, April 8, 2007, http://www.latimes.com/news/opinion/commentary/la-op-rodriguez8apr08,0,1081193.column.

125 See Lawrence Downes, "How Green Was My Rally," *New York Times*, December 10, 2006.

126 See also Ellen Barry, "In New York, the Irish Pack It In," *Los Angeles Times*, March 8, 2006; Bart Jones, "A Brogue Gets Heard in Debate," *Newsday*, April 2, 2006.

127 Erica Rand, *Ellis Island Snow Globe* (Durham, NC: Duke University Press, 2005), 46.

128 Ann DuCille, "The Occult of True Black Womanhood: Critical Demeanor and Black Feminist Studies," *Signs: Journal of Women in Culture and Society* 19, no. 3 (1994): 607.

129 Sonia Reyes, "Cafe Bustelo Effort Targets La Familia: Spanish Advertising Campaign for Rowland Coffee Roasters Brand Cafe Bustelo," *Brandweek*, July 2, 2001, http://findarticles.com/ p/articles/mi_m0BDW/is_27_42/ai_76443141.

130 Halter, *Shopping for Identity*, 148.

131 Rosemary Hennessey, *Profit and Pleasure: Sexual Identities of Late Stage Capitalism* (New York: Routledge, 2000), 95.

132 Rachel Ida Buff, "Introduction: Towards a Redefinition of Citizenship Rights," in *Immigrant Rights in the Shadows of Citizenship*, ed. Rachel Ida Buff (New York: New York University Press), 2.

133 Ronald Reagan, "Farewell Address," *National Review Online*, January 11, 1989, http://old.nationalreview.com/document/reagan200406052132.asp.

CONCLUSION

1 Tara Jefferson, "Junot Diaz Promotes 'Freedom University' on the Colbert Report," *78th Annual Ainsfield-Wolf Book Awards*, March 28, 2013, http://www.anisfield-wolf.org/2013/03/junot-diaz-promotes-freedom-university-on-the-colbert-report/.

2 "Junot Diaz: About," Junot Diaz.com, 2013, http://www.junotdiaz.com/about/.

3 Jefferson, "Junot Diaz Promotes 'Freedom University.'"

4 Hao Ying, "Writing Wrongs," *Global Times*, April 14, 2010, http://www.global-times.cn/metro-beijing/people/profile/2010-04/522054.html.

5 The United Nations confirmed that 50,000 people were killed under Trujillo's tyranny (1930–1961) before his assassination. See "Protest Aborts Dominican Tyrant's Daughter's Book Debut," *Dominican Today*, February 26, 2010, http://www.dominicantoday.com/dr/local/2010/2/26/34938/Protest-aborts-Dominican-tyrants-daughters-book-debut.

6 Edwidge Danticat, "Junot Diaz," *Bomb* 101 (Fall 2007), http://bombsite.com/issues/101/articles/2948.

7 Excerpts of book reviews at "Junot Diaz: *This Is How You Lose Her*," Junot Diaz.com, 2013, http://www.junotdiaz.com/books/this-is-how-you-lose-her/.

8 Junot Diaz, "Apocalypse: What Disasters Reveal," *Boston Review*, May 1, 2011, http://www.bostonreview.net/junot-diaz-apocalypse-haiti-earthquake.

9 Ibid.

10 Ibid.

11 Jodie Melamed, *Represent and Destroy: Rationalizing Violence in the New Racial Capitalism* (Minneapolis: University of Minnesota Press, 2011), 146.

12 For a summary of laws, regulations, and affected agencies, see "Creation of the Department of Homeland Security," Department of Homeland Security, www.dhs.gov, http://www.dhs.gov/creation-department-homeland-security.

13 *Uniting and Strengthening America by Providing Appropriate Tools Required to Intercept and Obstruct Terrorism Act of 2001* (USA Patriot Act), Public Law 107–56, (2001), https://www.gpo.gov/fdsys/pkg/PLAW-107publ56/pdf/PLAW-107publ56.pdf.

14 For elaboration of this point, see Rachel Ida Buff, "Deportation Terror," *American Quarterly*, special issue, David G. Guitierrez and Pierette Hondagneau-Sotelo, David G. Guitierrez and Pierette Hondagneau-Sotelo, eds., *Nation and Migration: Past and Future* 60, no. 3 (September 2008): 532–52.

15 Matthew Balan, "Nets Yawn at Obama's Patriot Act Renewal; Hyped Bush's 'Broad Powers,'" Newsbusters.org, May 27, 2011, http://newsbusters.org/blogs/matthew-balan/2011/05/27/nets-yawn-obamas-patriot-act-renewal-hyped-bushs-broad-powers.

16 Neda Atanasoski, *Humanitarian Violence: The U.S. Deployment of Diversity* (Minneapolis: University of Minnesota Press, 2013).

17 Melamed, *Represent and Destroy*, 149.

18 Rachel L. Swarns, "Failed Amnesty Legalization of 1986 Haunts the Current Immigration Bills in Congress," *New York Times*, May 23, 2006, http://www.nytimes.com/2006/05/23/washington/23amnesty.html.

19 Romano Mazzoli and Alan K. Simpson, "Enacting Immigration Reform, Again," *Washington Post*, September 15, 2006, http://www.washingtonpost.com/wp-dyn/content/article/2006/09.

20 Alicia Schmidt Camacho, *Migrant Imaginaries: Latino Cultural Politics in the U.S.–Mexico Borderlands* (New York: New York University Press, 2008), 317.

21 Michael Scherer and Michael Duffy, "The Role Model: What Obama Sees in Reagan," *Time*, February 7, 2011, 24–29.

22 Richard Norton Smith, "The Reagan Revelation," *Time*, February 7, 2011, 30–33.

23 Associated Press, "Obama Denounces SB 1070 after Meeting with Calderón," azstarnet.com, May 20, 2010, http://azstarnet.com/news/local/border/article_d6dcabeb-5eb0-5fa0-8dc5-db45d6b3a338.html.

24 "Immigration," *The White House: President Barack Obama*, 2009, http://www.whitehouse.gov /issues/immigration/.

25 Suzy Khimm, "Obama DREAMs On," *Mother Jones*, June 27, 2011, http://www.motherjones.com/politics/2011/06/obama-dream-act-deportations.

26 "Immigration," *The White House: President Barack Obama*.

27 Ian Gomez, "Senate Gang of Eight Releases Immigration Bill," *USA Today*, April 17, 2013, http://www.usatoday.com/story/news/politics/2013/04/17/senate-files-immigration-bill/2089879/.

28 Patricia Zavella, "Why Are Immigrant Families Different Now?" (Berkeley: UC Berkeley, Center for Latino Policy Research, 2012), 2, http://escholarship.org/uc/item/77k1morm.

29 Scherer and Duffy, "The Role Model," 26.

30 Eithne Luibheid, "Introduction: Queering Migration and Citizenship," in *Queer Migrations: Sexuality, U.S. Citizenship, and Border Crossing*, ed. Eithne Luibheid and Lionel Cantu, Jr. (Minneapolis: University of Minnesota Press, 2005), xi.

31 Hector Amaya, "Citizenship, Diversity, Law and Ugly Betty," *Media, Culture & Society* 32, no. 5 (2010): 801–17; 805.

32 Ibid., 810.

33 Gloria Anzaldua, "La Prieta," in *This Bridge Called My Back: Writings by Radical Women of Color*, ed. Cherrie L. Moraga and Gloria Anzaldua (Berkeley, CA: Third Woman Press, 1981), 220–33.

34 Amaya, "Citizenship, Diversity, Law and Ugly Betty," 808.

35 Isabel Molina-Guzman, *Dangerous Curves: Latina Bodies in the Media* (New York: New York University Press, 2010) 19.

36 Amaya, "Citizenship, Diversity, Law and Ugly Betty," 809.

37 The film earned a domestic gross of $1,759, 252; see "A Better Life," *BoxOfficeMojo*, http://www.boxofficemojo.com/movies/?id=abetterlife.htm.

38 See Roger Ebert, "A Better Life," RogerEbert.com, July 6, 2011, 2013, http://www.rogerebert.com/reviews/a-better-life-2011.

39 Monisha Das Gupta, "Dearly Deported: Sentimental Politics and Immigrant Rights," American Studies Association annual conference, San Juan, Puerto Rico, November 15–18, 2012, 5.

40 Clark Collins, "Holla Back," *Entertainment Weekly* 909 (November 22, 2006).

41 Mihi Ahn, "Gwenihana: Gwen Stefani Neuters Japanese Street Fashion," Salon.com, April 9, 2005, http://www.salon.com/entertainment/feature/2005/04/09/geisha.

42 Riane Eisler, *Sacred Pleasure: Sex, Myth, and the Politics of the Body, New Paths to Power and Love* (New York: Harper Collins, 1996.)

43 Tony Kashani, "Notes on Backlash against Feminism in Hollywood since Reagan," Tonykashani.com, 2008, http://www.tonykashani.com/?page_id=72.

44 Chon A. Noriega and Ana M. Lopez, eds., *The Ethnic Eye: Latino Media Arts* (Minneapolis: University of Minnesota Press, 1996).

45 David R. Maciel and Maria Herrera-Sobek, eds., *Culture across Borders: Mexican Immigration and Popular Culture* (Tucson: University of Arizona Press, 1998).

46 Lawrence W. Levine, "The Folklore of Industrial Society: Popular Culture and Its Audiences," *American Historical Review* 97, no. 5 (December 1992): 1399.

47 Molina-Guzman, *Dangerous Curves*, 8.

INDEX

ABOUT THE AUTHOR

Leah Perry is Assistant Professor of Cultural Studies at SUNY Empire State College. Her research and teaching interests encompass gender and sexuality, race and ethnicity, migration, and media and popular culture in the United States.